P. T. Barnum

AUTHOR'S PREFACE.

To my Readers: Although I have reached the evening of life, my heart is young, and the sweetest music in my ears is the merry laughter of childhood.

Before the parents of many of you were born, I entered upon my career as a manager of public exhibitions. I have catered to the instruction and amusement of three generations.

I have gathered from every point of the habitable globe the most marvelous curiosities in the realms of science art invention and the animal kingdom, and am still adding to my collection. I have expended millions in my efforts to educate interest and amuse. I have appeared before presidents kings queens emperors and rulers, and there are few if any places in the world where my name is unknown. Looking back through the long vista of years, it is a great satisfaction to know that my labors have been so well appreciated by those in whose behalf they were put forth. I have always given the public far more and better than was promised, thus demonstrating that "The Greatest Show on Earth" is in every respect worthy of its title. Recreation is one of the necessities of our being, and he who succeeds in making it instructive pure and elevating is a benefactor of his kind.

I have often thought that one of the most delightful means of instruction would be an illustrated history of the capture of the

wild beasts birds and reptiles which form
the Natural History department of my great
show. Such a history I present in these pages
in the form of a stirring Story, into which
is woven valuable information that I trust
will be acceptable and pleasing to my
friends everywhere.

P. T. Barnum

Waldemere Bridgeport Connecticut,
April 1888,

THE WILD BEASTS, BIRDS

AND REPTILES OF THE WORLD:

THE STORY of THEIR CAPTURE.

BY P. T. BARNUM.

Fredonia Books
Amsterdam, The Netherlands

The Wild Beasts, Birds and Reptiles of the World:
The Story of Their Capture

by
P. T. Barnum

ISBN: 1-58963-958-8

Reprinted from the 1892 edition

Fredonia Books
Amsterdam, The Netherlands
http://www.fredoniabooks.com

CONTENTS.

CHAPTER.		PAGE.
I.	DANGEROUS GAME,	11
II.	A WEAPON OF NATURE,	18
III.	HOW CURIOSITIES ARE CAPTURED,	23
IV.	MY AFRICAN EXPEDITION,	29
V.	THE CAMP IN BECHUANA LAND,	35
VI.	A STARTLING VISIT,	41
VII.	AN ATTACK IN THE REAR,	48
VIII.	THE CHAMPION OF STUPIDITY,	53
IX.	AN OVERTHROW,	59
X.	A DARING EXPLOIT,	64
XI.	A WONDERFUL PERFORMANCE,	68
XII.	THE WILD MEN,	75
XIII.	THE HUMAN BUCKLER,	80
XIV.	AFRICAN VERSUS AMERICAN,	84
XV.	A MASTERLY RETREAT,	89
XVI.	IN THE TREE TOP,	93
XVII.	A TIMELY ARRIVAL,	97
XVIII.	A STRANGE SCENE,	102
XIX.	IN THE NICK OF TIME,	108
XX.	A DISCOVERY,	114
XXI.	ON THE CREST OF THE HILL,	119
XXII.	A MISCALCULATION,	128
XXIII.	THE HORNS OF A DILEMMA,	135
XXIV.	THE WHIZZ OF A BOOMERANG,	140
XXV.	TURNING ABOUT,	144
XXVI.	"ALL TOGETHER,"	151
XXVII.	THE FRETFUL PORCUPINE,	156
XXVIII.	THE SECRETARY-BIRD,	162
XXIX.	A STRANGE SCENE,	167
XXX.	A FRIEND IN NEED,	172

CONTENTS.

CHAPTER.		PAGE.
XXXI.	"One, Two, Three!"	177
XXXII.	Concerning Snakes,	181
XXXIII.	A Reminiscence,	188
XXXIV.	Bears and Kangaroos,	194
XXXV.	A Thief of the Night,	207
XXXVI.	As in the Olden Days,	211
XXXVII.	"Good-by, Sweetheart!"	215
XXXVIII.	Funny Visitors,	220
XXXIX.	"I've Got Him!"	226
XL.	As to Baboons,	231
XLI.	Some Wonders of the Animal Kingdom,	241
XLII.	The Darkening Sky,	246
XLIII.	Out in the Night,	253
XLIV.	Peering Out into the Gloom,	258
XLV.	On the Trail,	264
XLVI.	The Glimmer of a Camp-Fire,	269
XLVII.	A Clever Stratagem,	273
XLVIII.	The Captive and his Captors,	277
XLIX.	At the Village,	282
L.	Lively Times,	286
LI.	The Rhinoceros-Hunters,	291
LII.	The Buphaga Africana,	295
LIII.	Turning the Tables,	300
LIV.	A Lost Hottentot,	305
LV.	Diedrick's Vicissitudes,	308
LVI.	A Whole Armful,	313
LVII.	The Behemoth,	317
LVIII.	The Crash of Splintering Wood,	322
LIX.	A Stroke of Fortune,	328
LX.	The Guns of Burrisaul,	332
LXI.	An Unpleasant Bedfellow,	337
LXII.	Bang! Bang! Bang! Bang! Bang!	342
LXIII.	Building Better than he Knew,	350
LXIV.	The Tiger-Hunters,	356
LXV.	The Tiger,	359
LXVI.	A Fortunate Shot,	363

CONTENTS.

CHAPTER.		PAGE.
LXVII.	A Frightful Occurrence,	366
LXVIII.	Caught in the Act,	371
LXIX.	Two Curiosities,	375
LXX.	Attacked in Front and Rear,	380
LXXI.	Jumbo and Toung Taloung,	391
LXXII.	An Interloper,	402
LXXIII.	A Flying Shot or Two,	408
LXXIV.	A Strange Experience,	412
LXXV.	Another "Close Call,"	418
LXXVI.	Dick Brownell's Last Exploit in India,	423
LXXVII.	In the Land of the Gorilla,	443
LXXVIII.	On the Edge of the Pool,	448
LXXIX.	A Strange Battle,	454
LXXX.	A Battle of Giants,	462
LXXXI.	A Camp-Fire Visitor,	469
LXXXII.	The King of the Jungle,	475
LXXXIII.	Home Again,	482
LXXXIV.	A Brief Résumé of my Life,	489
LXXXV.	How to Get Rich, and How to Live Long and Happy,	497
LXXXVI.	The Reason Why in Natural History,	501

LIST OF ILLUSTRATIONS.

PORTRAIT OF THE AUTHOR, . . Frontispiece.

	PAGE.
INITIAL VIGNETTE—TROPICAL LANDSCAPE, .	11
EAGER TO ATTACK, BUT AFRAID, ...	12
" HE LET FLY THREE TIMES IN SUCCESSION,".	14
THE LEOPARD, ...	16
VIGNETTE—" WAITING,"	18
BY THE STREAM, ...	18
DISPUTING THE WAY, ...	19
SHIPS OF THE DESERT, ...	24
A TROUBLESOME CAPTIVE, ...	27
THE JUNGLE AND SOME OF ITS DENIZENS, .	29
JACK HARVEY AND APACHE, ...	31
AFRICAN OX, ...	32
THE CAMP IN BECHUANA LAND, ...	36
THE HARTBEEST, ...	38
ONE OF THE NATIVES, ...	41
A RUSTLING IN THE GRASS, ...	42
THE KING OF BEASTS, ...	43
A STARTLING VISIT, , . , ...	44
THE DEATH SHOT, ...	50
" WHAT THINK OF HIM ? "	53
TRIUMPHANT, ...	56
OSTRICH HUNTING, ...	57
AN OVERTURN, ...	61
TURNING THE TABLES, ...	66
A WONDERFUL FEAT, ...	69
HOTTENTOT INGENUITY, ...	72
THE RHEA, OR AMERICAN OSTRICH, . . .	73
THE WILD BUSHMEN, ...	76
AN EFFECTIVE SHIELD, ...	81
THE POISONED ARROW, ...	85
IN COWBOY STYLE, ...	87
AN AFRICAN TOBOGGAN SLIDE, ...	97
GETTING DOWN TO BUSINESS, ...	99
SKELETON OF THE GIRAFFE, ...	100
THE CAPE BUFFALO, ...	103
THE BISON, ...	105
BUFFALO AND LION, ...	106
INGRATITUDE, ...	109
AN UNEXPECTED ATTACK, ...	110
AN EARNEST CONFERENCE, ...	112

	PAGE.
THE SPRING-BOK, ...	115
BLACK AND WHITE ANTELOPES, ...	117
THE GNU, ...	119
THE SABER ANTELOPE, ...	120
THE HARNESSED ANTELOPE, ...	121
THE ELAND, ...	122
THE AFRICAN ELEPHANT, ...	123
THE ORYX OF ABYSSINIA, ...	124
THE KOODOO, ...	125
" 'DOWN !' WHISPERED DICK,"	126
IN HOT PURSUIT, ...	129
THE SPOTTED HYENA, ...	130
A WARM RECEPTION, ...	131
THE STRIPED HYENA, ...	132
AN UNEXPECTED RECEPTION, ...	133
GONE CLEAN DAFT, ...	136
THE ADDAX, ...	138
" LOOK OUT ! HE'S GOING TO STRIKE !" . .	142
THE BOSCH VARK, . . , ...	145
THE WART HOG, ...	146
THE BABIROUSSA, ...	148
" HE FELL FROM THE BACK OF HIS STEED," .	150
THE QUAGGA, ...	153
BURCHELL'S ZEBRA, ...	154
" ME SHOW SOMETHING,"	157
THE TREE PORCUPINE, ...	158
THE TUFTED-TAIL PORCUPINE, ...	159
AN AWKWARD PET, ...	160
" I'LL LEAVE YOU HERE, APACHE," . . .	163
THE SECRETARY-BIRD, ...	164
A STRANGE COMBAT, ...	168
A DISMAL REGION, ...	169
A FRIEND IN NEED, ...	173
THE ORNITHOLOGIST, ...	174
VIGNETTE—CHAMELEON, ...	177
" THIRTY-ONE FEET, THREE INCHES," . . .	179
VIGNETTE—SNAKE, ...	181
THE BOA-CONSTRICTOR, ...	182
A PRODUCT OF OUR OWN COUNTRY, . . .	183
THE COBRA DE CAPELLO, ...	184
THE HORNED SNAKE, ...	185

LIST OF ILLUSTRATIONS.

	PAGE.
ANOTHER SPECIMEN,	185
A PIT VIPER,	186
VIGNETTE—A TREE-TOP FROLIC,	188
THE GRIZZLY BEAR,	189
"OLD EPHRAIM HAD COME TO TOWN,"	191
INITIAL—KANGAROO,	194
THE BROWN BEAR,	195
THE BLACK BEAR,	196
KANGAROO AND YOUNG,	197
THE MALAY BEAR,	198
THE POLAR BEAR,	199
THE BADGER,	201
THE ELEPHANT MOUSE,	202
THE KANGAROO MOUSE,	203
THE DUCK-BILL, OR ORNITHORHYNCHUS,	204
DINGOES HUNTING THE EMU,	205
A LEAP FOR THE CHAMPIONSHIP,	206
MEN HUNTING THE EMU,	208
"THE OUTLINES OF A MAN'S HEAD ROSE,"	213
AS IN THE OLDEN TIME,	216
THE TEST,	218
VIGNETTE—SPIDER MONKEYS,	220
THE BLOTCHED GENET,	221
"SOMETHING OUT THERE IN THE GRASS,"	222
A SLY THIEF,	224
A SECOND TOO LATE,	226
"I'VE GOT HIM!"	229
A FAMILY PARTY,	231
THE ORANG-OUTAN,	232
HEAD OF ORANG-OUTAN,	233
A CONCERT,	234
THE CHACMA,	235
THE GELADA,	236
THE DRILL,	237
THE MANDRILL,	238
THE HOWLERS,	239
LONG-NOSED MONKEYS,	240
VIGNETTE—THE TARANTULA,	241
THE ANT-LION,	243
THE ANT-LION'S TRAP,	243
THE CHAMELEON,	246
THE BELTED ARMADILLO,	247
THE BALL SHAPED ARMADILLO,	248
THE TAMANOIR,	249
THE AYE-AYE,	250
MARTENS,	251
"WE ARE READY!"	252
AN AFRICAN TEMPEST,	253
"IT VANISHED IN THE GLOOM,"	254
THE LIGHTNING'S FLASH,	259
"HE ALMOST FELL HEADLONG,"	261
"THE THREE LOOKED LONG AND CLOSELY,"	265
A STARTLING DISCOVERY,	267
"HE CAUGHT THE STAR-LIKE TWINKLE,"	271
"HIS ARMS WERE SUDDENLY SEIZED,"	275
CAPTIVE AND CAPTORS,	278
HUNTING FOR POISON,	280
THE PARLEY,	284
"'I SAW HIM!' EXCLAIMED BOB,"	287
LIVELY TIMES,	289
THE JAVANESE RHINOCEROS,	293
"HE CAUGHT SIGHT OF THE VAST BEAST,"	296
TURNING THE TABLES,	301
"HE SEES ME,"	303
TWO-HORNED RHINOCEROS,	309
A DOUBLE CHASE,	311
PONDEROUS GAME,	314
A TROUBLESOME CAPTIVE,	315
THE HIPPOPOTAMUS,	319
A RESISTLESS ATTACK,	323
"COME! HELP!"	330
"I PULLED TRIGGER,"	335
THE SACRED COW,	338
THE GAYAL,	340
MUSIC'S CHARMS,	343
"FIVE REPORTS RANG OUT,"	344
A WHOLE FAMILY,	346
A SERPENT-CHARMER,	347
AT HOME,	349
VIGNETTE,	350
IN A TIGHT PLACE,	351
TIGER AND BUFFALO,	355
A STRIKING TABLEAU,	361
WARM WORK,	364
DEATH OF THE POSTMAN,	368
CAUGHT IN THE ACT,	372
IN THE NICK OF TIME,	377
MOUNTAIN DOVES AND LIZARDS,	380
THE COCKATOO,	381
FAN-CRESTED PARROT,	382
THE HYACINTH ARARA,	383
GORAL ANTELOPE,	384
THE STEPPE ANTELOPE,	385
THE NYLGHAU,	386
FALCONER'S GOAT,	387
THE PANDA OF THE HIMALAYAS,	388
IN AMBUSH,	389
THE AOUDAD,	390
THE SACRED ANTELOPE,	392
A FAMILY OF ELKS,	393
FALLOW DEER,	394
JUMBO ON HIS TRAVELS,	395

LIST OF ILLUSTRATIONS.

	PAGE.
My Famous White Elephant,	398
A Battle in the Jungle,	401
Huge Sport	403
An Intruder,	405
"Royal Sport, Indeed,"	414
By a Hair's Breadth,	416
"But it was too late,"	419
"He laid him down,"	421
Golden Trogons,	423
The Critical Moment,	424
The Satin Bower Bird,	425
The Sociable Weaver Bird,	426
The Paradise Whidah Bird,	427
The Lyre Bird,	427
The African Barbet,	428
The Hornbill,	428
The Tailor Bird,	429
The Oven Bird,	430
The Stormy Petrel,	431
Panther and Her Young,	432
The Laughing Kingfisher,	433
The Dinornis,	433
The Brush Turkey of Australia,	434
The Apteryx,	435
The Great Bird of Paradise,	435
The Pelican,	436

	PAGE.
The Scissors Bill,	436
The Eagle Owl,	437
The Eared Grebe,	438
The Adjutant Bird,	439
The Common Octopus,	441
Inhabitants of the Deep,	443
Head of the Gorilla,	445
Discouraged,	447
Saurians,	451
"He jerked with might and main,"	455
Head of the Gorilla, Front View,	456
Chimpanzees,	457
Head of the Chimpanzee,	459
"Nip" and "Tuck,"	460
The Capture,	463
Might is Right,	464
A Tropical Tea Party,	465
A Fight to the Death,	467
Contentment,	470
Bulky Bathers	471
A Happy Mother,	476
The King of the Jungle,	478
A Little Fury,	479
Just too Late,	483
Dick,	485
Dick and His Pet,	487

INTRODUCTION.

THE subject and method of this book are indicated in the title, "Natural History From a New Standpoint." In its preparation two facts have been considered. First, no more effective method of instruction has been found than that which conveys knowledge through that love of the story which is characteristic of all children and youth. Second, in reading the book of nature, not only a knowledge of the teachings of science, but long experience and close, careful observation, are essential. The special fitness of Mr. Barnum to produce a book on this subject will be at once recognized. As he says in his preface, he has "catered to the instruction and amusement of three generations." The countless multitudes of people who have viewed the collections of animals which he has exhibited during this long period, have little appreciated the herculean labor and the world of dangerous adventure which has attended the capture of these animals — beasts, birds and reptiles — nor the minute and accurate study of their nature, habits and characteristics which has been involved in their care and training. It is plain that to hunt, find and capture these animals in their native wilds, to feed and care for them, preserve their health, subdue their wild natures, and teach them the many tricks which are performed, must not only have required great courage, patience, and a thorough knowledge of all that science can tell of them, but must have gained for those engaged in the work a far more close and familiar acquaintance with the nature of all these animals, and so a more thorough and accurate knowledge of actual natural history than has ever been given in any text-book on this subject.

It is from this vast storehouse of adventure and scientific information that the veteran showman and writer has drawn in the production of this work. In the form of a thrilling narrative he gives an account of the many exciting adventures which were experienced by those engaged in his expeditions made in search of wild animals, and at the same time presents a full and accurate description of the nature and peculiarities of these animals. The book is thus made a most efficient instructor in natural history, while at the same time it is a most fascinating narrative of adventure. Without preliminaries the reader is introduced to the exploring party under the direction of the naturalist, Carl Godkin, in the midst of an African jungle, and the story moves forward with an interest that never flags. The engravings which illustrate the text add much to its interest and value. The most striking incidents of adventure are illustrated by W. M. Cary, in a series of drawings which are considered by experts the best he has yet produced ; while the animals described are pictured by such artists as Specht, Kretschmar, Mutzel and others. The colored plates are from drawings by Specht. The work closes with a chapter entitled "The Reason Why in Natural History," which in the form of questions and answers gives much curious and interesting information.

Y young friend Bob Marshall was picking his way through the South African jungle, when he paused to look upon a striking but characteristic scene.

A beautiful leopard had run a short distance up the sloping trunk of a fallen tree, and then, turning about on a large projecting limb, faced a pack of hyenas that were eager to attack him, but afraid to do so. One rash fellow ventured nigh enough to receive a cuff from the defender's paw which knocked him a dozen feet away and caused him to keep a safe distance thereafter, while the others were equally careful to avoid those sharp claws and teeth.

Eager to Attack but Afraid—Page 11

Bob was inclined to raise his Winchester and fire upon the cowardly assailants, but he finally moved off without doing so.

"The leopard wouldn't appreciate my interference," was the thought of the youth, "and I don't believe he needs it anyway."

Bob was on his way back to camp, as the sultry day was drawing to a close, and he kept a close watch for danger.

"I can't see anything," he said to himself, holding his rifle ready for instant use, "but I have been in the Dark Continent long enough to know that *that* is no proof I am not in peril."

The listening ear caught the sounds of the myriad birds flitting among the exuberant branches overhead, and now and then the deep, resonant roar of some animal warned him that he was liable at any moment to be brought face to face with some of the fierce denizens of the wilds, always eager to fly at any intruder.

It was the growing conviction that something was stealthily following him which tried the nerves of Bob Marshall, for it is the unseen that tests one's bravery, since so long as it remains unseen it is unknown, and imagination gives it a form and substance ten-fold more fearful than reality.

He was sure that the limbs in the immediate vicinity contained no hideous python or boa-constrictor, for those reptiles must of necessity wind themselves around the trunk or branches of a tree, where the quick eye of the hunter readily detects them. And Bob was equally positive there was none of those frightful serpents approaching him through the jungle, for his hearing, trained to marvelous nicety, was sure to catch the soft rustling that invariably betrays the approach of a large snake.

"It must be some beast crouching so flat on a branch that his body is entirely hidden—helloa! there he is, sure enough!"

Barely thirty feet above the head of the youth, an immense limb put forth from a tree whose trunk was no more than a rod from where he stood. The diameter of the branch was sufficient to hide the body of a large animal, when stretched along its length, and such concealment it did afford to a brute whose ears, glowing eye-balls and open mouth protruded just far enough over the support to enable the young hunter to identify him as an enormous leopard.

So skillfully had the beast disposed himself on the limb that more than likely Bob would not have detected him, but for the low, threatening growl which he emitted.

Had the leopard held his peace and kept his head lowered, the youth would have walked directly beneath him, giving the treacherous animal a chance to bound down upon his shoulders with the irresistibility of a thunderbolt. But the leopard did not know enough to take that precaution.

His species, however, is among the most cunning of the animal kingdom, and, though it is probable that this specimen was now brought face to face with a Caucasian for the first time, he had sufficient subtlety to keep himself well shielded by the solid branch along which he was extended.

"HE LET FLY THREE TIMES IN SUCCESSION"   Page 15

" I think there is enough of your head in sight to make a pretty fair target," muttered Bob, bringing his rifle to his shoulder and sighting at the skull.

The distance was so short that there was hardly an excuse for missing, and yet that is just what Bob Marshall did do, though we can hardly censure him because of the failure.

By one of those rare coincidences that occasionally take place, the leopard, from some cause, which cannot be explained, ducked his head almost at the instant the weapon was discharged, the bullet cutting its way through the dense vegetation beyond and above the limb.

Keeping his weapon elevated, Bob instantly shoved another cartridge into place, and, as the threatening head rose to sight, he let fly three times in quick succession.

Bob did not score a " bull's eye" each time, but all the same, he hit the leopard, the balls ploughing their way through the outer portions of his head, and inflicting wounds which roused him to fury.

Confident that he had killed the beast, Bob lowered his gun and looked to see him fall. The leopard came down, but not as the youth expected.

Instead of tumbling from his perch, limp and lifeless, he emitted a snarling screech, and sprang from the limb straight at the astounded youth, who was almost paralyzed by the sight of the terrible head, streaked with blood, the ears lying flat and the jaws extended to their widest extent. The sharp, carnivorous teeth and needle-like claws were eager to rend the lad to shreds.

Had Bob Marshall stood motionless in his footsteps, nothing could have saved him, but, in obedience to what may be termed instinct rather than reason, he sprang back several feet, just as the leopard dropped lightly to the ground, and, crouching low, gathered his muscles for a second leap that was to land him on the shoulders of the youth.

It occurred to Bob that no more appropriate moment for shooting off a gun could be thought of, and I need not tell you that he was not long in acting upon this decision. The style in which he began pumping Winchester balls into the snarling leopard was enough to stampede a drove of elephants.

But it must not be supposed that the recipient of this bombardment remained quiescent. Hardly had Bob pulled trigger, after the beast landed on the ground, when the dreaded leap was made.

It was a moment of such fearful excitement that it was impossible for the lad to make his aim as unerring as it would have been had the animal remained stationary for a second or two. Almost before he was aware, the leopard bounded at him with a ferocity that can exist only when the fiercest of wild beasts is in his death-throes.

Bob had no time to recoil as he did in the first instance, but with admirable presence of mind, and with inimitable dexterity, he dropped to a crouching posture and darted a single step forward. As a consequence, the leopard went clean over him. Bob wheeled and again brought his gun to his shoulder; in fact, hunter and beast had exchanged positions.

The leopard must be kept off for a moment, for if those frightful claws were given but a single chance, they would play mortal havoc with the handsome face and athletic frame of the youth.

Three shots still remained in the magazine of the Winchester, and no three cartridges were ever discharged with more celerity. Every one, too, found a lodgment in the body of the beast, and they settled the business.

Deprived of the power of assault, and mortally wounded in half a dozen places, the brute rolled upon his back, with a rasping snarl, his claws beating the air like lightning for a few seconds, and then he became still and motionless.

THE LEOPARD.

With the coolness of Gordon Cumming himself, Bob Marshall stood aside and calmly surveyed his game, after all semblance of life had departed.

"That's the biggest leopard I ever saw," said he, "though Mr. Godkin tells me that he has seen larger in India, the home of the tiger. The usual length of the animal is four feet, with its tail a little more than half as much, but this fellow is fully five feet long, and he would have been a terrible foe if I had allowed him to close in with me."

I am quite sure all my readers have seen specimens of the leopard, which, like the cat, belongs to the *Felis* species. You have admired his rich, yellowish fawn color, paler on the sides and losing itself in the pure white of the belly. He is covered with numerous annular or oval black spots, the sides and part of the tail showing distinct roses, made by the near approach of three or four elongated small dark spots, which surround a central area, an inch in breadth, somewhat deeper in color than the ground on which it is placed. You may have noticed, too, that there are a few black lines on the lips, and bands of the same color on the insides of the legs.

The leopard is one of the most skillful climbers, and few animals can escape him by taking refuge among the tree branches. When wounded, he is a demon, and hundreds of people are annually slain by the species in India and Africa.

"I wonder how the rest have made out," muttered Bob Marshall, referring to his friends; "I have heard the reports of their guns more than once, and I suppose they have brought down something, but I don't believe there has been anything shot finer than this."

The youth noticed that the afternoon was wearing away, and, as he was a considerable distance from camp, he decided to set out on his return without delay. He looked longingly at the huge body, and, when he reflected what a handsome trophy the skin would make, naturally regretted leaving it behind.

"I promised to send Mr. Barnum something of the kind," he said, as he was on the point of turning away, "though I know he has more such presents than he knows what to do with, but I can't afford the time to skin him, and it may be that Mr. Godkin or Dick or some of the rest will bag something better."

And with this philosophical reflection, Mr. Robert Marshall slung his Winchester over his shoulder and set off for the encampment of his friends.

A goodly distance remained to be passed, and, since night was approaching, he thought it likely he would encounter more game before joining his companions.

This expectation received a startling confirmation within the succeeding quarter of an hour.

2

CHAPTER II.

As NEARLY as Bob Marshall could recall, he had to make his way for about a mile, in order to reach the camp where all members of the hunting party expected to pass the night. Ordinarily the task of traveling this would not be worth mentioning, but a portion of it led through the jungle, and he was obliged to make quite a circuit to avoid those exasperating thorny shrubs which travelers have named "wait-a-bit" bushes, and he knew that in that tropical country, where the twilight is so short, darkness was likely to descend before he could join his friends.

Not far from the spot where he shot the leopard it was necessary to cross a deep stream, too broad for him to leap, but it was bridged by a fallen tree, which he had used on his way into the jungle and which, of course, he expected to utilize on his return.

A less experienced hunter than Bob would have been almost certain to lose himself, because of the many changes in his course, but with the aid of the little compass which he wore as a watch charm, and by keeping his bearings in mind, he was generally able to avoid the dangerous blunder of going astray.

There was the stream, whose waters looked of inky blackness, which he came upon at the very moment he expected, and he had but a little way to go, when he caught sight of the fallen tree that had served him so well on his tramp thither.

"If nothing unexpected happens, I shall not be the last one to reach camp," he reflected, as he placed his foot on the trunk and began picking his way across, without paying heed to a sluggish snake twisting among some rotten sticks on the edge of the stream near by.

The base of the tree was several feet beyond the edge of the opposite shore, while the branches projected fully a rod behind where Bob began crossing, that part of the trunk which he used as a bridge being free from limbs.

DISPUTING THE WAY.

The youth had passed about one-third of the distance, with no thought of molestation, when, to his amazement, a leopardess issued from the undergrowth, and stepping upon the larger portion of the trunk, advanced to meet him.

This was a surprise indeed, and Bob stopped, in doubt for the instant what was the best thing to do. It flashed on him at once that this was the mate of the leopard he had shot, and whether she had learned the truth or not, it was manifest from her action that she was in a fighting mood. Indeed, the fierceness displayed by the two animals was exceptional, for, as a rule, leopards are not likely to disturb a man unless he first molests them.

The female advanced with the slow, cautious movement of her species, her head held low between her shoulders, which lumped up in a peculiar way as she walked, her jaws slightly parted, her eyes fixed upon the youth, while an occasional growl and her whole demeanor proved that she did not mean to give the road to him who stood in her way.

Bob saw the decayed bark of the tree crumble and break under the sharp claws that pierced it, as she approached, and none knew better than he what the result would be of a hand-to-hand encounter with such a ferocious foe.

But what cause had he to fear with his formidable Winchester, which he knew so well how to handle? A minute or two must pass before the brute could approach nigh enough to attack and that gave him abundant time in which to aim and fire.

The plan of turning to flee never once entered his mind, for such a course, in the presence of a wild animal, inevitably hastens its assault.

With that coolness which was one of the lad's most remarkable traits, he brought his rifle to a level, and was taking aim at a point midway between the glaring eyes, when he recalled that the magazine of his gun did not contain a single cartridge!

Bob had disregarded the fundamental rule of the hunter, which is, after discharging his gun, instantly to reload, so as to be ready for any emergency.

True, the task of preparing his breech-loader was so slight that this rule lost half its force, when the modern weapon was compared with the muzzle-loader of our fathers' days, but the youth felt he had no time in which to get his favorite weapon ready for the charge of the beast.

He was the owner of a fine, five-chambered Colt's revolver, thrust in his hip pocket, not to mention the knife at his waist; but he might well distrust the effectiveness of those weapons after his experience with the male leopard.

It was useless to regret his thoughtlessness, for at the moment he recalled it, it may be said the peril was upon him. He had not time to prepare his gun, nor did he wish to appeal to the revolver, though he hastily drew it, meaning to empty every chamber into the front of the leopardess, before she could fasten her claws upon him.

At such times a person thinks fast. Bob was handicapped by his position on the tree, and wished so strongly for more space in which to maneuver, that he began moving backward, trying to do so with such deliberation that his foe would not notice it.

But this was extremely difficult, as you can readily understand, because of the straitness of his support. It was necessary to step with the utmost care, and since he was not a trapeze performer, he found himself unable to retrograde, keeping his eyes on the beast at the same time. without imminent danger of being precipitated into the deep waters beneath.

At this moment, when it may be said matters had reached a crisis, a discovery flashed upon Bob with the suddenness of inspiration.

The leopardess looked up in his face, two or three times, with her body seemingly flattened along the log, and then darted her gaze away, as a child will do when it unexpectedly glances at the sun.

"I'll try it," thought the youth; "strange that I didn't think of it before!"

Bob now stood stationary on the log, but crouched in the attitude of a leaper, preparing for a standing jump. He stooped so low and his head was thrust so far forward, that, had you seen him, you would have felt sure (though wondering much thereat) that he was about to spring upon the head of the leopardess.

But I need not tell you that the wise youth never dreamed of throwing away his life in any such fashion as *that*.

What, then, was he seeking to do?

Assuming the fiercest expression at his command, he stared straight into the eyes of the beast. The latter met his gaze for an instant, as though she expected to look him out of countenance, but she was unequal to the test.

She kept up her snarling, while her extended claws showed a peculiar nervous twitching, the nails causing the crumbling bark to fall fast into the water, while she cast furtive glances at the rigid youth who seemed determined to look her through and through.

Again and again she looked at him, only to dart her eyes aside as if in actual fear, but she not only refused to retreat, but continued slowly advancing upon her enemy.

There could be no question that the female was clear grit.

Fully comprehending the situation, Bob Marshall now called into play his last resource.

With his head thrust forward, his rifle grasped in his left hand and his Colt in his right, he raised one foot and set it down several inches further along the log, his purpose being to give the step as much significance as possible.

It looked, for all the world, as if he had resolved to become the aggressor and assail the leopardess, instead of waiting for her to attack him.

Had he removed his glance but for a moment, while taking this bold step, the brute would have bounded forward and fastened teeth and claws in him, for beyond a doubt she was fully as courageous as her mate.

Such evidently was her intention, when, with a sharper growl than before, she partly rose to her feet and glanced at that terrible human countenance now so close to her own.

The battery of those burning eyes was more than she could stand, and turning nimbly on the log, she made a tremendous bound, which carried her back to the side from which she started.

Instead of running away, however, she crouched in the thin, tall grass near the trunk, with the evident intention of awaiting the advance of the young hunter, when she would try it again.

You will remember that night was closing in, darkness having actually begun, and, while there is no animal known that can be so easily subdued by the human eye as the leopard (especially the cheetah or hunting leopard), yet nothing is more evident than that the strange power cannot be exerted in gloom or darkness.

"I see you mean that I shall not use the log for a footbridge," said Bob Marshall, straightening up, "while I'm determined that I shall, and since I forgot to reload my gun, now is a good time to do so."

And balancing himself carefully on his narrow support, he took nine cartridges from his belt and placed them in the magazine. Then, bringing his weapon to his shoulder, he sighted at the velvety front of the beast just below her head, and drove three shells into the fatally weak spot with a quickness that could not have been surpassed.

They were more than enough.

The leopardess bounded several feet straight up in the air, just as if thrown by a powerful spring-board, making a complete somersault, or rather half a somersault, for she fell on her back, dead, almost as soon as she struck the earth.

"That teaches you that it's risky business to dispute the way with a young American gentleman when he has the latest pattern of the Winchester at command. The lesson comes too late to do *you* any good, but it couldn't have been better timed to suit me, and if some of your surviving kindred will read aright the moral of what they discover, it may serve them well."

As if to make amends for his former forgetfulness, Bob thrust three more cartridges in the magazine of his gun, so that as he moved across the stream, and stepped ashore on the same side with the carcass of the leopardess, his weapon was fully charged.

CHAPTER III.

"HELLOA, Bob! where are you?"

"I will be with you in a minute."

Bob Marshall recognized the call as that of his cousin, Dick Brownell, who, like several other members of the hunting party, was out alone for game. The youths, who were about the same age, were not far apart, and, a few minutes later, they met in the gloom of the gathering night.

Bob quickly related his adventure with the two leopards.

"That's lucky," said his friend, "for I am interested in them, or rather I was before they were shot."

"How is that?"

"The two kittens of the mother are tumbling about in

the grass by a rock just off yonder, and I've been waiting two hours to get a chance to shoot the parents before making off with the youngsters."

I am sure you will readily understand the methods by which the professional hunters secure most of the wild animals for my Great Show. I have despatched some of the most experienced sportsmen living, into the heart of the least known and most inaccessible regions of the globe, where they have been lost to their own kind for months. Sometimes, sad to say, they were lost forever.

Two of the best hunters I ever knew penetrated the dismal wilderness of interior Australia, mainly in quest of the kanga- roo, which is found there or in the neigh- boring islands. This was more than twelve years ago, since which time nothing has been heard of them, and there is little doubt that they fell victims to the many dan- gers that proved fatal to scores of explorers be- fore them.

SHIPS OF THE DESERT

I have sent parties into the mountains and table lands of Thibet, and hardly a year has passed for a generation that a company has not departed from Suakem or Massowah for the more salubrious climate of interior Abyssinia. These hunters always use camels, for it is impossible to employ any other means of conveyance.

The young that are captured are brought back on these "ships of the desert." Many of you remember the young hippopotamus which was with my show some years ago. It was secured in the Upper Nile region and carried all the way to Suakem, on the African coast of the Red Sea, suspended in a hammock between two camels, the weight of the young monster being too much for a single beast of burden.

I have always drawn freely on India, where many of the fiercest animals abound (and which is the home of the royal Bengal tiger, the most fearful of all creatures), not to mention Ceylon, Farther India and many other portions of the earth.

Africa, however, is the great source of supply, and many a hundred thousand dollars of my money has gone to the Dark Continent, that I might bring you curiosities that are interesting, entertaining and instructive. I have had agencies at Port Natal, Cape Town, on the Gold Coast, at Cairo and other points, and have now sat down to write the history of the most famous expedition I ever sent into Southern and Central Africa, India, or indeed into any part of the world. I will give you particulars further on.

One simple rule governs the hunters who are in quest of wild animals. You can understand that it is impossible in most cases to capture the full grown tiger, leopard, giraffe, ostrich, lion, and indeed any large quadruped except, perhaps, the elephant, which can be readily brought under subjection. Most of these beasts, in their savage state, will fight to the death before yielding. At any rate, the difficulty of securing them shuts out most attempts to do so.

The rule of the hunters, therefore, is to seek the place where the young are receiving the attention of the mother, and then, lying in wait, shoot her, and quite often the father, too, when he is in the neighborhood.

The parents being disposed of, the helpless offspring are taken from their quarters, carefully looked after, and sent to the sea coast, where they are kept until strong enough to be shipped across the sea to England and thence to this country.

Now, you will see that Bob Marshall, when he shot the two leopards, to use a common expression, builded better than he knew. Beyond a doubt, they were the parents of the kittens of which his cousin spoke, and the way was thereby opened to carry off the valuable young.

That was what the two youths and their companions were in Africa for, and they lost no time in following instructions. Dick Brownell led the way through the tall grass to an immense rock, at the base of which was a cavity partly filled with dead vegetation, arranged with some system by the mother of the leopards.

Enough light remained for the cousins to observe two forms, resembling chunky dogs, nosing around in the grass, emitting strange mewing sounds, as they vainly groped for their mother. They were hungry and could not understand why their usual supper was denied them.

"That's a piece of good luck," said Bob, stooping down and griping one of the kittens by the loose skin at the back of the neck, which, as you know, is the spot where the *Felis* species seizes their young when they wish to carry them any distance.

Dick Brownell did the same with the other kitten, which was a solid fellow indeed. The baby leopards were quick to learn that it was not their mother that was handling them, and they began fighting with a vigor which gave a vivid idea of what they would be able to do a few months later.

However, they were too infantile to cause much harm, and soon ceased their struggles.

When one of the cat kind is obliged to carry its young an unusual distance, it frequently sets it down for a few minutes on the way. I suppose this is not for the purpose of resting the mother, but to relieve the little one from the discomfort of being transported for a long time by the neck. How much better the arrangement if the parent would carry its young on her back, like the hippopotamus, but it is not for me to find fault with the wonderful provisions of nature.

The youths grasped the little leopards, and strode off rapidly in the direction of camp. But it was not long before the kittens began to squirm with discomfort and the boys set them on the ground.

"My gracious!" exclaimed Bob, "that youngster is heavier than I thought; my fingers and arm ache."

"So do mine; let's try another plan, for it seems to me their necks must feel uncomfortable."

So they shoved their prizes under their right arms, just as I have no doubt you have done when trying to carry a large watermelon, which, I believe, is the most awkward thing in the world to transport in that fashion.

Of course each held his rifle in his left hand, so as to leave his other free to manage his prize, and they soon found it was needed.

The young leopards ought to have been grateful for the change, but, somehow or other, it did not seem natural, and they twisted about with a vigor that was astonishing.

"Look out! there goes your chap!" called Bob, with a laugh, to his cousin, as he noticed the youngster wriggling his way forward.

Hardly were the words uttered when the uneasy captive plumped to the ground like a huge doughnut at the feet of Dick Brownell, despite his frantic efforts to check the fall.

"Confound him! why don't he know when he is well off and keep still?" muttered Dick, stooping down to recapture the fellow.

Bob Marshall broke into merry laughter.

"If I couldn't manage a baby leopard I'd give up all pretension of being a hunter— OAGH!"

Bob was so interested in the dilemma of his companion that he failed to give proper attention to his own prize, which, instead of working to the front, shoved backward with such deftness that it slipped from the lad's grasp before he suspected it.

With a seeming knowledge of the state of the case, the young brute had no sooner landed than it leaped upward and buried its sharp teeth in the leg of Bob Marshall, above his boot. The lad, with a howl of dismay, sprang several feet in air, kicking his limb forward as if to free himself from some venomous serpent that had fastened its fangs in his flesh.

"Why can't you behave yourself?" he demanded, angrily catching up his tormentor and raising his hand to give it a cuff.

But the blow did not descend, and he joined in the laugh of Dick, who was certainly warranted in turning upon him in that fashion.

It is not to be supposed that the young creatures knew enough to mourn the loss of their parents, could they have been made to comprehend that they had actually lost them; they were simply hungering for their usual evening meal, and had it been in the power of their captors to supply that want, they would have been as docile as lambs.

"I don't think you will starve before we get you

A TROUBLESOME CAPTIVE.

back to camp," remarked Bob, picking up his prize more carefully than before; "and when we once land you there, we'll stuff you to your ears."

It was not to be expected that such addresses would exert a very soothing effect upon the captives, and the youths were not long in finding they had essayed anything but an easy task in carrying them to headquarters.

Before half the distance was passed the night was fully come; the faint moon in the sky gave all the light needed, for they had left the dense jungle behind and were pushing through a portion of the country so open that no trouble was experienced in keeping the right course.

But you must bear in mind that they were in a part of the world where they were continually exposed to danger. While guarding their treasures, therefore, with such care, it was necessary to keep their senses on the alert for other forms of peril.

Several times Dick, who was in advance, stopped and listened, fancying he detected something threatening; but fortunately they were not molested, and finally the end of their somewhat laborious journey was reached, without any mishap either to themselves or the prizes in which they were so much interested

CHAPTER IV.

MY AFRICAN EXPEDITION.

IT is now time I gave you some information about the expedition whose adventures in Southern and Central Africa and India I have set out to tell.

The rule with the hunting parties which leave Suakem for the interior of Abyssinia is to take thirty days for the journey into the desert and forty days to return, the greater period being necessary to transport the captures made.

The expedition which I sent into Southern Africa, however, was much more elaborate in its make-up and more ambitious in the results sought.

It consisted of ten natives, respectively known as Pongo, a Bushman (whose people show some resemblance to the Chinese); Diedrick, a Hottentot; Abdallah, from Senaar, and Govozy, Wart, Adz, Bormo, Divak, Valmur, Orak and Gooboo, gathered from the wild tribes near the south-eastern coast. The first three could talk English quite well, the others having such an imperfect knowledge of the language that they rarely attempted to make their meaning known, except by a gibberish that was as hard for Pongo, Diedrick and Abdallah to understand as for the American members of the company.

The three of whom I have particularly spoken were experienced hunters, Pongo having been acquainted with Gordon Cumming and the lamented Livingstone, while Diedrick was with the famous missionary when he died. The others were simply servants who were counted upon to do what may be called the menial labor of the expedition.

Carl Godkin was the director. He entered my service when a boy, and was sent to India before he reached his majority, which was thirty years previous to the most important enterprise in which he engaged and of which, as I have said, I have set out to give you the history.

Although nearly fifty years old, he was so toughened by his many years of exposure that he seemed proof against the frightful African climate, which proves fatal to so many foreigners. He was intelligent, well educated, possessing great resources and knowledge of natural history, and was one of the most successful sportsmen that ever lived. When I add to this that he was an American, thoroughly honest and devoted to my interests, you will approve of my course in placing him in charge of the expedition.

In addition to the natives named, Mr. Godkin took with him three other Americans as his main assistants. The first of these was Jack Harvey, a Texan cowboy, ten years younger than himself, but his equal in many and his superior in other respects. He was a consummate horseman, could throw the lasso with the skill of a Comanche chieftain, was a wonderful shot with his Winchester and revolver, and went into danger from pure love of the excitement it afforded.

I made Jack's acquaintance in San Antonio, ten years previous to the time I introduce him to you. His handsome, manly appearance, and his extraordinary coolness and courage, rendered him famous among those whose chief claims to admiration lie in that direction, and when he announced his wish to enter my service, I gladly made room for him.

Jack's first ambitious attempt was in New Guinea, where he secured two kangaroos and acquitted himself so well that I was pleased to send him into Africa with Mr. Godkin and his party.

I should mention one peculiarity of Jack: in all the enterprises in which he engaged, he stuck to his cowboy costume, refusing to accommodate himself to the particular country where his duty led him. So you will picture him always as a sinewy, athletic cowboy, with a Roman nose, big mustache, chin whiskers, broad sombrero, rattlesnake band, flowing hair, thick flannel shirt, belt around the waist, containing cartridges, bowie-knife and two revolvers, while his Winchester was hardly ever absent from his strong right hand.

You have had a partial introduction to the remaining members of the expedition — Bob Marshall and Dick Brownell — cousins and both slightly more than seventeen years of age. These young gentlemen have made me promise not to give much information about them, though I can't understand why they should feel any objection, since all that I could tell would be to their credit.

I will say this, however: they were strong, athletic youths, belonging to good families, bright, honest, manly, and relatives of one of the dearest friends I ever had. It was their intention, should they be spared to return from the perilous enterprise on which they entered with such zest, to become students in Yale College, where they were sure to make a creditable record for themselves.

There is considerable more interesting information that I could give about these young men of whom I am so fond, but they won't let me. They are unwilling even that I should mention the commendable fact that neither has ever

JACK HARVEY AND "APACHE."

tasted liquor, smoked or chewed tobacco, and that a profane word has never polluted their lips; that they are affectionate and dutiful sons — but really I must proceed no further, or I shall have an account to settle with them when my good publishers place this volume before you.

Bob and Dick followed the advice of Mr. Carl Godkin, the leader of the expedition, in all things. Like him, they wore the hunting costume most sensible for Southern Africa, consisting of the helmet hat, the light but serviceable hunting coat and trousers, which, like those of Jack Harvey, were thrust in the top of their cavalry boots. The latter were not the most comfortable for that climate, and many hunters use only sandals, without stockings, while others go entirely barefoot, like the natives.

But the tough leather had saved every one of the four more than once from the bites of venomous snakes, and I cannot help thinking they were wise in retaining them. At any rate, I have made up my mind that if ever I engage in a similar hunting jaunt, I shall adopt a similar costume.

The party took with them three wagons, all of which, as some would say, had been "salted," that is, they were seasoned by service under the flaming sun of

AFRICAN OX.

Africa, and were not liable to break down until thoroughly worn out, when, like the Parson's famous "one-hoss shay," it might be expected they would go to pieces all at once.

The latter half of these wagons was covered with canvas, and the front open. Each was drawn by two span of oxen, there being two extra span for emergencies.

There were also a half dozen goats to furnish milk for such animals as required nursing before being able to digest their natural food. The supply from the goats proved a blessing many a time to the hunters themselves.

Attached to the expedition were six fleet, active, intelligent ponies for the use of the four Americans, two being extra. It was characteristic of Jack Harvey that he took his mustang, which he called "Apache," from Texas, with him. Carl Godkin assured him that it would succumb in the trying climate of Africa, but the Texan replied that in that case he would be no worse off than if he hadn't taken him, since the company was furnished with two extra animals.

Up to the date of which I am writing, Jack's steed was as vigorous and service-able as when bearing his rider across the Llano Estacado in pursuit of the mur-dering Apaches, and his owner was confident that, barring accident, he would take him safely through his campaign in the Dark Continent.

All were armed with Winchester repeaters, beside which there were two double-barrel shot-guns, full choke, intended for use in shooting birds and smaller game, especially for the pot. Each man also carried a five-chambered revolver, Colt's pattern (Jack Harvey being the only one who used two), and a long, keen knife, indispensable in that country.

Of course there was a full supply of cooking utensils, a number of simple medicinal remedies and articles which it is not necessary to particularize. One of these, I may say, however, was a Texan lasso that Jack Harvey carried with him when careering across the country in search of animals. You shall speedily receive proof of his skill in the use of this peculiarly American contrivance, so popular on the Southwestern border.

The natives expected to do little hunting and generally traveled on foot or took turns in riding in the lumbering wagons. They were armed with spears and knives only, there being one notable exception in the case of Pongo, who carried a boomerang, or rather three of them.

He could throw those singular weapons with the skill of a native Australian, though where he got them and by what means he acquired his dexterity were a puzzle which neither Mr. Godkin nor any of his friends was ever able to understand, since that most remarkable implement is almost unknown outside of Australia.

Such is a general description of the party which entered the wilds of Africa in quest of curiosities for The Greatest Show on Earth, and whose adventures, exploits and achievements form one of the most romantic episodes in the history of marvelous enterprise.

The company made its start proper from Port Natal, which, as you may know, is on the eastern coast of Africa, in latitude 30° south. Moving northwest to Peter-maritzburg, they made their way through the Drakenberg mountains, which form the boundary between Natal and the Orange Free State, and thence through the southern part of the Transvaal into Bechuana Land.

This of itself was a great journey, the history of which would be interesting, but the real work of the expedition did not open until they were several hundred miles from the coast, and the space at my command will not permit me to give in detail the adventures of my friends on their way thither. Mr. Godkin, Bob Marshall and Dick Brownell kept full journals of their doings, from which I have been enabled to write this history. Had I left that work to any one of the three individuals, his modesty would have prevented him appropriating full credit for his own exploits; but, possessing, as I do, the narrative of all, and, intimately acquainted, as I am, with the excellences of each, I am quite sure I have placed the credit where it properly belongs.

Then, too, it must be borne in mind that many portions of Natal, the Orange Free State and the Transvaal Republic have been settled and developed to such an astonishing degree during the last few years that the laborious journey of our friends lacked the stirring features which awaited them further in the Dark Continent.

CHAPTER V.

IT was a merry party which formed the camp in Bechuana Land, near the Kalihari Desert, and almost under the Tropic of Capricorn. It was the most favorable season of the year, and every member of the original company had reached this distant point without serious accident. Naturally, therefore, all were in good spirits and full of high hopes. Ah, if I could but say the same a short time later !

What was still more remarkable, not a horse or ox had been lost, and the wagons proved they had been thoroughly "salted." One of the goats wandered too near a boa-constrictor one day, and the reptile darted his head from the limbs of a tree in which he was coiled and gathered in the poor capricornus with the quickness of lightning.

The indignant Jack Harvey put a bullet through the eyes of the enormous serpent and gave him his quietus, but that didn't bring the goat back to life. As it was, however, our friends could not but admit they had been extremely fortunate thus far, and they prayed heaven that their good fortune might continue.

The camp was on one of the many tributaries of the Hart River which ultimately finds its way, by means of the Great Orange, into the South Atlantic Ocean. The wagons were placed near the bank of the stream, which was several rods wide, the animals collected in an irregular circle within them, while two large fires were kindled with the intention of keeping them burning until daylight. The horses and oxen had become so accustomed to the perils of the country that they required little attention, except when actually threatened by the attack of wild animals.

The natives busied themselves by attending to the fires and preparing the evening meal. The abundance of dry grass and wood near at hand rendered the gathering of fuel a comparatively easy matter, while one of the double-barrel shot-guns had been turned to such good account by Mr. Godkin that there was a full supply of palatable antelope steak.

The animals had advanced to this point at such a leisurely pace, and had been given so many opportunities to crop the luxuriant grass on the way that they lacked nothing, and the oxen contentedly chewed their cuds as they lay on the ground, before sinking into slumber.

The evening meal being finished, the natives sat apart, where most of them could chatter in their own peculiar fashion and see that the fires were not allowed to die out. The four Americans, having looked after their ponies, also assembled in a group by one of the fires, to engage in conversation as was their custom at the close of each day.

The Camp in Bechuana Land — Page 35

Before doing so, however, the boys surrendered the leopard kittens to Pongo and Diedrick, who declared them to be two of the finest specimens they had ever seen. They were given a hearty meal of goat's milk, after which they curled up in the strong cage brought for such purposes in the rear of one of the large wagons, and sank into dreamland, pictures of contentment and peace.

Jack Harvey had been off on a ramble with his mustang, and had twice started in pursuit of ostriches, but found it impossible to get near enough for a successful shot. Consequently, he came back empty-handed, and, since Mr. Godkin hadn't tried to capture anything, it will be seen that the success of the party for the day was attained by Bob and Dick alone.

The first thing done by Mr. Godkin, after the conclusion of the meal, was to light his pipe, for he was an inveterate smoker. Jack Harvey did the same, since he was also fond of the weed, while Bob and Dick lolled in lazy attitudes, which were very restful after their long tramp.

"We've made a pretty good beginning," remarked Mr. Godkin, "for I agree with Pongo that we have two fine specimens of leopards which I hope will safely reach The Greatest Show on Earth, though the voyage is a long and trying one to the animals."

"I don't think we ought to call this a beginning," said Dick Brownell, "for Jack lassoed a fine young hartbeest further east and we got an eland last week."

The hartbeest, as you may not be aware, is found in the flat wooded districts of South Africa, the eland also belonging to that part of the continent. The latter is one of the largest and heaviest of all antelopes, and its flesh is excellent eating. My friends disposed of many of them while pushing their way through South Africa.

Some years ago one of the Earls of Derby attempted to domesticate the eland in England, but I believe he did not meet with encouraging success.

"We caught them so easily," said Mr. Godkin, replying to the remark of Dick, "that I hardly count them."

"But they are valuable none the less."

"Yes, and they, too, are doing well. I hope we shall be equally fortunate with what else we secure."

"I had an easy job with that hartbeest," said the Texan; "the little fellow started to run off, and I lassoed him as easy as if he had been a child. Then he gave up right away and hasn't made any trouble, I believe."

"He make no trouble — he good," remarked Pongo, walking over from the other group and joining his employers; "wait till we cotch oders — then they *not* so good."

"I think we shall have some fun to-morrow," observed Jack, removing his pipe from his mouth and sending several rings of smoke toward the stars.

The others looked inquiringly at him, but he smiled grimly and shook his head with the remark:

"I ain't going to give anything away; there may be a slip-up, but whether there is or isn't, you've got to wait and see for yourselves."

It was useless to question him when he spoke that way, and no one did so. The cousins were all eagerness, for, truth to say, though they had fully entered one of the wildest regions of the globe, where the largest animals known abound, they had not encountered as many as they anticipated.

"Have patience," said Mr. Godkin, when they referred to this fact; "you will get your fill of adventure, and probably more too, before you see salt water again."

"That may be," replied the sprightly Dick, in a tone which implied that he doubted whether it was possible for him and his cousin to obtain more than they desired, "provided we push northward through the Congo State into the Gaboon country, the home of the chimpanzee and gorilla."

THE HARTBEEST

The boys and Jack looked at the director of the expedition to observe how he received this feeler. The sagacious fellow shook his head.

"I'm afraid you don't understand what you say. We shall find all we can attend to in this part of the world. To travel from the Tropic of Capricorn, through the heart of Africa, to the Equator, is a task which I don't believe was ever accomplished by mortal man, though a great deal of the country has been explored. We are here to hunt curiosities for Mr. Barnum, not to penetrate unknown regions, and, if we undertake what you seem to favor, he would not only lose the fortune he has invested in this exterprise, but we should lose our lives."

"But," Bob Marshall hastened to say, "no one has any idea of attempting the journey you speak of, though Dick has referred to it."

"What, then, is your plan?"

"It seems to me that after we have captured about all we came for in this part of the world, we shall be as near the Atlantic as the Indian Ocean coast. Instead of going back to Port Natal, it will be as easy for us to journey to the western shore."

"I hadn't thought of that," replied Mr. Godkin, after a moment's pause, "though I am better acquainted with the country through which we have come than that to the westward."

"I don't see that that makes much difference," observed Jack, "for we can't know much about a region that we've been through only once, and, as long as we're in the same latitude, it isn't likely we shall find many changes in the country itself."

"After reaching the Atlantic coast," said Dick, "we can take sail to Loango and get to the Gorilla country without trouble."

"You've put the matter in a shape that will bear thought," replied Mr. Godkin. "I suspect," he added with a smile, "that you two young gentlemen have been discussing the matter when I wasn't present."

The boys laughed and admitted that the project was a favorite one with them. They had informed themselves, so far as they could, before leaving home, as to the habits, peculiarities and home of the wonderful gorilla, and they had talked to Jack Harvey so long that he was won over.

While those three would not have hesitated to plunge northward through the heart of the Dark Continent to the Gaboon country, under the Equator, I am glad to say that Mr. Carl Godkin was immovable in the sensible position he took.

Not to mention the peril from wild men and beasts, this journey would have taken them into regions as pestilential as the famed valley of the Upas tree, and from which they would have stood no more chance of emerging than if flung overboard in the middle of the Atlantic.

But the plan, as outlined by the cousins, was not without its possibility of success. The powerful motive with Mr. Godkin was that of securing some specimens of the chimpanzee, but especially of the gorilla, and there was hardly a danger he would not have faced for the purpose of obtaining them for me.

No doubt many readers of these pages have seen one or more chimpanzees, but I am quite sure that few have ever gazed upon a gorilla, because no one has lived to be brought to this country. By special invitation, I spent considerable time in inspecting the male gorilla that was on exhibition some years ago in London, but he died shortly after, and it seems impossible to preserve them for any length of time, after removal from their native haunts. I have expended many thousand dollars in the attempt to secure one of the pets, which I consider as more interesting and valuable than the famous white elephant of Siam, which cost me over two hundred thousand dollars, and whose death by fire at Bridgeport in November, 1887, didn't cause me a pang of regret.

However, the time hasn't come just yet to talk about the Gorilla country, but I'll have something interesting to tell you of that region and those strange creatures before you finish these pages.

CHAPTER VI.

THE custom adopted by Mr. Godkin, after entering fairly upon his work in Africa, was to place himself or one of his friends on guard during the first half of the night, with two of the natives as assistants. At midnight a change was made, another American and a couple of servants assuming care of the camp until daylight.

ONE OF THE NATIVES

Such an arrangement was easily carried out, and caused little discomfort to the sentinels, who, if they felt the call for extra sleep, had opportunity to secure it during the day.

It fell to the lot of Dick Brownell, Pongo and Diedrick to look after themselves and the rest during the first portion of darkness, after which Jack Harvey, Abdallah and Govozy were to take their places.

A RUSTLING IN THE GRASS.

The conversation around the camp fires did not last long, for our friends had learned the wisdom of regularity in their habits. It was quite early when Mr. Godkin and Bob Marshall stretched themselves out in one of the wagons and sank into the deep, restful slumber which always waits on health. The Americans made it a rule to slumber in the wagons, where they felt safer, but the natives preferred to lie on their blankets on the earth, sometimes dispensing with the covering altogether.

Two hours, therefore, before midnight, Dick Brownell, with his Winchester over his shoulder, was pacing back and forth near the animals and wagons, and within the circle of light thrown out by the camp fires. Pongo and Diedrick sat a short distance off, smoking their pipes and occasionally talking in low tones. They did not feel it necessary to keep in motion to preserve their wakefulness, and probably it was not always needed in the case of the Americans. Some nights before, however, Bob Marshall, while standing guard, had sat down for a few minutes, fallen asleep and endangered the safety of all, for the native assistants, supposing him to be awake, left a part of the duty to him. After that, it was understood that the practice of sentinels elsewhere, and of the watch on board ship, would be strictly followed.

Everything went well until near midnight. The servants, stretched upon the ground, were asleep, and there could be no doubt of the unconsciousness of the Americans in the wagons. The animals were equally oblivious to their surroundings, and the glance which Dick cast in the direction of the Bushman and Hottentot caused a suspicion that they were also taking an excursion into the land of dreams.

He walked over to where he had heard the murmur of their voices.

"Just as I suspected," he said with a smile; "the camp, therefore, is under my charge and I ought to feel the responsibility, as I think I do. Pongo and Diedrick have done unusual work to-day and were more tired than they thought. I'll let them sleep till it is almost time to change the guard, and then wake them up so as to save their reputation, unless some danger appears——"

The thought had hardly found expression, when a rustling in the tall grass, just

The King of Beasts

beyond the area of illumination, warned Dick that the utmost watchfulness was required. By this time, the moon was so low in the heavens that it gave scarcely any light at all.

In the direction of the stream was a rank growth of high grass, which offered the best of hiding for wild animals. This fact had been so apparent to the party, when forming camp, that they had moved several rods back from the water, where

A Startling Visit — Page 45.

the ground was more open. That in the opposite direction contained nothing more than a stunted growth of vegetation, only a few inches in height.

Instantly Dick was on the alert, and, holding his rifle ready for immediate use, he peered toward the water.

He could see nothing, but he was none the less certain that some kind of animal was there. More than that, he was almost positive as to its species.

In the repressed excitement of the moment, the youth forgot about awaking the natives. His whole anxiety was to learn the nature of the danger that threatened himself and companions.

Suddenly two small, round circles of light flickered in the grass and then vanished, almost before they were seen.

Dick knew they were the eyes of a huge lion, whose orbs at that instant reflected the light of the fire, the head immediately shifting its position, so as to hide the phosphorescent glow from the watchful youth.

The cunning beast did not growl, and was evidently trying to steal upon the camp unawares. But for Dick's vigilance the king of beasts would have accomplished it without detection.

The gloom in the grass was too deep for the lad to locate the massive head or lithe body, and, uncertain whether he had changed his position or not, he dared not fire. He was standing in this attitude of doubt when the lion did an astounding thing.

He had not changed his position, but, crouching low in the grass, where he was invisible, he gathered his mighty muscles and made a prodigious bound upon the one marked for his victim.

This was not Dick Brownell, as you might suppose, but the native called Orak, who lay sleeping the farthest from one of the fires and the nearest to the beast.

It was while the youth was trying so hard to penetrate the gloom, that he suddenly saw the lion rise from the grass, as if he were lifted in air, and then come over in his terrible parabola toward the unconscious African, who was slumbering less than a dozen feet from where Dick was standing.

The lion did not utter the slightest roar, seeming to know that prudence forbade, for he was too intelligent to attack such a large company when on their guard.

It seemed singular that the beast did not assail one of the oxen or ponies or goats, but it is a strange fact connected with the lion, that he generally prefers to attack a native African, even when other game is more convenient.

At the instant the beast was at the highest point of the appalling arch, Dick Brownell let fly with his Winchester. A horrible growl left no doubt that his bullet had found its mark, but, the enormous animal having started, nothing could check his prodigious bound while in air. He landed astride the sleeping Orak, and, dropping his massive jaws, fastened them in his shoulder, whirled about and galloped off in the darkness, as lightly as if carrying a kid.

His action was as quick as a cat's, but as he wheeled, Dick continued firing, sending two more shots into him before he passed beyond reach.

Poor Orak uttered a piercing screech as the teeth of the beast sank in his shoulder, and he was lifted from his feet and borne off with his knees dragging along the ground.

The report of the rifle, the cry of the native and the shout of Dick roused every one in camp. Jack Harvey, who had learned the need of awaking like a flash, on the plains of Texas and New Mexico, bounded from the wagon, gun in hand, while Mr. Godkin and Bob Marshall were at his heels.

The natives leaped to their feet, as if the ground had suddenly become red hot, and stared bewildered around them.

"Where is he? What is it?" demanded the Texan, dashing after Dick, who had started to overtake the lion.

"It's a lion; he's got Orak! look out or you'll kill him instead of the beast."

"Which way did he go?" asked Jack, staring into the gloom without catching sight of the monster.

His question was answered by a wail from the poor African, struggling vainly in the grasp of the merciless beast.

All four Americans and most of the servants ran at their highest speed in the direction of the cry.

Mr. Godkin seized a brand from one of the fires, and, swinging it above his head, took the lead, the others seeing the indispensable advantage the torch gave him.

"He is badly hurt," called Dick, "and I don't believe will run far."

"Look out! we're close on him!" called Jack, in a warning voice, fearful that Mr. Godkin's haste would lead him into inextricable peril.

But the veteran knew what he was doing. Holding the torch above his head, he circled it swiftly, so as to add to its flame, and, bending his head forward, stood still and peered into the gloom beyond.

"Here, Jack!" he called in a low voice; "I see him! Fire quick!"

It was important to keep the torch aflame, since an unerring shot could not be made without it. Mr. Godkin, therefore, though he held his gun in one hand, made no attempt to fire, since to do so successfully he would have had to cast aside his torch or pass it to some one else.

There were too many good marksmen at his elbow to render this necessary.

"Hold your light a little higher," said Jack Harvey, bringing his rifle to his shoulder and striving for a better view of the lion.

"Be careful you don't hit Orak," admonished Dick, who had restrained his own fire through the fear of injuring the native.

The lion, as he frequently does under such circumstances, had run but a short distance, when he crouched on the ground to devour his victim.

He had halted near a clump of bushes, wheeling about so as to face his pursuers, who approached within fifteen or twenty yards. The native had been laid on the ground between his paws, where he had almost fainted from the pain of his wounds.

But the lion had also been badly hurt, and, as Orak lay in that frightful position, he felt the warm, crimson drops from the king of beasts, as they dripped upon his breast and shoulders, while the muttering growls proved that he had his share of pain.

Orak did not dare move, for he knew the instant he made the attempt he would be crushed by a blow from one of those paws that were powerful enough to smash the skull of an ox, as though it were a rotten apple.

He remained motionless, aware even in that awful situation that his friends had rushed to his help and that his only hope was in them ; if they failed, he was doomed.

CHAPTER VII.

JACK HARVEY, the Texan, formed a striking figure, as, with his left foot thrust forward, he brought his Winchester to his shoulder and aimed at the massive front of the lion.

Mr. Godkin stood at his elbow with the flaring torch above his head, striving to give him all the light necessary, while Dick Brownell, Bob Marshall and the terrified natives were grouped just back of the couple, intently watching the exciting scene.

Jack was cool and meant that the single shot when fired should be all-sufficient.

The couchant lion held his paws, so as to inclose his motionless victim. With his dripping head raised and staring at the hunter, he gave utterance to threatening growls, as if daring the avenger to do his worst.

Suddenly the bony finger pressed the trigger, a sharp report rang out, and the sphere of lead, entering midway between the blazing eyes, plowed its path through bone, muscle and brain into the vitals of the beast, which sprang convulsively to its feet, whirled around like lightning and rolled over as dead as Julius Cæsar.

Then the whole group ran forward and bent over the prostrate Orak. A groan showed he was conscious, and while Mr. Godkin held the torch, he was tenderly lifted from the ground and borne to the camp, apparently more dead than alive.

Half the distance was passed, when an outcry from the three natives that had stayed behind proved that some new danger had burst upon the camp.

"What's up now?" demanded Jack Harvey, breaking into a run.

"Wild animals seem to travel in couples in this part of the world," replied Bob Marshall, who had caught a glimpse of a second beast by the light of the camp fires.

He was right, as the others saw before he uttered the words. The lioness had been lurking in the vicinity at the time of her mate's daring charge. Taking advantage of the diversion created by him, she made a foray into camp, where she caused indescribable consternation.

The horses, oxen and goats were roused by this time, and were so frightened that there was danger of them breaking into a stampede, in which many would be irrecoverably lost.

Like the lion, his mate fixed her attention upon one of the natives, this time it being Divak, the smallest and most insignificant member of the party.

He had just risen to his feet, when the female was upon him. Though he was armed only with a spear and knife, he made the best defense possible.

Confronted by the raging beast, he let drive with his javelin, which he handled with the deftness of a Zulu warrior. He aimed at the center of the animal's breast,

48

but she turned slightly aside at the moment of his effort, and the point sank several inches in her shoulder, inflicting a maddening wound which intensified his own peril.

Had his companions shown equal bravery, all might have been well with Divak, but they were overcome by terror, and instead of rallying to his help, ran shouting after those who had gone to the aid of Orak.

The Americans saw the situation, and lost no time in hastening to the assistance of the servant, who was confronting, single-handed, the enraged lioness.

The latter made such a fierce leap to one side, when the spear entered her body, that the weapon was wrenched from the grasp of Divak, who was left only with his long-bladed knife.

This was whipped from the upper part of his breech-cloth, where he carried it, and he struck desperately at the animal as she bore him to the ground. Like the former weapon, it inflicted a bad wound, but not a mortal one, and, sad to say, everything done by the brave fellow really added to his own peril.

Instead of carrying off the prostrate native, as the lion had done with his victim, the female struck him a blow which shattered his skull as though it were an egg-shell, the fellow dying with a suddenness almost like that caused by a lightning-stroke.

But, if it was the last fight of Divak, so was it the last stroke of the lioness' paw. Hardly was the fearful blow delivered, when the crack of a rifle sounded above the tumult, and the stricken beast, with a wild struggle, rolled over in the agonies of death.

It was Dick Brownell, who had outrun his friends, and, pausing at the moment he saw the native borne to the earth, gave the finishing blow to the raging beast. Alas! that it came just an instant too late to save her victim.

As may be supposed, all was excitement for a few minutes, though the elder members of the party retained their presence of mind.

The chattering and affrighted natives flocked to the spot, Pongo and Diedrick devoting themselves to soothing the animals and preventing the dreaded stampede, while the Americans, seeing that Divak was past help, placed Orak in one of the wagons, where he received all possible attention.

"Watch for more lions," admonished Mr. Godkin; "I will attend to him. We may receive another visit "

The advice was good, though the danger was an improbable one.

A few minutes later, something like quiet was restored. The rush was averted, and the natives regained something of the self-possession that had left them so suddenly a short time before.

Convinced that all peril for the time was past, the members gathered around the vehicle where Mr. Godkin was attending to the wounded native.

By the aid of the torch, he had effected a careful examination of the hurts of his patient. Jack Harvey now took charge of the light, leaving both hands of the director free to complete the work of the good Samaritan.

4

THE DEATH SHOT — Page 48

Greatly to the relief of all, Mr. Godkin said that, though Orak had been badly hurt, he was likely to recover. No bones were broken, though his shoulder was shockingly mangled and he was weak from the loss of blood.

From the stores of the expedition were brought bandages and an excellent medicated wash, which were applied by Mr. Godkin with a skill acquired by practice in India and other parts of the world. Then a gentle stimulant was administered to the sufferer, who was assured that if he remained quiet and kept a brave heart, he would soon be himself again.

Having done all that was possible for him, Mr. Godkin descended from the wagon and approached the still form around which the rest were collected, silent and awed by the sudden death.

"All that we can do is to give him decent burial," he remarked, looking down on the body, "and we may as well do it without delay."

A couple of the natives were set to work, the soft soil requiring the use only of the shovel, though among the supplies were several picks that could have been employed if required.

The grave was made deep, to protect the remains from being dug up by hyenas and other wild beasts, and into this cavity the remains of poor Divak were tenderly lowered, there to remain until summoned forth by the last great trump which shall call us all to judgment.

The terrifying incidents of the evening drove off all disposition to sleep on the part of our friends. In the discussion that followed, Dick Brownell was obliged to make known the fact that Pongo and Diedrick had so far forgotten themselves as to fall asleep when it was their duty to keep awake, but the generous youth insisted that the censure should be visited upon him, since he ought to have awakened them.

Jack Harvey, Bob Marshall and Mr. Godkin assured him, however, that no blame could attach to him, since he had acquitted himself manfully, and he had done much to save Orak from the frightful death that at one time seemed certain to overtake him.

Several times during the remaining hours of darkness, the roar of lions was heard, and you need not be told that a keen lookout was kept for another visit from the dreaded beasts; but the sounds in every case were distant, and the animals, if they ventured nearer, did not disturb any of our friends or their property.

A probability naturally suggested itself to the hunters: since the male and female lion were slain, and since an examination of the latter showed that she had been nursing young, a chance to obtain one or two specimens was at the command of the hunters. The attempt was to be made at daylight.

Pongo had displayed a remarkable aptitude in tracing the dens and lairs of wild beasts, his long experience as a hunter having given him a skill not possessed by the rest. A few trained hounds would have been of great assistance, but since they were liable to be devoured by some of the game they set out to find, none had been brought with the party.

At the earliest streakings of light, the Bushman, without waiting for his morning meal, walked along the bank of the stream, until he reached the highest point, when he paused and scrutinized the surrounding country.

Dick and Bob watched him with no little interest.

"He knows so much about the habits of wild animals," remarked Bob, "that he can easily locate their dwelling-places."

"I suspected he possessed some secret of tracing them, but I guess you are right—ah! he has discovered something."

The next moment Pongo broke into a loping trot, like that of an American Indian, taking a course that led him farther up stream.

His shoulders were seen regularly rising and falling, until the slope of the ground shut him from sight. He had left his spear in camp, but he carried his three boomerangs, the longer portions of which had been thrust in his clothing at his waist, where they could be withdrawn the instant needed.

CHAPTER VIII.

THE CHAMPION OF STUPIDITY.

A HALF hour later, the Bushman was seen approaching camp, where the members were engaged at breakfast.

"By gracious! he's got something," said Bob Mar-

'WHAT THINK OF HIM?'

shall, springing to his feet, his cousin doing the same. "Yes, and it's some kind of animal," added Dick

53

"It looks to me," added Jack Harvey, "as if he'd found a baby that has lost its mother."

"That's just what he *has* got," said Mr. Godkin, who identified the prize before any of the others.

Pongo, instead of carrying his captive by the nape of the neck, as the boys had done most of the distance with the young leopards, held it in his arms, where, possibly because of some skill he possessed, it did not struggle or give any trouble.

"What think of *him?*" he asked, stooping over and placing it on the ground.

All were delighted, for the baby lion was a vigorous specimen that would have pleased the heart of any showman. When put on its feet it looked like a bull pup or chunky kitten, and was not without a certain incipient majesty, as it raised its head and peeped inquiringly around in the faces of those that were surveying it with so much interest.

Pongo had an interesting story to tell. He had found the "lion's den" without trouble, among a mass of rocks a short distance up the stream. There were two young ones, or rather had been, for one was dead.

I must tell you a singular fact regarding lions. From one to three are born at a litter; if three, two are males, and if two, there is one of each sex. Out of every four females born, one dies in infancy from teething, while the male has little if any difficulty from that source. As a consequence, in countries where lions abound, the males greatly outnumber the females.

The young one of that sex which Pongo saw had succumbed to the impossibility of cutting her teeth, and had been flung out of her quarters by the mother, while the brother was in prime condition, suffering only from hunger, as had been the case with the leopard kittens the evening before.

For several days after her young are born the mother never leaves them for an instant. It is not long, however, before they are able to trot by her side, and then she takes them out for a walk. Before their return she furnishes them a dainty meal of some kind of tender flesh, which is carefully shredded so as not to hurt their gums.

It is said that the owners of domestic animals in South Africa know when the young of lions are born by the havoc their mothers make among the youngest of their flocks.

This animal, known as the king of beasts, is nocturnal in his habits, keeping his lair from sunrise to sunset, unless drawn out by thirst. He is indisposed to attack when the moon is shining, so much so indeed that at such times the oxen are not generally tied up. When there is no moon, however, look out!

Faint as was the orb on the night of the visit I have just described, the lion and lioness would not attack until it had almost entirely disappeared.

The strength of the lion is amazing. The blow which crushed the skull of Divak was only an ordinary one. A male has been known to seize a buffalo, after disemboweling it, and trot off with only a portion of it dragging on the ground.

His teeth, like all the carnivora, the quadrumana and man, are composed of bone and enamel, the entire crown being covered with the latter. His tongue, as is the case with the tiger, is so rough that a few licks will scrape the skin from your hand.

Pongo gave it as his belief that the specimen captured by him was three or four weeks old — old enough to care nothing for babe's food. This was proven when some of the uncooked antelope was dissected and placed in front of him. He ate with as much zest as my young friends devour pies and puddings.

The arrangement was now made for a hunt by Jack, Bob and Dick. each mounted on his horse. Mr. Godkin was invited to go along, but he did not feel easy about Orak. The fellow had a high fever, and the crisis in his condition was evidently at hand. The director said they would stay in camp until the following morning, since all their surroundings were favorable and to move the native in the wagon would increase his peril. It was characteristic, therefore, of the kind-hearted Mr. Godkin that he should remain with the sufferer, so long as there was a prospect of helping him by doing so.

The rest of the natives of course stayed behind, for it was impossible for them to appreciate the eager enjoyment with which the Americans entered upon a hunt that promised to be spiced with personal danger.

Mounted on their fleet, tough ponies, and keeping well together, the three friends galloped at an easy pace in the direction of a ridge of hills which the Texan had passed just before dusk the day before, and, in crossing which he had observed something that induced him to take his companions to the spot in the hope of showing them a species of sport which they had not yet enjoyed.

He persisted in refusing to give them any inkling of its nature, and they were left to indulge in all sorts of surmises, Jack simply smiling and replying with some remark that bore no relation to their questions.

Good as well as ill fortune seemed to wait on our friends, for the game that Jack was seeking was found awaiting him and his comrades.

Riding up the first slope, they looked down in a valley about half a mile wide and three or four times as long, the hills which formed its boundary sloping away at each end until they sank to the level of the plain. Halting their animals at a point about midway between the ends of the valley, and, gazing before them, they saw five ostriches quietly plucking the grass.

The "camel birds," as they are sometimes called, were within a third of a mile of the northern opening of the valley, and consequently much nearer it than were the hunters.

You will naturally conclude that the huge birds were not in any danger, for the way of escape was open and the speed of the ostrich is so great that in a fair, straight-away chase, no horse can run him down.

But of all fools that were ever created, I think the ostrich is the champion. Among birds and beasts I have never met any with such monumental stupidity. Were it otherwise, I don't see how so many of your sisters and lady friends would

TRIUMPHANT!

be able to wear the glossy plumes that we all admire so much, for it would be almost impossible to secure them.

You have read accounts of the manner in which the Bushman hunts the ostrich. He gets himself up so as to resemble, when viewed from the side turned toward the bird, the ostrich itself, and manages to insinuate himself among a herd, when he clubs his victims to death.

Such zanies deserve to be clubbed.

The plan of Jack and the youths was to ride down the hillside into the valley, taking care that the ostriches should see them. The horsemen would head toward the opening furthest removed from the game. Then the latter had only to turn

OSTRICH HUNTING.

about and run out of the egress near them into the broad, level country beyond, where they could laugh at every effort to overtake them.

But what do you suppose they did?

The hunters had no more than fairly started down the slope, when one of the ostriches threw up his head and stared at them. Then a second, third, fourth and fifth did the same. Standing motionless a few seconds, they deliberately started on a swift trot in the direction of the outlet which was a mile beyond the horsemen and nearly two miles from themselves.

I have asked many of my hunters for their explanation of this stupidity on the part of the bird. Carl Godkin probably states the truth when he repeats the general belief of hunters, that the action of the sportsmen, when they head toward the avenue of escape which is the hardest for the ostrich to reach, leads the bird to think there is some trap or snare at the other opening into which the sportsmen are trying to drive him.   He therefore runs the opposite way, even though it is certain to bring him in collision with the very enemy he seeks to escape.

Thus Jack, Bob and Dick were galloping toward the same outlet of the valley which the ostriches were seeking to gain, with the distance nearly twice as great for the game as for the hunters.   The routes must of necessity converge, but the birds were sure to keep straight on, though they saw the foes rapidly nearing them, and when, too, they had only to turn about and take the opposite direction to insure their safety.

"There they come!" called out Bob, hurrying his horse through fear that the great speed of the birds would carry them to the outlet before he could reach it.

"The ostrich is the biggest fool that goes on legs," remarked the disgusted Jack, "but, all the same, don't you forget that when you get him into a corner, he will fight like fury."

"I suppose these are too big to capture," observed Bob, "so we can only try to bring down two or three."

"I've a notion to try an experiment," said the Texan.

"What's that?"

"Fling a lasso over the head of one, yank him 'round, and see whether I can't persuade him to sheer off on another route."

"I don't believe you can do it, and it will be a good deal like lassoing a loco-motive."

"I ain't afraid on *that* account," replied Jack, with a confidence which promised ill for his enterprise, since he had never hunted ostriches, though, like his young comrades, he had informed himself as thoroughly as he could concerning their habits.

Pongo was an old hunter of the birds, and had told them so much that the three felt something of regret because they had not persuaded him to join them in what promised to be a most exciting experience.

CHAPTER IX.

AN OVERTHROW.

FOR most of the distance down the slope, the ponies kept well together, but, before reaching the southern outlet, the Texan began to draw away from his companions. His mustang was one of the fleetest of his kind, and, when given free rein, as his rider gave him now, he never failed to prove his superiority. He steadily forged ahead of Dick and Bob, who could have remained side by side, had they wished, but they deemed it best to separate.

The cause for this parting was the action of the ostriches, which showed a difference of speed that was as marked as it was unexpected.

One of the immense birds took the lead, gaining so fast that by the time he reached the opening he was fully a hundred yards in advance of the others. The latter were also scattered, the flock streaming through the valley in Indian file, with the rear nearly a furlong behind the leader.

"You're my game," muttered Jack Harvey, fixing his eye on the foremost, a huge male, and, therefore, the most formidable of the group.

You have all seen an ostrich, and can easily picture the fellow that knew no better than to run into a trap with his eyes open, and to lead the rest of his friends thither. With his comparatively small head thrust far forward, not with his neck curved, but straight and leaning like a post out of plumb, his short, stumpy wings partly outspread and his muscular legs doubling swiftly, he gave a display of fleetness that would have made the chase hopeless, had he but possessed enough sense to use the advantage at his command.

Now, I don't wish you to form a poor estimate of the sense of the Texan cowboy, for he is to-day, as he always was, among the coolest and most level-headed gentlemen I ever knew, but we are all liable to make blunders, and one of the greatest of his life was committed when on his ostrich hunt.

He was in earnest, at the time he assured his young friends that he meant to lasso one of the birds, and, by way of experiment, seek to reverse his line of flight.

It cannot be said there was anything specially foolhardy in this, since he possessed admirable means for making the test, but, when he displayed his contempt for the ostrich, by declining to take the precautions he showed in lassoing wild horses and other animals, he was guilty of an indiscretion for which he deserved to suffer discomfiture.

Instead of securing one end of his lasso to the support on his saddle (as he could have done either before or after flinging it), he wound it around his left arm. Jack was proud of his horsemanship, and spurned the thought that any ostrich was able to unseat him.

As was his custom when he required the use of both hands, he slung his Winchester over his back, whence he could bring it with the same amazing quickness with which a Texan secures the "drop" on an enemy by whipping out his revolver.

Jack's mustang was not only swift, but intelligent. He needed no prodding to understand that his rider wished to be brought within lasso distance, as it may be called, of the giant ostrich that was leading the herd. The steed proceeded to do so with the skill that he had displayed in placing the cowboy many a time alongside of a plunging buffalo bull. The reins lay on his neck, and Jack held himself ready for the hazardous exploit.

Our friends were "making history" with a rush. The mustang and the leading ostrich were converging with a mathematical surety that, if continued, was sure to bring the two in collision, but at the moment when such a meeting seemed inevitable, the steed, of his own accord, swerved slightly to the left, so that the lines of flight immediately become parallel. The fugitive did not vary an inch to the right or left. Had a stone wall suddenly risen in front of him, more than likely he would have dashed out his brains against it.

That is, if it can be believed the ostrich is the owner of any brains to dash out.

The mustang was slightly in advance of the bird, which was where his rider wished him to be. He was still on a dead run, but the game was steadily gaining.

Already Jack Harvey was circling the loops of the lasso above his head, just as one does when preparing to cast it around the neck of a fleeing fugitive.

Swifter and swifter hummed the loops until they resembled the misty spokes of a rapidly revolving wheel. Then, like the coiled serpent, they shot forward, straight at the projecting head of the king ostrich.

The aim was unerring, but the bird ducked and escaped the loop by a hair's breadth, the rope dragging along the ground as the Texan hurriedly gathered it in, knowing that, with the astonishing speed of the bird, it was impossible to secure more than a second chance to lasso him.

Now, don't make the mistake of supposing it was the sagacity of the ostrich that led him to dodge the whizzing coil. The sudden lowering of his head was an instinctive movement, caused by the sight of the arrowy rope shooting toward him.

It was Jack Harvey that showed his mental keenness by reading the act aright. He meant to take that into calculation when making his second throw.

I need not tell you that no time was lost. The ostrich had come abreast of the mustang and passed beyond, before Jack, with all his dexterity, could gather in the rope and fling it again.

The pony was running for all he was worth. He must have experienced an emotion of wonder when he entered into a contest of speed and saw that his antagonist could outrun him, but, with a pluck characteristic of the gallant steed, he strained every muscle, as though there was a fighting chance of reaching the goal first.

As I said, Jack Harvey, when throwing a second time, took into calculation the probability that the ostrich would duck his head as in the first instance.

Now, if the fugitive had held his neck motionless, the lasso would have failed once more, but, just as the Texan expected, he ducked and thereby brought about his own overthrow.

Having displayed his stupidity by his peculiar flight, it was eminently proper that he should sustain that reputation by inserting his head into the snare that was dangled in front and above it. In it went, very much as you thrust your hand into a hollow tree to draw out a shrinking squirrel.

In accordance with his training, the mustang, the instant he saw the success of his rider, threw himself on his haunches and braced himself for the shock that was

meant to bring down the ostrich, or instantly check his flight. Jack, as I told you, had wound several feet of the tenacious rope a-round his left arm, so that he, too, was pre-pared for the shock.

It was terrific. The

AN OVERTURN.

ostrich was brought up with such suddenness that he fell on his side, where, struggling savagely for a second or two, he scrambled to his feet again.

In the general smash-up it so happened that he rose with his head turned pre-cisely the opposite way from that which he had been following. He started back-ward a step or two, then stopped and stared around, in a bewildered manner, and, all at once, wheeled and resumed his flight in the same direction he was following when so roughly interrupted.

Jack's experiment, therefore, had answered the question that was in his mind when he set out on his hunt after the idiotic birds.

But the end was not yet.

When the crisis of the collision came, and the bird tumbled to the earth, Jack Harvey thought his arm was jerked from the shoulder, and had not his sagacious mustang yielded a little ground, the rider would have been snatched from his stirrups.

As it was, he recovered and sustained himself by a skill which not one horseman in a thousand possesses.

Unfortunately, Jack did not heed the lesson, and, instead of coiling the other end around the knob of his saddle, he still relied on his arm to withstand the second wrench, which he believed could not be as powerful as the first.

But never did a man receive a ruder awakening.

It was not the ostrich that was overturned this time, though he was almost whirled off his feet, but before the Texan knew what was coming, he was roughly snatched out of his saddle, as if by the hand of a giant, and sprawled headlong on the plain.

Not only that, but the ostrich continued its flight as though unconscious of the drag weight he was drawing, and Jack went bumping and bounding over the ground, like an anchor thrown out from the rear of an express train.

It took him but a moment, however, to unwind the rope that held his arm, when he lay still, and the ostrich serenely continued his flight, with the lasso trailing after him.

" Well, I'll be hanged," muttered the Texan ; " I thought the ostrich was the biggest fool on earth, but he aint,—there's another whose name is Jack Harvey, from San Antonio, Texas."

Without-stirring or attempting to rise, the cowboy drew his rifle around in front, it having suffered no injury during the owner's rough usage. Still lying flat on the ground, he raised his shoulders just enough to give him the needed room, and aimed at the author of his discomfiture.

The distance was considerable, and, since the Texan scorned to shoot at any part of the bird except its head, the shot was a difficult one,—that is, difficult for most persons.

But when Jack pressed the trigger, the bullet sped true to its aim, and went through the skull of the ostrich with the accuracy and fatal effect of a stiletto.

The elevated head instantly dropped, and, resting on the ground, while the legs continued their motion, the ostrich resembled some strange-fashioned plow, ripping up the soil at locomotive speed.

But not for long.

You can understand how a plow, driven at such prodigious rate, is liable to take a header, on striking some immovable obstruction. That is just what the ostrich did. Actually turning a half somersault, and kicking his legs for a minute or two in air, he departed this life.

Jack's mustang, reading aright the stirring incidents, trotted toward his master and waited for him to remount.

The action of the pony seemed to say:

"I'm ashamed of you for such work as this."

"I don't feel very proud myself," remarked the Texan, rising slowly to his feet and moving toward the fallen bird for the purpose of recovering his lasso; "but I've learned a lesson to-day which I won't forget very soon. I wonder how Bob and Dick are making out."

Aye indeed, how *were* they making out?

CHAPTER X.

IT is not necessary to tell you that in the ostrich hunt there was no intention of trying to capture any one of the gigantic birds as a curiosity for The Greatest Show on Earth.

Such an exploit would have been almost impossible : the creatures can be secured only when young, or hatched from eggs.

Our friends aimed to have some exciting sport, and it proved, in the case of each, far more so than any anticipated.

As they galloped down the slope, Dick and Bob, like Jack, selected the particular bird to which he meant to give his undivided attention. Bob fixed upon the second, which, as I told you, was about a hundred yards behind the leader.

The youth was not in the lasso business, and, while galloping toward his victim, he decided to try his revolver instead of his rifle upon him.

It would seem that the smaller weapon ought to have been sufficient, since the fight was sure to be at close quarters.

Recalling the remark that Jack had made about the impossibility of changing the line of flight of a frightened ostrich, Bob made up his mind to test it, though necessarily in an indecisive way.

Instead, therefore, of galloping up beside the ostrich, as the Texan had done, he forced his pony directly across the course of the bird and brought him to a stand-still.

But the horse was uneasy, as any animal would naturally be when halting in the course of a charging enemy of the size of the ostrich. He snorted, reared, and finally, despite all the rider could do, made a tremendous bound that carried him far to one side of the line of flight.

Bob whirled him about so as to face the bird, and, afraid that it would escape him altogether, whipped out his revolver and discharged all the chambers in rapid succession.

Fearful that he would miss, because of the restlessness of his pony, the youth did a thing which was as reckless as the conduct of Jack Harvey.

Leaping from his saddle, he ran forward, so as to place himself in front of the approaching ostrich, which showed no evidence of having been struck by the pistol balls, brought his gun to his shoulder and aimed at the small head which was bearing down upon him like a cannon ball.

Now, Bob knew better than to keep precisely in the path of the game, since a dangerous collision would have been sure to follow, but he placed himself just far enough to one side to allow the bird to pass him, his intention being to give him the fatal shot at the moment he came opposite.

The plan was not without its good features, and, had the ostrich done what was expected, the result would have been all that the youth desired. But, unfortunately for Bob, it did the unexpected thing.

Unlike Jack's game, the bird changed the line of flight.

One or two of the pistol balls fired by the lad had really wounded the ostrich, whose native stupidity did not prevent him comprehending that an enemy was on the ground within reach.

At the instant, therefore, that Bob brought his rifle to a level, the bird swerved to one side, and, before the lad could understand what was coming, delivered a kick which sent him sprawling a dozen feet away.

Bear in mind that the ostrich kicks forward, just the same as you do. The prodigious muscularity of the bird enables it to do this with a force sufficient to break the ribs of a lion or smash the breast of a hunter.

It was a wonder that Bob Marshall was not killed outright. All that saved him was his gun leveled in front. That acted like a shield, parrying the full force of the kick, which, however, was sufficient to make the recipient feel as though he had been struck by the lightning-express, when striving to make up lost time, on a descending grade.

A million stars danced before his eyes, everything turned of inky blackness, and, falling outstretched upon the ground, with his gun knocked out of his hands, he lay for a minute or two senseless.

When he recovered and rose on one elbow, the game that had knocked him out so scientifically was nowhere in sight. It had disappeared through the southern opening of the valley, very little if any the worse for the pistol balls, which had drawn but a few drops of blood.

"I've had enough ostrich hunting for one day," concluded Bob, climbing to his feet, with a dozen aches and pains in different parts of his body. "I hope Jack and Dick have done better than I, though it looks to me as if matters haven't gone just right with them."

Dick Brownell picked out the ostrich at the rear of the flock as his special prize, and, withdrawing all attention from what his companions were doing, centered his energies on bringing down this bird, which, despite its slowness of gait, was fully the equal of the leader that had given Jack Harvey such a tough tussle.

It really seemed as if each of the three hunters had determined on risking their lives in the most reckless fashion while engaged in the ostrich hunt. I have told you what Jack and Bob did, but Dick surpassed them all in daring hardihood.

Unlike his companions, he remained undecided as to his line of action until, it may be said, it was forced upon him.

He noticed the size of the rear ostrich, and wondered why his speed was less than his companions', though he was rather glad of the fact, since it gave him better opportunity to arrange for the combat, which he meant should take place before the bird joined the rest.

Dick reached a point directly in front of the ostrich, while he was still several rods distant, and, like Bob, he decided to try to compel him to head the other way.

The result in every respect was surprisingly different.

Dick's pony held his ground, as immovably as a veteran, and the ostrich, instead of coming straight on and banging against him, suddenly checked himself, when no more than a dozen feet distant, wheeled squarely about, and, contrary to all laws that govern his species, headed toward the northern outlet, through which he might have fled on the first appearance of the hunters.

Dick was astonished, and, determined that the game should not escape, he spoke sharply to his pony, which made a tremendous

TURNING THE TABLES.

bound that landed him alongside the ostrich, the latter not having time to strike his pace before the leap of the steed.

Bird and horse were now almost close enough to touch. This proximity, how-ever, could not continue more than a few seconds, since the game, though slower than his companions, was sure to draw away from the horse, even though the latter should run at his topmost bent.

A strange impulse seized Dick Brownell at that exciting moment. Had he pos-sessed one minute for reflection, he would have dismissed the thought before it was fairly formed, but, unfortunately for him, that minute was not his.

Freeing his feet from the stirrups, he flung one leg over the front of the saddle, and, while both pony and ostrich were on a full run, he took a flying leap from the back of the former to the latter.

The daring bound was executed with wonderful dexterity, and he landed with his legs astride of the bird, which no doubt was never so amazed in all his life.

Feeling that he must retain his seat at every hazard, the youth dropped his rifle, threw both arms around the neck of his steed and held on for life.

It is hard to imagine the sensations of the pony, which witnessed the action of his master, but probably he was disgusted, for he emitted a snort, and, trotting after the couple a few paces, flung up his head with another whinny, and galloped toward Jack and Bob and the rest of the ostriches.

Dick was no more than fairly in his seat, with his arms about the neck of the bird, when he realized what he had done, though his whole body was still thrilled by the excitement of the novel ride.

The ostrich was heading in the opposite direction from that taken by his com-panions, and, terrified by his burden, he struck a pace greater than he had yet shown, and fully the equal of that of the leader who had met his fate a moment before.

"I wonder how long he will keep this up," reflected Dick, when he was able to look about him, and saw that he was swiftly nearing the northern outlet of the valley; "if he don't give out, he will land me in the Congo State, where I can join Stanley, if we ain't stopped by the mountains and rivers in the way."

Now an ostrich cannot run forever, though he possesses great endurance, and, no doubt, Dick's steed would be compelled, in time, to drop to a slower pace, which would allow the lad to leap to the ground without danger from the fall; but, in that event, it is more than probable the bird would have attacked and killed him, before he could bring him down with his revolver.

But the conclusion of this adventure was more startling than Dick Brownell dreamed.

CHAPTER XI.

IF you have ever enjoyed the thrilling sensation of sitting on a locomotive engine, and thundering across the country, at the rate of a mile a minute, you can understand the emotions of Dick Brownell, when seated astride the front of the ostrich, that was careering across the plain at such a tremendous rate. I do not mean to say that its speed equaled that of the engine, for no animal lives that can hold its own with the iron horse, but it *seemed* as great, for the smoothness of the wonderful machine far surpasses that of any living creature's gait.

The wind swept by the face of the lad in a gale, and he dared not release his grasp, through fear of losing his hold, and going to the earth with a violence that would have broken his neck.

The only thing possible to do was to hold on until the ostrich exhausted himself, then to take a flying leap, and, in case of an attack by the bird, to defend himself with his revolver.

Dick had hardly reached this decision, when he saw a man standing at one side of the opening of the valley through which his winged steed was carrying him.

A second glance showed that it was Pongo, the Bushman, who must have come from camp to observe what the horsemen were doing. He seemed to be transfixed with wonder at the sight of a lad riding a terrified ostrich.

Dick uttered a shout, and saw Pongo trot briskly down the slope, as though he intended to head off the bird, but that could not have been his purpose, for his gait was not rapid, and he was too far off. The native did not speak, but, when a hundred yards separated him from the lad, he stopped suddenly and faced partly away from him. As he took this singular position, Dick observed a sudden sweep of his right arm, as though he had struck a violent blow at some object behind him. A second or two later, came an indescribable whizz and zip-like sound, and he knew that something extraordinary had taken place. With an amazement beyond description, he saw the next instant that the ostrich was as completely decapitated as if his neck had been held beneath the descending blade of a guillotine!

A glimpse of an odd-shaped implement whirling end over end at one side of the line of flight, the head itself having vanished under the feet of its owner, told the story.

The Bushman had hurled his boomerang, with such marvelous precision that it clipped off the head of the ostrich as smoothly as the sword of a Crusader ever clove, at a single blow, the neck of a Saracen.

Now, it is not to be supposed that even so stupid a creature as the African ostrich can make out very well without its head, even though that head contains but a modicum of brains. The bird's pace suddenly slackened, became wabbly, and then down it went, just as Dick was able, in a slight degree, to prepare for the shock.

With the extaordinary advantage given him, the youth went over on the plain, very much as many of you have taken a header from your bicycles when indulging in a spin over a country road.

By the time Dick had climbed to his feet, Pongo was at his side, his sallow face showing the solicitude he felt. His countenance lighted up when he saw that Dick was not seriously injured, while Jack Harvey and Bob Marshall, who had re-mounted their ponies, the lad having gathered up the gun and horse of his cousin on the way, galloped up, relieved beyond measure to find how well the whole party had escaped the serious peril that threatened them.

Mutual congratulations followed, and Pongo fairly blushed at the compliments of his deftness in throwing the singular Australian weapon. The modest fellow trotted some distance away to recover the boomerang, which he valued too highly to lose.

"It's my opinion," remarked the Texan, when the native returned, "that we've all got a better opinion of the confounded ostrich than ever before. I was never yanked out of the saddle till now, though I came pretty near it once."

"When was that?" asked Bob, who, like his cousin, was always interested in the reminiscences of the Texan.

"The time I was out with General Crook after Geronimo and his murderers. One moonlight night, when I was scouting in the Mogollon Mountains, an Apache whirled a lasso over my head and had me half out of the stirrups, before I could cut the rope and let moonlight through him with my Winchester."

"The ostrich beat the Apache," remarked Bob, with a smile.

"You may well say that: it was lucky I hadn't on my Sunday clothes, for they would have been ruined, though I settled with him for the way he used me."

"You seem to have had your hands full," remarked Dick, looking at his cousin.

"Yes; my customer let me have a kick that a mule would envy; if it hadn't been for my gun, that parried the blow, he would have staved my breast in."

"Never forget, ostrich kick *this* way," said Pongo, striking forward with his foot; "don't get before him."

"I don't think I'm ever likely to forget it," replied Bob, rubbing his shoulder; "the fact of it is I knew it before, for one day, last summer, when Mr. Barnum was telling me something about his largest ostrich, the fellow kicked at us in the same way, and Mr. Barnum referred to the peculiarity."

While this conversation was under way, our friends had adjusted themselves in their saddles, and "taken an account of stock," so to speak, while Pongo stood near, ready to accompany them to camp.

But the horsemen noticed that he was gazing off over the plain as though he saw an object which interested him.

Peering in the same direction, all observed something whose nature neither of the three could determine. It resembled a curiously formed animal, approaching at a moderate gait, evidently with the purpose of joining them.

"What in the name of creation *is* it any way?" asked Jack, who, shading his eyes with his hand, looked long and earnestly at the remarkable creature.

"I can't guess," replied Dick, who, like Bob, was gazing across the plain, which was quite sandy, at a distance of less than a mile. "It looks like an animal with a humped back that is walking on its hind legs."

It was evident, from the peculiar smile on the face of the Bushman, that he penetrated the mystery, though he chose to wait the few minutes before it would become clear to his comrades.

Suddenly the horsemen broke into hearty laughter, and well they might.

Diedrick, the Hottentot, was the only African belonging to the expedition who sported the European luxury of trousers. He had received a present of a pair of coarse canvas ones from Mr. Godkin, who saw the longing looks he cast upon them while at Petermaritzburg.

Diedrick was as proud as a child over his present and wore them continually. He had left the camp that morning earlier than the horsemen, unnoticed by them. He had been born and reared in the home of the ostrich, and the signs which he saw the previous day told him the birds were in the vicinity, even though, unlike the Texan, he had not been able to catch sight of any one of them.

When he departed, it was not to hunt ostriches, but their eggs, of which he was very fond.

I have expressed a poor opinion of the intelligence of the ostrich : let me give you another illustration.

When a Bushman discovers one of their nests he steals all the eggs but one or two, taking care to leave no other evidence of his visit. Even though, when the mother went off for a time, she left a dozen, she has not enough sense to comprehend that nearly all have been abstracted, but resumes laying, only to have her nest depleted by regular visits from the Bushman, who watches for her departure.

The native keeps this up for weeks and months, and the stupid bird continues laying from June to October, never suspecting that all the time she is steadily contributing to the support of a thieving Bushman and his family.

While the hunters were having their own sport with the ostriches, Diedrick was despoiling a nest that he found without difficulty. In it were more than a score of eggs, which he resolved to take into camp.

But how to carry them was the question. A single one is considered the equivalent of two dozen ordinary hen's eggs, so you can easily see that the task was considerable.

But Diedrick was equal to the emergency. In a twinkling, he had doffed his beloved trousers, and, tying the bottom of the legs in a knot, he deposited the plunder within, the space required being all that could be spared in the legs and some of the portion above the bifurcation of the garments.

Then, slinging his odd load over his shoulders, he started back. Catching sight of the horsemen, he changed his course so as to join them, when, as I have told you, he was received with much merriment, which was increased by the solemnity of the Hottentot's visage. He had never been known to smile, and seemed to be mystified by the high spirits of his companions.

But he was complimented on his achievement, and the party set out on their return to camp. When they arrived, their pleasure was heightened by learning from Mr. Godkin that the wounded Orak was much better, and, in all probability, would recover in a brief while.

The ostrich, when full grown, is eight or nine feet tall, and I have known some to weigh between three and four hundred pounds. Its only weapon of defense is its powerful legs, about which I have already told you. Its eye-sight is very keen, and its elevated head gives it a wide range of vision.

The male is of a glossy black color, with the exception of the large plumes of the wing-feathers, which are a pure, rich white. These are the chief objects of ostrich hunting.

In the female, the feathers are of a grayish brown, fringed here and there with white. The cry of the bird is coarse and gruff, its legs are strongly jointed, and its hide is capable of being tanned into strong leather.

The nest of the ostrich is of the simplest description, consisting of a rude cavity in the sand, five or six feet wide and twenty inches deep. The eggs are packed on end, so as to economize space, as many as fifty having been found in a single nest. These are the product of several birds, which take turns in sitting

HOTTENTOT INGENUITY.

upon them, the male standing guard at night, to fight off the jackals, which are among its numerous enemies. The average weight of an egg is about three pounds,

and, as I have said, it is considered the equivalent of two dozen hen's eggs.

The young, as soon as they emerge from the shell, are about the size of pullets, and are able at once to follow their parents. They quickly acquire an astonishing capacity for speed, previous to which, if frightened, they will squat down and remain immovable until the danger is past. At such times, the parent bird having them in charge sometimes displays unexpected cunning, by feigning lameness, with a view to drawing pursuit to himself or herself and away from the helpless ones.

The ostrich is easily domesticated, and I am sure you have heard of the attempts in that direction in this country. In the southern part of Africa are many ostrich farms, whose owners have done well in rearing the birds and selling their plumes.

Their voracity is not their least remarkable characteristic. Gravel, stones metal keys, knives, and, I have been told, horse shoes, have sometimes formed a few of their articles of diet.

It is the feathers of the bird that constitute its chief value.

THE RHEA OR AMERICAN OSTRICH.

It requires seventy of these to weigh a pound, and, since twenty or twenty-five marketable feathers is the largest number that can be plucked from a single ostrich, you will appreciate the difficulty of supplying the demand for these luxuries.

But the price (from ten to fifty dollars a pound) is enough to spur the native of Damara or Bechuana to his utmost to procure them.

March and April is the principal feather season, the birds having then recovered from their moult, while their plumage is vigorous and elastic. In order to preserve their value, they are plucked from the ostrich, immediately after it is brought down by the artifice already described, and while the body is still warm.

Despite the speed of the bird, it is so worn out and spiritless on the approach of the rainy season that a single horseman can easily ride it down. Its energy is insufficient for it to fight, and it often stands still until brained by the native's shambok or knobby stick.

The rhea, or American ostrich, is a native of South America. Three species are known, and the male is sometimes kind enough to arrange the eggs and perform the whole duties of incubation. Their favorite home is along the La Plata River, where they are generally seen in pairs, though sometimes associating in flocks. They are timid and fleet-footed, but, when hunted, show little more intelligence than their African relatives, running aimlessly in different directions until the natives bring them down with their "bolas," which consist of a cord with a ball at the end, which is thrown at the bird, and coils around its neck and legs, so that it stumbles to the ground.

CHAPTER XII.

THE WILD MEN.

A DISAPPOINTMENT awaited our friends on reaching camp. The eggs captured by Diedrick had been sat upon so long by the parent birds that they were unpalatable. Diedrick and Pongo, however, found several of the latest laid, that were acceptable to themselves and the other natives. The best of these were cleverly prepared for the suffering Orak, who relished them greatly.

But the *suspicion* of staleness ruins an egg for eating purposes with most of us, and not one of the Americans would so much as taste them. The eggs of the ostrich are naturally strong, and, even had these been perfectly fresh, I doubt whether our friends would have partaken of them. Several of the shells were preserved for use as cups.

By the time the eggs were disposed of, it was near noon, and, although Mr. Godkin deemed it safe to move Orak, yet he decided to adhere to his first resolution of remaining where they were until the following day. The rest thus secured was as grateful to the animals as the men. The natives showed their appreciation of the indulgence by climbing into the wagons and spending most of the hours in sleep, of which it seemed impossible for them to secure a surfeit.

The oxen and horses were so well trained, that, when turned out to graze, they never wandered off. At night, of course, all were gathered close to camp, where their owners could defend them against wild beasts.

The temperature was oppressive during the middle of the day, at which time the train often paused for several hours' rest. Had the season been the hot one, it would have been almost intolerable.

The situation of the camp was such that an extended view was afforded north and south, but it was shortened to the westward on account of the hills beyond which occurred the encounter with the ostriches. To the east, also, it was interfered with by the bank of the stream, which rose to a height of a couple of rods before sloping down to the water.

Mr. Godkin, who took in all the points of any business in which he was engaged, referred to this curtailment of their vision as a disadvantage.

"We are in the land of the Bechuanas and Bushmen, who are as treacherous as the American Indian," said he in explanation; "and we must keep a lookout for a visit from them."

"What reason have you to fear that?" asked Jack Harvey, while Bob and Dick were on the alert.

"Pongo saw signs, when he went out to watch your sport with the ostriches; the fact is," added the director, "I suspect that was his purpose, instead of taking a hand in clipping off the heads of camel birds."

75

The Wild Bushmen — Page 77.

The listeners looked inquiringly at the Bushman, but, instead of replying, he walked over to the wagon where Orak was lying. The fellow had many peculiarities, and one of them was, at times, a dislike to exchange words with his employers.

"What did he tell you?" asked Bob Marshall.

"Nothing, except that when he stopped on the slope of the hill, he learned that a large party of mounted Bushmen were hovering in the neighborhood. He gave no particulars, for I don't suppose he had much more to tell."

"That's curious," remarked the cowboy, "for I took a good look 'round the country for more game, and I didn't catch a glimpse of any two or four-legged creatures."

"There's nothing strange in that, for, if you and Pongo were on the plains of New Mexico or Arizona, it would be *you*, and not he, who would be the first to discover the approach of danger."

Jack, however, was not prepared to admit that his skill was any the less because he happened to be in the Dark Continent, instead of galloping over the prairies of his own glorious land.

But the declaration of the director of the expedition received a striking confirmation before the Texan could say much in the way of protest.

Naturally, while the Americans sat on the ground, discussing the situation, their eyes turned toward the range of hills where Pongo had detected signs of the presence of his warlike countrymen. Along the crest of the nearest range, fully a score and a half of Bushmen suddenly appeared, rising to view as simultaneously as if they formed a line of trained cavalry that had come up the slope on a walk.

Every one of the hunters seemed to detect them at the same moment, several expressions of surprise being uttered. All, with the exception of Orak, instantly sprang to their feet and stared wonderingly at the savage horsemen.

The latter formed a picturesque sight. Their animals were small and of a dark color, their riders being naked, with the exception of a kind of breech-cloth of sheep-skin. Their heads looked large, because of the spread of bushy wool above, and the only armament of half of them was a single long spear, while the rest carried bows and arrows. The bows of the Bushmen are small, and they carry their arrows thrust in their head-dress, from which they can snatch and fire them so rapidly that one of the insignificant warriors often has two or three missiles in the air at the same time.

These did not seem to be formidable weapons, but, when you learn that each spear and arrow was tipped with deadly poison, you will understand the dread in which they are held by their enemies.

The bows were short and sturdy, but the Bushmen who use them do so with surprising accuracy, while those who throw the javelins display a skill hardly less than that of the warriors of antiquity.

Certainly there was no such emotion as fear among the American members of the hunting party when they surveyed the row of native horsemen on the crest of the hill. Fully armed as were the whites, with their modern, improved weapons, they could afford to despise a native force three times as numerous.

"I wish the ragamuffins would attack us," said the Texan, who, to show his contempt for the party, deliberately brought his gun to his shoulder and fired at the group.

The distance was too great to do any execution, and it is not probable the Bushmen knew the meaning of the demonstration, for they kept their places, moving their heads and arms in a way that showed they were holding a vigorous conversation, of which, no doubt, the hunting party was the subject.

All at once, the war party moved forward down the slope in the direction of the camp. Their horses walked slowly, and Mr. Godkin, who brought his binocular to his eyes, said that there was not the most primitive bridle or saddle in the whole party. The Bushmen needed nothing of the kind to hold perfect control of their steeds.

"I wonder whether they mean to attack," was the inquiring remark of Bob Marshall, as he looked at Mr. Godkin, who still held his glasses before him.

"They may, but not in that shape. They know better than to charge upon the camp, where they are sure to receive a welcome that will tumble half to the ground before they can come within striking distance. Nevertheless, we will be ready for them."

Little was needed in the way of preparation. The natives showed some trepidation, and, with the exception of Pongo and Diedrick, wanted to crawl into the wagons, after the manner of a child who draws the bed-clothes over his head when scared.

A sharp sentence, however, from Mr. Godkin, prevented any such exhibition of cowardice, which was likely to encourage the Bushmen to attack the camp. He ordered them to be ready with their javelins to help repel an assault, while Mr. Godkin and the other whites looked to their own weapons to make sure they were in shape for any emergency. Pongo and Diedrick, who possessed some experience in the use of fire-arms, would have done good service with the shot-guns in case of a fight.

The Bushmen advanced with a slow regularity that aroused the admiration of the spectators. The thirty-odd kept side by side, the ponies stepping with an evenness that was not without a certain element of majesty.

While the hunters, including Pongo, were wondering as to the cause of this singular demonstration, the wild men halted.

They were within about two hundred yards, and stood absolutely motionless for a full minute, during which the curious sounds meant for words could be plainly heard by the hunters, who disdained to seek shelter against such a force.

The language of the Hottentots sounds like the clucking of hens more than anything else, and there is some resemblance between it and that of the Bushmen.

It was easy to single out the leader of the party, for he was not only of larger stature than the others, but showed, by his manner, that he controlled them. While they held their places in a mathematical line, he rode several paces in front, and began swaying his arms in such a peculiar way that the whites looked to Pongo for an explanation.

The friendly Bushman, however, said nothing, but, standing erect beside his friends, looked fixedly at the chief, as if he was also at a loss to interpret the gestures.

"I believe he wants to hold a parley with us," remarked Mr. Godkin, lowering his glass and looking also at Pongo, as if he meant him to understand that he must give an opinion.

"Yes, that is it," replied the native.

"Why doesn't he speak?"

"He don't know we understand him; he don't know me Bushman, like him."

"Call to him in your native tongue, and ask him what he wants."

Pongo did so, to the evident astonishment of his fellow-countrymen, who had no suspicion that any member of the company could talk by means of words with them.

Pongo was right; the leader of the Bushmen desired to hold converse, though it is hard to guess how he expected it to be done without an interpreter.

"Let him say what he has to say," remarked Mr. Godkin.

"He asks me to go out, so that me and him talk alone."

"You don't think of running such a risk, Pongo?" asked the director.

"Yes, me do it," was the startling reply.

CHAPTER XIII.

THE HUMAN BUCKLER.

ANOTHER characteristic of Pongo, the Bushman, was his obstinacy. Ordinarily he was quite amenable to discipline, but when he set his mind upon some course, it was useless to try to change it.

The fact that he belonged to the same tribe with the wild men may have been some reason why he decided to gratify the wish of the chieftain, and there was a possibility that such a meeting would accrue to the benefit of the hunting party, though Mr. Godkin did not believe it.

"Go ahead," said he in his quiet way, "and pay the penalty with your life."

Pongo uttered no reply, but went forward, as calmly as he would have gone to the edge of the stream, to help himself to a drink of water, by tossing it from the palm of his hand to his mouth, a foot away, in a style which no white man can imitate.

"You can make up your mind there's going to be trouble," said Jack Harvey in a low voice; "let's be ready to give him help when he needs it."

The distance was not too great for the Texan to bring the chieftain from his pony, in case of treachery, though the savage might manage to place Pongo in peril from the same shot intended to bring him down.

The chief carried a long spear instead of bow and arrows, and the moment he saw one of his countrymen advancing, he settled down into a stationary position to await his approach.

The spectators on both sides fixed their attention upon the couple, or rather upon Pongo, who, by his own act, had become the object of solicitous interest.

Our friends felt that, whatever the issue of the extraordinary interview, it devolved upon Jack Harvey to take care of their native servant in his own peculiar way. His skill in marksmanship fitted him pre-eminently for the task.

Meanwhile, Pongo walked out on the plain with the same even step he had shown at first. He left his spear behind him, but in the girdle at his waist was thrust a single boomerang,—the same with which he had decapitated the running ostrich. His deftness in handling that peculiar weapon made it as dangerous at short distances as when separated a long way from his enemy or intended victim.

The course of Pongo was foolhardy from the beginning, and it must have been that the sagacious fellow was deceived by the protestations of the leader, whom he had met before and who knew him well.

Understanding, as he did, that the Texan was covering him with his rifle, and that he would not hesitate to shoot the savage from his horse, on the first sign of treachery (and possibly before), Pongo made known that fact, while yet a full rod from the Bushman.

AN EFFECTIVE SHIELD. — Page 82

It would seem that this ought to have been sufficient to defeat any scheme of betrayal, but, unfortunately, the only purpose it served was to place the horseman on his guard against the single real danger that threatened him.

He was unusually large and powerful for a native, being fully six inches taller than Pongo, who was of the ordinary size.

It may be interesting for you to know that, until lately, there were only two known races with a mean height below five feet,— the Negritor, of the Andaman Islands, and the Bushmen of South Africa. There has been another race discovered, however, which is still smaller,— the Akkas, of the Monbuttu country, Central Africa. Emin Pasha obtained two of the skeletons, and Schweinfurth discovered them in 1870. They are the smallest people upon earth, their height being less than four feet.

The party of Bushmen which confronted our friends were, on the whole, above the average in height, the leader especially being almost equal to a Caucasian in stature, and, therefore, a giant among his own people.

When several paces separated the friendly African from the savage, a misgiving came over him. He saw he had committed a mistake that was likely to cost him his life; but it was too late to retreat. If he should turn about, and dash back toward his friends, he would be filled with poisoned javelins and arrows, any one of which was sufficient to cause death. Nothing remained, therefore, but to put the best face possible on the matter and suppress all evidence of distrust, while taking every possible precaution against the peril that threatened him.

Within two minutes after the meeting of Pongo and the chief, Jack Harvey exclaimed :

"By gracious ! Pongo is gone !   The scamp has outwitted us all !"

With every seeming of friendship, his ugly countenance made still uglier by a vast grin, the chieftain leaned over the side of his horse, and extended his hand to his fellow-countryman after the most approved civilized fashion.

Our friend was surprised, knowing that his people are not addicted to that style of greeting ; but, being familiar with it himself, he reached up his right hand, with no suspicion of the real meaning of the salutation.

The fingers of the chieftain closed about those of the footman with a grip like iron, and, in a twinkling, Pongo was lifted clear off the ground and forced upon the back of the pony, directly in front of the savage, who thus made a shield of his body.

Quick as was the Texan to catch on to all such deviltry, he was not quick enough to prepare for this daring perfidy. By the time he could bring his Winchester to his shoulder, the whole front of the leader was covered by the form of Pongo, who did not struggle, knowing that instant death would follow any such act on his part.

"Never mind," muttered Jack, " I'll let him have it when he turns with his horse."

But he didn't turn with his horse. No more striking proof could have been given of his control over the animal, for, without anything bearing the slightest resemblance to a rein, and by the mere sound of his voice, he caused the steed to step backward keeping his head turned toward the hunters, and thus enabling the chief to guard himself effectively with his human buckler.

Jack Harvey uttered an expression too forcible for me to record.

"If the grinning imp would only show his head, I'd let daylight through him, but he's too cunning; well, I ain't done with him yet," he added, keeping his rifle at his shoulder, and on the watch for the first chance to get in his work, as the expression goes.

The steed of the chieftain retrograded until he had taken his place among the others. Then, at a word from him, the whole party wheeled about and dashed toward the hills whence they came.

"I'll be hanged if I can stand *that!*" exclaimed the Texan, with the old thrill which had nerved his arm many a time on the South-western prairies; "I'll make it lively for them if I can't do anything more!"

Leaping to where his saddled and bridled mustang was standing, he vaulted into the seat, and, facing the Bushmen, started in furious pursuit of the whole party.

"He goes to his death," said Mr. Godkin, "but I cannot desert him."

"And *we* can't desert either of you," added Bob Marshall, echoing the sentiments of his cousin, who was equally prompt in making a break for his pony.

Jack Harvey did not expect the help of his friends, in the daring effort to save Pongo, nor did Mr. Godkin, in his chivalrous essay to aid the Texan, look for the assistance of the youths; but, all the same, it was given as eagerly in one case as the other.

Jack's horse was the only one that was ready for the brush, but the rest were prepared in a twinkling. Before the Bushmen had passed over the ridge, with Jack Harvey close behind, the other three were stringing after them.

Had the wild men divided their party, and sent one portion, by a roundabout way, to the camp, they would have had little trouble in destroying every native left, and driving off or killing the stock.

Mr. Godkin thought of this danger, but he felt it more important to save the life of the Texan than to stay behind to defend the natives and the property.

Exasperated as was Jack, he did not lose his presence of mind, and he understood the difficulties that confronted him. He had just seen an evidence of the cunning of the Bushmen, and he meant that, whatever took place, he would not run into such a trap as had ensnared Pongo.

The wild men went over the hills just as he started up the base. He saw several glance around at him, and the instant they vanished, he changed the direction of his mustang, so that, instead of coursing to the top where the Bushmen expected him to appear, he reached the crest more than a hundred yards away.

Not only that, but he decreased the speed of his pony, so as to be prepared for any sudden movement on the part of his enemy.

Well, indeed, was it for him that he did so.

CHAPTER XIV.

AFRICAN VERSUS AMERICAN.

ALL three of the Texan's friends had their gaze fixed on him the moment the Bushmen vanished. They noted the abrupt slackening of the mustang's pace, and how, before attaining the top, he stopped short, while Jack rose in his stirrups and peered over the crest.

The moment he did so, his friends saw him duck his head, and caught a glimpse of an arrow which sped, with almost invisible swiftness, over the back of the mustang, apparently cleaving the very spot where the sombrero of the cowboy had been but an instant before.

Discharged from a lower point, and aimed upward, the missile shot high in air, like a rocket, the youths noticing its course, as it curved far above them, turning and falling several rods beyond where they had also slowed their steeds.

It seemed as if it had been driven with enough force to pass entirely through the body of a man, though a puncture of the skin would have been all-sufficient to cause death.

"I'm afraid Jack has undertaken a bigger contract than he can carry out," said Dick Brownell, as he and his companions drew their horses close together and continued their cautious advance.

"The Bushmen have halted in the valley beyond," remarked Mr. Godkin, "and are waiting for him."

"Why don't they kill Pongo and have done with 't?" asked Bob.

"They may prefer to keep him prisoner awhile, but you can depend upon it, they will punish him for joining those whom they look upon as their enemies."

"I don't suppose they have any fear of losing him—"

"Look!" interrupted Dick.

Jack Harvey had given the spurs to his mustang and was going over the hill as if shot from a catapult.

We all despise cowardice in any one, but there is sometimes equally great danger in over-confidence. The Bushman leader, after galloping beyond sight with his prisoner, and surrounded by his own warriors, seemed to conclude that it was a work of superfluity for him to make such haste to get beyond reach of his single pursuer.

Hardly had the first elevation been placed behind them, when, at a single word, the entire party halted and wheeled about, so as to face the rash horseman that was dashing so ardently in pursuit.

The best archer of the company took his place, bow and arrow ready, to launch a shaft at the white man the instant he came in sight, for, though they might despise a solitary foe, they were ready to use any treacherous means to bring about his downfall.

You will see, therefore, that if Jack had dashed up and over the hill, he would have been met by a poisoned missile, which, with all his dexterity, he could not have dodged.

As it was, his head appeared at a totally unexpected point. The dusky bowman made instant shift of aim,

THE POISONED ARROW.

and was so quick, indeed, that the Texan had no time to spare in giving it room to pass.

I have referred to the quiescence of Pongo, the prisoner, and explained the reason.

Had he been alone with the chieftain, he would have given him lusty battle, but, knowing that the least advantage on his part, over his much more powerful country-man, would be met by an attack from the warriors, he was only prudent in refrain-ing from anything of the kind.

He knew that Jack Harvey was trying to do his utmost for him, and, though he did not see how any possible help could be afforded, yet his faith in the American's amazing prowess was so deep that he was not without hope.

The Texan was astonished, on peering over the hill, immediately after the shot, to see that the leader had actually challenged him to battle.

His warriors were drawn up in line, beyond the base of the hill, and Pongo was standing motionless, a short distance in front, while the Bushman was riding his horse at a deliberate walk, to meet the approaching white man.

Need I tell you how eagerly Jack Harvey accepted the gauge of battle thus thrown down? Could he have been assured of the least resemblance to a fair contest, nothing would have delighted him more than to engage the chieftain single-handed.

He was none the less ardent because he knew he was confronted by subtlety and cunning, but he must needs be more on his guard.

The Bushman held a spear in his hand, that being the only weapon he wished, though he also carried a curved knife at his waist, the handle, of elephant-ivory, plainly showing.

The Texan could have brought him down with his Winchester, or, indeed, with one of his revolvers, before drawing near enough for the savage to use his javelin, but there was something unfair in taking such an advantage, and Jack refused it.

In fact, it was not the chieftain he had so much to fear as the warriors behind him. The white man was compelled to advance so far that he must be dangerously close to the horsemen, who would be quick to seize every possible advantage.

It was with this knowledge that Jack strove to equalize, to a slight extent, the chances of the two, by bringing his mustang down to the slowest possible walk. Besides inspiring his antagonist with the suspicion that he held him in fear, he hoped it would draw him farther from his supports.

But the Bushman was shrewd, and probably read aright the purpose of his foe, for he, too, moderated the gait of his steed, until to have made it less would have brought his animal to a standstill.

Before the moment came for a demonstration on the part of either, Jack Harvey had decided what to do.

"If that confounded spear wasn't poisoned," he said to himself, "I'd close in on him and settle up this business in the style of one of our Kansas cyclones — *helloa!*"

A slight twitch of the Bushman's right hand indicated that he was about to call his javelin into play. Possibly it was merely a feint, but Jack could not be too careful.

All at once, and, while both horses were slowly approaching each other, up went the dusky arm, and the javelin was poised over **the** shoulder of the sinewy Bushman. Jack dodged **his** head, apparently as if in a panic, and the pleased savage grinned with pleasure.

But, rather singularly, this time it was a feint on the part of both. The Bushman did not mean to throw his weapon, and Jack's movement was only a pretense of terror.

Hardly had the enormous grin bisected the face of the warrior, when he observed his white antagonist circling a serpent-like loop, with bewildering swiftness, around his head.

He had never seen a weapon of that kind, and did not know what it meant. He learned right away. Flinging back the hand which grasped the javelin the savage prepared himself with incredible quickness to drive

In Cowboy Style.

the poisoned missile through the chest of the Caucasian. But, on the point of launching the spear, the upper part of his arms was griped by a ring of fire that seemed burning its way through flesh and bone.

Jack Harvey meant to coil the loop about the neck of the savage, but the leveled shaft interfered to that extent that the rope enclosed the shoulders. The instant it did so, it was jerked taut with the quickness of lightning.

No doubt the Bushman was accustomed to think fast; but, before he could grasp matters, he was jerked off the bare back of his steed, sprawling like a frog on the ground, with his legs beating the air, the shock of the fall being so violent that, for a few seconds, he lay motionless and stunned.

His horse was bewildered by what took place, and, flinging up his head with a whinny, started back to his companions.

In doing this he headed toward Pongo, whom he must have mistaken for one of his own people.

Pongo saw that his chance, desperate though it was, had come. With a couple of bounds, he met the animal, and a single leap landed him on its back. In a twinkling, he headed it the other way, and, understanding so well how to manage its kind, he sent it flying at headlong pace up the slope toward the encampment of his friends.

Expecting to be filled with arrows and javelins until he resembled a porcupine, Pongo flung himself forward on the neck of his new steed, and shut his eyes, while the throbbing animal beneath him thundered up the hill with the speed of the wind.

Two singular causes intervened to help him.

The fall of the Bushman leader filled his followers, for the moment, with consternation. Seeing him motionless on the ground, they seemed to think he had been slain by some new and mysterious weapon in the hands of the white man With cries of rage and grief the party galloped toward him, while several, noting the thief making off with the best steed of the tribe, despatched a number of arrows in that direction.

In doing so, however, they were handicapped by the fear of killing the noble animal, which they hoped yet to recover for their leader, provided the latter was alive. These factors in the problem, appearing at the critical moment, saved Pongo, who passed beyond reach of his infuriated countrymen, not only without a scratch, but the owner of the finest native horse he had ever bestrode.

But as for Jack Harvey, as he expressed it, he was not yet out of the woods; in fact, he had only fairly entered them. He had unhorsed his opponent in emphatic style, and nothing would have been easier than to despatch him, as he lay on the ground; but the Texan's chivalrous nature recoiled from such a summary course toward a foe that had not only shown a certain bravery in sallying forth to meet him, but at that moment was helpless.

CHAPTER XV.

A MASTERLY RETREAT.

IT was a time for coolness and nerve, and no man possessed more of those desirable qualities than Jack Harvey, the Texan.

Quick to learn from the example of the Bushman chieftain himself, he spoke a few words to his mustang, and the sagacious animal instantly began retreating up the slope which he had descended but a short time before.

Jack had managed to draw the noose from the shoulders of the savage, and he rapidly hauled in his lasso, while his pony withdrew, with his face toward the enemy. That done, Jack coiled the rope loosely over the hook on his saddle, and brought his rifle to the front.

He knew the leader was only stunned and would quickly be himself again. His own escape must be effected during the few brief moments of the Bushman's unconsciousness.

Had he wheeled about and dashed up the hill, he would have brought a shower ot arrows after him, with the chances all in favor of receiving a number in his body. His purpose, as you will see, was to get as far off as possible, before the Bushmen could recover from their flurry, and then, at the critical moment, spur away at headlong speed.

Everything went with a rush. Like a trained circus horse, the mustang walked backward up the incline — one of the most difficult of all tasks for a horse, while his rider held his rifle prepared to shoot, and with his eyes fixed on the wild men, all of whom were in his field of vision.

Jack had retreated several rods when he detected a threatening movement. It was at the moment when the war party were grouped around their fallen leader, and the two that helped him to his feet saw he was not dead nor even seriously injured.

On the outer edge of the party, one of their number, seated on his horse, began carefully adjusting a poisoned arrow to his bow.

It was the same archer that had launched a missile at the Texan when his head first showed over the crest of the hill. He was an expert, and the distance between him and the white man was so much less than before, that he was sure to impale Jack if allowed to fire a single arrow.

"*Hands up!*"

There was something so absurd in the command, under the circumstances, that Bob, Dick and Mr. Godkin, who were watching the thrilling scene, smiled, the latter remarking:

"A man's early training is sure to show itself."

The savage to whom the order was addressed could not be expected to grasp the meaning of the peculiar border command, and he continued his preparations for shooting.

While the rest of his companions were interested in their chieftain, who was still somewhat groggy on his feet, the bowman was the only one disposed to attend strictly to business.

It took him but a few seconds to make ready, when he extended his left hand, grasping the middle of the bow, and began sighting carefully at the horseman, whose steed had now backed a considerable distance up the slope.

But before the Bushman could complete his aim, Jack Harvey had pressed the trigger of his rifle, and you need not be told that he made no miss.

That which followed seems incredible. The Bushman archer uttered a rasping shriek, and went over backward from his pony. In the act of doing so, he instinctively discharged the arrow, but it was aimless, and, instead of speeding in the direction of the white man, it bounded straight up in air with diminished momentum, turning, at a height of less than a hundred feet, and descending among the startled group, where the point punctured the shoulder of one of the Africans, who, for the moment, could not understand whence came the deadly hurt.

This was the crisis for which Jack Harvey had been waiting, and, wheeling his mustang around, he sent him toward the crest of the hill like the arrow discharged toward him a few minutes before.

The fugitive expected several of the venomous shafts, and threw himself forward on the neck of his horse, keeping his gaze on his enemies, so as to dodge their missiles if necessary; but, extraordinary as it may seem, not a single one followed him.

The death of the archer, taking place before the party had fully recovered from the mishap of its leader, rendered the confusion, for a moment, greater than before, and, ere the Bushmen could understand all that had taken place, the Texan's mustang had whisked over the hill and joined the other ponies.

All three felt that duty did not require them to wait longer in that neighborhood, and they lost no time in riding back to camp and joining the sorely frightened natives, whose fears had been increased, rather than diminished, by the arrival of Pongo on his captured steed : for the latter, thinking he might be of some service to his chivalrous rescuer, had immediately wheeled about and rode back, meeting and joining the three friends on their return.

Hardly had the five horsemen reached camp, when the Bushmen reappeared on the hills as before, and looked down upon the hunting party that had given them such a chastisement. But they had learned an important lesson : it was perilous to trifle with men who owned such mysterious and awful weapons.

The leader of the Bushmen was compelled to share a seat with one of his warriors, where he looked far less impressive than when he bestrode his own steed. He had lost his valued horse, not to mention his best bowman and another warrior, and was sure to suffer still more if he attempted further molestation.

The natives had had enough, and, after indulging in a number of peculiar cries and gestures, wheeled about and disappeared.

"Are we likely to be bothered any more with those tenderfeet?" asked Jack Harvey of Mr. Godkin.

"Not during the daytime, for the lasso and Winchester have filled them with a healthy fear of us. The chief may attempt to revenge himself by stealing up to the camp at night and sending in a few shots, but I think even *that* is doubtful."

Pongo, being appealed to, was of the same opinion as the director. The fellow was so grateful to his friends, for their help in getting him out of the clutches of his countrymen, that he was ready to give them any information at his command.

He said that he and the chieftain were old acquaintances, and that the latter was uttering words of friendship when he griped his hand and violently lifted him upon the horse, in front. Pongo knew the mistake he had made before he reached the leader, but it would have been fatal to turn back, and he therefore went forward, as I have already described.

"You acquitted yourself nobly," said Mr. Godkin to Jack Harvey, who, like the best specimens of cowboys, was always modest when his own exploits were referred to.

"I don't see that there was anything so wonderful about it, but I was uneasy because of the poisoned arrows. I thought, when I rode over the hill, Apache would catch some of the confounded things, even if *I* didn't."

"Pongo has learned something as well as his countrymen," ventured Bob Marshall; "he deserved bad usage for his foolishness in walking into such a trap."

The Bushman grinned and nodded his head to signify that he agreed with the sentiments just utteged.

"It strikes met here is no company in the world," said Dick Brownell, "in which it is plainer that strength lies in union "

"Not merely strength," observed Mr. Godkin, "but safety. We must separate at times, while hunting, but it won't do to wander too far from each other to be unable to yield mutual support."

"Good advice," replied Jack, "but I know it won't be followed by any one of us. We're in a country where there are enough birds, beasts and reptiles to stock all the shows in creation, and it's our business to scoop in what we can for Mr. Barnum. When we get fairly at work we'll be sure to forget all about the confounded wild men."

"But they won't forget about *us*, you may depend on that."

The site of the encampment, as I have stated, was not favorable in all respects, for it offered too good an opportunity for their enemies to steal upon them during the darkness. It would seem an easy task for one of those sallow warriors, creeping up the bank of the stream, to hurl a poisoned javelin or arrow into the group, inflicting a mortal hurt, and getting off before a return shot could reach him.

It will be understood, therefore, that our friends were in anything but a comfortable frame of mind when night shut in, though the closest watch they had been able to keep through the day failed to disclose the first sign of the Bushmen.

Jack Harvey, Bob Marshall and two of the natives took charge during the first half of the night, with the intention of alternating with Mr. Godkin, Dick and two others for the remaining hours of darkness.

The Texan's experience in Indian campaigning in the Southwest convinced him that if any demonstration was made, it would be from the direction of the stream flowing near the camp.

Accordingly, he located himself in the grass on that side. He did not hesitate to lie on his face, for he had learned long before to do that through the entire night without falling asleep. The confidence of his friends in him was such that they felt that, despite the peculiar peril to which the approach was exposed, it was really the safest spot while under his guardianship.

Sure enough, just before the turn of night, Jack detected several dusky figures stealthily moving along the stream, close to the water, and he knew they were his old enemies. The instant he was able to locate them, he opened with his repeater, launching the whole nine shots in such rapid succession that the recipients must have believed an old-fashioned bombardment had opened.

This volley of Jack's accomplished its purpose. The terrified Bushmen skurried out of reach with the utmost precipitation, and, though Jack remained on guard till morning, he saw nothing more of them.

CHAPTER XVI.

WITH the coming of day our friends were in high spirits, for the repulse of the skulking Bushmen was complete. They were invisible, and all felt that no further thought need be given them.

Orak was doing so well that he stepped down from his couch in the wagon, and announced, as best he could, his intention of walking several miles for the purpose of stretching his legs. His fever was almost gone and he possessed an excellent appetite, the best evidence that he was rapidly recovering from the rough usage received from the lion a couple of nights before.

The specimens in natural history were lively, and promised to survive the long journey before them, provided no untoward accident occurred. The natives understood the nature of the curious little pets, and could be depended upon to give them all possible care.

It was yet early in the day when the train took up its lumbering course, it being the intention of Mr. Godkin to trend toward the Atlantic coast, with a view of ultimately striking it south of the Congo State. Although he made no mention of his purpose, he meant that a part of the expedition should enter the Gaboon country in search of the chimpanzee and gorilla.

Noon had not yet come, when Pongo, who rode in advance, on the horse captured from the Bushman leader, made known that giraffes, or camelopards, were in the neighborhood. He pointed out several well marked spoors, though nothing of the animals was seen.

One of the curious facts connected with this creature is the difficulty that hunters experience in identifying it at even a moderate distance. Its peculiar shape renders a sportsman liable to mistake a tree or high stump for it, such errors being common with those that have spent years in Southern Africa.

The temperature was uncomfortably high, when Mr. Godkin brought the train to a halt, intending to resume the journey toward the middle of the afternoon. The stop was near a stream of water, broader than that from which they had drawn their supply the preceding night. It was believed to be a tributary of the Zambesi, whose delta is on the shore of the Mozambique Channel, in latitude 18 degrees south.

The stream was fully an eighth of a mile wide, winding and sluggish, with a growth of tall, rank weeds on both sides and with the shores so level that little fear was felt of the stealthy approach of wild men, despite the shelter afforded by the growth alongshore.

The parties who set out to hunt giraffes were the two youths, Jack Harvey,

Carl Godkin and Pongo. Diedrick staid behind to look after the camp, agreeing that, if anything should rise to demand their presence, he would signal them by firing both barrels of one of the shot-guns. It was not believed, however, that any such emergency was likely to occur, since no Bushmen or wild men had been seen since the previous night.

The hunters were mounted on their own animals, Pongo carrying his three boomerangs, while the Texan, as a matter of course, took his lasso, which had done such good service more than once before.

Mr. Godkin consented, after they had ridden some distance across the level plain, that they should separate and enter the extensive jungle in front at different points, insisting, however, that they should not allow their interest in the chase to lead any one beyond reach of the support of his friends, whose help was likely to be needed in securing some of the specimens for which they were searching.

The jungle was found to be so open that their horses made their way through it without difficulty, and the plainly marked spoor of the giraffes was seen so often that each member of the party was confident it would be his good fortune to discover one or more of the coveted animals before the rest came up with them.

It was Bob Marshall's luck to secure the first meeting with several of the most extraordinary members of the animal kingdom.

He had picked his way but a short distance among the tall, column-like trees, when he observed that the ground was slightly rising and the trunks were becoming more scattered. If this continued, he must soon enter an opening, or natural clearing.

Sure enough, that was what followed. Within fifteen minutes after parting with his comrades, he found himself on the edge of a comparatively open space, several acres long, and about half as wide. The surface was covered with a stunted, yellow grass, that seemed to have been withered by the flaming African sun. Near the middle stood a tall cameeldorn tree, the species being abundant in the wood through which the youth had reached the spot.

Beyond this tree were others of smaller growth. Dismounting, Bob examined the ground with the closeness of an Indian scout, and became convinced that the impressions which he saw had been made by the feet of giraffes. He was filled with a strong hope by the fact that some of the tracks were quite small, suggesting that young ones were among the old.

If this should prove the case, it was encouraging, for it promised a chance of obtaining some of them to add to the menagerie they were gathering in the Dark Continent, to be sent to the other side of the world.

But it was annoying, after such a long ride and search, and after reaching this clearing, where the animals had passed so recently, that he was unable to catch sight of a single one.

"They can't be far off," was the conclusion of the lad, who, leaving his pony on the edge of the jungle, walked to the green cameeldorn tree, with the intention of making use of it to help him extend his survey over the surrounding vicinity.

Instead of carrying his rifle at the side of the saddle, as is sometimes done by hunters, Bob followed the custom of his friends, who slung their weapons over their backs, by means of a strap, whence it could be quickly brought to the front in case of need. Thus he would have the full use of both arms when he wished it, and, in climbing a tree, could carry his chief weapon with him.

That was what Bob did. It took but a few minutes to ensconce himself among the branches of the cameeldorn, whose leaves were as green and cool-looking as though the roots were perennially supplied with moisture.

The youth ascended until the strength of the limb on which he rested permitted him to go no farther, when he paused, to take a survey of the neighborhood.

The result, at first, was disappointing. His vision extended less than he expected, though it swept over considerable space; but it showed nothing of what he hoped to see.

"It must be," he thought, "that the giraffe holds its head so high and has such sharp eyes, like the ostrich, that it discovers the hunter long before he can detect the animal. There may be a herd of them that have observed us long ago, and are keeping out of our way. Helloa! somebody is luckier than I."

This exclamation was caused by the sound of a gun, a short distance to the left. He suspected the weapon was Dick's, though, of necessity, it was guesswork on Bob's part.

Suddenly, the latter's heart gave a throb. Two hundred yards off, in a direction opposite to that where he had left his horse, he saw something moving. It was at the farther end of the clearing, where all became jungle again, and the objects were so hidden by the vegetation that, for some minutes, it was impossible to identify them.

By and by, however, a male giraffe, fully eighteen feet high, and two females, three or four feet less in stature, moved into plainer sight and began cropping some of the acacias that were plentiful in that section.

The youth debated with himself what he should do. The animals were too far off to risk a shot from his perch, and he hesitated to shoot them down in mere sport, when there were no young in their company. The spoor convinced him that some infant camelopards were not far off, and it was important that the older ones should not be scared into fleeing with them.

Bob was indeed in a quandary, and he ardently wished that his friends were within call, so that some plan for making the important capture could be agreed upon. But he was afraid to signal them, lest he should frighten off the animals. He therefore waited and cogitated over the matter, hoping all the time that the giraffes would come closer.

While still attentively watching them, he made the discovery that fully half a dozen others were near. He could catch glimpses of their long, awkward necks now and then, as they thrust their heads hither and thither among the acacias, while cropping the succulent leaves; but they persisted in keeping so obscured that he could not learn whether or not they were accompanied by any young, the probabilities, however, being that more than one baby giraffe was in their company.

"I can't see why Dick and the rest don't work their way over nere," thought he, "for most of the animals must be near me, though I know they sometimes travel in herds of thirty or forty. We could surround the whole lot, and Jack, with his lasso, would be able to gather in one or two of the young — "

At that moment he heard a slight rustling, and turning his head, was so startled by what he observed, that he came within a hair of losing his balance and falling to the ground.

The most extraordinary object he had ever beheld was moving among the leaves. It showed no legs or arms, but from the front was thrust a tongue, fully a foot long, that, wrapping about the green leaves, tore them off in handfuls and shoved them into its capacious mouth. The oblique and narrow nostrils were protected by strong hairs, and surrounded by muscular fibers that could close the organs of smell against the entrance of the sand dust which sometimes sweeps, with fatal effect, over portions of the Dark Continent. A pair of beautiful eyes were so placed that the owner could gaze in any direction without moving his head.

This remarkable object was gliding here and there among the leaves of the cameeldorn tree, with a certain smooth grace that proved it was controlled by some power beneath. Those lustrous eyes could not fail to see the lad, crouching on the other side of the trunk, and peering around, as though in doubt whether he ought to appeal to his weapons or drop from his perch and run for life. But no notice was taken of him. The object, whatever its nature, glided hither and thither, sometimes approaching and sometimes receding from the boy, and acting all the while as though it cared naught for him or anything else.

CHAPTER XVII.

A TIMELY ARRIVAL.

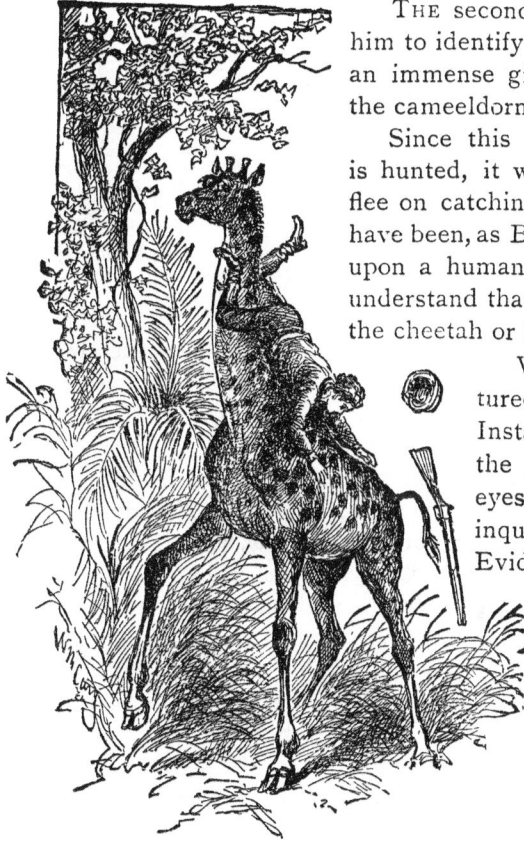

An African Toboggan Slide.

THE second glance of the affrighted Bob enabled him to identify the strange sight: it was the head of an immense giraffe, that was cropping the leaves of the cameeldorn tree in which he had perched.

Since this animal is one of the most timid that is hunted, it was singular that he did not instantly flee on catching sight of the young hunter. It must have been, as Bob suspected, that he had never looked upon a human being before, and, therefore, did not understand that he was ten-fold more dangerous than the cheetah or lion.

Wondering at his temerity, Bob ventured to move a few inches toward him. Instantly the head became stationary, and the long tongue motionless, while the fine eyes contemplated the stranger with an inquiring stare, not unmixed with fear. Evidently the creature was on the point of fleeing, though the lusciousness of the leaves tempted him to remain.

Bob kept still, and the giraffe resumed feeding, though, for a few minutes, he did not approach any nearer the lad. The latter, watching him closely, was able now and then, when the head parted the branches, to follow the long neck, as it sloped downward to the ground where the body was standing. Bob was sure, too, that others of the kind were there, though the thick growth of leaves prevented him seeing plainly, and he was afraid that if he shifted his position, he would drive off the male which showed such confidence in him.

By and by the latter edged over to where the astonished youth was holding to the limb. Bob felt just enough misgiving of the extraordinary head to wish to avoid too close company with it. Of course, he could have shot the beast, but, before doing that, he wished to satisfy himself that such an act would not shut out all chance of capturing some of the young.

Still closer came the head until it was so nigh that Bob shoved himself further out on the limb, intending to swing his arm and frighten the animal into preserving a respectful distance; but the youth forgot that the branch on which he was resting was already taxed to its utmost.

The consequence was, that it snapped off like a pipe-stem, close to the trunk, and, in an instant he began his descent through the limbs, to the ground.

The flurry startled the giraffe into an awkward leap, directly under the descending lad, who struck the giraffe's neck just back of his head, and shot down the whole length of the animal, from head to tail, with the velocity of a sled going down a toboggan slide.

Bob realized instantly what was coming, and, dropping his gun, instinctively threw out his arms to grasp the neck and stop his accelerating descent. Had it been any other animal, he must have succeeded, but the inclination of the giraffe's body, from his head to his switch of a tail, approached too nearly the perpendicular to permit.

Faster and faster went the youth, despite his efforts of resistance, until he shot off the spine of the startled animal with such momentum as to strike the ground a dozen feet distant, where he made a backward somersault, just in time to escape the vicious kick of the giraffe's hind foot, which, had it landed, would have done serious damage.

Before Bob could clamber to his feet, the sharp crack of a Winchester sounded on the air, and the huge giraffe made a frantic lunge forward, falling dead on his face, his brain pierced by a shot from the rifle of Jack Harvey, who dashed forward the next moment on his mustang, and with his lasso whizzing about his head.

For Bob was not mistaken in believing there were others of the same kind beneath the tree which he had climbed. There were a female and two young, the mother grazing from the branches so much lower down that the youth had not seen her head. The young were feeding still lower,—that is, they were imbibing their mother's milk, while she was helping herself to the vegetation.

Even in that exciting moment, the hunters were touched by the sight. The mother stared around in a bewildered way, and then, with a vague consciousness of her danger, started off, with her offspring trotting at her side.

But she went only a few paces, when the merciless coil settled round her neck, and she was jerked backward with such force that she fell on her side, where she kicked and struggled violently for several minutes.

"Don't kill her!" called Bob, his heart full of pity for the young ones, too much stupefied by the calamity to flee.

"I don't want to," replied Jack, leaping to the ground, "but we've got our hands full. Where the deuce is Pongo?"

The Bushman at that moment bounded from among the trees on foot. He ran forward to the struggling giraffe, and, halting by its head, jumped up and down, swung his arms, and emitted a series of the most hideous sounds that can be imagined.

These were intended to frighten the captive, and accomplished that purpose. Either from exhaustion or fright, she became still. The pleading expression in her large soft eyes, as she looked up at her captors, would have touched a savage.

"I'll be hanged if I can kill her, though I expected to do it," said Jack Harvey; "them eyes are too human. If she'll behave herself, and let us lead her back to camp, I'll spare her."

The flurry caused by this incident started the other giraffes in the vicinity, and they went skurrying away at their highest bent. No attention was paid to them, for our friends had all they could attend to in looking after their captives.

GETTING DOWN TO BUSINESS.

It seemed a pity that the male had been killed, but it was impossible to capture him. He was so large and strong that he would have continued fighting for freedom, while there was promise that the mother could be managed through her affection for her young.

While she lay on the ground, the two babies stood quietly by her side, looking down in such a wondering way that it was plain they were grieved and unable to understand the meaning of the sad sight.

Finally, at the suggestion of Pongo, the mother was allowed to rise. She came to her feet in a hurry, and immediately started off again, but was checked without any help from the mustang, to whose saddle the end of the lasso was still secured.

"Do you think you can lead her?" asked Jack, of the Bushman.

"Me can," he replied, with a nod of his head.

"I guess I'd better keep her tied to the saddle for a time; I don't think she can run away with me and Apache. Bob, warn't you trying to slide down the back of the male when I came in sight?"

"No; I was trying to keep from sliding down it, but I couldn't help myself, because the roof was too steep."

"He *is* got up in curious style," remarked the Texan, surveying the inanimate figure on the ground. "I saw one of the critters in Barnum's show, when it was in Texas, and tried to study out what sort of joke nature was trying to get off when she shaped him up in that fashion, but I couldn't make it out.

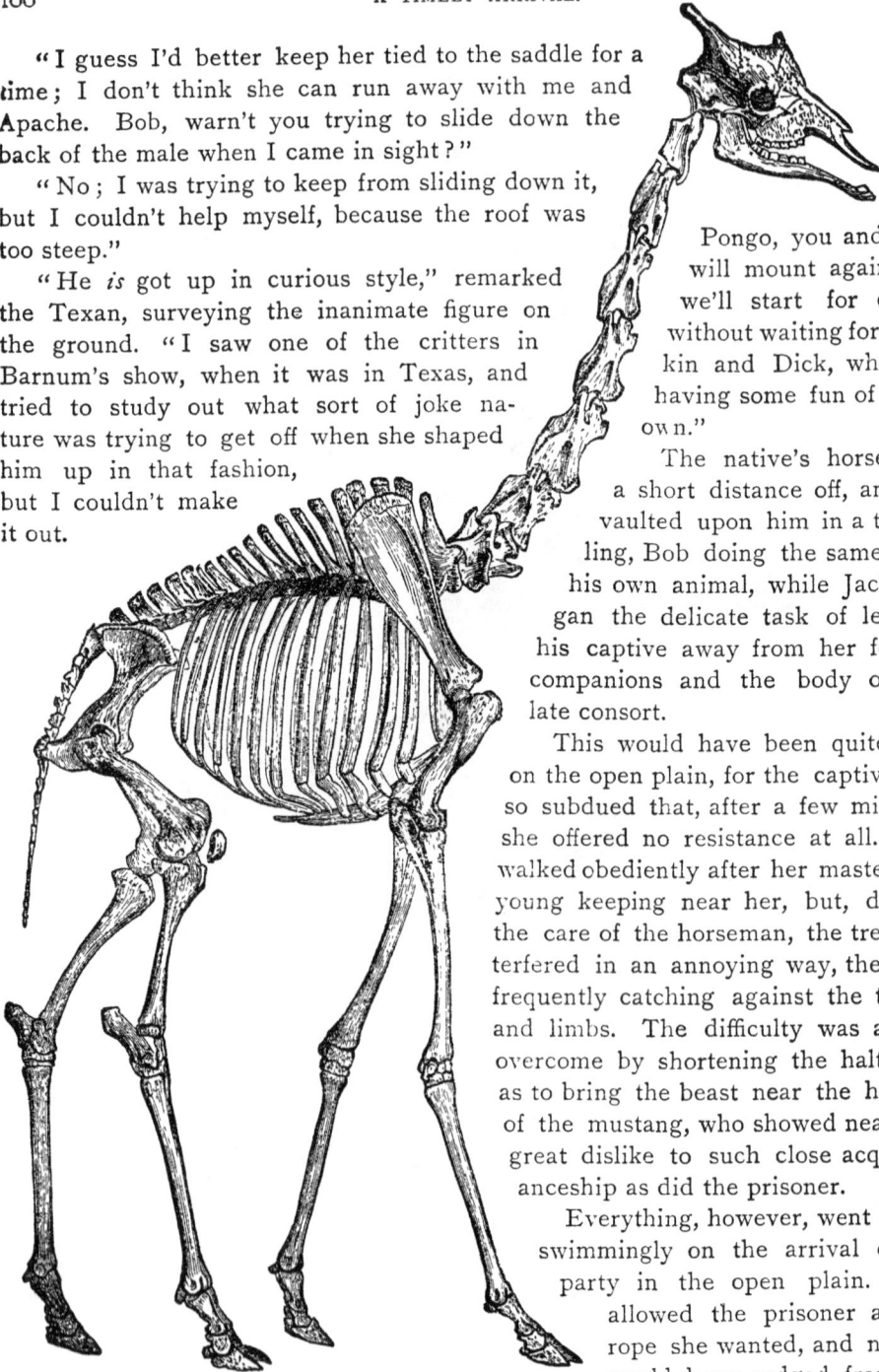

Pongo, you and Bob will mount again, and we'll start for camp, without waiting for Godkin and Dick, who are having some fun of their own."

The native's horse was a short distance off, and he vaulted upon him in a twinkling, Bob doing the same with his own animal, while Jack began the delicate task of leading his captive away from her former companions and the body of her late consort.

This would have been quite easy on the open plain, for the captive was so subdued that, after a few minutes, she offered no resistance at all. She walked obediently after her master, her young keeping near her, but, despite the care of the horseman, the trees interfered in an annoying way, the lasso frequently catching against the trunks and limbs. The difficulty was almost overcome by shortening the halter so as to bring the beast near the haunch of the mustang, who showed nearly as great dislike to such close acquaintanceship as did the prisoner.

Everything, however, went along swimmingly on the arrival of the party in the open plain. Jack allowed the prisoner all the rope she wanted, and no one would have judged, from her

SKELETON OF THE GIRAFFE.

demeanor as she followed her captors, that she was an unwilling member of the company.

Bob and Pongo rode at the rear of the strange procession, studying the animals, which, you will admit, are among the most interesting of those found in the Dark Continent.

I am quite sure you have formed the opinion that the fore legs of the giraffe are much longer than the hind ones, when, in truth, they are about the same in length, as you can see from the representation of a skeleton of one of them. In walking, the neck is stretched in a line with the back, and the animal looks very awkward, but this disappears when it runs. It lifts its hind legs alternately with the fore, and they are carried outside and far beyond them. Under a full gallop, the fore legs are stiff in rising and falling. It prefers the open country, and loves to wander in large herds over the plains of Nubia, Abyssinia and South Africa.

When he wishes to eat something on the ground, his posture is the most awkward imaginable. He spreads his fore legs far apart, his hind ones retaining their usual position, and thus manages to grasp the twig, or grass, in front of him.

The giraffe is the sole living representative of the *Camelopardalidæ* family, and, unlike the deer, has no supplementary hoofs on its feet, nor has it any canine teeth.

The male and female have each two short frontal horns, covered with hairy skin, ending in a tuft of hairs. Their color is a light yellow, with large brown spots. The tallest specimen I ever saw was about eighteen feet, which is a third higher than the late lamented Jumbo, the largest animal ever known.

CHAPTER XVIII.

A STRANGE SCENE.

ALTHOUGH it fell to the lot of Bob Marshall to have the most resultant meeting, as it may be called, with the giraffes, yet, Dick Brownell was really the first member of the party to catch sight of the interesting animals.

I have told you that the camelopard is fonder of the open plain than the wooded sections, but they frequently enter the groves, in quest of the succulent leaves, of which they are fond. It so happened that fully a score were engaged in feeding in the jungle into which the five men rode at different points.

Dick was advancing slowly, his senses on the alert, and in the momentary expectancy of catching sight of one of the creatures, when his horse suddenly pricked his ears and stopped short.

The young rider instantly saw the cause of his alarm. A huge male giraffe was standing a short distance off, with his head thrust among the lofty branches, and gathering in the leaves, just as was the male which so startled Bob Marshall a few minutes later. Had not the animal been so much engaged, with the leaves rustling about his ears, he would have discovered the approach of the hunter before the latter could have seen him.

Dick was so flustered by the sight, that he hurriedly brought his rifle to his shoulder and fired. Inasmuch as he could not see the head, hidden among the vegetation, he aimed at the point where he supposed it to be, but where it was not.

The report roused the animal, which withdrew his head like a flash, and, observing the horseman, turned in the other direction and made off at a speed that was astonishing.

Dick galloped after him, and once more raised his gun, but lowered it without pulling trigger. He was confident of his ability to bring the tall creature to the ground, but, knowing its gentle disposition, he felt little desire to do so. He continued his pursuit a short distance, when the fugitive disappeared, being able to make better time through the jungle than could his fleeter-footed pursuer.

Dick felt little regret over its escape, and, checking his pony, he turned the other way, with the intention of rejoining his companions, when he was mystified by a series of sounds which he could not understand.

They seemed to consist of a number of short, thunderous bellows, mingling with the brief roars evidently uttered by another kind of animal, and were so near that he looked in the direction, knowing he would catch sight of the beasts, whatever they might be.

An immense buffalo bull was standing at bay, with his back toward a large rock, and facing a couple of male lions, that were evidently resolved to make a meal of

him, but, at the same time, were well aware that it could be done only by a desperate fight with the magnificent fellow that defied them.

The African buffalo is one of the most dreaded animals that roam the plains
and jungles of the Dark Continent. He is the true buffalo, the name being a mis-
nomer as applied to the species, now nearly extinct, on our Western prairies, and

THE CAPE BUFFALO.

which are properly called bisons. He is of great size, very powerful and active,
courageous, swift of foot, with an enormous spread of horns, that curve outward and
upward to sharp points, which, backed by the prodigious strength of the animal,
become the most formidable of weapons.

It has been said by more than one native of South Africa that one should rather stand fifty yards in front of a rifle, aimed and fired at his breast, than to hold the same position, unarmed, in front of a buffalo; for, in the former instance, the weapon might miss, but, in the latter, death is inevitable.

From this statement you can form an idea of the beast, which, finding itself assailed by a couple of lions, coolly backed against a rock and faced them.

Now and then the bull flirted his head in a savage way, with a short, muttering bellow, to which the lions answered with a somewhat similar cry. Then the assailants began creeping stealthily forward, their bodies close to the ground, and the ends of their lashing tails thumping angrily against their ribs.

Either could have made a leap that would have landed him on the shoulders of the bull, but, though they seemed to meditate an assault of the kind they hesitated to attempt it.

The bull, as is a favorite custom with his kind, had been wallowing in the mud until his entire body was coated. This coating had been baked by the sun, and, since his violent movements had dislocated many of the flakes, his appearance could not have been more unsightly. But he was "game" all the way through.

The first glance that Dick Brownell obtained of the stirring sight showed that the bull was attended by a small bird, which, unmindful of the peril of his huge friend, kept industriously garnering the insects that swarmed along his spine. When the latter charged, the bird rode with him, more interested in obtaining his own meal than in the strange combat going on.

It is claimed by some that the *textor erythrorhynchus*, as scientists have named this bird, warns the bull of the approach of danger, but I believe the weight of authority is against the assertion.

The strange contest (if at this stage it could be called a contest) had probably continued some time when Dick Brownell arrived on the scene, though he saw no proof of any wounds having been given or received by any of the combatants, not one of which paid the least heed to him.

The larger of the assailants appeared to be growing impatient. While his companion was darting forward, and then quickly retreating a few paces, he stood erect, as if debating whether the best thing was not to him to dash in, and, with a short struggle, end the business.

His decision seemed to be hastened by the retreat of his comrade, for, with another threatening growl, he trotted straight toward the bull. The latter, instead of awaiting his assault, advanced to meet him.

This, evidently, was more than the lion had counted on, for, standing his ground but a moment, he dropped his tail, and ran back, afraid of the frightful horns that were coming toward him with the momentum of a battering-ram.

The bull was too wise to be drawn far from the rock and placed at a fatal disadvantage. Having followed the lion, therefore, a short distance, he trotted swiftly back to his first position, holding his head high, so as to be prepared for any demonstration of his foes. Then he instantly wheeled and faced them, defiant as ever.

The smaller of the lions was more cunning than the other. Leaving the latter to confront the bull, he began sneaking around to one side of the rock, with the manifest intention of assailing the brave fellow from the rear.   This could be easily done, for the rock was not high, and, while the bull was engaged in fighting his more chivalrous foe, the other could pounce down on his shoulder, and, clinging fast, keep free of his dreaded horns and kill him.

THE BISON

In making this flank movement, the beast approached the side of the rock near-est Dick Brownell, whose sympathies, naturally, were with the bull.   The lion did not notice him, — the chief cause for the oversight being his interest in the singular struggle for a dinner.

"That ain't fair!" muttered the youth, reading the meaning of the course of the king of beasts: "I won't allow anything of the kind."

And, without hesitation, he deliberately raised his Winchester, and drove a bullet back of the fore leg of the beast, who was killed instantly, so that he had barely time to make a single leap.

Dick expected the report of the gun to draw the attention of the other lion to him and his horse, and he held himself ready to meet him with the remaining cartridges in his rifle; but, to his surprise, both the lion and bull acted as though they had not heard the sound, nor witnessed the downfall of one of the assailants.

In fact, the larger lion and bull had feinted and faced each other so long that they were rapidly becoming infuriated. They cared nothing for what was going on around them: they had only eyes for each other.

"Now matters are on a fair basis,"

BUFFALO AND LION.

thought Dick, observing that he was receiving no attention from either of the combatants, "and may the best fellow win." The savage brutes did not delay in getting down to business.

Once more the lion trotted toward the bull, who, as before, eagerly advanced to meet him. As he did so, he again lowered his head, turning it sideways, so as to present one of the magnificent horns to his assailant.

The latter halted suddenly, when a few paces distant, and, dropping part way to the ground, made a quick jump, meant to carry him over the lowered head and upon the body of the buffalo. Had he done so,—and the plan was feasible,—nothing could have saved the brave old fellow; for, unable to use his horns upon his clinging enemy, he would have been at his mercy.

But the bull read aright the purpose of his foe, and met it in a singular way. Instead of throwing up his head, as Dick expected him to do, he leaped lightly to one side, and, the instant the lion landed, went at him like a demon.

The brute had no time to gather himself for effectual resistance. While striving to do so, he was shoved on his side and knocked over again, still snarling and striving desperately to regain his feet.

Seeing the lion was helpless, the bull jammed his side a third time with such fury that one of the long horns was driven almost through the body.

It was a fatal wound, but the king of beasts in his dying struggles inflicted more than one serious hurt on his conqueror, who, drawing back his massive head, rammed him again, even after all semblance of life had departed, until, with a fierce snort, he flung the senseless body a dozen feet away, as though it were a bundle of rags.

"Hurrah!" shouted the excited Dick, swinging his hat; "you made a gallant fight, and I feel as though I would like to shake hands with you——"

The youth's congratulations were cut short, for, at that moment, he became aware that the buffalo appeared to have made up his mind to "shake hands" with a vengeance.

CHAPTER XIX.

IN THE NICK OF TIME.

THE bull, having vanquished his foe, seemed fired with the resolve to reconstruct the neighborhood.

Dick Brownell was swinging his hat, and giving utterance to his congratulating shouts, when the snorting animal lowered his head, and came for him and his steed like a cyclone.

"Confound you!" muttered the youth; "if that's the way you treat a friend, I'll turn enemy."

And drawing up his rifle, he pulled the trigger. The aim was perfect, the ball entering the lower part of the skull, and tearing its way along the spine.

The bull took a single bound forward, staggered like a drunken person, went down on his knees, and then over on his side, where, with a single bellow, he died.

"I would have been glad to spare you," said Dick, "but I couldn't see my way clear to do it."

The youth observed Mr. Godkin approaching among the trees. The reports of the gun had brought him to the vicinity, and he arrived in sight at the moment the bull was shot.

"You ought not to have killed him," said he, jocosely, "for he would have been a valuable curiosity for Mr. Barnum."

"Yes; I should like to see the man, or party of men, who could make him prisoner; it would be like trying to chain a blizzard."

"Jack Harvey is an expert in the use of the lasso."

"He does seem to have an itching to try it on every wild animal he sees. It would be just like him to drop the coil over a buffalo's horns, but I don't think he would do it a second time."

"No; the African buffalo is among the most dangerous game in the country. To me he always seemed as bad as the Asiatic tiger."

At Mr. Godkin's invitation, Dick seated himself on a fallen tree beside his friend, who, it was evident, had something to say to him. Dick was always glad of the chance to talk with the gentleman.

"I haven't had a shot," Mr. Godkin remarked, "since we parted company, though I got near enough to three giraffes to bring one or two down. But there is something so innocent and helpless about the animals that I dislike to kill them."

"I feel the same; I fired in such a hurry that I missed, but I didn't try a second shot. But," added Dick, "you would have been interested had you seen the buffalo gore that big lion to death."

"I've seen it done," quietly replied Mr. Godkin; "a lion is a fool that, single-handed, attempts to bring down a bull buffalo."

INGRATITUDE. — Page 108.

"But there were two of them."

"At first; but, if I'm right, you shot one."

"Yes; I wanted to make the fight more even."

"A cow buffalo, defending her young, is fiercer, if anything, than a bull," remarked Mr. Godkin.

AN UNEXPECTED ATTACK

"I don't see how that can be," said Dick, with a look at the prostrate foe that had assailed him so savagely.

"I hope you will never have the chance of seeing it. I have known a cow to fight two lions, save her young, and finally drive off both her assailants. The bulls, as they grow older, are inclined to wander off by themselves into the swamps and jungles, and the hunter who meets them must be on his guard. Do you note that bird ? "

The little feathered friend of the buffalo was industriously hopping about the inanimate form, in its never ending hunt for food. During the charge upon Dick it had kept its place on his back.

" I noticed it on my first glance at the bull."

" They seem always to be in attendance on their fierce majesties, but are not like the birds that warn the rhinoceros and hippopotamus of the approach of danger. Do you know," continued the director, rousing to animation, " that I have seen a buffalo whip an elephant ? "

" It seems incredible."

" It's a fact, nevertheless. I was once riding a medium-sized elephant, with Pongo, when we routed a bull from a thick clump of bushes, where he seemed to be fighting off the insects, rather than seeking food. He came at our steed with a rush, and, striking his shoulder, knocked him to his knees."

" Didn't he gore him ? "

" That was the strange part of it. You know the horns spread so far apart that there is a good deal of space between. It must have been that the ends of the horns thus missed wounding the elephant, while the impact of their bony base was enough to capsize him."

" What were *you* doing all this time ? "

" I had my rifle, of course, but I told Pongo that if the elephant couldn't save himself from an animal so much less in size, I didn't feel like helping him. The big creature trumpeted with terror, and, getting to his feet, wheeled about and lumbered off like a whipped dog."

" He must have run fast to get away from the bull."

" He made good time, for an elephant can travel rapidly, but he wouldn't have done so well but for the help of the buffalo. He delivered his second charge against the hindquarters of the bulky fellow, who was pushed forward so violently that he came near being thrown to his knees again, with us flying over his head. By this time the elephant was in a panic. He trumpeted so pitifully that I knew the horns had inflicted a hurt the second time ; so, to save our steed and ourselves, I sent a couple of bullets from my unsteady perch, which ended the matter."

" You make me quite proud of my achievement in bringing down such a dreadful fellow," said Dick, with a smile and another glance at the lifeless form.

" You may well boast of it ; had you missed killing him the second time, there is a certain young gentleman in South Africa, of whom Mr. Barnum thinks a great deal, that would never shake his hand again. But," added Mr. Godkin, coming to the matter of which he intended to speak in the first place, " I have done more thinking than hunting during the last hour or two, and have come to the conclusion to make a permanent camp where we have now halted."

The youth looked at his friend, as if uncertain of his full meaning.

"We are in the heart of the best hunting region of South Africa," he explained, "and we cannot improve our situation by penetrating farther, while to do so makes the return the more laborious, and dangerous for the young that we hope to take

AN EARNEST CONFERENCE.

back to the coast. By making our camp permanent, that is, during our hunt for curiosities, we can be secure against the attack of wild men and beasts, can give our oxen and horses abundant rest, and, when we have gathered all that we can well take care of, we shall be in good form for the long journey to the sea coast. That, after all, is the most trying ordeal before us. If we can reach port with our prizes I snall feel that nine-tenths of the real work is successfully finished."

"Then, from the camp, we will make excursions through the surrounding country, in search of what we want?"

"That is my plan; what do you think of it?"

"It strikes me as good, since, as I understand it, we cannot hope to find any more desirable prizes farther north, nor, indeed, in any direction, without traveling much farther than you ever intended to go."

"You are right. Then, too, we can give the young better care in camp than while dragging them across the country."

"There is enough in South Africa to keep us busy."

"I rather suspect so. The list is a long one, embracing, as I am sure you know, hyenas, rhinoceroses, monkeys, zebras, porcupines, wild boars, koodoos, the secretary birds, hornbills, ichneumons, elands, hippopotami, not to mention the leopards, lions, antelopes, and giraffes, and other animals with which we have already come in collision."

"You have omitted one," said Dick, significantly.

"If my list were twice as long, it would omit scores."

"But I conceive this to be the most important of all."

"What is that?"

"The gorilla."

Mr. Godkin smiled in return, and said:

"We shall see."

CHAPTER XX.

A DISCOVERY.

IT was not wise to press the matter too far, much as Dick Brownell and Bob Marshall desired to enter the gorilla country; but Mr. Godkin had given them reason to hope, and, when Dick told his cousin what the director had said, the enthusiastic youth declared that, barring accidents, the question was already settled in their favor.

Mr. Godkin was delighted, on reaching camp, to learn of the important captures that had been made, thanks to Jack Harvey's skill in handling the lasso. If the female giraffe and her young could be transported safely to the coast, they would form valuable prizes for the Greatest Show on Earth.

But a good deal remained to be done, and all saw the wisdom of the director's decision. They might hunt a good while without finding so favorable a spot for a long halt. Grass was abundant for the animals, while the stream, flowing near, provided water for all. Besides, the country was so open on every side, that if only ordinary vigilance was used, it would be almost impossible for any of the wild men to steal upon them, either by day or night.

The decision having been made, no time was lost in the preparations. The three wagons were placed so as to form part of a large circle, the property carefully stowed away under the strong canvas covers, and everything made as secure as possible against those tremendous storms which sometimes devastate the African plains.

One of the most important steps was the preparation of new quarters for the young animals they had captured, as well as for those that they expected to secure. The cages, with which our friends were well provided, being intended for use in transportation, were necessarily small, and the active young were sure to suffer from their cramped quarters. Strong stakes were therefore driven into the ground, so as to inclose a fourth of an acre, and this was subdivided into what might be called apartments, each embracing a square rod, more or less. These stakes were so tall, and pointed at the top, that a lion could not have leaped within the inclosure. They were therefore, sure to keep the captives safe inside, while affording room for exercise.

The section devoted to the giraffe and her young needed to be lofty to hold her secure. As it was, her small head, with its odd horn and bristling hairs, was often seen roaming along the upper end of the stakes, like some creature creeping unsteadily over an uncertain pathway.

Had you been a member of this expedition, you would have appreciated the services of the natives at this time. The stockades for the captives were mostly made by them, and it now became their duty to look after the wants of the wild as well as the domestic animals. It was their province, as they understood it, to keep watch of the grazing oxen, and prevent them wandering too far from camp; to look out for wild beasts and men; to provide grass and leaves for the giraffe, flesh for the young lions and leopards; to take care of the goats, and furnish their milk for the table, and such of the captives as might need it; to provide fuel, attend to the cooking, and, in short, to do everything except hunt.

SPRING-BOK.

In other words, since the four white men meant to devote their energies to that business, they arranged that all other work, in and about camp, should be done by the natives, who had been brought along for that purpose.

Two exceptions should be named, in the persons of Pongo, the Bushman, and Diedrick, the Hottentot. They were more intelligent than the others and their previous experience in these wilds rendered them valuable assistants. The extra ponies were intended mainly for their use, though the prize Pongo had secured in that line left another spare horse for future contingencies.

It was a cause of thankfulness on the part of all that the wounded Orak mended so rapidly. Even Mr. Godkin, with his slight knowledge of medicine, would not have dared to prophesy such speedy recovery as the African showed. Orak offered to give help in building the stockade, but that could not be permitted.

Respecting Pongo and Diedrick, the arrangement was that one of them should be in camp during the absence of the hunters. The servants needed some one to direct them; and especially if any unexpected danger should threaten, either the Bushman or Hottentot was competent to assume charge of matters until the return of one or all of the white men.

The only weak point about the encampment lay in the tall grass which I have told you skirted both banks of the stream running near. These offered the best of concealment for wild beasts or men that might try to steal within striking distance of the party at night.

Mr. Godkin's uneasiness was such that most of the second day was spent in cutting off the grass nearest the camp, and between it and the river. It was a relief when so much had been removed that they felt tolerably secure against the descent of any poisoned missiles in the night time.

During the afternoon following the capture of the giraffes, and the next day, none of our friends engaged in hunting, but they gave their help to the erection of the stockade, and to putting everything in good form against the descent of the storm that was liable to come up at any time.

The feeling of security which diffused itself in camp was somewhat shaken at the close of the second day, by a discovery of Abdallah, the native from Senaar. He was wandering along the bank of the stream, where he was quite sure several hippopotami had been but a short time before, when he stumbled over a raft, drawn against the bank at a point precisely opposite the camp.

This structure consisted of a dozen or more large logs, from which the branches had been partly cut, bound together by ropes of twisted grass, which covered the top like the thatched roof of some humble dwelling. Its buoyancy was sufficient to float several men.

The party would have been glad to believe the raft had lain where it was found since some date previous to the arrival of themselves, but that was impossible. Mr. Godkin, as well as Jack Harvey, had made careful examination of the shore immediately after the halt, — so careful, indeed, that they could not have overlooked such a large object. Failure to discover it was proof that it had not been there.

Pongo explained that the Bushmen, Bechuanas, and other native tribes, sometimes used such craft in descending rivers, even for short distances. They rarely constructed them for the single purpose of crossing, and never attempted to employ them against a strong current, since they were too unwieldly for that purpose.

They were handled as we handle similar structures — that is, by means of long poles, pressed against the bottom of the stream on which they were floating.

It was noticeable that there were no poles on or about the raft, — the meaning of which no one for a time guessed.

"It must be," said Mr. Godkin, "that, in spite of our watchfulness, a party of natives have come down the river and landed here."

"And, inasmuch as the raft is on this side," added Bob Marshall, "they must also be here."

BLACK AND WHITE ANTELOPES.

"Undoubtedly."

"And where are they now?"

"That is what I should very much like to know; but it was easy for them to steal up or down stream, through the tall grass, without any of us detecting them."

Pongo and Diedrick had hastily examined the surroundings, but were unable to identify anything that looked like the footprints of natives. They attributed their failure to do so to the tracks made by themselves in tramping back and forth, while the wet ground, for some feet from the shore, so quickly filled all indentations that it was impossible to tell whether they were caused by the feet of men or animals.

"Nothing is to be feared from an open attack," remarked Mr. Godkin, after considerable discussion, "but it is these sneaking scamps that will crawl just nigh enough to launch one of those pestilent arrows, and then scoot off before the shaft comes down on your head."

"We have been exposed to that risk before entering Bechuana Land, and even while we were in the Transvaal," said Dick Brownell.

"That may be," replied his cousin, "but I suppose Mr. Godkin means to say that the danger he speaks of is one of those we can never become used to — what's the matter with Jack?"

The Texan had walked apart from his friends, and was prosecuting an investigation independent of them.

The fact was, the cowboy was utilizing his experience on the plains of the Southwest when campaigning against Geronimo and his miscreants. The occasion was one which called for that sort of knowledge, and the sagacious Texan was turning it to good account.

First, he went some distance up stream; then, turning to one side, so as to pass clear of the party near the water, he returned to the bank at a point below. Thus, it will be seen, he followed a line which, at some point, must have been crossed by the wild men, after disembarking from the raft.

While thus engaged, he scrutinized the damp ground with the penetrating eye of a Kit Carson. He detected no trail beside that of his friends, whose footprints he was able to identify, because of the peculiar footgear they wore.

Returning to Mr. Godkin and the others, he observed the absence of poles from the raft, besides which, it lay so lightly against the bank that a slight push would have set it free.

It was enough: Jack Harvey had formed his conclusion.

"That raft has drifted down stream ; there wasn't a rascal on it ; the current carried it against the bank, where it caught fast."

CHAPTER XXI.

ON THE CREST OF THE HILL.

THE GNU.

WHEN Jack Harvey explained the reason for his conclusion, his friends were satisfied, only wondering that they had failed to note the signs that guided him so well.

It followed, therefore, that while no immediate danger from the source threatened, there were wild men not far off, and no precaution against a visit from them was to be neglected.

The following morning, the four white persons, accompanied by Pongo, the Bushman, rode to the top of an elevation, about a half mile from camp, to gain a survey of the surrounding country, and to settle upon their plan of campaign, as it may be termed. Reaching the crest of the circular hill, covered only with grass, the view was most extended and interesting.

They found themselves in the center of a genuine South African landscape. Far to the northward rose a ridge of mountains, whose crests almost pierced the snow line, while the scores of square miles in other directions were broken by winding streams, jungles, broad sweeping plains, swamps, and groves that gave a variety to the scene that would have delighted the heart of a painter.

While the rest employed their eyes in the pleasing task of surveying this delightful picture, Mr. Godkin made good use of his glasses, which had served him on former occasions. He possessed more experience than any of his companions in hunting wild animals, and few points escaped him. It may be said that his view was a business one, for, in spite of the sport and adventure that must of necessity accompany their stay in the Dark Continent, the expedition had its definite purpose in coming so far, and there was no time to be thrown away in diversions or side issues.

The most interesting feature of the landscape was the animate portion which gradually impressed itself upon the vision of the spectators.

It would be impossible to enumerate the different animals which, at various times, were discerned from this elevation. From the accounts sent me by Dick and Bob I name the following:

The spring-bok; hartbeest; black and white antelopes; saber antelopes, whose horns, indeed, resemble formidable weapons; the koodoo, with its long, spiral horns; the curiously marked animal called the harnessed antelope; the eland, of which you have already learned something; and the gnu.

To the north, in the direction of the high mountains, and near the edge of a grove, standing close to the bank of the stream which passed by the camp, was a

THE SABER ANTELOPE

herd of elephants, evidently feeding. Still farther off could be discerned a half dozen small animals in the middle of a grassy plain, which the glass proved to be elands, a graceful species of antelope, many of which had been previously met on the way to this point.

Far beyond these, so far, indeed, that the glass failed to identify them of a certainty, were several moving specks, which it was generally agreed were horse-men, probably the party of Bushmen with whom our friends had had such a stirring encounter a short time before. Inasmuch as they were receding, and must soon pass out of the field of vision, no uneasiness was caused by sight of them.

To the east and west, at varying distances, were other antelopes, while, as Mr. Godkin declared, the thick grass along the streams and the muddy waters was likely to give shelter to hippopotami, rhinoceroses and crocodiles. It was not likely, either, that much of a search was required to beat up lions, panthers, hyenas and leopards from their hiding-places.

THE HARNESSED ANTELOPE

That which specially interested the hunters, at the conclusion of the general survey, was five animals, grazing less than a mile off, near the stream that wound around the foot of the elevation. The spot was comparatively free from the tall weeds so abundant in the vicinity of the camp, and evidently afforded excellent pasturage.

"What the mischief do you call *them?*" asked Jack Harvey, handing the glasses to their owner.

"Oryxes; if you propose to make a capture of any, you will find it no easy task."

"Why?"

"The oryx is the fleetest quadruped in South Africa," said Mr. Godkin. "With the exception of Apache, my mustang," said the Texan.

"I am not so sure about that, when you are upon his back. But he is a beautiful creature, and I wish we could secure one or two."

"He is the animal that is sometimes called the gemsbok?" was the inquiring remark of Bob Marshall.

THE ELAND

"That is because of his resemblance to the chamois or *gemse* of Europe," remarked Dick Brownell.

The director nodded his head to signify that his young friend was right, and added.

"The oryx is found in the central and western parts of South Africa, being rare even so far east as this. The male is not quite four feet high, and is of a pale buff color. You can notice their peculiarities by aid of the glass."

Further inspection showed that the head of the animal was shaped like that of the wild ass, while his mane and tail were those of the horse. Several black bands about the head suggest that the oryx continually wears a stall-collar.

One of the most notable characteristics of the oryx is its horns, which are a yard in length, ringed at the base, curving very slightly backward, and of a glossy black color. These constitute the most effective of weapons, as our friends were destined to learn sooner than they anticipated.

The female's appearance differs from that of the male only in height, which is a few inches less, and in the horns, which are more dainty and tapering. These are

THE AFRICAN ELEPHANT

so exactly similar that when the oryx is viewed from the side, it appears to have but a single one.

"I am going for them," Jack abruptly declared; "they are so slight in size and strength that the question of danger doesn't enter into the business."

"You will think different if you run against those horns, which are as bad as the tusks of the wild boar."

"I don't see any need of running against them," quietly replied the Texan, "for I judge the critters won't attack us."

"They are not apt to unless driven at bay."

Although the elevated situation of the party rendered them conspicuous, there were no evidences that they had attracted the attention of any of the animals in sight.

"You see that grove of timber, about a fourth of a mile to the north of where the oryxes are feeding," said Jack; "well, I'm going to make a circuit, so as to enter from the other side.   As soon as I get beyond the wood, I want you, Bob and Dick, to ride toward the critters from this side.   They'll be likely to make for the grove, and I'll wait till they enter or start to turn off, when I'll bring the old lasso into use once more."

ORYX OF ABYSSINIA.

Looking upon the matter as settled, Jack started off, circling so far to the left that a ride of several miles was necessary before the youths could leave their position.

Mr. Godkin smiled. "He hasn't left anything for you and me to do, Pongo," he said to the Bushman, "but I don't think we need remain idle.   Let's take a turn to the southeast, where I suspect we shall find something worth attention."

Pongo was glad to hear this, for nothing displeased him more than to remain inactive, even during the sultry hours of midday. He nodded his head to signify he was waiting his employer's pleasure.

Wishing his young friends success in their enterprise, the director bade them good-by, and the next minute the boys were left alone on the crest of the elevation.

THE KOODOO.

"I think," said Bob, "that it is best to move a little farther back, so as to run no risk of being seen by Jack's game."

The suggestion was followed. The youths slipped from the saddles, after moving their ponies so far down the slope behind them that they were out of sight of everything on the plain to the north. Then they seated themselves in the short grass, where it would have required a wonderfully keen eye to discern them from a point a few hundred yards away.

The objects which interested them to the exclusion of everything else were the orxyes and the Texan, since those parties promised to become involved within a comparatively brief space of time.

The animals were still cropping the grass, some of the number occasionally raising their heads and looking around. The action, however, was due to a habit of precaution, and not because they suspected the presence of any danger.

The lads wondered that they had not detected the hunters on the elevation, for the oryx, like all the antelope kind, is a suspicious animal, some of the family being extremely difficult to approach, even by the most experienced sportsmen.

"DOWN!" WHISPERED DICK

The Texan formed a picturesquely graceful figure as he galloped away on his beautiful mustang. The animal rose and sank with an even motion, which he was able to continue for hours without fatigue, while Jack's body swayed in unison with that of his steed. His broad-brimmed sombrero, the rifle slung over his shoulder, and his athletic figure, would have awakened admiration anywhere, though it is safe to say that he was the introducer of the cowboy costume in South Africa.

He steadily bore to the left, for the success of his plan depended on preventing the oryxes taking alarm before he reached the shelter toward which he wished them driven.

At the moment when he was at the farthest point west of the game, and was beginning to bend his course around and beyond the grove, the whole five gemsboks suddenly threw up their heads, and looked so fixedly at the hill on which the lads were sitting, that they believed, for the moment, they were discovered.

"Down!" whispered Dick, sinking lower in the grass, "or we shall scare them away."

The two almost lay on their faces, holding their heads only high enough to keep the animals in sight.

Gazing toward the hill for a half minut₋ or so, the creatures next stared so earnestly in the direction of the distant horseman that there could be little doubt they observed him.

"I wonder what they think of Jack," said Bob, unconsciously lowering his voice, as though he feared that any tone above a whisper would betray them.

"If they're capable of thinking, they can't help admiring the handsome fellow."

"That is well enough, if they are not frightened off."

"Jack is so far away that they must believe there is no cause for fear. There! that's what I suspected."

The oryxes resumed grazing, and, a few minutes later, the Texan passed out of sight beyond the grove.

CHAPTER XXII.

A MISCALCULATION.

THE disappearance of Jack Harvey, beyond the grove, was the signal for the lads to start the oryxes in his direction. Since they were liable to move to the west in their flight, Bob Marshall headed his pony to the left, following a course parallel to that of the Texan, though not so far westward, while Dick moved directly upon the creatures.

By this action, the game's most natural line of flight would be toward the timber, because the stream was on their right, and they were not likely to swim it, unless hard pressed.

Such was the calculation of our young friends, but, as is often the case in this world, the result proved very different from what was anticipated.

Dick adopted a slower pace than Bob, because he had less distance to go, and he did not wish to start the animals too soon, but he had hardly reached the base of the hill, when the oryxes threw up their heads with such manifest alarm that he stopped.

The moment he did so, the five began running 'round in short circles, as though bewildered. Then, instead of fleeing toward the grove, where Jack Harvey was awaiting them, the herd broke for the west.

Dick uttered a shout, to warn his cousin, but he had already observed the move, and tried to check it, by swinging his hat, throwing up his arms, shouting and galloping toward them.

His success was less than expected. Three of the oryxes dashed off at their highest speed, taking a course neither toward him nor the grove of trees, but midway between, there being abundance of room for such maneuvering.

The other two, after making several feints at Dick and the river, finally headed for the grove, thus giving a pleasant expectation to the Texan, who was attentively gazing out upon the plain from among the trees.

Bob Marshall was surprised by the obduracy of the three, who acted as if they had some suspicion of the trap laid for them, though that was hardly possible. He determined to force them to do as he wished, and, putting his pony to a dead run, he aimed to intercept the trio.

Despite what he had learned of the fleetness of the oryx, he was confident of his ability to do this, since he had much the advantage, on account of the shorter distance to travel.

But the fugitives mixed matters once more by separating. At the first, they ran in Indian file, a large male at the head, and formed an exceedingly pretty picture, skimming, with the speed of the wind, across the plain. Two, after edging farther and farther from the horseman, finally circled still more, so as to double on their own trail, and ran back toward the spot where they had been grazing a short time before, only to be still further terrified by Dick Brownell, who sent them skurrying down the stream on a line which, if followed, must carry them clear of the grove.

But the male, who was evidently the leader of the small family party, showed an unwillingness to be driven in that fashion. He bent his line of flight, to keep out of the way of the horseman trying so determinedly to head him off, but he would

neither turn back nor veer so much as to follow the other two, that were making for the grove.

"I'll see whether you can't be stopped," muttered Bob, compressing his lips and urging his steed to the utmost.

Never was the lad more astonished at the speed of any animal than at that of the oryx. With his head thrown back, so that the points of his long horns seemed to be resting on his haunches, he fairly flew over the ground, his graceful legs doubling beneath his body with a swiftness that rendered it almost impossible for the eye to perceive them.

Since his course converged with that of his pursuer, the male steadily bore to

9

the right, while Bob pushed his pony still harder.   He was confident of interposing himself across the path of the game, until he found that, despite his desperate exertions, he was bound to fall short after all.

When fifty feet separated pursuer and fugitive, the oryx shot by, like an arrow discharged from a bow.

Immediately the course of the youth became parallel to that of the fleeing animal, and, though his steed was doing his best, he steadily fell to the rear.

"I could shoot you easily enough, but I won't," said Bob, slackening his pace,

THE SPOTTED HYENA

"for you are too pretty to harm.   I wonder whether Jack could overhaul you with his mustang."

The lad kept up the pursuit a short distance farther, more to compel the oryx to continue its astounding speed than with any idea of running it down; but the pony, seeing the idleness of pursuit, voluntarily slackened its pace, until it drew down to a moderate gallop, which soon ended in a halt.

The fugitive ran but a short distance farther, when he came to a graceful stop, broadside to his pursuer, at whom he looked with an exultant air, as if to say:

"Well, young man, if you think you've got an animal there that knows anything about running, I'm ready to give him another

A WARM RECEPTION

lesson." "I salute you," said Bob, raising his hat in mock homage, "for you have done what I didn't believe possible. But," he added, the next minute, "look out, or you will get into trouble that you don't dream of."

The flight of the male had carried him into taller and ranker vegetation, that rose to his head. A short distance beyond the stationary animal, Bob detected a movement which showed that some other creature was in the grass.

He could not see distinctly enough to identify it, but it was evident that it had fixed its attention on the oryx, and meant to attack him. The strange beast looked like a large dog, and was creeping so stealthily forward that the oryx appeared to be unaware of his danger.

Bob's sympathies were entirely with the graceful creature, and he was on the point of raising his rifle to venture a shot in his behalf, when he saw it was too late. The beast that was stealing upon the oryx was a spotted hyena, such as are found only in South Africa. But a few paces separated it from its intended victim, when Bob descried the animal, crouching low in the grass to escape observation.

He wondered that the gemsbok failed to see his danger, though, judging from what followed, it is not improbable he had descried it before the horseman.

At the moment the latter was in the act of raising his rifle, the hyena moved forward several paces with extraordinary quickness, and leaped at the oryx, which was standing with his head turned away.

Escape was impossible, but, at the instant the hyena rose in air, the oryx seemed to brace his legs firmly, and, without shifting his position, gave a single backward flirt of his head. The hyena landed on the points of both horns, which slid into its body as if they were daggers, as indeed they were.

Before the assailant could make use of his claws, the oryx, by a dexterous flirt, shook him off his crimsoned horns, and, leaping back a few feet, lowered his head, and, with one bound, drove the fearful weapons again into his side.

The hyena was dying before the second stroke was delivered, though he struck venomously at the oryx, which easily avoided him, and, standing back, lowered his head once more. But he did not advance again, seeing there was no call to do so.

Bob Marshall's admiration deepened. It seemed to him, when the oryx was in full flight, that he was the most harmless of animals. So, indeed, he was, but he

THE STRIPED HYENA

had proven what he could do when forced to defend himself. Standing erect, with the blood dripping from his graceful horns, towering so far above his head, he became an object of respect.

Bob could now appreciate Mr. Godkin's remark about the skill of the gemsbok in using the weapons with which nature provides him. Gifted with such extraordinary speed, in addition to his means of defense, the exploit of bringing down or capturing his kind is one worthy of a veteran sportsman.

It is a fact that an oryx and lion have been found dead together, mutually slain, the king of beasts by his impalement on those sharp-pointed horns, and the gemsbok

An Unexpected Reception — Page 134.

by the shock of the collision. Our representation of the reception of a leopard by one of the plucky animals has been verified more than once in the Dark Continent.

As the animal confronted Bob Marshall, he saw a danger which he had not suspected up to that moment. What would become of him, or rather his steed, if the beast should charge?

The antelope had already demonstrated his superiority in speed, so that the pony could not escape by flight, and a single thrust of those bony swords would be fatal.

"There's one weapon, however, that beats his," added the youth, following his train of thought. "If he attacks, I will meet him with a few charges from my gun, and they will stop him before he can reach us."

It was fortunate, therefore, for this particular oryx, that, though his blood was roused, and he was quite ready to assail the hunter, from whom he had fled in such fright a few minutes before, he decided to leave him and his animal alone, provided they returned the compliment.

Bob, however, kept an eye to windward, as he rode off to join his friends, not feeling secure against a demonstration until a long distance separated him from the oryx. But the latter, after holding his ground a few minutes, turned away, as though he had forgotten the recent stirring incidents as well as the fact that the members of his family had become pretty well separated during the flurry.

Looking toward the grove, Bob descried Dick, who had halted a short distance from it, and was evidently awaiting him. Nothing of the other oryxes was seen, and the youth was uncertain whether they had plunged into the grove, to stir up matters with Jack Harvey, or had made their escape long before.

Dick, as may be supposed, was deeply interested in the story his cousin had to tell.

"Something has taken, or is taking place in the wood," remarked the former, "and, from what you have related, I shouldn't wonder if Jack has found his contract bigger than he thought. Let's find out."

CHAPTER XXIII.

THE HORNS OF A DILEMMA.

THE young hunters struck an easy gallop toward the grove of timber, whither they had driven a couple of oryxes for Jack Harvey to capture.

Despite their confidence in the Texan's bravery and skill, they were not without some misgiving, based on the natural mistake any one was liable to make respecting the graceful, fleet-footed animals that know how to use their horns so well.

This uneasiness was suddenly increased by what took place while they were yet some distance from the timber. One of the creatures dashed into sight, leaping and cavorting in the most extraordinary manner. It seemed to be standing on its hind legs, then balancing itself on its front ones, whirling around, darting hither and thither, and, in fact, disporting itself like an oryx gone clean daft.

There was a hint of the cause of this frantic performance, for the sombrero of Jack Harvey was pierced through the top by both horns, and it had slid down to their base, where it had settled over the pretty eyes of the creature.

The oryx was in the situation of a man that has a hat jammed inextricably over his face, and its wild performances were with a view to relieving itself of the exasperating annoyance, which seemed to baffle its frantic efforts.

About all it could do was to strike at it with its fore feet, and flirt its head. Several times the hat, with its rattlesnake band, appeared to rise a short way up the supports, as if about to part company with them, but settled back in place, and resisted every attempt to dislodge it.

But for the serious phase of this performance, the boys would have made the wood ring with laughter, for a funnier exhibition cannot be imagined; but they were too much alarmed about the Texan.

"I am afraid he has been gored by the gemsbok," said Bob, in a scared voice, "and is in need of help, if indeed he is not killed."

"There is little time to lose," added Dick, as much terrified as his cousin; "we'll leave our ponies here, and stop just long enough to capture this animal, which looks like a female."

On reaching the other side of the grove, where he had stopped to secure one of the oryxes, Jack Harvey had dismounted and left his mustang at the farther boundary. The intervening trees and vines were sufficient to shut out all view of the plain on which the animals were feeding. Knowing the timid nature of the antelope kind, he deemed it necessary to keep himself and horse out of sight as long as he could.

By leaving his steed, he was invisible to the approaching creatures, until they should penetrate the grove for at least half its width. The density of the timber rendered it almost impossible to use the pony to advantage in capturing any animal within the wood. Consequently, it was wise, in more than one sense, to follow the course he adopted.

The Texan paused, lasso in hand, with rifle slung over his back, about a dozen yards from the edge of the timber which the gemsboks were approaching. He stood

GONE CLEAN DAFT.

behind the trunk of a tree, which hid his entire body, and peeped out at the plain where the game were feeding.

He saw the scattering of the drove, and followed Bob Marshall with his eyes as he chased the large male to the westward, and noted the break that two others made for the strip of land between the grove and the river. The next minute, he perceived that a couple were heading toward the spot where he was standing, and were quite sure to pass within reach.

"That suits me," he said to himself; "I only wish they would come close enough to lasso both at the same time."

The Texan had not long to wait. The pretty creatures approached at a swift gallop, the male leading the dainty female by a few paces, and entered the grove at a point which would bring both within a biscuit's toss of where he was standing.

Whizz !

At the critical moment the loop dropped ever the long horns of the male, and Jack quickly coiled the other end round a sapling at his elbow.

The oryx was checked so suddenly that he was thrown to the ground with considerable force. Before he could rise, his captor was kneeling over him with one of the horns grasped in either hand. He was afraid the noose would slip along the smooth length, and allow the animal to free himself and dash off.

The instant his muscular hands closed around the glossy horns at the base, Jack gained a vivid idea of the capacity of those weapons to do harm. They felt warm at the base, as though throbbing with the vitality of the owner, which continued his fierce effort to rise to his feet. Not only that, but he tried to strike his enemy with the horns, curving his nose between his fore legs and flirting the weapons outward. His position, however, prevented any effectiveness, and Jack found no difficulty in holding his advantage.

That his precaution was wise was proven by the fact that, the moment he seized the horns, the noose, which had closed tightly around the base, slipped half way to the tips. Had the horns been spiral, like those of the koodoo, or had they spread at the top, they would have formed an excellent support for the lasso, but I have referred to their perfect similarity and evenness, which would have made it easy for the oryx to slide the rope off, had he been free to make the attempt.

Holding the beautiful head flat against the earth, Jack whipped the noose over the fore leg of the prisoner, where, by drawing it taut, he could hold him fast against all struggles. The flesh was yielding, and the irregular contour of the limb prevented the rope being shaken off.

The task would have been simple for the cowboy, but for an unexpected interruption.

At the moment the male was thrown, the female whisked by in full flight. The sight of the mishap of her mate, however, brought her to a sudden stop, and, wheeling about with her head aloft, she stared wonderingly at the scene.

With more devotion than most animals would have shown under such trying circumstances, she rushed to the help of her overturned lord. Jack noticed her dancing around and preparing to gore him. He saw that she must be given attention, if he wished to save himself from exceedingly unpleasant consequences.

But he did not dare rise from the ground until he had the male fast, for he was determined to hold him at all hazards. The necessity of keeping an eye on both made this difficult. He could have ended the trouble by killing the female with one of his revolvers, but her affection for her companion gave him the hope that he might also secure her. At the moment the latter lowered her head with the intention of goring him, he snatched off his sombrero and tossed it toward her, intending to bewilder her until he could secure the male. His skill with the lasso enabled him to drop the hat in place, and the upward flirt which she gave at the same moment sent the points of the horns through the crown, the hat sliding down to the base and veiling the lustrous eyes of the lady.

"That's rough on my old sombrero," said Jack, laughing at the success of his essay, "but I don't believe she will hurt it past mending, which wouldn't be the case with *me*, if she should jam those confounded horns through my body."

THE ADDAX.

Instantly the female forgot her helpless partner, and began frantic efforts to disentangle the hat from her horns. She pranced about, now on her hind feet and then on her fore ones. She inflicted more than one severe bruise on herself, by striking the trees and branches about her, and quickly emerged on the open plain, where her grotesque performances attracted the wonderment of Bob Marshall and Dick Brownell.

It took Jack Harvey but a few moments to secure the male, when he stepped back and allowed him to rise. He bounded to his feet as nimbly as an acrobat, and, dropping his head, plunged at the astonished Texan, who leaped behind the large trunk, just in time to escape the charge.

Instead of giving up the effort, the oryx followed Jack, who never traveled around a tree so quickly in all his life.

Fortunately, this performance speedily "wound up" the animal, else the Texan might have received more than one sharp puncture.

"While you're unwinding," he said, "I'll take a look at my sombrero — that is, if enough is left to look at."

Reaching the edge of the wood, he saw that Bob and Dick had also dismounted, and, leaving their horses free, were trying to capture the cavorting female.

"Look out for her horns!" he called, observing that they were trying to get near enough to seize her.

"Don't fear for us," replied Bob, who, like his companion, was immeasurably relieved to see their friend unharmed.

"I'm obliged to you for your efforts to save my hat, but I don't want you to run too much risk: shall I lend a hand?"

"Attend to your own animal and leave us alone —— "

While the words were in the lad's mouth, he made a sudden bound and grasped one horn of the female, Dick instantly doing the same on the other side.

It was no easy task for their united strength to hold her captive, and, had she not been well-nigh exhausted from her struggles, she might have escaped.

Dick whipped off the troublesome hat, and flung it aside for its owner. The instant the female saw her captors, she renewed her resistance, and for a minute or two it was an even thing; but the youths were plucky, and held on till she surrendered.

Jack ran forward, picked up his hat, and went back to his own prize.

He found him pretty well subdued, though he stamped and lowered his head in a threatening manner for some minutes. Finally, seeing he was worn out, the captor released him from the fastening, and whistled for his mustang to follow him.

The steed came forward, causing another panic on the part of the oryx. He made no move, however, against Jack, who speedily led him out on the plain, where a brief consultation was held with the youths, who were grimly holding fast to their prize.

It was decided to leave the ponies to follow them to camp, while the three gave their undivided attention to the prisoners. Bob walked on the right, grasping one horn, while Dick did the same on the left. Jack Harvey kept close to the head of the male, so as to seize his weapons should he become obstreperous.

The return to camp was tiresome, but it was reached without mishap, and the two prizes were safely placed in a portion of the stockades reserved for captives.

I may state just here that the addax of North Africa, as you will observe from the illustration, bears some resemblance to the oryx.

CHAPTER XXIV.

THE WHIZZ OF A BOOMERANG.

JACK HARVEY and his young friends having selected their field of operations, Mr. Godkin did the same for himself and Pongo, the Bushman.

Fully a mile southwest of the elevation where they had parted company, stretched a jungle several miles in extent. Most of it appeared to be on higher ground than the rest of the plain, and within its gloomy depths were sure to be found birds, beasts and reptiles without number.

"We'll go there," was the decision of the director, who struck his horse into a brisk gallop, closely followed by his assistant. A short distance passed, and they came abreast, continuing thus until close to the jungle, where they meant to make their investigations.

"Now," said Mr. Godkin, when they drew up their ponies, for a moment, on the margin, "the trees are too close together, and there are too many vines for us to ride in there. We will dismount and look around on foot. Do you think your horse will stand?"

"Yes — he stand," replied the Bushman, who had learned enough of the sagacious animal to feel full confidence in him.

"Provided he isn't disturbed by some wild beast or reptile, when we would expect him to take care of himself."

Numbers of birds, with brilliant plumage, were seen hopping among the branches overhead. It was noticeable that those with the most gorgeous dress possessed voices of hideous harshness. To have sat within the hearing of their discordant screeching would have driven a person almost wild.

But the hunters had no special interest in them, though they expected to obtain some valuable specimens before their return.

The horses, being left free, began cropping the grass, which was green and succulent, close to the margin of the jungle, where it was partly screened from the sun's scorching rays. Possibly they incurred some risk in doing this, but, since it may be said they were always in danger when traversing the Dark Continent, they had to take care of themselves, at times, as best they could.

The men stepped as guardedly as a couple of Indian scouts in an enemy's country, peering into the dismal depths of the jungle, on the watch for anything that promised game or plunder.

"St!" hissed Pongo, stopping short, directly behind his employer, "me see somethin' then."

"What did it seem to be?" asked Mr. Godkin, who had detected a suspicious rustling. "Snake — dere he be!" said Pongo.

The white man had caught sight of the reptile at the same moment. It appeared to have been stretched in a small open space, near the plain, where the light could strike it, for some of the poisonous serpents of Asia and Africa find enjoyment in the glare of the sun far beyond the power of a white person or ordinary animal to stand.

The hunters were advancing directly toward the spot where it lay, when it reared its head a few inches and swiftly crawled into the jungle. Instead, however, of continuing its flight, it halted on the margin, coiled itself like the American rattlesnake, and waited for the couple to come nigh enough for it to strike.

Some persons see beauty in snakes, but I confess I never could feel anything but horror and disgust in looking at them. There is something in the sight of a crawling reptile which sends a shudder over me, and I believe the feeling is shared by nine-tenths of mankind.

But those who can find beauty in the creature whose head, the Scriptures say, the woman's seed shall bruise, would have been charmed with the reptile on which Mr. Godkin and Pongo gazed.

It was about four feet in length, slender and tapering, with crimson and yellow bands along its back, which changed to greenish colored spots at the neck and tail. The belly, as is the rule, was of a whitish tint.

The head was reared nearly a foot, from the center of the coil, and was as broad and flat as a child's hand. Just back of the small, glittering eyes rose two horny protuberances, of the oddest imaginable appearance. The mouth was disproportionately large, and, at intervals, partly opened. From this darted forth a crimson tongue, or rather a double tongue, for it seemed to be bifurcated at the root. It curled about hither and thither, with such quickness that, at times, the mouth appeared to be crossed by several tiny streaks of blood.

"I have seen just such a snake as that in the Deccan," remarked Mr. Godkin, after studying it a minute, "and it is one of the most venomous in the world — fully as bad as the cobra de capello."

"Want to catch him?" asked Pongo, with a grin.

"No, sir; I ain't hunting snakes for Mr. Barnum; there are plenty of them in this part of the world, but I'll let him buy what he wants of Reiche, in New York, or his old friend Hagenbeck, in Hamburg. But do you think you could catch him, Pongo?"

"Yes, me catch him."

"How?"

"Kill him first."

"All right; the best use you can put such creatures to is to kill them; that's always my motto."

The particular specimen of which I am writing quickly proved its demon-like viciousness.

Its action in coiling and rearing its head was a challenge to the hunters to attack it. It made not the slightest sound, but its bead-like eyes scintillated with rage, and it plainly wished and expected them to come closer. Mr. Godkin feinted to do so. Instantly its head rose several inches, and was drawn back, just as a man does when about to deliver a blow.

"No; I thank you," laughed the white man, recoiling; "I don't mean to give you a chance to knock me out in that fashion."

The failure of the parties to advance seemed to convince the serpent that they were afraid of it, and it now endeavored to coax them into coming closer. Uncoiling, it crawled slowly in the jungle, its head raised but a few inches, and its whole manner that of alarm, as if fearful of being pursued.

And yet nothing was clearer than that it was seeking to draw the hunters after it.

"Look out! He's going to strike!"

Pongo now took a step in advance. Instantly the reptile stopped, but it did not resume its coil, afraid that if it did so, the man would be frightened into retreating again. But another pace forward and the snake would have gone into coil like a flash.

The Bushman took that step, bringing himself fearfully close to the little demon, which looped itself like Jack Harvey's lasso, the head instantly rising fully eighteen inches, and thrown far back, until it almost touched the ground on the farther side of the native.

What a lightning-like blow he could deliver from that position!

"Look out! he's going to strike! You're too near!" called the alarmed Mr. Godkin.

But the action of the reptile was no quicker than that of the Bushman, who let fly with his boomerang, clipping off the head of the serpent with such precision that it followed the implement for a dozen feet, dropping in the bushes, just before the boomerang struck a tree, a few feet beyond.

The body whipped and threshed the ground for a few minutes, and then became still.

"Oogh!" muttered Pongo, with an expression of disgust, as he came back, after recovering his favorite weapon; "me don't like kill snakes with him — don't want to get him blood on it."

"I intended to practice a little with my revolver, but you took the sport out of my hands."

The director suggested that the hunt on which they were engaged could be prosecuted with better success if they separated. That is, while he continued along the side of the jungle in one direction, Pongo should take the opposite. The chance of discovering something would thus be doubled, while neither would go too far to run to the help of the other, if needed.

A sight which pleased each followed this brief parting. The two horses had been left behind, cropping the grass, but when Mr. Godkin's saw him moving off alone, he followed him, keeping some distance behind and out on the plain, as though he knew he ought not to interfere with any plan he had in view.

Pongo did not expect his own pony to show any such regard. He was, therefore, interested and expectant as he saw the handsome creature standing, with head elevated, and watching him approaching, his course necessarily leading him toward the animal.

Affecting not to see him, the Bushman passed beyond, but had not gone far, when the sound of hoofs told him he was followed, as though the animal was unwilling to part company with his new master. The African stopped and awaited his approach.

The pony came forward without timidity, and extended his nose for his master to stroke his forehead. Pongo did this for several minutes, adding several playful pats on the neck, much to the pleasure of the animal.

In a country where man seemed arrayed against, not only those of his kind, but all the natural inhabitants, as they in turn were arrayed against him, there was something touching in this exhibition of affection on the part of a dumb animal for one whom a few days before it had never seen.

The Bushman was not indifferent to such proof of the confidence of the beast, and he forgot, for a brief while, the duty that had taken him hither, and devoted the time to petting the faithful animal, as he would have done with a member of his own family.

CHAPTER XXV.

HARDLY more than a hundred yards from the spot where Pongo had stopped to pet his new steed, he came upon a large, branching tree, standing not on the edge of the jungle, but fully a rod out on the grassy plain. He recognized it as one that bore a peculiar fruit, something like the hazel-nut of our own country.

But it was not the tree which interested the native so much as that which he saw under it.

One of the largest wild boars on which he had ever gazed was feeding upon the nuts, of which he was very fond. Some of the branches of the tree spread so far as to enter the jungle, and since the animal happened to be browsing beneath this point, he had been invisible until the Bushman ran almost against him.

There could be no mistaking his identity. He stood as high, almost, as a cow, was long, gaunt and thin, of a dark brown color, and covered with bristles, which seemed to stand erect along the spine.

The most noticeable feature of those animals is their immense tusks, which, curving outward from the lower jaw, reach a length of eight or ten inches. Backed by the prodigious strength of the brute, they are like a couple of Damascus blades in the hands of a master swordsman.

The boar is hunted in the forests of Germany and the jungles of India and South Africa. The favorite weapon is a spear, and the sport should always be conducted on horseback. The hunter of Bengal uses a weapon less than seven feet long, the shaft being of bamboo, weighted with lead at the upper end and with a broad, strong blade. It is held firmly, with the point projecting beyond the stirrup-iron, so that when the boar charges, he runs on the spear. In Bombay and Hyderabad, the spear is longer and lighter and is carried underhand. The animals are hard to kill, and, even when wounded, they often escape the most experienced sportsmen.

The wild boar is afraid of no living creature. He has been seen to refuse to give the path to the lion or tiger, both of which beasts are generally wise enough to turn out and let him go by unmolested. With those frightful tusks he can disembowel a panther or bear as easily as you can cut apart a piece of cheese. I have known one of them to drive his tusk through the middle of a sapling, splitting it into kindling wood.

A curious fact regarding the wild hogs is that when they are young they are beautifully striped. These markings entirely disappear as they grow older.

The bosch vark, or bush hog, belongs to Southern Africa, and is a formidable animal, resembling the wild boar in many respects, but with several points of difference as you can observe from the illustration.

The babiroussa belongs to Malacca. Nature is kind enough to furnish him with four effective tusks. Those of the upper jaw, instead of having their sockets point downward, are curved upward, so that in filling the curvatures of the socket, they pass through a hole in the upper lip, curving so sharply over the face that they are useless as a means of defense.

The wart hog ranges over the tropical regions from Abyssinia to Caffraria. His appearance is so grotesque that I am sure you have often been amused in viewing him.

THE BOSCH VARK.

Being well acquainted with the wild boar, Pongo stopped at a respectful distance to survey him. His more prudent horse halted several rods beyond.

The boar continued crunching the nuts, which were quite abundant, though he had been engaged so long in feeding that the supply must have been considerably reduced. You will perceive that Pongo was not loaded for boar, and he did not care to open fight with this one, though confident he could turn his boomerangs to account against him.

10

The hog was in continual motion. At first his haunches were turned toward the native, then his side and next his head. The tough snout occasionally plowed up the earth, which was ridged in many places, but he showed no interest in anything except the delicious food with which he was filling himself.

Suddenly he threw up his snout, and holding his jaws motionless, with the dirt dropping from his nose and the partly crushed nuts from his jaws, he stared at the man, whose presence he seemed to discover for the first time.

THE WART HOG.

Pongo laid his hand on one of his boomerangs, for he felt the situation was becoming interesting. None knew better than he the power of those beasts, for the long, ridged scar on his hip was made by the tusk of a boar that clove the body of the horse he was riding half asunder.

It seemed to the Bushman that the tusks before him were fully a foot long. White, solid and gleaming, they were embedded in bone that was backed up by irresistible muscle.

A brief survey was enough for the brute to take in all the points of the intruder upon his domain, and, without lowering his head, and emitting only a slight snort, he started on a moderate trot toward the presumptuous hunter. The latter thought it a good time to make a change of location, and he proceeded to do so, without lingering on the way.

Pongo's first impulse was to take to one of the trees, into which he was confident of clambering before the tusks could reach him. But, observing that his pony was near, he started for him. Before, however, he could come up with the steed, he perceived that the boar had given up the pursuit, and had returned to crunching nuts beneath the tree. It looked as if he was afraid the visitor meant to root out the food from under his nose, and he only cared to keep him at a distance.

Pongo walked slowly back, stopping farther away than before. Had he possessed a gun, he could have brought down the hog without trouble. He could use the boomerang with effect against him, but you can understand that it was an awkward weapon to be employed for such purpose, since there was too much neck to be cloven in two, as he had done with the ostrich and serpent.

All at once, the boar stopped eating, and, without looking at the native, began walking along the side of the jungle, in the direction that Pongo had been following when he came upon him.

The Bushman now ran out to where his horse was grazing, and, springing upon his back, started after the boar, not directly behind him, but a short distance away from the trees, the courses of the two being parallel. The animal was on its return to his lair, which could not be far off. A rocky portion of the jungle, a furlong ahead, most likely was the location.

The Bushman was at a loss what to do. He was eager for a bout with the hog, but he held him in considerable awe, and Mr. Godkin was too far off to be summoned to the spot. A few minutes more would be enough for the fugitive, if he may be called such, to reach his home, from which it would be impossible to dislodge him.

At such times, when the boar is worried, he will make a sudden dash out upon the dogs, rip several of them to death, maiming a horse, perhaps, and then dart back to cover before any of the hunters can drive a spear into his body.

Astride of his fleet steed, Pongo felt safer than when on foot. Determined to give the animal a bout, he whipped out one of his boomerangs and let fly.

True to its aim, the weapon circled around in air, as though aimed at any point except the one where it was intended to strike, but turned as intended, and landed against the ribs of the hog with a thump which gave out a sound like that of a bass drum.

It was so violent, indeed, that it jarred him perceptibly, though it inflicted no cut, nor was it meant to. The boar never stopped, but glanced around, as if to determine the point whence the blow came. He did not diminish his speed, acting as if he would like to suggest to the hunter to try something better if he hoped to annoy him.

Pongo now urged his horse, and he broke into a gallop. Before the intervening distance was much lessened, the boar also increased his pace.

He did not gallop, but trotted with astonishing swiftness, and with the smoothness of a dog following his master's carriage. The pony, realizing what was wanted, let himself out, and the fugitive did likewise, his pace quickly becoming an amazing one.

A moment later, the horse was on a dead run, and the distance between him and the fugitive diminished sensibly.

Pongo did not stop to recover his boomerang, intending to do that on his return, nor did he throw a second one, for nothing was to be gained by pounding the hog. Possibly he might have hewed off a leg, but, I am glad to say, the hunter, even though a native African, was not inclined to mutilate a creature in that fashion.

Such a race must, of necessity, be brief. The boar speedily reached a point opposite the rocks which the pursuer had fixed upon as containing his lair. That

THE BABIROUSSA

he was right, was shown by the action of the brute, which came down to a moderate trot, with his snout groping along the slightly worn path, as if searching for the door to his dwelling.

From some inexplainable cause, he seemed to have lost his bearings for the moment, for he turned about and came back several yards, then wheeled, and resumed his advance, with as little regard to the horseman seeking to harass him, as though he were a hundred miles away.

The Bushman could not help reflecting on the splendid opportunity that a properly-armed hunter would have seen in the bewilderment of the hog. Indeed, the chance was so good that he decided to give him another whack with a boomerang, just to keep things moving.

He was in the act of drawing the weapon from his waist, when a faint shout caused him to turn his head. Looking around, he saw that Mr. Godkin had mounted his horse, and was galloping toward him.

The native wondered whether, with the aid of his glasses, he had learned what was going on, or whether he wanted assistance in some emergency that had arisen.

Although the boar had made one demonstration against him, Pongo was not looking for anything of the kind, since his whole purpose seemed to be to find the entrance to his home. The native was still gazing inquiringly at his master, when a snort and prancing of his pony brought his attention back again.

The hog seemed to have become enraged at his failure to find the opening for which he was looking, and, probably, in some dim way, he associated the horseman with his trouble. Be that as it may, while the latter was looking back, the fierce brute charged upon him like a hurricane.

When Pongo caught sight of him, he was no more than twenty feet off, and coming at a terrific pace. His small eyes glowed like fire, his jaws were parted and dripping with foam, and, altogether, a more fearful object cannot be pictured.

The Bushman had no time to use his weapon, which, as I have said, was an awkward one for such an emergency, nor had his nimble pony a chance to wheel to the right or left, nor to turn and flee, as he would have done had his rider discovered his peril a second sooner.

"He Fell from the Back of his Steed."— Page 151.

CHAPTER XXVI.

"ALL TOGETHER."

BEFORE the pony could change his direction, the brute was upon him. He was the embodiment of fury, as, with his jaws dripping froth, and the frightful tusks agleam, he charged like a cyclone; but the steed had seen his peril before his master, else he would have been ordered to flee in time easily to escape.

At the instant when it seemed that nothing could save him, the horse, squatting low, made a tremendous leap, which carried him and his rider clean over the head of the boar that thundered beneath.

The effort of the pony was entirely unexpected to Pongo, who had no time to prepare himself, and, being without saddle, he fell from the back of his steed, striking the plain with such force that, for a few seconds, he was stunned.

The pony ran several rods, snorting with terror. Then he circled about, and, though apparently anxious to give his master help, was afraid to attempt it.

The boar made a vicious upward flirt of his terrible tusks as he shot under the belly of the steed, and must have grazed the glossy hide of the animal. Then, quick to realize his failure, and seeing the prostrate form on the plain, he wheeled and made for that.

The Bushman was not entirely senseless, though unable to rise or defend himself. In a vague way, he knew what was coming, and, instead of resisting, lay perfectly still.

The scene that followed was extraordinary. The boar, when directly upon him, stopped as abruptly as if he had run against a stone wall.

He had but to lower his head and give a single upper cut, to cleave the breast open, or rip the thigh to the bone, but he made no sign. Standing motionless a second or two, he uttered a sniff as of disgust, and then turned and trotted toward the entrance to his home, which he had discovered at last.

The wild boar sometimes displays a strange chivalry toward a fallen foe. In the midst of a terrific fight, when the hunter sinks helpless to the earth, suffering, perhaps, from fearful wounds, the brute will halt and wait for him to rise, before assailing him.

He does not always do so, but, aware of his occasional forbearance, and, knowing he could not resist him successfully, the Bushman lay still. The hog waited a brief while for his enemy to rise, but, as he did not, he left him.

At the moment of his vanishment among the rocks, Mr. Godkin was close enough to reach him with his rifle, but he made no attempt. He saw and understood the courtesy, and he would have been less than a gentleman had he refused to reciprocate.

"You were fortunate," he remarked, halting his pony beside Pongo, who climbed to his feet, none the worse for his violent fall.

"Yes; he good hog," was the satisfied reply of the native, who remounted his animal a moment later.

"If it had been any other brute, you would not have fared so well, which inclines me to remark that a wild boar isn't always the hog that some other animals are."

The face of the Bushman showed that he hardly grasped the full meaning of the facetious remark, though it cannot be supposed he failed to appreciate the chivalry of his foe.

"My gun was at my shoulder when he turned to leave you," added the director, "but I hadn't the heart to shoot, after seeing how kindly he treated you."

The brisk encounter with the boar did not drive from the minds of the sportsmen the errand that had taken them thither. They drew their ponies close to the edge of the jungle, and held them down to a walk, while their eyes searched the gloomy depths for whatever could be found.

As Mr. Godkin anticipated, they had not gone far when they discerned a denizen of the most frightful kind, in the shape of an immense boa-constrictor, coiled around the limbs of a tree so close to the plain that they sheered to the left, to avoid tempting him to make a dart at them.

The director had no thought of attempting to capture any such specimen as that for my exhibition, but he paused and debated with his assistant whether they should give it a shot or two. Standing at a safe distance, the white man could have riddled its head with balls, without any risk to himself, but he did not care to do so; preferring that Bob Marshall and Dick Brownell should see the monstrous reptile before disposing of it.

This conclusion was hastened by the sight of a drove of zebras, grazing and frisking at the base of the hill from which the party had taken their observation of the surrounding country. A second glance showed there was at least one colt among them, and Mr. Godkin was hopeful that, by careful maneuvering, they might be able to make it and its mother captives, somewhat after the manner of the taking of the giraffes, though they had no prospect of the use of Jack Harvey's lasso.

You are so familiar with the zebras, that I am sure you will not expect me to give a description of them. You have seen its black and white stripes, with the same colored rings around its legs. The quagga is brown, with black stripes, and with white belly and legs, while the animal known as Burchell's zebra differs from the ordinary kind only in having white legs.

There was nothing to be feared in attacking these animals, which are among the most harmless in South Africa, though almost untamable. Their peculiar appearance renders them interesting members of any exhibition, and Mr. Godkin would not have felt his work finished until he had secured at least one specimen.

"You see the dam with her foal?" he said to Pongo, as they drew near the drove, which did not notice their approach until they were quite close; "we must separate her from the rest and drive her to camp."

The Bushman nodded, to signify he understood, and was ready to give all the help he could. Striking their animals into a sharp gallop, they headed directly for the drove.

The female zebra, with her young, was at the rear, busily cropping the grass, while her colt helped itself to maternal nourishment, flirting its tail, jamming its head, and frisking about the parent in a way that, now and then, called forth a protesting whinny or kick, which, however, inflicted no hurt.

THE QUAGGA.

It was curious that the colt was the first to discover the presence of the strangers. Suddenly it looked toward them, with the milk dripping from its black muzzle, and with such a comical expression that even the glum Bushman smiled.

The youngster emitted no cry, probably not knowing enough to give the alarm, but the whole drove were startled the next moment by the tramp of the ponies' hoofs and the sight of the horsemen bearing down upon them.

Up went every head, and away they galloped, taking exactly the contrary course from that desired by the sportsmen.

The zebras showed considerable speed, and would have led the pursuers on a smart chase but for the colt, which, being unable to run as fast as the others, soon fell behind. The mother, of course, kept it company, showing a natural solicitude for its safety.

This was what Mr. Godkin wanted and what he had counted upon. When an opening of several rods appeared between the couple and the rest of the drove, he

BURCHELL'S ZEBRA.

and Pongo forced their horses between and turned the heads of the parent and colt in the opposite direction.

This was to the south of the elevation, and, if it could be continued long enough, would lead to camp. But it was not to be hoped that the zebras would keep the course after descrying the peril in front; they could not be taken without the help of the friends there.

Circling round the hill, the horsemen had to ride but a short distance, when they came in full sight of the camp. By that time the Texan and the lads had arrived with their oryxes, and were quick to discover the chance to secure new prizes.

Jack showed an instant perception of what was needed. A large gap was made in one side of the stockade, at the farthest portion from the camp, the natives moving hastily from the spot. Then Jack, Bob and Dick vaulted into their saddles and spread out on the plain to help drive the zebras into the inclosure.

This proved anything but an easy task, for it was not to be expected that any wild animal would willingly approach a place like the encampment of the hunters. The mother snuffed the air, pricked her ears, looked right and left, stopped short, and then started at a brisk trot over her own trail, the colt following closely at her heels, for, even in her fright, she accommodated her gait to that of her offspring.

But she had time to go only a short distance, when she was confronted by Pongo, who swung his arms and shouted so hard that she quickly shifted her course, only to find her path barred this time by Mr. Godkin, who disported himself like a frantic person.

Once more the zebra headed for camp, approaching quite close, but the sight was too terrifying and she wheeled with such a determined effort to flank the shouting Bushman that she would have succeeded, despite his efforts, except for the opportune appearance of Bob Marshall and Jack Harvey, who were riding so near together that the way was closed.

By this time the zebra was panic-stricken and seemed to forget about her colt, in her wild desire to extricate herself from the snare into which she had run.

Jack had his lasso in hand, but it looked as if the capture could be completed without that, though he was ready to use it at any time.

The only way open was that leading to the inclosure, and the mother started thither with the young one still at her heels. She saw the opening, but showed renewed misgiving as she neared it. While still several yards off she stopped short, snuffed and shook her head, as if to say she could not be fooled.

This was a critical moment. "All together'" called Mr. Godkin, and the five horsemen bore down on the hesitating animal with such shouts and outcries, that she bounded forward, and the next minute she and her little one were safe within the stockade.

CHAPTER XXVII.

THE FRETFUL PORCUPINE.

MR. GODKIN carefully examined the stockade to make sure the captives were secure, when he rejoined his friends, highly pleased at the success that had attended their efforts. He gave it as his belief that if the good fortune continued for two or three weeks longer, the expedition would be ready to start on its return to Port Natal, or, possibly, to some point on the western coast.

But he reminded his friends that the work already done was but play compared with that before them. Although they had had a memorable brush with a couple of lions, not to mention the encounter with the leopards, there were far more serious tasks in encountering the elephants, rhinoceroses, hippopotami, "and," he added,— "possibly the gorillas."

When he came to tell about the boa-constrictor discovered in the edge of the jungle, waiting for prey, the boys were all eagerness to see the reptile, which the director pronounced the largest of the kind he had ever looked upon, and he had met some big ones in India.

"We have met plenty of the smaller species," said Dick Brownell, "and I have wondered why we haven't seen some of the big ones, since we are in a section where there are plenty."

"They are not so numerous here as nearer the Equator, and I am glad of it : I would be pleased if there were fewer."

"I suppose you expect me to lasso the critter," said Jack Harvey, with such a serious countenance that his hearers doubted whether he was in earnest or not

"I have been thinking about that," replied Mr. Godkin, without the trace of a smile on his face, "but I'm afraid there will be some difficulty in dropping a coil over the boa-constrictor's head."

"Of course it would be difficult for *you*, but what trouble can it be for *me* ?"

"Suppose the snake should lasso *you* at the same time? You know he is built something on the order of a cable rope, and it doesn't take him long to coil himself around his game."

"In that case I'll give him a few lessons in the business; I never yet met a chap that could beat me with the lasso, and I don't propose to knock under to any snake, if he is as big around as a barrel, and hooks his tail into a tree before he sends out his noose."

"Of course," said Bob Marshall, perceiving the drift of their friend's remarks, "you wouldn't need to fasten the other end of the rope to your saddle."

"Certainly not ; I would wind that round my arm, so if the critter tried to get away, I could draw him to me."

" But if, with you pulling one way and the constrictor the other, the rope should happen to break ? " suggested Dick Brownell.

The Texan solemnly shook his head.

" No snake is strong enough to break *that* rawhide : I had it made on purpose for me by one of Mr. Barnum's friends. After I once get it around the varmint, *he'll be there* — depend on that."

" Yes — and that would be the trouble, but to end this jest, of course we'll kill the constrictor, for I always feel it my duty to extinguish such reptiles at every opportunity."

" Them's my sentiments," said Jack, so heartily that there could be no doubt of his sincerity.

"ME SHOW SOMETHING."

While this conversation was under way, Diedrick, the Hottentot, was busy examining all sides of the inclosure. It will be remembered that the camp had been left in his charge while the whites were absent with Pongo, and he did not seek to throw off the responsibility with the return of his friends.

It took some time to replace the stakes that had been removed from one portion of the stockade, to make wider the door through which the zebras had been driven. While Diedrick was thus employed with several assistants, the mother showed such a frantic desire to get out, that, but for her solicitude for her colt, she would have galloped right over the natives ; but, since the young one declined to take such risks, she finally huddled in the farther corner, where she stayed until all chance of escape was gone.

Mr. Godkin decided to wait several hours before hunting out the boa-constrictor, which might have changed its quarters since he saw it. The sun beat down with such power that all were glad to seek the shade within reach.

The cousins had just crawled beneath one of the wagons, when Diedrick approached, and, with a significant expression, beckoned them to follow him.

"I wonder what's up now," said Bob, with a laugh.

"I've no idea, but it's something worth seeing, or he wouldn't have invited us to follow him." The youths lost no time in joining him.

THE TREE PORCUPINE.

"What is it?" asked Bob.

"Me show something," was the vague reply.

"We don't doubt that, but we want to know what it is."

"Come wid me; soon see."

"All right; go ahead."

The Hottentot led the way around the large inclosure, and toward the stream of which I have spoken so many times. He did not continue to the water, nor indeed to the tall weeds that lined the banks, but, following the course of the river a little way, and at a considerable distance from it, he paused and pointed to the ground.

His companions saw a burrow in the earth, with several openings, but no evidence of any living creature. "Well, what of it?" asked Bob, looking up inquiringly at the native. "There isn't any snake in there, I hope, for if there is he can stay, for all I care."

"No snake; no snake," replied Diedrick, with several shakes of his head.

"Is there anything at all?" asked Dick, half suspecting the Hottentot, despite his glum disposition, was playing some trick on them.

"Yes; you see, you see," replied the native, with some excitement, catching each by the arm and pushing him back. An agitation of the dirt showed that, whatever it was that made its home in that place, it had started to come to the surface, doubtless unaware of enemies so near at hand.

TUFTED-TAIL PORCUPINE.

The instant it came forth the boys recognized it as a porcupine, a creature that you have all seen, since varieties are found in both the new and old world. It bristled with long spines, elegantly ringed with broad bands of black and white, and its short, muscular limbs carried it over the ground faster than most persons would suppose it capable of traveling.

It had gone several yards from the entrance to its subterranean home, before it observed the three figures standing behind it, and watching its movements.

It instantly turned and started to run to its retreat, but Bob stepped forward and shut it off. Finding itself driven at bay, and believing it was about to be attacked, it resorted to its peculiar means of defense. Being without teeth or talons for fighting, the porcupine turned its back to its enemies, and, burying its head between its fore legs, erected its spines and shook them violently.

You may have heard the belief, common in many quarters, that this creature, when attacked, defends itself by throwing its quills at its assailant. While this is an error, yet it is a natural one, since there is reasonable ground for the belief.

Horses that have shown too much curiosity in snuffing about the odd-looking creature, have come away with a number of the needle-like spines sticking in their noses, where they were believed to have been thrown by the porcupine.

How this mistake originated was clearly brought out by Dick Brownell within a few minutes after the discovery of the creature. Understanding its nature quite well, for he had seen specimens in his own country, he felt no fear when he stooped down and extended his hand toward the animated burr.

"Have a care," admonished his cousin, still acting the part of a guard over the approaches to the underground home.

"He isn't a very nice thing to handle, but I guess I can do it," replied Dick, reaching carefully toward the porcupine.

The most venturesome person might well hesitate as to the best manner of seizing the creature, and the youth's hand was an inch or two from it, when he snatched it back with a cry of pain. As he did so, several of the spines were seen to be clinging to his palm. It looked for all the world as if the porcupine had flung them at him, but such was not the fact.

AN AWKWARD PET.

At the moment when the hand was closest to its body, the specimen of the *hystrix cristata* (whose head, you will remember, was turned away from the youth) made a sudden leap backward a few inches, bringing its longest spines in sharp collision with the hand.

These animal javelins are loosely imbedded in the skin, besides which it probably was on the point of shedding some of them, so that when Dick drew his hand away, the quills stuck to it.

The wounds inflicted were enough to cause any one to cry out, for the sharp points brought blood, which trickled from Dick's palm as he gave it such a flirt that the quills flew a number of feet.

"Confound it," he muttered "I didn't expect him to do business in *that* style."

"Look out! he's coming again!"

The porcupine, aware of the effective blow it had struck, was making ready to repeat it. It was cautiously backing toward the youth, so as to get close enough to make another retrogressive hitch that would dispose of some more of its spines. But Dick took care to keep out of the way. Diedrick, who had darted off a moment before, now reappeared, carrying a strong scoop-net at the end of a pole, such as are in common use along our sea-coast for crabbing, and the porcupine was deftly captured, without a chance to inflict any further injury.

The tufted-tail porcupine has shorter quills, which lie flat against the body. Its tail is scaly, and has a tuft at the end which looks as if composed of narrow strips of parchment. This animal is found in Fernando Po, and in India and Malacca.

CHAPTER XXVIII.

THE SECRETARY-BIRD.

WHEN the time had come for hunting the serpent, Jack Harvey, to the surprise of his friends, said he had concluded not to go with them. It was his wish to make some investigations that he thought advisable, because of the craft that had floated down stream and lodged near camp.

You will perceive that there was something congenial in this work, for it was on a line with his training in the Southwestern section of his own country. The Texan was an Indian fighter who had been on some of the severest campaigns, and he had learned the art of trailing an enemy and of reading "signs," as they are called, that are invisible to ordinary eyes.

The hunters had gone into camp in this remote section of the Dark Continent with the intention of staying several weeks, if not months. They had taken the utmost precaution against peril, but, after all, the real danger which impended over them was that from their own kind.

It was for the purpose of learning the truth about the wild men that Jack Harvey decided to take the time, which his companions devoted to the boa-constrictor, to delving into the matter. The readiness with which he had solved the cause of the raft lying against the bank proved his skill in that direction, and inspired his friends with such confidence, that they were glad, without exception, to learn his purpose in staying behind, or rather in going off on an expedition of his own.

"I want you to remember one thing," said he, when they were about to separate: "it may take me not only all the afternoon, but the night; so don't fret if I don't put in an appearance before some time to-morrow."

His friends opened their eyes. They had not yet been separated a single night from each other, and the prospect was not pleasant; but Jack had a reason for saying what he did, and none was so competent to understand that, in such an undertaking as he was about to enter upon, no calculation could be made regarding the time required.

So with pleasant words they parted. Jack headed up the stream, mounted on his mustang, and with his favorite lasso coiled at his saddle. The business on which he was engaged promised little use for the rope, but it had done him so many good turns that he was unwilling to go without it.

Avoiding the weeds near the river, the Texan followed its course, keeping far enough from the bank to escape entangling himself in any of the natural obstructions in his way.

Since the ranger had made previous investigations in this section, it was not until he had gone a half mile that the scenery became new to him.

That which first attracted his notice was the sinuous course of the river, its windings being so many that the wonder was how the raft had floated so far without

"I'LL LEAVE YOU HERE, APACHE"

striking the bank. The fact that it had done so caused Jack to fear the wild men were not so distant as he had hoped.

Within less than a mile from camp, the stream made a regular horseshoe, so that if one should cross it where the raft had lodged, and go straight westward, he would meet the same current at no great distance.

It was here, also, that the dense weeds and tall grass merged into dense timber, which continued indefinitely up the river, much farther, at least, than the eye of Jack could follow.

"I wonder if the varmints are in there," he said, drawing his mustang; "they couldn't get a better hiding-place, but I don't know why they would want to hide themselves so long."

Reason suggested that if there were any hostile natives in the neighborhood, they were not likely to stay long in camp; and if they had been in this jungle, they must have left long before; but the Texan had learned, during his stirring experience on the Southwest border, that it was often more prudent to follow what may be called instinct than reason. He therefore determined to investigate.

As he had anticipated, his mustang was able to force his way only a short distance before the vines and trees became so dense that he was forced to stop.

"I'll leave you here, Apache," said he, addressing the steed, "and will expect you to be near when I come back, even if it isn't till to-morrow morning: do you understand?"

The face of no animal could have shown more intelligence than that of the mustang, when thus addressed by his master, who felt no doubt that he comprehended the question put to him. Jack did not remove the saddle, lasso, or any of the trap-pings. He never used a bit with Apache, who was left free to graze or employ himself as he preferred.

Jack Harvey, therefore, as he began picking his way farther into the jungle, carried his Winchester, two revolvers, and knife and was as " well heeled " as any of his countrymen could desire.

It seemed to him that if any of the savage natives were in the wood they were likely to be near the river. The fact that they had employed one raft at least, to-gether with the further fact that it is the custom of all people, whether barbarous or civilized, to make all possible use of water com-munications, led him to be-gin working his way toward the stream.

While thus employed, as a matter of course, he was alert. Knowing, as he did, the number of venomous serpents and all manner of savage beasts, he meant that none of them should steal a march on him.

Here and there were beautifully-colored birds, disporting among the branches, some with a plum-age that was bewildering in its brilliancy. He would have been glad to capture a few of them for the show, but he could conjure up no means, unless, perchance, he might come upon some nest and rob it of its young.

THE SECRETARY-BIRD.

The cries were so discordant that more than once he uttered an impatient ex-clamation, and was tempted to fire at them; but, since he could have caused no appreciable diminution in their numbers or harshness, he refrained.

It was this careful scrutiny of the upper branches that disclosed to him a broad collection of twigs in the tuft of a tree which he thought was the nest of a bird. It was so well hidden that he would not have discovered it had he not been searching with such care, and even then he was not sure he was right until he had made a circuit around the base of the tree, and studied the object from every point of the compass.

"Yes," he said to himself, "it's a bird's nest as sure as my name is Jack Harvey, but since, as near as I can figure, there are about seventeen hundred million of the critters in this country, I can't feel sure what kind of a bird this is."

Several times, in peering upward, Jack fancied he saw the parent bird looking down at him. It was a queer front, as he caught a glimpse of it now and then, the eyes being very bright, and the head showing a resemblance to a crest.

The size of the nest left no doubt that the occupant was very large; and, brave as was Jack, he might well hesitate about climbing the tree and combating it, since, more than likely, its mate would hasten to its assistance.

Since the bird was sure to keep her place as long as danger threatened her castle, the Texan resorted to strategy to draw her forth. He turned about and walked away until beyond her sight, when he came back from another direction, taking care in doing so, and halting behind a trunk, large enough to hide his body.

This artifice was successful. He could not see the parent bird, for her head was turned away from him, and it was not likely she was looking for any danger.

All the same, however, she discovered it with a quickness that amazed the watcher, especially when he found he was much closer to peril than to the nest.

An enormous bird appeared on the edge of the latter, coming into sight with the suddenness of a jack-in-the-box. Its head was turned sideways, proving that it was gazing downward.

Naturally, Jack's first thought was that it had detected him again though that seemed improbable, but, while he was still puzzling over it, the question was settled in rather a startling manner.

No more than a dozen feet off was a serpent, some six or eight feet long, quite slender, brightly colored, and with an appearance that left no doubt of its venomous nature.

It must have been crawling toward Jack, and it might have come nigh enough to bury its fangs in his body before he suspected his danger, so absorbing was his interest in the bird among the limbs above.

As yet, the snake showed no signs of being aware of the man's presence, but it saw her who had hopped upon the edge of her nest so promptly and was now gazing down at the reptile.

"By jingo!" muttered Jack, "there's going to be a fight!"

Sure enough, the thought was hardly formed, when the huge bird fluttered downward through the branches, landing on the ground less than a rod from where the snake prepared tself for the battle that was sure to be to the death.

The presence of the bird so near Jack Harvey gave him a chance to study its appearance closely, without frightening it away. It bore a likeness to the eagle and crane, the head resembling the former, and the body the latter, and was fully three feet tall. Ten or a dozen dark-colored feathers projected from the back of the head, hanging loosely like a pendent crest, and were erected or depressed at pleasure.

This bird, as you may have suspected, was the famed secretary-bird of South Africa, so named by the Dutch because of the fancied resemblance the tuft of feathers bears to a pen thrust behind the ear.

The Hottentots call it the serpent-eater, its scientific name being the *serpentarius reptilivorus,* and that the name is an appropriate one, I think can be shown by what Jack Harvey witnessed a few minutes after its descent from its nest to the earth.

CHAPTER XXIX.

A STRANGE SCENE.

THE secretary-bird took but a second or two to scan the serpent, which did not coil, like the rattlesnake, but reared its head, with its tongue darting back and forth, its tiny eyes flashing, and its whole appearance showing its intense rage. It knew that it was to be attacked, and was ready for it.

There was no sign of fear on the part of the bird, but she was cautious, her situation being something like that of our friends when fighting the Bushmen. They despised the foe, but dreaded their pestilent missiles.

She stepped slowly toward the reptile, and, before arriving within striking distance, thrust the point of one of her wings forward. This, as was proven the next moment, was for the purpose of parrying the blows of her enemy.

Having thrown up her guard, so to speak, the bird pushed farther, for the purpose of drawing the attack of the snake. Sure enough, the horrid head suddenly shot forward, with a quickness that the eye could scarcely follow, the blow being twice repeated with the same marvelous swiftness, but each time it was parried by the pinion, and turned harmlessly aside.

Seeing its failure, the snake crawled slowly toward the bird, so as to secure a better chance of landing its blows, but the feathers had already caught its spare venom, and some time was necessary for nature to replenish the supply.

Well aware of this, the secretary-bird promptly met the snake, and, leaping upon the writhing form, quickly clawed a part of its body to shreds, instantly driving out all semblance of life.

This done, the serpent-eater proceeded to make her dinner at leisure, while Jack Harvey, carefully screening himself from sight, watched the performance with a profound admiration for the prowess of a bird that could vanquish a large, venomous serpent in such thorough fashion.

An incautious movement on the part of Jack caused the secretary-bird to turn like a flash. That she saw him for the first time, was evident from her manner, which showed, too, that she was as ready to attack him as the serpent.

The Texan smiled at its combative manner, but he chose to use discretion, not that he felt any fear of the bird, but because he held it in too great respect to wish it harm.

"There is no need why you and I should have any trouble," he said, carefully withdrawing, with his face toward her, "but I'll remember this spot, and I shouldn't wonder if we saw each other later."

The mother did not follow him, though, if he had ventured to approach, she would have flown at him with the fierceness of a tigress defending her young. In a few minutes Jack was out of sight, and once more gave attention to the business that had led him to penetrate the jungle thus far. Carefully noting his bearings, he resumed his advance toward the river, which he reached a short time later.

It was a dismal place, rendered more so because the long, sultry day was drawing to an end, and the somber gloom of twilight was closing over jungle and river

A STRANGE COMBAT.

The trees on both sides grew near the stream, which at this place narrowed to a width of barely a hundred yards, so that the inky current must have been unusually deep. The desolation and silence, with the exception of the occasional screeches of the birds flying overhead, were such as to impress as unsentimental a person as the Texan, who stood for a minute or two, rifle in hand, gazing on the lovely scene.

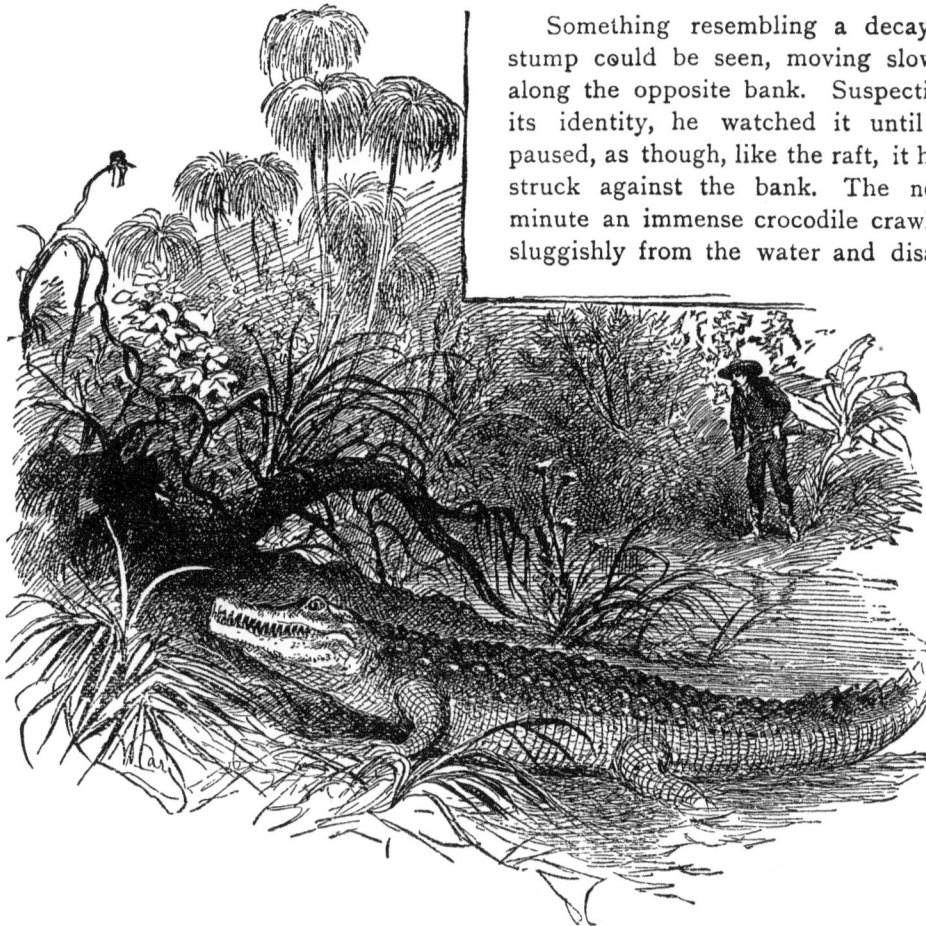

Something resembling a decayed stump could be seen, moving slowly along the opposite bank. Suspecting its identity, he watched it until it paused, as though, like the raft, it had struck against the bank. The next minute an immense crocodile crawled sluggishly from the water and disap-

A DISMAL REGION.

peared among the trees and undergrowth on the edge of the river. He would have given it a shot as it came into view, but for the fear of attracting the attention of the wild men he suspected were in the vicinity. He could not afford to allow any side issues to draw him from the real business of his exploration.

He was standing in this incertitude, when his blood was set tingling by a cry so sharp and agonizing that he started and glanced around, with a gasp of affright.

The cry came from a point close at hand, slightly behind him and no more than a few rods up stream.

Possibly it might be that of some wild animal, but to his ears it had the semblance of a man in mortal suffering. Glancing at his weapons, to make sure they were right, he began picking his way up stream, resolved to penetrate the mystery without delay.

The solution came sooner than he expected.

Peering through the dense undergrowth, he saw fully fifteen of the most savage beings on which he had ever looked, gathered around a hapless prisoner, whom they had evidently determined to put to death with great torture.

The main party were not Bushmen, but belonged to another tribe in the vicinity. They were quite small in stature, with enormous, bushy heads, most of them entirely naked, while a few had the skin of some animal bound around their loins. Their wrists and ankles were clasped by bracelets, cunningly constructed of ivory, and the masses of wool were ornamented with long, brilliantly-colored feathers, stuck in place much after the manner of the American Indian. Huge rings, apparently of gold, hung from their ears, besides which, each bore a similar ornament suspended from the end of his broad, flat nose.

The bulbous lips, retreating chins, low foreheads, bulging eyes and protuberant cheek-bones were so marked that it is hard to imagine how any human beings could be more repulsive in appearance.

Every one of the fifteen carried a long, pointed spear, and they were performing a wild dance around the prisoner, who lay on the ground, with his wrists and ankles bound by some vine, as thin, and almost as strong, as iron wire.

As the party moved about the captive in a circle, they stooped down, and now and then one of the warriors reached forward and pricked him with the point of his spear. Some of the punctures were so light that the victim bore them in silence, but now and then the leader gave such a sharp thrust that the poor fellow emitted a cry of pain. It must have been a particularly vigorous jab that caused the yell which had startled the listening Texan, a short distance off.

The scene recalled an incident in Jack's career, when campaigning in Arizona From a hiding-place where every moment he expected to be discovered, he witnessed the death of a comrade at the hands of Geronimo, that prince of miscreants, and his warriors. Jack dared not lift a finger to save his friend, for he expected to share his fate, but the present situation was different, for these savages were not Apaches, and he felt little fear of them while retaining his magazine-rifle and two revolvers, the three weapons giving him almost a score of shots.

The prisoner was as swarthy of complexion as his tormentors, but he differed so much in other respects, that there remained no doubt he belonged to another tribe. Jack noticed that he had no ornaments in nose or ears, or on his wrists or ankles.

The Texan's theory, probably, was the right one: he was a member of some hostile people, and having fallen into the hands of this party, was doomed to suffer the most frightful of deaths at their hands.

The Texan watched them but a short while before acquiring a knowledge of the state of affairs.

The savage who bore twice as many feathers in his wool as any of his warriors, whose breech-cloth was stained of various hues, who carried a longer spear, with a bundle of feathers tied at one end, and who was of a taller stature than the rest, was the chieftain.

Furthermore, he had reserved to himself the sweet privilege of inflicting all real suffering upon the victim. The others were allowed to prick him smartly, but it was the chief who indulged in a jab, now and then, which forced a cry that the bravest man could not have suppressed.

"I can't stand that sort of thing," muttered the Texan, compressing his lips; "if you would give the poor fellow a show, I would say, ' Let the best man win ;' but for fifteen knaves to bear down on a tenderfoot who has his arms and legs tied, why, it ain't the square thing, and I mean to have something to say about it."

This characteristic decision was no more than formed by Jack Harvey when the chieftain precipitated the crisis for which the watcher was waiting.

The prisoner must have suffered a good deal before the single spectator arrived. The grotesque circling and chanting suddenly ceased, and all came to a stand-still. Every eye was fixed on the poor wretch lying partly on his side, awaiting his doom. He did not struggle, except to shrink, in a convulsive way, whenever the cruel spear-points were pressed against his quivering flesh.

It was manifest that the chief was growing impatient, and had determined to bring the sport to a close, or, at least, to give it a more enjoyable phase.

All at once the suspicion flashed upon Jack that this was a party of cannibals, and that, after slaying their captive, they would make a feast upon him. There is reason to believe he was correct in his conclusion.

Standing in front of the prisoner, the rest of the warriors some paces to the rear, the leader of the savages addressed a few sentences to the victim. What they were can only be guessed, but his manner indicated they were in the nature of taunts, another fashion which, as you know, prevails among the American Indians.

The prisoner did not answer, therein differing from one of the American race in a similar situation, for he would have replied with taunts equally exasperating.

The address lasted but a minute or two, the victim never once parting his lips, when the chieftain raised his long spear with the intention of giving the finishing touch to the frightful scene.

CHAPTER XXX.

A T this moment, the sharp crack of the Texan's Winchester rang out, and the leader, with a frantic shriek, flung up his arms and fell headlong across his intended victim.

Jack Harvey sprang from behind the tree, and, with a wild shout, dashed at the natives, who, tarrying only long enough to catch a single glimpse of the terrible figure, fled into the jungle, as if death itself was at their heels. The rescuer had no wish to harm any one beside the leader, who was in the act of putting a fellow being to death, but, had the others shown hostility, he was ready to open on them.

Jack was used to scenes of violence, but it was with a shudder that he drew the inanimate form from the prostrate figure, which seemed as much terrified as were his tormentors by the sight of the white man who had interfered in his behalf.

A flirt or two of the keen knife and the prisoner was free, but he lay still, too much overcome to move. "Come, old chap, it's a good time for you to leave," called Jack, seizing his arm and lifting him almost bodily to his feet.

The poor fellow stared at him for a moment, and then, with a howl, ran to the river, leaped in, and began swimming frantically for the other shore. As he did so, his friend, who stood on the bank calmly watching him, laughed outright at the affrighted glances he cast over his shoulder, several times diving beneath the surface, as if he expected that the weapon which had destroyed the chieftain was about to be turned against him.

"I'm afraid he don't appreciate what I've done," was the conclusion of the Texan, "and, if that is so, he won't be the first person that has been in that fix."

There was no need of staying in the vicinity, especially since he believed the savages were likely to rally from their panic and return to the spot, with the probability of making it unpleasant, to say the least, for him. Accordingly, the Texan started to return to his mustang.

He had taken but a few steps, when he found himself face to face with two of the warriors who had fled in such panic but a few minutes before.

They seemed to have recovered from their terror, and become very combative. Their huge mouths were parted in hideous grins, which displayed their stained teeth, and one of them brandished his spear threateningly.

"I'm agreeable," called Jack, with another war whoop, making a tremendous bound toward them. At that moment, the fellow with his uplifted spear flung it, but he was so disconcerted by the unexpected charge, that the weapon went wide of its mark, without any dodging on the part of Jack Harvey, who whipped out one of his revolvers and let drive with a couple of charges.

He purposely missed, though he felt some doubt about the wisdom of such leniency toward those who knew nothing of what mercy meant; but the Texan was not of a cruel disposition, and he wished to injure no one, unless it was clearly his duty to do so. Whether he would have been attacked again, had he stayed where he was, can only be conjectured, but he saw nothing more of the natives, and lost no time in leaving the spot where he had witnessed such a stirring scene.

He had solved the question more promptly than he had anticipated on leaving camp, and was hopeful of rejoining his friends before night closed in. So he picked his way as fast as he could through the jungle, returning over his own trail, which was marked so plainly that it was no trouble to follow it.

A FRIEND IN NEED.

The walk was not long to the tree in which the secretary-bird had its nest. He approached with much caution, for he was hopeful of finding the mother absent, and, if such should prove the case, he meant to visit her home.

It was a difficult question to settle, for, if the bird was on guard, it would be dangerous to disturb her. The hunter would be at much disadvantage while climbing the tree, and, in case the mother attacked (as she was sure to do if she detected him), he would have to shoot her in self-defense.

He did not wish to do that; so, after looking upward awhile, without seeing anything of the bird, he announced his presence by swinging his sombrero and calling to her. Since she remained invisible, he broke off a piece of rotten limb and flung it aloft, coming quite close to the nest, though branches of the tree prevented an accurate aim. Still the parent bird made no sign.

THE ORNITHOLOGIST.

"She don't appear to be there," muttered the sportsman, his heart throbbing with hope; "but if she is, I reckon I'll learn it afore I reach the nest."

The day was waning, and there was no time to lose. He was too cautious to leave his gun on the ground, and indeed there was no need of it, for it was readily slung over his shoulder, as he was accustomed to do when using his lasso, while riding his mustang.

He feared that some of the natives might follow to the spot and attack him while in the tree. He had watched and listened for pursuit, but discovered nothing to cause alarm.

However, some risk was inevitable, and, being convinced that the bird was absent, though likely to return any moment, Jack began climbing the tree with the nimbleness of a monkey.

Having effected the start, he pushed forward with all the energy possible. The height was considerable, but he soon found himself near the structure from which the bird had descended to attack the serpent.

The nest was composed of sticks, was fully a yard in diameter, and was lined with wool and feathers. The most difficult part of the climber's task was when he found himself directly underneath the nest, for it covered so large a space that it required considerable skill to climb around it. He succeeded at last, and gained a peep of the interior. A pleasing surprise awaited him.

The eggs of the secretary-bird are about the size of those of a goose. There had been four in the nest, but two of them were hatched, the others evidently being on the eve of liberating their captives.

It was singular that the mother had absented herself at such a time, especially as she had feasted so recently, but it may have been she was seeking suitable food for the little ones. She was certain not to be away long, and Jack had no time to speculate over the matter.

Parting his shirt in front, he quickly shoved the little ones within, and began making his way down the tree again. The brave fellow had not been so nervous in a long while. Having secured the young birds, he was anxious to get away with them, for to him the species was one of the most interesting curiosities obtainable.

"I wonder whether she can figure any better than the ostrich," thought the hunter, picking his way to the ground, on his guard against an assault by the mother he had just robbed. "'Cause if she can't, she won't be able to cipher out that two of her beautiful children are missing, though, it seems to me, it must get through her head that something is wrong.

"I don't care about banking on the idea that she won't smell a mouse — helloa! by jingo! *there she is!*"

Jack had reached the ground and moved a few steps, when a whirr and rush overhead told that the parent bird had returned to her nest. By this time there was so much gloom in the jungle that the hunter was greatly favored. He was resolved that, having succeeded thus far, he would not surrender his prizes. If the parent should attack, he would shoot her, which would only be in accord with the hard rule that the sportsmen in search of natural curiosities must follow. In that event, he meant to climb the tree and take the other eggs.

The bird had not observed the pilferer below, who stealthily withdrew from the vicinity of the tree, hopeful of eluding her, but it was evident from her manner that she saw something was amiss. There was a good deal of fluttering, with some queer squawking, which speedily brought the male bird home to learn the cause of the excitement.

What followed it would be impossible to say, since Jack Harvey passed beyond hearing at this stage of the proceedings, and saw nothing more of those whom he had despoiled.

The felicitation which he felt was marred, on arriving at the margin of the wood, by his failure to see his mustang. He feared some of the wild men had stolen him, but this misgiving quickly vanished when, in response to his signal, the pony came trotting toward him, with a glad whinny.

An instant later the Texan was in his saddle, and once more he felt at home. The young birds, which he had placed within his clothing, appeared to be well satisfied. They uttered a tiny squeak or two, fluttered about a little when disturbed by the motion of his body, but made no effort to free themselves, nor did they protest against their confinement.

At the moment of taking the saddle, Jack looked across the plain in the direction of the encampment. There could be no mistaking its location, since its light glowed like the beacon that tells the sailor of the harbor he is approaching.

His friends were surprised and pleased on seeing their valued comrade, as he drew up his mustang, sprang to the ground, and asked them not to embrace him too warmly, since he carried something brittle near his heart.

The tiny birds were produced, and examined by all. Bob and Dick could not guess their species, and, though Mr. Godkin studied over it for some time, he was wrong when he gave his opinion.

But Pongo and Diedrick hit it the first time. Young as were the birds, one of them showed signs of the picturesque plumes at the back of its head, and it was this fact that revealed the secret.

Having related his own experience, the Texan was prepared to listen to what had befallen the others.

CHAPTER XXXI.

"ONE — TWO — THREE !"

BOB MARSHALL, Dick Brownell, Mr. Godkin and Pongo set off in the direction of the jungle, where they had seen the enormous boa-constrictor, and all were in high spirits.

"How do they catch the snakes that we see in museums?" asked Dick, while they were still some distance from the wood.

"It is not difficult for those who understand the business," replied the director. "I have taken a hand in capturing several in India. You have only to wait until they are in a torpid condition from gorging themselves, then slip up and fling a blanket over their heads. At the same time, a strong net can be used, and a little dexterity will secure the reptile without much trouble."

"Did you ever try chloroform?" asked Bob.

"No; although I do not see why it might not be turned to good account."

"Some years ago," remarked Bob, "when I was in New York, a big snake, that a man was wheeling in a box, was set free by the upsetting of the barrow in the City Hall Park. You ought to have seen the people scatter, though I don't think any of them got out of the way quicker than I did. There was a panic for a time, until one of the trained men from Reiche's place, in the Bowery, appeared, threw a blanket over the snake's head, and then easily lifted him into the box."

"I once asked Mr. Reiche the size of the biggest snake he ever had,"said Dick, "and he told me eighteen feet. I judge, from what you have said, that if we find the one you saw this forenoon, we shall look upon a much larger one."

"You will, indeed; too large for any company of men to think of capturing, though I have felt inclined, more than once, despite my dislike of the reptiles, to secure one. We have no chloroform with us, so we cannot try the experiment you speak of, and, on the whole, I think we'll give that class of curiosities the go-by."

"I hope so," replied Dick, "for, to my way of thinking, they would form the one disagreeable feature of our menagerie."

Before reaching the immediate neighborhood of the spot where the constrictor had been seen, all four dismounted. Pongo took the lead, and, remembering the place well, went straight to it, but, to the disappointment of all, the reptile was not in sight.

"He can't be far off," said Mr. Godkin, following the native among the trees, "and we shall soon find him."

Despite the director's warnings, the Bushman walked so fast that he drew away from them. Mr. Godkin was on the point of ordering him to return, when a low whistle was heard, and Pongo came back with such a flurried appearance that all knew he had located the constrictor.

"Me find him," said he; "big fellow—eat horse—eat ox—eat us!"

"I hope he won't undertake all that," said Bob, with a laugh, glancing at his rifle.

"Since you have found him," said Mr. Godkin, "you may lead the way, Pongo."

This suited the native, who willingly assumed the duty of guide.

Only a short distance had been passed, in a guarded fashion, the three following close at the fellow's heels, when he paused and pointed up among the branches of one of the trees. Following, with their eyes, the direction, our friends looked upon an amazing sight.

The most enormous boa-constrictor on which they had ever gazed was coiled around the trunk, at a height of less than thirty feet from the ground. He was just above the spot where a number of big branches put out, in different directions. He surrounded the tree four or five times, while fully a dozen feet of his neck and head were extended along one of the limbs.

The reptile was motionless from head to tail, though, if it chose, it could have unwound itself with great rapidity.

The four sportsmen stood for a minute, gazing in silent awe.

"Did you ever see the like?" asked Bob.

"Never," replied Dick, "and I can't say that I'm anxious to see it again."

"And yet there are plenty of them," remarked Mr. Godkin.

"Do you think it sees us?"

"Likely enough, for it is on the watch for game, and they have a keen vision."

"Suppose it should unwind and come for us?"

"It would be a good time to leave," was the half jocular remark of Mr. Godkin; "but I don't apprehend anything of the kind, unless we venture nearer."

The flat, hideous head was far out on the branch, which bowed considerably, under the unusual weight.

While the party were surveying the vast reptile, the front of the head was observed to rise a few inches, the base remaining on the support.

It looked as if he had espied the parties below, and was saying: "You'll do very well; please come a little closer."

"Well, Mr. Godkin," said Bob, "shall we try it?"

"Yes; the mark is so fair that we can't miss."

"It seems impossible for a single bullet to kill such an enormous creature as that," said Dick, "but I suppose it will do so, if it is rightly aimed."

"That is at the head?" asked Bob.

"Yes, though there is the heart, which would do as well, if we could only locate it. But we will try the head, and we must shoot together, so as to give him a triple dose."

"'THIRTY-ONE FEET, THREE INCHES."

The preliminaries were quickly settled. It was agreed that when Bob and Dick were sure their aim was accurate, they were to utter a slight exclamation. Then Mr. Godkin would count slowly, and at the word " *Three!* " all would pull trigger.

The boys kept their bodies well hidden behind the broad trunk at their side, while Pongo watched the hunters with a vivid interest, which possibly may be imagined.

Carefully and coolly our friends pointed their rifles at the head of the reptile. Holding them stationary for a few seconds only, the cousins softly spoke:

" *Now!* "

" *One — two — three!* "

The three reports sounded like one, and the bullets tore their way clean through the constrictor's head, each taking a fatal course, and only a few inches apart.

The monster did not stir for perhaps five seconds. It must have been that that length of time was required for it to discover that its "time had come."

All at once, it was seen to be winding and unwinding its body with lightning-like rapidity, whipping among the branches with a fury that looked as if it must splinter everything within reach.

"It may come this way," remarked Mr. Godkin, who saw that it was gradually working toward the ground, where, when it arrived and continued its struggles, it would be like the piece of pyrotechny known as a "chaser," which darts in the most unexpected directions. The snake was liable to make a plunge toward the spectators, without meaning it, but, in such an event, the results were sure to be disastrous.

Every one moved nimbly back a couple of rods, where the sight was partly obscured, observing which, Mr. Godkin again stepped forward, determined to miss nothing.

The terrific threshing lasted but a few minutes, when it gradually ceased, and all became still.

"I believe the creature is dead," said the gentleman, stepping a little nearer and peering carefully through the undergrowth.

"Have a care!" admonished Bob; "you can well afford to wait until certain."

The advice was good and was heeded. All, however, went far enough to observe that the reptile lay on the ground, contorted and partly coiled and as motionless as when it was first descried in the branches of the tree.

"He dead," said Pongo, who showed his faith by going forward and kicking the body. A nervous twitching of the tail caused the others some misgiving, but there remained no doubt that the boa-constrictor was lifeless.

The next wish, after inspecting it, was to ascertain its length. This was rather difficult, owing to its twisted posture on the ground, but Pongo with some effort stretched the snake at full length upon the ground, and Mr. Godkin applied his tape measure, from the tip of the tail to the extremity of the head.

Shall I tell you the precise length?

"Thirty-one feet, three inches."

CHAPTER XXXII.

CONCERNING SNAKES.

"WOULDN'T Mr. Barnum open his eyes if he could see *that?*" said Jack Harvey that night, as he sat with his friends, talking over their experience with the boa-constrictor.

"So would any person," replied Mr. Godkin: "there are authentic instances of pythons growing to a length of twenty-eight and thirty feet, but they are rare."

"I'm glad we have nothing of the kind in our country," said Bob Marshall, "though I've heard of some pretty big ones in Jack's State."

"Yes, we have a few healthy rattlers down in Arizona and Texas and around there, but they are always manly enough to give warning before they strike."

"I've seen a black-snake kill the *crotalus horridus*," said Dick, "if you will allow a technical term.'

"How was that?" asked Mr. Godkin; "I have met both kinds, but never witnessed that."

"The black-snake, you know, is a constrictor, and therefore not poisonous, but he is a good deal more lively than the rattlesnake. When they go for each other, the black one easily dodges the blows of the other and soon squeezes him to death."

"How large a rattlesnake have you seen?"

"None with more than a dozen rattles, which is a pretty good size, but I know a Mr. Hall, who, when riding through Illinois, many years ago, on horseback, saw a great snake crawling across the road ahead of him. There was no fence on either side, but the serpent crept in among some tall dry grass, where his eye could easily follow him. Mr. Hall dismounted, leaving his horse alone, for there was nothing to tie him to, picked up a hoop-pole from a pile at the side of the road, and started after the fellow. He saw that he was a monster and he meant to kill him.

"Running up as close as he dared, he hit him a smart rap, for a slight blow will kill a rattler. It instantly coiled to strike, but he jumped back out of the way. The snake started on and the gentleman ran forward and struck it again. He said the hoop-pole was so slender that it bent as he brought it down, and the blow was too weak, therefore, to be effective.

THE BOA-CONSTRICTOR

"The snake repeated its tactics, but it was easy enough to keep out of its way. By and by he caught the white gleam of its belly, and he knew that his blows were telling. So he rained them faster and faster, and in a few minutes the reptile was as dead as a door-nail. He said the snake, a short distance below its head, was as big around as his leg above the knee. He cut off the rattles, and kept them for many years. I saw and counted them."

"How many?"

"Thirty-two."

[I may state, parenthetically, that the story told by Dick Brownell is strictly true. Mr. Hall killed a rattlesnake with thirty-two rattles, as described, in the State of Illinois, in 1842.]

A Product of our own Country

"I never saw any as large as that," said Mr. Godkin, "though one of them that buried his fangs in my finger had half as many rattles."

"What did you do for the bite?"

"I drank nearly a pint of brandy."

"At what time of the year was it?"

"Quite early in summer."

"You probably would have done as well without any medicine at all, for the rattlesnake's bite is not very deadly except between the first of August and the time he goes into winter quarters. You know how sluggish he is, and that he never bites without warning, and then only when he is disturbed; but the cobra, for instance comes crawling into a hut when its inmates are asleep, and lets fly with that hooded head and his bursting poison-sacs, the instant he gets a chance, and his bite is deadly at *all* times."

"Yes; he is one of the worst known. How many orders are there of serpents, Dick?"

"About a thousand, I believe, which is just a thousand too many."

"Do you know of any method of telling whether the wound of a snake is poisonous, since you cannot always identify the species by its appearance?"

"If the wound consists of numerous punctured orifices placed in two curved lines, the snake-bite is harmless, but when there are only two punctures, you may make up your mind that it is a venomous snake that has inflicted them, though there are some harmless ones whose two long fangs are not perforated in front."

"How many species are there of the *viperidæ* family?"

THE COBRA DE CAPELLO

"About twenty-two; all have a single perforated tooth on each side of the upper jaw, and belong to the Eastern Hemisphere, especially in Africa."

"Yes," said Mr. Godkin, "it was one of that species which is credited with causing the death of Cleopatra. The horned snake of Egypt is one of the most remarkable species."

"I saw a specimen in Mr Barnum's museum. A little horny spur projects above the eye, and the snake was about two feet long, with a sandy red color and irregular brownish markings. They are very fond of the heat, and will luxuriate in the flaming sands of the desert, where almost any other creature would die."

"The European species is the only venomous reptile found in Great Britain, and even that is not very dangerous. So that England is more favored in the respect you name than are the United States, while Ireland is ahead of every other country. Speaking of the rattlesnake, however, can you tell me of how many species the *crotalidæ* family consists? I will let Bob answer, if he pleases."

"About forty pit vipers," replied the lad with a laugh, for he, too, had studied the subject quite fully, "so called from having a deep pit on the side of the snout. They are absent from Europe, Africa, and Australia, but are plentiful in America and of course, some of them are found in Asia and the East Indies."

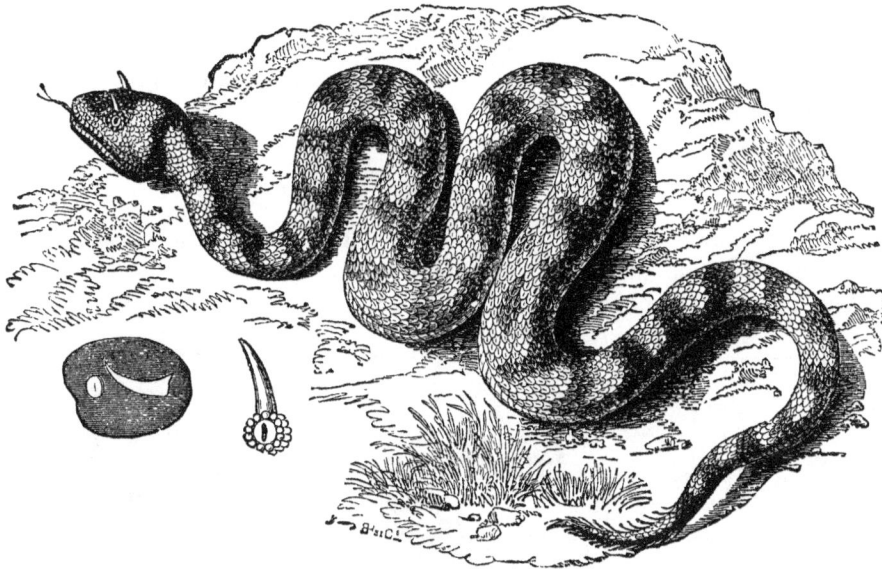

THE HORNED SNAKE

"The Asiatic species of pit vipers are a good deal smaller in size than the American species," remarked Mr. Godkin.

"And a great deal more dangerous," added Bob; "they lack the rattle, though the genus *halys* comes pretty near it. The genus *trimeresurus* are so vicious when aroused, that they will strike at everything within reach and will sometimes bite themselves, which is a habit to be encouraged. There is a species found in Java and Siam, a single one of which has been known to kill two persons, who died within five minutes of each other."

"Hold on! draw it mild," said the wondering Jack Harvey.

"Did you see any of the *hydrophidæ* on your way here?"

"No, I wasn't introduced to any of them," replied the Texan.

"I have noticed quite a number between Calcutta and Ceylon," said the director.

"They are abundant in the Indian and Australian seas, for the whole distance between Madagascar and Panama. Those which I saw were all of the *pelamis bicolor* species. None of them was more than three feet in length, and they never leave the water.

"I believe there are about a hundred species of the *elapidæ* family, to which the cobra belongs," added Mr.

Godkin; "and from the knowledge you boys have displayed of the subject, I don't suppose it is necessary for me to say that plenty of them are met with in Australia, and the Egyptian cobra is often seen in Cairo. There is one group which I am quite sure you have not seen, boys."

"What is that?"

"The *acrochoridæ.*"

"No; we never saw any specimens."

"There are only three or four species belonging to the *acrochoridæ* or wart snakes, but, of course, they abound in Southern India."

"Yes; and in Singapore, Borneo and New Guinea."

A PIT VIPER.

The conversation had drifted into this scientific channel without premeditation on the part of any one. Mr. Godkin's study and experience had given him a knowledge of the animal kingdom above the ordinary, and now and then he liked to quiz his young friends, who showed by their replies that they had given much attention to the same interesting subject.

During the talk, Jack Harvey quietly smoked his pipe and listened in awed wonder. He had never heard such terms used, and consequently they were Greek to him. Now and then he uttered a protest, and at the last remark of the director turned such a reproving look upon him that all laughed.

"I hope you'll catch that critter," said he, "but you'll never be able to get him across the water alive."

"Why not?"

"His name will be the death of him. What others are there?"

"There is the *acrochordus javanicus*."

"What sort of 'cus' is that?"

"I never saw one, and indeed but a single person that had looked upon one. The serpent belongs in Java and is about eight feet long. Its face resembles that of a thorough-bred bull dog, and it is believed to live on fruit, though very little is known about it. However," added Mr. Godkin, with a sigh, "we haven't half exhausted the subject, for there are the other families, including the pythons, boas-rock-snakes, blunt-head snakes, whip snakes, tree snakes, desert snakes, dwarr snakes, flesh-eating snakes (found in Penang, Singapore, Gamboja, Sumatra, Java, Celebes and Borneo), short tails, blind snakes, double-enders and scores of others. But we have had enough."

"A little too much," said Jack Harvey; "what is the fancy name for a grizzly bear?"

"*Ursus horribilis*."

"That ain't right," said the Texan, decisively.

"What is it, then?"

"Old Ephraim."

CHAPTER XXXIII.

A REMINISCENCE.

"YES, sir," added Jack of the grizzly is Old Eph- out hunting with any of wouldn't be well to forget Harvey, "the right name raim, and, if you ever go the boys in Californy, it that fact.''

"Do you know," said Bob Marshall, "that to hear you speak of the grizzly bear makes me homesick? It comes like a breath of air from the Rocky Mountains; no other country in the world can produce the magnifi- cent grizzly bear, and I am proud of it."

"So am I," added Dick Brownell, with a radiant countenance; "I've heard the animal called Old Ephraim, and it gave me a pleasant thrill when Jack pronounced the name. Here we are in the Dark Continent, with a climate that half the time is like an oven, with snakes and all sorts of horrible creatures around us: how can I help thinking of my own glorious West, with its snowy mountains, its green, rolling prairies, and its grizzly bears. Ah, me!" added the youth with a sigh, which was shared in spirit by his friends, "I sometimes wonder what possessed us to come to such a country as this."

"The same reason, or lack of reason, which prompts the arctic explorer that returns from the land of desolation, broken in health, to sigh to return again," replied Mr. Godkin, who repressed the longing that often came over him to hasten to his beloved America, thousands of miles away.

"Tell us something about the dear old grizzly bears," said Bob, with such a pleading look at the Texan that he could not resist the appeal.

"The only trouble," said Jack, "is that I've been in so many scrimmages with the Old Ephraims, that it's hard work to pick out the most interesting."

"Let us hear about the first time you met him," suggested Mr. Godkin.

"Well, that's about as entertainin' as any of the other fights, leastways it was so to me, for it happened a good many years ago, afore I had learned to sling the lasso, but not afore I thought I knowed a good deal more than I'm sure I know now.

The Grizzly Bear

"Me and Bill Lamokin picked up a sick miner in 'Frisco one day, and took the best care we could of him. He had some sort of fever, that the doctors couldn't handle, but the main trouble with the poor fellow was that he'd got it into his head that he couldn't live, and when a sick man is in *that* shape, he's sure to pass in his checks, in spite of a cityful of doctors.

"Howsumever, me and Bill done the square thing, and was with him when he died.   The chap felt so thankful like, that he give us a slip of paper with a lot of figgers and marks on it, and explained that if we'd follow the directions there, arter reaching a certain part of the Sierra Nevada, we'd strike it rich.   There was plenty of gold dust, and it wouldn't take us long to scoop in enough to buy out the bigger part of 'Frisco.

"Well, arter the poor miner was shoved under ground, Bill and me got ready to look into the matter.   I reasoned that we was so blamed poor that we couldn't get any poorer, so that if we made a miss of it, we wouldn't be any worse off than we was afore we started.

"The upshot of all this speculatin' was that at the end of a month we was close to the hidden gold mine.   We each had a mule, but we concluded that, if we struck a pile of the dust, we'd cache it and then come back with a big enough drove of mules to carry it to the mint in 'Frisco.

"To tell the truth, Bill didn't seem to have as much faith in the thing as I did, and he insisted that we should prospect while we was on our way there: that was the reason why we was so long in getting fairly into the Sierras.

"As near as I can figger, we couldn't have been more than twenty miles from the spot, when we went into camp, in one of the wildest places I ever set foot on

"It was early in the afternoon, and we was as hungry as 'get out.'   Bill agreed to start the fire and put the camp in shape, while I set off to hunt supper.   Antelope, elk and deer was plenty, and I was sure of shooting all I wanted without long hunting.

"Howsumever, the animals was so shy that it was a full hour afore I got a shot at one of the critters, and then he give me such a long run that I got mad and let him go. He had led me a good distance up among the rocks, into one of the wildest places I ever seen.   It was right on a high precipice that overhung a deep stream, a long ways below, which made me fairly dizzy when I looked down at the water.

"I wasn't very good-natured, you may depend, when I turned about to hunt for other game, but all thoughts of my disappointment were knocked out of my head when, after walking a few yards, I found myself face to face with an Old Ephraim, as big as Samson, that old grizzly Adams used to show in Barnum's Museum.

"That was the first time I had ever looked on the critter, though I was in a region where they was quite plenty, and you needn't wonder when I tell you that it fairly knocked my breath from me for a minute or two.

"He was standing right in my path, as I wanted to leave the high place among the rocks, though it looked as if there was a chance for an active young gentleman like me to dash around him.

"I had a good gun with me, but it wasn't a Winchester.   It was a single-shot breech-loader, and I knowed how to handle it pretty well.   I reckoned that one bullet, when I had the chance to take good aim, was enough to settle the hash of any critter, whether he was Old Ephraim or not, and, as the weapon was ready for use, I can't say that I felt shaky at looking him in the eye, with only about fifty yards between us.

"Old Ephraim Had Come to Town" — Page 192.

"The critter seemed as surprised at first as I was. He stood with a stupid, inquiring look for a minute, and then rose on his haunches, and began pawing the air in a playful way, as if to coax me to go up to him, and let him give me a reg'lar old-fashioned hug.

"Not much, I said to myself, raising my gun, and, sighting at the place where I 'sposed his heart was, I let drive, and then banged the stock of my rifle down on my foot, and looked up to see him keel over like a meeting-house when its foundation gives out.

"But he didn't keel. He pawed at his flesh as though the wound was a splinter which he was trying to pull out. I was sure he would turn up his toes the next minute; but, while I was watchin' for it, he dropped down on all fours and lumbered toward me at a gait that left no time to load my gun again.

"If there ever was a scared young man, it was Jack Harvey about that time. Right behind me was the precipice, with the deep river far below. The grizzly was in front, and, coming so fast that I couldn't load up again nor get by him. The only weapons left was my hunting knife and revolver.

"Yanking out the pistol, I emptied every chamber into him when he was less than twenty feet away. I'm sure, too, that each bullet lodged in his big body, and yet, for all the effect they produced, they might as well have been fired against a stone wall.

"By the time I could get out my knife, Old Ephraim had come to town.

"I knowed it was no use trying to fight him with only my knife, for he could chaw me up afore I could prick him. Feeling that I had made a mistake in not jumping over into the water, I started; but what held me back was the fear that the stream was not so deep as it looked. In such a wild place a current is likely to have all kinds of depths — that is, in some places it would take a pole fifty or a hundred feet to touch bottom, while right alongside it a p'inted rock might push up within an inch or two of the surface.

"Now, if I should happen to drop on one of them p'ints, you can see that it would be rather bad for me, and it was that which kept me from jumping until it was almost too late.

"Just as I turned, Old Ephraim grabbed me, with the intention of crushing my ribs into a pulp, and I knowed that the question had to be settled in the next minute or two. I put forth all the strength I had to break loose, but I couldn't Howsumever, I done that which was next best. The grizzly was so close that I upset his balance, and over we both went.

"Well," added Jack Harvey, with a sigh at the recollection, "that was a good many years ago, but I don't think I'll forget about it if I live to be as old as Godkin there. It seemed to me that we were about an hour and a half falling through the air afore we struck the water, and, when we done so, it must have sounded as though the top of the mountain had tipped over into the stream.

"I remember that at the minute we went off the ledge, I tried to bring Old Ephraim under me, so that if we did stop too suddenly, he would get the benefit of it, but, lucky for me, the water was so deep that we must have sunk twenty feet afore I felt my foot touch the rocky bottom.

"I lost my hold of the grizzly when I struck the water, for I had gripped him by the long hair at the back of his shoulders, and I hoped to get to the surface again ahead of him. But, when I come up, there he was, and he went for me with a rush.

"I had a better chance in the water, and, dropping down, I dove under him, taking care when I came up to grab the hair on his back, and held on with both hands.

"Wasn't he furious? He growled and began swimming round and round after me, but, since it was easy enough to hang on, it was like a kitten chasing its tail, and he never quite reached me, though he was so close more than once that I expected he would.

"Well, this thing went on till Ephraim began to get it through his head that he couldn't draw a hand that would win. Then he headed straight for the other shore with me towing after him, as though he was playing the part of a steam-tug.

"I wasn't yet out of the scrape, for if we should both land, the grizzly would have me foul, and I couldn't swim back to the shore behind me, for that was a solid stone wall where a rat couldn't land.

"So I gently let go, just afore we reached land, took a long dive, only allowing my nose to come up for a niff of air, went down again, and, when I finally opened my eyes, I was a dozen yards below Ephraim.

"Would you believe it? There he stood on the shore, with his snout out over the water, waiting for me to come up within reach. He didn't know enough to look down stream for me, and, by managing things right, I drifted so far off that, before long, I was able to leave the stream without danger from him.

"It was a long journey round to the top of the rock where I had left my rifle, and, by the time I laid hands on it again, it was growing dark, and I had to go back to camp without anything for supper."

CHAPTER XXXIV.

BEARS AND KANGAROOS.

 HE gold mine in the mountains — what of that?" asked Mr. Godkin, who, like the boys, was much interested in the story of the Texan. The latter uttered a sniff of disgust.

"I've no doubt it is there just where the chap said it was."

"Why, then, didn't you find it? — or, perhaps, you did, and you are a disguised millionaire," remarked Bob Marshall.

"Remember," added Dick, with mock eagerness, "that we are your friends, and will stand by you as long as the money lasts."

"Do you know," said Jack Harvey, looking up almost angrily, "what that confounded Old Ephraim did?"

"He got away from you."

"Worse than that."

"What was it?"

"He made me lose the paper that had the directions to the gold mine. Somehow or other, it got out of my pocket during the circus in the water, and I never laid eyes on it again. Bill and me spent all next day in searching 'round the spot, and then made up our mind that Old Ephraim found it and chawed it up on purpose."

"I should have thought you would have remembered everything on it from reading it so often."

"That's what we both thought; but, when Bill studied it, he must have held it upside down, or else I did, for our recollection didn't agree very well. Neither Bill nor me was much of a scholar, and I suppose the truth of it was we got things mixed. But it's sure that, though we spent weeks in the mountains, we never found any place that answered the description of the miner, and we come back to 'Frisco the worst-looking tramps you ever laid eyes on."

"It seems to me," said Bob, "that the bear is one of the most widely distributed of animals."

"Yes," replied the director, "he is found in many different parts of the world, and you know we have several varieties in our own country, besides Old Ephraim that Jack has just told us about."

"Bob and I have hunted the black and brown bear," said Dick, "and there are few sportsmen in the Eastern States who cannot tell you of some adventures with them."

"What is there peculiar about the Malay bear?"

"He is called Bruang by the Malays, and is a native of Sumatra, Borneo and Java and the Malayan Peninsula. He is about four feet long, and two feet high at the shoulders. He is remarkable for his power of protruding his lips. He has a long tongue and claws, and is very fond of honey, which is also a weakness of other bears."

THE BROWN BEAR

"Why are some of them called sun bears

"Because of their fondness for basking in the sun instead of keeping in their dens during the daytime."

"The sloth bear, I believe, belongs to India," said Bob.

"Yes; he is found at Nepaul, Benares and the Southern Mahratta country. When he was first taken to Europe, a good many took him for a sloth. He, too can protrude his lips to a considerable extent. His muzzle is elongated, and, like the ends of the feet, is whitish or yellowish.   He is fond of fruits, honey and white ants, and in captivity is mild and melancholy."

"The polar bear seems to be able to stand warm weather as well as cold," remarked Dick, "for I know Mr. Barnum has hardly ever been without one in his show, which does most of its business during warm weather."

[As a proof of the ability of the polar bear to undergo high temperature, I may add that "Dick," now in my possession and eight years old, was the only bear that survived the great fire at Bridgeport, in November, 1887.]

"Mr. Godkin," said Bob Marshall, "how long have you been in the employ of Mr. Barnum?"

THE BLACK BEAR

"It's a long time," he answered, "dating away back from before either of you were born.   It so happened that I landed in India just previous to the breaking out of the great Sepoy mutiny of '57."

"Were you there through that war?" asked Dick.

"Through a good deal of it, and I had one of the strangest adventures that ever befell a person.   I won't tell you about it this evening," he added, observing the expectant looks of his friends, "but some time I'll give you the story."

"You have been in Africa before?"

"Yes, I made a visit to Bechuana Land some years since, and I spent one season in Australia."

"Hunting for kangaroos, I suppose?"

"That was the principal business, but Australia can furnish a good many
curiosities besides the kangaroo, though I think that animal leads them all in

interest. However, I suppose you young gentlemen know so much about the
creatures," said the director with a smile, "that you won't care to hear anything
from me."

THE MALAY BEAR

The boys hastened to protest against any such view, and plied their questions
so fast that Mr. Godkin laughingly waved them back, and made known some facts
which, I think, are new to you.

"The young of the kangaroo are born in an embryotic state, and are placed at
once in the curious *marsupium*, or pouch, belonging to the mother, where they attach

themselves to the nipples. There they cling till their limbs are gradually formed and they are able to go alone. It is pleasing to see the odd-looking creatures hopping about their mother, and, on the first appearance of danger, dodging into the friendly pouch, where they stay till it is past, perhaps peeping out now and then to observe how matters are going."

THE POLAR BEAR.

"That certainly is a remarkable provision of nature."

"But not every one understands the most wonderful features about it. The embryotic kangaroo at its birth is less than two inches long, and, although it has the power to grasp the mother's nipple, it isn't strong enough to draw nourishment therefrom."

"How in the mischief does it get along?" asked Jack Harvey, "that is, if you can tell a fellow without the use of any of those big Dutch words."

"You will allow me, however, to say that it belongs to the genus *macropus*. Well, since the young one cannot pump her own supply of milk, the mother does it for it,—that is to say, while the little one is simply clinging to the nipple and unable to do anything else, the parent injects the milk into its tiny mouth."

"It seems to me," said Bob, "that that would interfere with its breathing."

"So it would, except for an astonishing provision of nature. Since the mother cannot know when the little one is trying to draw sustenance, and is, therefore, unable to time her injection with that effort, nature has arranged the air passages of the fœtus so that it can breathe and imbibe at the same time."

"How long does the young one stay in the pouch?"

"At the end of eight months it begins to peep out its head to see what the world looks like. Now and then it crops the grass, at the same time that the mother is grazing, and by and by hops out upon the ground, ready, however, at any instant to rush back to its refuge.

"It relies upon the mother for shelter and supplies, until it weighs nearly a dozen pounds. Occasionally it thrusts its head into the pouch for its lacteal fluid, even though another fœtus may be inside clinging to the second nipple."

"How does the kangaroo rank as to intelligence?" asked Dick.

"All marsupiated animals, as you may know, stand at the bottom grade as respects intelligence. They seem to be incapable of forming friendships, and will recognize their attendant no more than a stranger. They hardly ever utter a sound, though I have heard a muttering growl now and then from one of them. But the giraffe is silent even in its death agonies.

"I believe kangaroos are found in a few other places besides Australia.

"There are plenty in New Guinea, where Jack saw them, and in Tasmania and the adjacent islands, fully sixty species being known. The great kangaroo was discovered in 1770, during Captain Cook's first voyage, while passing on the coast of New South Wales to repair his ship."

"How big is he?"

"A full-grown male measures between five and six feet, from the tip of the nose to the root of the tail, the female being considerably less. When in full flight, they will jump fifteen or eighteen feet, their bodies and tails being outstretched, the latter serving as a balance. Its fore legs are so short that they are useless for traveling, but mighty convenient for digging."

"Those that you are talking about," said Jack Harvey, "I believe are the largest kind."

"Yes; the *macropus giganteus* heads them all as respects size. Mr. Barnum was always interested in them, and has six now in his menagerie. Then there is the antelope kangaroo, with short fur, and stiff hairs, found in North Australia, the brush kangaroo, so plentiful over all Australia that thousands of its skins used to be sold at a trifling price; the yellow-legged kangaroo, often met in South Australia, and entirely nocturnal in its habits, and the two species of the tree kangaroo, natives of New Guinea. Their fore legs are almost the size of the hind ones, and are furnished with powerful curved claws, which make climbing easy. They have very long tails and coarse hair."

"What is meant by Le Brun's kangaroo?" asked Dick Brownell.

"It is the animal which Le Brun observed in 1711, and was the first of the

THE BADGER

family with which naturalists became acquainted. Le Brun saw it in captivity at Batavia. Its tail is shorter than its body, is thick, ringed with scales and naked toward the apex. It is not nocturnal, and is found in New Guinea and the Aru Islands."

"What about the lunulated kangaroo?"

"I consider that the prettiest of all. It is only about two feet high; is slender and graceful, with short fur, very prettily marked. Then there are the hare kangaroos, of small size, in Southern Australia, while the Tasmanian rat kangaroo is more diminutive, but a hardly less interesting animal."

"I believe the badger is an Australian bird," said Jack, who felt more interest in the conversation than he was willing to admit.

"The Indian badger is met with in Assam and Arakan; the common badger is found in the British Islands; the American badger in the western part of our own country, but the Australian badger, or wombat, is very different from any of them. He has a heavy body and short legs, and waddles along like a fat bear. You will find him in almost every part of Australia. He keeps out of sight during the day, burrowing so deep that few natives have the patience to dig him out."

THE ELEPHANT MOUSE.

"I judge the kangaroo rat to belong, also, to the same country," said Dick Brownell.

"He is very plentiful in New South Wales, but he is small, his head and body being only fifteen inches long, with the tail about two-thirds as much, and is covered with scales, with a few stiff hairs forcing their way through, here and there."

"What is the gerboa?"

"He belongs to this part of the world, upon the sides of the mountains, where he lives in burrows that he tunnels for himself in the ground. In many places you will find the earth honeycombed. They hardly ever leave their tunnels until after sunset. The natives are fond of their flesh, and secure them by drawing them out of their holes."

"Is the elephant mouse so called on account of his size?"

"Rather on account of his trunk-like nose. We shall probably see some of them in this part of the world, though they are found as far north as the Zambesi and Mozambique."

"Australia has one creature," said Dick, "which has awakened more interest than anything else: that is the duck-bill, or ornithorhynchus."

"It belongs there or in Van Dieman's Land, and is known as the mullingong, or platypus. It is less than two feet long, and is an aquatic and burrowing animal. It has a broad, flat bill, thick, soft fur and webbed feet. It can use its fore feet

THE KANGAROO MOUSE.

equally well for digging or swimming, and in digging it employs its bill as well as its feet. The males are furnished with a flexible spur for their hind feet, which can be folded up so that it is out of sight."

"Since Australia is the land of the kangaroo," suggested Bob, "I suppose you had some adventures with those animals?"

"Plenty of them, though none was so stirring as my experiences in India and this part of the world. Kangaroo hunting is a favorite amusement of the colonists and natives. The latter make use of the boomerang, to which Pongo is so partial, and they throw it with the skill he shows.   Sometimes they surround a herd of the animals, drive them together, and then make a rush upon them with clubs and spears.   But the right way is to hunt on horseback, with trained dogs, in regular fox-hunt style.

"It happened that I was alone, when my two hounds started a large male, which went bounding over the grassy plain with amazing speed.   His course led toward

THE DUCK-BILL. OR ORNITHORHYNCHUS.

a stretch of open woods, where he was so hindered that the dogs caught up with him.   What did the animal then do but turn at bay on the edge of a large stream, seize the first dog that came within reach, and, pushing him under the water, hold him there till he was drowned?

"Flinging him aside, he then jumped for the other, which kept out of his way for awhile.   The dog might have dodged the kangaroo altogether, but he was too plucky for his own good, and, leaping at the throat of the game, was caught, like

DINGOES HUNTING THE EMU -- Page 206.

A LEAP FOR THE CHAMPIONSHIP.

his predecessor, in those short arms, and ripped to shreds by the hind legs, that are provided with claws as effective as bowie-knives.

"I was somewhat bewildered by the sounds of my dogs, not feeling sure what they meant. I supposed they were able to take care of themselves, but thought it prudent to hurry and learn how they were making out.

"I dismounted, and had penetrated only a short distance in the timber, when, to my surprise, I caught sight of the kangaroo, who was returning over his own trail, by a series of moderate jumps. I stopped short, and he did not see me until within a couple of rods. Then, instead of turning aside, as I expected him to do, he put on more steam and came directly for me, making a tremendous bound that carried him over my head. I was so startled that he came near escaping altogether, but I dropped him just before he reached the open plain. I might have spared him, if I hadn't been so angry over the loss of my dogs.

"Some time later I shot the female, who had two vigorous, partly grown young ones, which I sent to Mr. Barnum. They grew into fine large fellows, which traveled thousands of miles over the country with him."

The emu is another interesting curiosity whose home is in Central Australia. It is very fleet of foot and resembles the ostrich in many respects. The dogs which are trained to hunt it, wait until it is exhausted before attacking, when they spring at its throat, thus avoiding its dreaded kicks, which are delivered sideways and backwards, instead of forward, as is the case with the ostrich.

The height of the emu sometimes exceeds six feet and it is a good swimmer. It is hunted so persistently that it is dying off rapidly, and in a few years will probably be extinct, like the famed dodo, and also the bison of our own country.

The fierce native dogs of Australia, known as dingoes, follow the same method as the trained dogs in running down the emu, which fights them in vain.

CHAPTER XXXV.

A THIEF OF THE NIGHT.

THE African night wore on. Its mildness was such that there was no need of protection, nor of the fire that had been kindled for cooking purposes and kept going because of the cheerful appearance it gave to everything.

So long as it blazed and crackled, the friends could see each others' faces, and you who have not been similarly placed cannot realize the pleasure of meeting the kindly countenance of a friend whenever you turn your eyes in a certain direction.

The moon had grown to proportions that afforded considerable light, so much so, indeed, that the hunters felt safe from the lions that would have been on hand except for the orb of night.

But a single fire was burning, and that did not throw out a strong area of illumination. Horses, cattle and goats had been gathered in secure quarters, and everything made snug for the night. There was some apprehension that the captured animals in the stockade might be looked upon as legitimate prey by prowling wild beasts, but in such an event, before the marauders could tear down the stakes, the prisoners would be sure to give notice of their danger, and the defenders could rally to their defense.

Orak was recovering so rapidly that he insisted on keeping company with his friends and in taking his part as sentinel. His comrades did not object, for, as you will see, it produced a slight but perceptible lightening of their own labors.

It fell to the duty of Jack Harvey and Mr. Godkin to keep guard the first half of the night, with the two natives, Wart and Adz, as their assistants. They compelled the latter to keep moving about, so as to prevent themselves falling asleep, but the Americans were confident of their own ability to keep awake while sitting by the fire, smoking their pipes.

Bob and Dick became so drowsy, despite their interest in the narratives of Jack Harvey and Mr. Godkin, that they bade them good evening and retired.

You would think that the experiences they had gone through during the day would have kept them awake. So they would, had that been their first night in the African wilderness, but you know how readily we can become used to any danger. Soldiers will lie down and slumber on the battle-field, though not until they have become accustomed, in some degree, to its horrors.

And thus it was that Bob Marshall and Dick Brownell, after a prayer of thankfulness to God for his mercies, and a plea for the continuance of them to themselves and their friends on the other side of the world, sank into a slumber as sweet and refreshing as any they had ever known in childhood at home.

Both the youngsters assured me they never once dreamed about the enormous boa-constrictor they had taken part in shooting, nor indeed could they recall that their rest was disturbed by any visions at all.

"Carl," said the Texan, when the two were entirely alone, "I want to come to an understanding with you on one point."

"It shall not be my fault if we do not."

"You know the boys have set their hearts on making a visit to the Gaboon country, for chimpanzees and gorillas."

MEN HUNTING THE EMU.

"There can't be and doubt of their wishes on that point, nor," added the director, "of yours."

"Well, I'm free to say that I feel a good deal as they do; what I want to know, if what *you* think about it, for it is yours to decide."

"If we are as fortunate as I hope to be, I shall arrange to go upon a gorilla hunt."

"How will you fix it?"

"Well, after we have captured all that we can get in this part of the world, I'll start the train for Port Natal."

"Will all of us go with it?"

"That's a point on which I haven't fully made up my mind, and I'll be glad to hear your views. Will it be prudent for me to turn the train over to the charge, say of Pongo, while you, I and the boys push for the western coast to take ship to Loango?"

This was the first time Mr. Godkin had given an intimation of the plan he had in mind, though it had been suspected by his friends.

"As near as I can judge," replied the Texan, "we're about a thousand miles from the Atlantic."

"It is not as far as that — say, some seven or eight hundred miles."

"Then what is the distance to Port Natal?"

"Nearly twice as far."

"I hardly thought it stood that way," remarked Jack, as if musing with himself.

"You had a proposition in your mind : let me hear it."

"I was about sayin' that if there wasn't much difference 'atween the roads to the Atlantic and the Indian Ocean, why not all go back together to Port Natal, see the animals safe on board ship, and then take Pongo and Diedrick, if you thought best, with us, and sail from Port Natal for Loango?"

"I am inclined to think we will do that even as it is — the only objection is the great time it will consume. We could strike the highlands of Great Namaqua Land, and reach the coast long before the train would arrive at Natal."

"Why not continue to the westward with the train itself, and ship our animals from an Atlantic port?"

"I would like to do so, but there are grave objections. In the first place, my knowledge of Great Namaqua Land is to the effect that it is very rough and mountainous, especially that portion directly west of us. The great Orange River receives one of its chief tributaries from the mountainous region of Upper Great Namaqua Land; the country abounds with wild men, and, I am afraid, many parts are impassable for wagon trains."

"It can't be worse than the portion of the Transvaal through which we worked our way. We hadn't got fairly into Petermaritzburg when we were among the Drakenberg Mountains. We met little else till we struck Bechuana Land, and we've found plenty of them here."

"It is true we have had a rough time of it, though we got through with good fortune, but the country, bad as it is, is more favorable for traveling than that to the westward. There is another objection, almost equally serious," added the director.

"What's that?"

"No matter what point we might strike on the Atlantic coast, it would not be half so advantageous as Port Natal. I have shipped animals — as have others — from there many times. Plenty of vessels are always at the place, and no difficulty will be encountered in sending off our curiosities. But it is all the other way on the western shore. I know of no ports between Cape Town and Benguela, or Angol, where we can count upon obtaining ship, though it might be that a small party could secure passage northward."

14

"You mean to say, then," said Jack, "that if four or five of us should head westward, we are likely to reach the Atlantic, obtain ship to the north, and save weeks and months of time?"

"That is my view, but I have already named the greatest objection to that course. We have secured a lot of valuable prizes for whose care I am responsible, and, if I turn them over to a party of natives, and calamity should befall them, Mr. Barnum would never excuse me. No," said the director, with a compression of his lips, "it will never do."

"You're right," added the Texan, decisively; "we will see the train safe out of the woods, or, at least, do all we can to see it out, and then we'll look into the gorilla business."

I may say that I was surprised to learn from Mr. Godkin that there had ever been any question in his mind as to the proper course for him to pursue. Having reached a decision, he himself wondered that he had ever wavered on the point. I suspect that his strong desire to gratify the wishes of his young friends interfered, to a slight extent, with his natural level-headedness in such matters; for I trust I have told you enough to make clear his coolness and good sense in such crises as he was continually meeting.

It was not yet midnight when the director announced his conclusion in such emphatic language. He and Jack refilled their pipes, and smoked as though they would never tire. Wart and Adz, the natives, were dimly seen in the faint light of the fire and moon, as they plodded back and forth on the edge of the camp.

They did not encircle it in their tramping, as they should have done, but their beat covered a small space at the side and a few yards from where the white men sat discussing the future movements of the expedition.

The fire had smoldered so low that the two could hardly see each other's faces. Mr. Godkin stepped forward and stirred the wood with his foot, so that it broke forth into a large, crackling blaze. There was plenty of wood within reach, and he flung a lot on the flames.

"We don't need it," he said, resuming his seat on the other side, and facing the Texan, "but it is so cheerful that I prefer to keep it going. I wonder what time it is."

He drew out his watch to answer his own question, and found that midnight was but half an hour distant.

Once more he settled back, but, before he could add anything to what he had just said, Jack Harvey spoke in the most matter-of-fact tone:

"Don't stir; there's a wild man right behind you; I'll attend to him."

"What do you mean to do?" asked Mr. Godkin, with the same coolness, as he deliberately puffed his pipe.

CHAPTER XXXVI.

"I MEAN to steal round behind him and try the lasso."

"Then I think I'd better take my seat by you, so that I'll face him, instead of having my back toward him: I'd like to have a chance, too, to see the fun."

"Be careful that you don't scare him away."

"I'll look out for that."

No one would have supposed from viewing the two men, and overhearing, without understanding their words, that there had been the least change in the subject of their conversation. Both were smoking, and the murmur of their voices sounded the same as before in the ears of the native guards.

The latter were walking back and forth on the side of the camp opposite the wild man, who was so cautious in his movements that there was no fear of his being discovered by either of the other sentinels.

It was at the moment that the fire flamed up so high, under the stirring given it by Mr. Godkin, that the keen-eyed Texan caught the outlines of a head and shoulders as they dropped down in the shadow behind the director.

The single glimpse was enough to explain the nature of what he saw. It was evident that the wild man was reconnoitering, or, more likely, seeking a position close enough to allow him to hurl his spear, or discharge his bow and arrow, and then make off before he was seen.

Mr. Godkin sauntered to the other side of the fire, and sat down on the ground beside Jack Harvey.

"How many are there?" asked the elder.

"I saw only one, but there's no telling how many others are sneaking about in the darkness."

"There can't be many, or Wart and Adz would have learned it. How are you going to work it?"

"I mean to steal behind the chap and nab him."

"I don't believe you will succeed, but go ahead; we'll have some sport, anyway."

"I'll leave my gun here," said Jack, laying down his pipe and the weapon, "for I want the free use of my arms, and I'll take along the lasso."

"You may need the free use of your rifle," suggested Mr. Godkin, "and you had better do as you are accustomed to when on horseback."

The Texan, however, moved off without his chief weapon. If he ran into any trouble, he had his revolvers, while he was close enough to friends to call them to his help.

No one could have understood better than he the care necessary in leaving the vicinity of the camp fire. No doubt the wild man had his eyes fixed upon him, and any movement would be watched with suspicious eyes.

Jack Harvey, therefore, sauntered off as though he had no purpose other than to stretch his limbs. His course led straight away from the interloper, and consequently took him across the beat of the native sentinels.

They looked at him as he approached, doubtless wondering what he wanted. Since neither could speak English, conversation was out of the question, except in the most disjointed way.

Still, Jack's purpose was to make the wild man believe he wished simply to say something to the sentinels, and he, therefore, paused and uttered a few words, to which the others made the best replies they could, which were not much.

Into the gloom beyond, the Texan strolled, gradually circling toward the river, until he entered the tall grass that had been the cause of so much misgiving on the part of all.

Had the wild man undertaken to follow him, he could have done so without detection, since he appeared at a point between the camp fire and the edge of the tall weeds, and was on the ground where it was almost impossible to see him. On the other hand, Jack was erect, and the act of stooping was likely to awaken suspicion.

But the gentleman from Texas reasoned that there is considerable difference between a native African and an American Indian.

Had he taken the course I have described in the presence of an Apache or Comanche scout, the redskin would not have been deceived for an instant.

The question which bothered the Texan was, whether there was one or a dozen wild men. If the latter, the case was serious, for they might launch a shower of poisoned arrows or javelins into camp at any moment, while, if there was but a single person, he was likely to maneuver a longer time before making any demonstration.

Though he could not be sure he had removed all misgiving the intruder may have felt on witnessing his movements, Jack was so certain such was the fact, that he acted on it without hesitation.

Not until he was fairly in the tall grass did the cowboy feel the confidence he showed on his Indian campaigns. Finding himself in "cover" similar to that which had often served him so well in his own country, he made no mistake.

He now stole through this grass in a stooping posture, with the purpose of getting behind the stranger and bringing him in a direct line with Mr. Godkin.

That point gained, he would creep upon the savage, who would have to be an amazingly spry fellow to escape him.

You will perceive that the Texan was acting on the theory that he had but one enemy in front of him : should there prove to be more, his plan of campaign must undergo modification.

No serpent could have moved through the weeds with less noise than he. He might have passed within arm's length of a watchful redskin without betraying himself.

"I guess this is about the spot," thought Jack, slowly raising his head above the grass, so as to get his bearings; "if that darkey had half the brains of an injin, he would have tumbled before this, but there ain't anything decent in this country, compared with ours."

"THE OUTLINES OF A MAN'S HEAD AND SHOULDERS ROSE SLOWLY TO VIEW."

Jack ought not to have forgotten that the little enterprise on which he had started was not yet concluded.

It was an easy matter for him to reach the edge of the grass without detection from any one. There he paused, with a space of perhaps a hundred yards between him and the camp-fire that he had left some time before. Most of this had been grown over with the grass that was cut off as a matter of precaution, and somewhere on this space, he was convinced, the native was crouching, with his baleful eyes fixed on the white man, who, he little dreamed, knew of his whereabouts.

Jack found the intervening plain shrouded in more gloom than he had anticipated. Over most of it the unaided eye could not have detected any person unless he stood on his feet, so as to be thrown into relief against the light of the camp fire.

It may have been that Mr. Godkin, who could be plainly seen by the Texan, suspected his embarrassment, for while the latter lingered on the edge of the open space, he saw him rise to his feet, fling more wood on the fire, and stir it.

"Good for him!" muttered the pleased scout; "he knows just what I want, and he done it for me."

The increased illumination, however, did not light up every portion of the little plain, and the keen eyes of the Texan, roaming over the ground, failed to locate his man.

"I wonder if he's lost," thought Jack, "or has he smelt a mouse and dusted out afore I could give him a boost. Ah —"

In the gloom between him and the camp, the outlines of a man's head and shoulders rose slowly to view.

Jack had located his fellow at last.

"Yes, he's there," he chuckled, "and the band will begin to play mighty soon."

The savage was crouching at a point about two-thirds of the way between the scout and the fire. This showed he was moving forward and did not suspect the meaning of the white man's movement.

Jack felt a tinge of alarm as he realized that the savage was so near Mr. Godkin that he could easily have launched a poisoned missile before the gentleman could get out of range.

Should he make the attempt, Jack was without his rifle to anticipate him; but his revolvers were at command, and he reflected that he had learned to use them with considerable promptness in an emergency.

The question whether there was one or more savages had not yet been solved, and it was that which chiefly occupied Jack as he began creeping toward the camp-fire.

Once free of the grass, he crouched lower than the native in front of him. The Texan had discovered in his Indian campaigns how to move silently over the ground, with his chin but a few inches from it. By this means, too, he brought his man into clearer relief against the yellow flame beyond.

"I'm satisfied," he concluded, after progressing some way, "that, no matter how many darkeys may be in the neighborhood, there's only one atween me and Carl, and he's the one I've got to deal with ; I'll 'tend to the others afterward."

The savage, having shown himself, now sank down again and became almost invisible. This meant that he was advancing upon the camp. When he straight-ened up, it was to note his progress and bearings.

A few minutes later, the head and shoulders reappeared, this time so much nearer the camp that all doubt of the native's hostile purpose was removed. He meant to slay Mr. Godkin, and was steadily advancing to do so.

Indeed, he was so near that Jack was sure the director must be able to see every movement, a fact to which the wild man was singularly blind.

At any rate, he had approached so close that there was no call for him to go closer, and that such was his own conclusion was proven by the next step he took.

CHAPTER XXXVII.

"GOOD-BY, SWEETHEART."

THE wild man rose higher than before, straightening up until his body was visible to the waist. The act showed that he was armed with a javelin and was gathering himself to throw it.

The fire was not burning as brightly as before, though the savage would not have stood so nearly erect but for the necessity of balancing himself to hurl his missile.

The opportunity must have been a tempting one to the African, for the only two sentinels who made a pretense of attending to their duties were still tramping back and forth without suspicion of his presence. The white man was sitting cross-legged on the ground, smoking his pipe, and apparently gazing into the fire in a dreamy reverie, though I need hardly say that he was giving far more attention to the sneaking native just then than to anything else.

As he afterward said, it seemed to him that Jack Harvey was altogether too deliberate in his movements, and, in fact, matters were getting into too fine a shape for him to feel comfortable, knowing, as he did, that the delay of the skulking African was solely that he might make his aim unerring.

Strange that the continued absence of the second white man from the camp had not awakened the suspicion of the native.

Jack Harvey allowed the scamp to raise the javelin over his head, with his arm drawn slightly back, when he let fly with his rawhide. The whirr of the lasso alarmed the African, who quickly turned. At the sight of the Texan his alarm became a wild fright, and he dropped the javelin and ran at full speed. The noose was true to its aim, however, and in less time than it takes to tell it, the savage was ensnared so tightly that he almost strangled.

The violent pull brought him over on his back with a force that fairly made him bounce. Before he could help himself, or utter more than a few gurgling sounds, the Texan was upon him, angry enough to crush his head under his heel.

"You're a scamp from Scamptown," he exclaimed, catching the bare arm and jerking him to his feet; "the best use I can put you to is to practice on you with my revolver."

The wretch was so terrified that he could not offer any resistance. As his captor loosened the noose he would have gone down in a heap but for the sturdy Texan, who yanked him to his feet as a pedagogue would handle a snarling school-boy.

"Stand up, confound you!" called Jack, giving his ears a smart cuff; "if you don't know how to walk, I'll teach you."

The castigation frightened the fellow into obedience, and he trudged beside his captor as meekly as a lamb, on the watch, however, for a chance to dart off in the darkness.

"Here he is," said Jack, addressing the interested Mr. Godkin, who had risen to his feet, and come part way to meet him; "and don't you think he's a beauty — well, I'll be hanged!"

The Texan recoiled in amazed indignation. By the light of the camp-fire he recognized the native as the one he had saved from death by torture that same afternoon.

"There's gratitude for you," he said, after explaining the matter to his friend; "now, there isn't any question that he ought to be knocked in the head, though I've no doubt his skull is so thick that it'll take a pile-driver to crack it."

"I don't see that there is any ingratitude about it," remarked Mr. Godkin, seeking to appease the wrath of his friend, "for it wasn't *I* who saved his life."

"But you are my friend."

"How could he know that?"

"But he saw me sitting with you when he began crawling up to camp, and I shouldn't wonder if, after all, it was *me* that he was after," added Jack, looking wrathfully at the shrinking native.

AS IN THE OLDEN TIME.

Wart and Adz thought the situation warranted them in leaving their posts and approaching the camp-fire, and Wart became so excited at what he beheld that he rushed away to arouse the sleeping cousins.

"The poor wretch is entitled to the doubt," said Mr. Godkin with a laugh, unable to share the anger of his friend. "Who knows but that if you had stayed where you were, he might have come forward and offered his hand in friendship?" Jack Harvey cast such a scornful glance upon the director that the latter came near waking the camp with his merry laughter.

"Let me look at that spear," said he, reaching his hand for the weapon which Jack had picked up from the ground.

The director carefully examined it. The handle was made of hard, smooth wood, resembling bamboo. The head was symmetrical in outline and secured immovably in place.

"These people have some way of obtaining iron," remarked Mr. Godkin, noticing that the head was constructed of that metal. "It may be they understand how to make it, or more likely they get it from the traders."

Inspecting the point by the light of the fire, Mr. Godkin fancied he could see a yellowish substance on the end, though he was by no means certain.

"I know a good way of telling whether it's p'isoned," said Jack Harvey.

"How?"

"Give him a jab with it; if it don't kill him, it isn't p'isoned, while, if it does kill him, you can make up your mind there's been some fooling with it."

Mr. Godkin pointed the weapon at the naked breast of the native, as if about to make the test Jack suggested. He expected the prisoner to shrink and show every sign of terror, but there was nothing of the kind. He had been frightened from the first, but when the point of his own spear almost pricked his chest, he assumed a smile that was childlike and bland.

"Why, Jack, you have done the fellow an injustice," said Mr. Godkin, handing the weapon to Wart, who had just returned from a reconnoiter of the camp, "that weapon is an honest one."

"It does look that way," replied Jack, not fully satisfied, however, that the director's conclusion was correct; "but, even if the spear isn't loaded, it wouldn't be a pleasant thing to have run through your body."

"Well, he is our prisoner; what shall we do with him?"

"Ask *them*," replied the Texan, pointing to Wart and Adz, who were interested spectators of the scene.

The question had to be propounded in pantomime, but it was easy to make the native understand that their opinion was wanted as to the proper way to dispose of their captive.

The answer of both was unmistakable. They favored the severest measures toward the African, who had been arrested in the very act of launching his weapon at the director of the enterprise, for whom they held a strong affection.

Wart reached out his hand for the javelin, and, gently touching the point with his finger, shrank back as though it had given him a distressing wound.

"He believes it is poisoned," said Jack, with a laugh; "you can't fool him, for he is a native of this country."

"They seem to think we ought to punish the fellow, but I didn't agree to follow their wishes. Jack, I am sure you would not consent to slay the wretch in cold blood."

"No, I confess I wouldn't, though I was mad enough when I flung the lasso to strangle him."

"You came pretty near doing it as it was."

"We ain't in this country to capture Africans," remarked the Texan thoughtfully, "though Mr. Barnum is anxious for anything worth seeing in that line. He spent a great deal to secure the Siamese twins and the Sacred Hairy Family of Birmah."

"He might exhibit you and this fellow: he as the wild man of Bechuana Land, and you as the one who prevented him killing me."

"I'm afraid the people wouldn't take much stock in him, and as for *me*, they would set me down as a fraud right off."

THE TEST

"Well," said Mr. Godkin, with another laugh, "I have made up my mind what to do."

"What's that?"

"I turn him over to you to do what you please, without hindrance on my part."

The director understood what he was doing. No one knew the nature of the gallant Texan better than he. He had proven himself a demon in more than one hand-to-hand encounter with the red men of the Southwest, and in the memorable campaign against those miscreants, there was no braver scout and soldier in the commands of Generals Crook and Miles than he.

And yet his was the heart of a woman. No **ear** was more open to an appeal for mercy, and his adventurous career had never been stained by an act that ought to bring the blush to his cheek.

Mr. Godkin believed Jack's anger toward the captive was partly assumed, and it was without the least misgiving that he surrendered the prisoner to him for disposal.

There was a mysterious smile on the face of Jack as he said: "All right; let me have him."

Wart and Adz recoiled a step or two, doubtless convinced that the wild man's hours were numbered, but the cousins, who, like the director, knew Jack better, had no such idea.

The javelin was retained, and I may as well state that the investigations afterward made proved that it was tipped with one of the deadliest poisons in existence. Had Mr. Godkin but pricked the wild man's skin with it, he would have died within a few minutes.

But he was a cunning dog, and knew how to help his own cause by an assumption of innocence at the critical moment.

Taking him by the arm, Jack Harvey walked slowly to the edge of the encampment, pausing at a point where there was just enough light from the fire to reveal his actions.

His friends walked a few steps after him, so as not to lose the sight.

"*Good-by, sweetheart!*"

As the Texan uttered the words, the captive stood directly in front of him. Simultaneously with the farewell, he delivered a kick which lifted the African from the ground and sent him half a rod forward.

As the wretch landed, he uttered a yell like that which had escaped him when the native chieftain punctured him with his spear, and vanished in the gloom of the night at headlong speed.

I think Jack Harvey did exactly right; at any rate, no member of the expedition ever saw the scamp again.

CHAPTER XXXVIII.

FUNNY VISITORS.

ALL through this characteristic incident, not one of the sleepers would have been awakened but for Wart's excitement.

It was now considerably past midnight, and time for a change of sentinels. Wart and Adz were directed to crawl into one of the wagons, while Pongo and Abdallah were aroused to take their places. Jack Harvey and Mr. Godkin gave way to Bob and Dick, who had expressed the wish that they might keep each other company.

As the Texan was about to creep into his quarters, he stopped a minute to admire a small animal, which ran under the wagon and vanished in the darkness. It was beautiful and graceful, of a gray color, with an admixture of yellow, and covered with dark patches, with alternate bands of black and white on its tail.

The creature is the blotched genet, which has retractile claws, and is found not only in South Africa, but in the southern part of France.

The investigation of the Texan satisfied him and the director that no other wild men were in the vicinity, and nothing further was said about the exciting incident

THE BLOTCHED GENET.

which had so recently occurred. The discussion, they thought, would keep until a more opportune season.

The guards stationed themselves precisely as before, despite the resolution the lads had previously formed that they would insure wakefulness by keeping in motion; but, having had several hours of sound slumber, and being in one another's company, there certainly was little likelihood of their losing consciousness.

Pongo and Abdallah paced back and forth like professionals, while the boys, after stirring the fire, sat down in the positions occupied by the two men in the earlier portion of the evening.

"I don't think we are likely to have any more disturbance," remarked Bob, "since everything appears to be quiet, however, it won't do to take anything for granted in this country."

"I've no doubt that some of the natives have had a look at the camp, and probably have made up their minds that we are too well prepared to make it pay them to attack us."

"I noticed to-day," said Bob, "that the raft which caused so much alarm is still lying against the bank, where it caught fast the other day."

"From what I heard Mr. Godkin say, I think he means to use it to take us across the river, so as to hunt in a new section, after we have harrowed over this one pretty well."

"There is plenty of game left. We haven't had anything to do with elephants, and I know there are rhinoceroses and hippopotami not far off."

"How can you be sure of that?"

"Pongo told me this evening that he had seen signs of both, and you know he isn't the fellow to make a mistake like that."

"The raft is likely, then, to come into use,—at any rate for hunting hippopotami—helloa! what's up?"

The question was caused by Pongo's hurried approach, his manner showing that he had made an important discovery. Abdallah remained at his post.

"What is it, Pongo?" asked Bob Marshall, half rising to his feet.

"Something out there in grass — think they wild men."

"If that's the case," said Dick, "we must wake Mr. Godkin and Jack."

"Ain't sure," added the Bushman; "come see."

The boys, rifles in hand, followed their guide to his station. As they did so, they reflected that they were exposing themselves recklessly, for the firelight must have shown them clearly to any one looking in the direction of the camp, while the intruders themselves were hidden in gloom.

The boys noticed that their

"SOMETHING OUT THERE IN THE GRASS."

guide led them to the side of the camp facing the tall grass along the river,— the place where the single wild man had appeared some time before, and most likely to be used as a screen by a party of them.

"Don't go too far," whispered Bob. "for remember we are in plain sight of any one in the grass."

Pongo halted, and the three stood peering into the obscurity.

Everything seemed quiet and motionless, not the slightest object being in sight. But Pongo was not the one to be misled, and the cousins were as certain that danger lurked in the vegetation as if they beheld it with their own eyes.

The three had stood in the attitude of intense attention but a few minutes, when a soft rustling in the grass proved that the Bushman was right; something was there.

"It seems strange," whispered Dick, "that the wild men should betray themselves like that."

"They haven't betrayed themselves as much as we."

"But they know — sh! see there!"

The slightest possible glimpse was caught of a head as it rose above the vegetation, instantly dropping out of sight again.

There was just enough moonlight to enable the watchers to trace the outlines, which, dim as they were, awakened the wonder of the three by the fact that, instead of being covered with a huge mass of bushy hair, the head appeared to be bare and smaller than one of their own.

Before anything was said about this peculiarity, the head popped up again, then another and another arose, until fully half a dozen had come to view, all going up and down like so many jacks-in-the-box.

What did it mean?

Pongo was heard to laugh softly, and he uttered one word which solved the mystery:

"*Monkeys!*"

A party of the creatures appeared to have ventured out from the adjoining jungles, with the intention of investigating the encampment that had been near them for several days.

Our friends had seen hundreds of monkeys since entering Bechuana Land, but gave them little attention, because they considered it more important to capture other game. Monkeys are plentiful in many parts of the world (even the poor organ-grinders being able to afford them), and they can be obtained without difficulty.

For this reason, Mr. Godkin decided that none would be captured unless they came upon some rare specimens.

"I guess it's safe to go back and sit down," remarked Dick Brownell with a laugh, as he turned about, followed by his companions.

"I wonder what has possessed them to pay us a visit?" said Bob, as they resumed their seats, Pongo returning to his station.

"Mischief; the monkey is the most mischievous creature in the world; they are looking for sport, and will get it, if possible, before they leave."

"Look at them!"

As suddenly as if they had sprung from the earth, fully twenty of the animals appeared at the camp-fire. They were on all sides except that under the immediate protection of Pongo and Abdallah, and some showed a disposition even to crowd them.

"They are not monkeys," said Dick, after carefully studying them a minute or two.

"What are they?"

"Baboons; notice how large several of them are. Their muzzles are elongated like a dog's, and the hands and feet are short, with long thumbs."

"They have manes, too, and their tails end in tufts of long hair. Yes, they are baboons, but there's little difference, after all, between them and the regular style of monkeys."

"There's a funny-looking one," added Bob.

His friend had noticed the animal before his attention was directed to it. It was unusually large, and the abundant mane, instead of being of a plain, dark color, was oddly flecked with white, as though the creature was becoming gray in spots.

A SLY THIEF.

The baboons were going through all sorts of performances, hopping over each other, running toward the fire, as if they meant to jump into it, skurrying off again into the high grass, where, after being out of sight for a few moments, they suddenly shot into view once more, and then, standing still, some of them indulged in the luxury of making grimaces at the amused lads.

Nothing would have been easier than to have opened a fusillade on the funny creatures that would have quickly decimated them; but nothing, at the same time, would have been more cruel, and the youths had no idea of anything of the kind.

Pongo and Abdallah scorned to pay attention to them. The animals were beneath their notice, and the sentinels had more important business on hand than to give heed to them.

While the lads were trying to obtain a better view of the odd-looking creature, he vanished, as if conscious of the notice he had attracted and anxious to escape it.

"I wouldn't mind capturing him, if we had a chance," said Bob, peering about in the gloom; "but he is so big that I suppose he would fight like a wild-cat."

"If we only had Jack's lasso, and knew how to throw it, it would be easy enough —confound it!"

The youth made a frantic clutch at his hat, which just then was whisked from his head as deftly as any school-boy ever performed the trick. Bob broke into laughter, for he had seen the spotted baboon sneaking up behind his cousin, and, suspecting his purpose, held his peace.

The look of dismay on his companion's face caused even the glum Pongo to smile.

"Bring that back!" called Dick, half amused and half angry; "that's the only hat I've got, and we have a hot sun in this country."

The thief, on securing the trophy, had scampered off among his companions, all of whom now indulged in the liveliest of chattering, as if delighted with the exploit.

"How shall I get that again?" queried Dick, surveying the fellow, who had halted a few steps away, as if to invite him to make the attempt.

The lad did not hesitate, but began cautiously approaching the baboon, who held his ground until he was almost within reach. Then he slowly edged off.

Dick made a quick jump and shot out his hand.

He came very nigh catching the thief, but missed him by a hair's breadth, and once more Bob and Pongo laughed. Abdallah may have been amused, but he failed to make it manifest.

"You'll have to run a race with him," remarked Bob; "I don't think I would feel very proud of letting a baboon steal my hat—hold on!"

Off went Bob's head-gear, snatched from his possession by another of the animals as cleverly as the first had performed the feat for his cousin.

CHAPTER XXXIX.

"I'VE GOT HIM."

IT was Dick's turn to laugh, and you may be sure he did so with as hearty mirth as he ever enjoyed in all his life.

Both boys were bareheaded, with little apparent chance of recovering their property.

"That beats everything," was the rueful exclamation of Bob Marshall; "I expected an attempt of the kind, but was sure I couldn't be outwitted."

"There's one way we can secure our hats," added Dick, who was on the point of losing his temper; "and that is to shoot the thieves, and I'll do it, too, if we don't get them pretty soon."

"They only mean it for fun, and we won't shoot them unless we have to. Watch me while I go for this fellow."

The baboon that had stolen Bob's property was smaller than the other thief, but seemed more venturesome. Halting less than a rod distant, the impudent fellow reached out the trophy, chattering and making the funniest of grimaces, as if inviting the owner to try to regain it.

Bob imitated his cousin's tactics, but, taking lesson from his failure, sought to get closer before snatching it back again.

A SECOND TOO LATE.

The creature allowed him to come quite near, and, instead of making a quick grab at it, the youth slowly extended his hand, in the hope of throwing him off his guard.

But the animal was not to be deceived that way. As the hand advanced that of the baboon receded, and the distance between the two was not diminished.

Suddenly, as Bob was on the very point of darting his fingers after it, the thief had the impudence to turn squarely around and begin walking off, with a mincing gait, glancing over his shoulder at the discomfited youngster, in a way that tantalized him beyond endurance.

"Take that, then!"

Bob made one bound, and, concentrating all his strength in his right leg, delivered a kick which, had it landed, would have lifted the animal several feet in air.

But the creature was too nimble to permit the boot to land. He hopped out of the way, and the kick was so tremendous that Bob's foot shot of ward, lifting him clear off the ground, and dropping him on his back with a resounding thump.

Dick Brownell sank down, so overcome with mirth that, for the moment, he could hardly stand.

I am sorry to say that Bob lost his temper, though I think that you or I would have done the same if in his situation. He brought his gun to his shoulder with the intention of shooting the animal that was having such sport at his expense.

Before he could aim, however, Dick sprang up, and, grasping the barrel, turned it aside.

"'They only mean it for fun, and we won't shoot them unless we have to,'" said he, quoting the remark Bob made only a minute before.

"But this is carrying a joke too far," growled his cousin; "how are we going to get our hats without shooting the thieves? And, if we have got to shoot them, what's the use of waiting?"

"You have read the story of the trader, who went to sleep under a tree with a lot of caps beside him, and, when he awoke, found that a number of monkeys had stolen them all, and were frolicking among the branches of the trees overhead."

"What did he do?"

"He chased them till he got mad, and then spitefully threw down the only hat he had left. The monkeys did the same, and he got back all his property."

"And you propose that we try the scheme?"

"Yes."

"How can we do it, when we haven't a hat left?"

"Almost anything will answer. I'll fling down my knife as though I am disgusted, which is the fact, and may be they will do the same with our hats."

Drawing his large knife from the belt at his waist, Dick slammed it on the ground, while the two watched to see its effect on the baboons.

The spotted animal kept his distance, and made no motion by way of imitating the action. The smaller one, that had removed Bob's hat, ran nimbly forward, as if he intended to lay the trophy at the foot of Dick.

Such, however, was not his purpose. He meant to secure possession of the knife also.

But he was just a bit too eager. He ventured so close that, before he could withdraw, Dick had seized him by the arm.

The captive emitted a number of sharp screams, and began biting and scratching with such fierceness that Dick administered a couple of sound cuffs and allowed him to scamper off, though not until he had regained his prize.

The other baboons uttered similar cries, and danced about in such excitement that it looked as if they were about to attack the youth who had laid violent hands on one of their number.

The quick release of the captive, however, averted that unpleasant turn of affairs.

"There!" exclaimed Dick, catching up the hat and throwing it toward his cousin, "I got your property for you, and you ought to get mine for me."

"I'll be only too glad to do so, if I have the chance."

"I don't think flinging down anything we can lay hold of will help matters. The others didn't venture near, and I don't believe that fellow would have tried it, if he had taken a second or two to consider the matter."

During these stirring incidents, Pongo and Abdallah kept their beat, though they stopped several times in tramping back and forth to survey the scene.

It is remarkable how closely a lot of monkeys or baboons will imitate the antics of a number of mischievous boys.

Having failed to catch the spotted-maned thief, Dick Brownell refrained from repeating his attempt in that form. He stood still, meditating whether any plan, after all, except the hard one of shooting the pilferer, would answer.

The latter, noticing him standing thus, now began to coax him to venture again. He walked slowly toward him, holding out the hat, as if saying that the youth need but to stretch forth his hand to take it.

"Stand quiet," said Bob, in a low voice, "and see how close he will come."

Dick followed the suggestion. The baboon halted a few steps off, but the lad, looking sideways at him, never stirred a muscle. The creature came still closer, but remained just beyond reach. Without shifting his feet, he leaned over and extended his paw a little farther.

Dick was tempted to spring at him, but his cousin warned him to wait.

The baboon seemed to realize he stood on the very "death line," and that it would not do to venture an inch nearer.

He leaned as far as he could, with the extended hat, grimacing and chattering in a way that would have exasperated a person less cool than Dick Brownell.

Still, the animal went no nigher, though he seemed on the point, more than once, of risking it, and still Dick, in obedience to Bob's counsel, stirred not.

At this critical juncture, several of the baboons that were attentively watching the scene seemed to lose their patience. One of them sneaked behind the spotted thief, and, with a view of ending the "dead-lock," gave him a slight shove.

It is not easy to push down such a nimble creature as a baboon, but this one was so nicely balanced that he toppled over at the feet of Dick.

"Now's your time," called Bob.

No need of the cry. Dick pounced upon the knave like a flash, and snatched the hat from his grasp. Throwing it to his cousin, to guard for him, he hurled the baboon to the ground and endeavored to pin him fast, as a prize for the Greatest Show on Earth.

But the contract proved rather extensive.

It was a strong animal, and he fought like a tiger, using his claws with such vigor that he inflicted considerable damage. But Dick was plucky, and held on.

The other baboons became frantic. Their champion was in the grasp of an enemy, and fighting, as may be said, for his life. They chattered and ran back and forth, making demonstrations toward the youth which were sure to turn, very soon, into a savage attack upon him.

Events moved swiftly, but it must not be supposed that Bob and the two natives remained idle during the perilous struggle of their friend. They saw his danger and lost no time in running to his help.

They were not a moment too soon. The other animals began closing around the combatants, when the three reached the spot, where they applied feet and hands with such vigor that the assailants were hurled right and left.

The tumult, by this time, had roused Mr. Godkin and Jack Harvey, who scrambled from their quarters and rushed forward to take a hand in the disturbance.

Dick Brownell was a skillful wrestler, and he was making a good fight with his contestant. They were on the ground, and the lad had twisted one leg around the lower limbs of the baboon, so as to hold them motionless. He had also secured a grip about the arms, as they may be called, which were so imprisoned that the owner could make no use of them.

But the lad's danger was from the teeth of his fierce foe, which made such efforts to bite him that it was hard work to protect his face, and, at the same time, hold the claws motionless.

"I've got him!" called the brave youth, seeing his friends around him, "and he won't get away either!"

"We can leave you alone, if you enjoy it so much," said Mr. Godkin with a laugh, "but I reck-on we'd better interfere."

"I'VE GOT HIM."

With the help of the men, it was an easy matter to secure the obstreperous baboon. His legs, both fore and aft, were tied as though his captors were handcuffing an ordinary malefactor, and he could only screech his rage and helplessness.   His companions continued running and capering about, but the company had assumed too formidable proportions for them to assault, glad as they would have been to help their leader.

"We've got a cage that will just fit this fellow," said Mr. Godkin, "and he is no insignificant prize."

Five minutes later the big baboon was safely lodged in a strong structure, his fate being another illustration of the truth that the way of the transgressor is hard.

CHAPTER XL.

A FAMILY PARTY

THE baboons continued their excited demonstrations for some time after the caging of the big captive, but finally they seemed to comprehend that nothing could be done for him, and that they themselves might be in danger. They scampered off into the tall grass, and, no doubt, soon betook themselves to the jungle, where they must have had a startling story to tell their friends of their experience by the camp-fire of the intruders.

The flurry drove away what disposition Mr. Godkin and Jack Harvey may have felt to sleep, and, lighting their pipes, they sat down by the fire to keep company with the boys, to whom they told the whole story of the Texan's experience with the wild man previous to their being aroused.

The cousins laughed as they did when they recalled their own efforts to recover their stolen hats.

"I think my tussle with that fellow," said Dick, "gave me good practice for hunting the genus *Troglodytes*, which means, Jack, the chimpanzee and the gorilla," the lad added, observing the startled look of the Texan.

"Why don't you call 'em by the right name?" growled Jack.

"He is right," remarked Mr. Godkin with a smile, knowing the distaste of their friend for technical words; "we may as well compare notes when discussing these matters. You know Mr. Barnum rightly contends that his menagerie is the best school in natural history, and there is no reason why we shouldn't brush up our knowledge on the subject. What about the genus *Simia*, Bob?"

The latter scratched his head a moment or two, but brightened up.

"I believe there is but a single species of that genus, and he is the orang-outan, or mias, found in Northern Sumatra and in Borneo."

"Borneo is considered its home, for they are very rare in Sumatra. He is a

231

THE ORANG-OUTAN.

terrible brute, and it is said that the only creatures that dare attack him are the crocodile and python."

"And how do *they* make out?" asked Jack Harvey.

"He kills the crocodile by main strength, and doesn't find it hard to do the same with the python. In fact, he comes closer to the gorilla, in most of his characteristics, than any animal of which I have knowledge. The next genus of the ape family is that of *Hylobates,* so called because of their power of walking nearly erect. They have several species known as *Gibbons,* or long-armed apes. They

HEAD OF ORANG-OUTAN

live in troops among the upper branches of trees in upland districts, the different species being found in Assam, the Malay Peninsula, Java, Sumatra, Borneo and Cambodia, Hainan. It isn't worth while to discuss them, for we are more interested in the animals with which we have just had some experience."

"I believe they come under the family of sacred monkeys?" was the inquiring remark of Dick Brownell.

"No; there are two genera of that family, but the baboons belong to the family of cheek-pouched monkeys, the most widely distributed of all the Old World monkeys, one variety being found as far north as Gibraltar, and others in North

China and Eastern Thibet. There are seven genera belonging to the family, with seventy species."

"Since you have started," said Jack Harvey, refilling his pipe, "go ahead; I can stand it if the rest can."

"I don't want to appear to air my knowledge, and, when I see any weariness, I will stop. We will drop the monkeys, so called, for, when you come to give the list found in the New World, it is almost endless. What I have to say, therefore, will relate to the baboon branch of the family. They are found in every part of Africa, and one species in Arabia. The latter has a tail ending in a large tuft of hair, and the neck and shoulders of the male are largely maned. It has long, slate-colored whiskers and is of an ashy-gray color. They live in large herds, and

A CONCERT.

are met in the mountains of Arabia, throughout Abyssinia, in Senaar, the home of Abdallah there, in Kordofan and Darfur, sometimes at the height of a mile and a half."

"I believe the ancient Egyptians considered the baboon sacred?" said Bob Marshall.

"The Egyptians worshipped and embalmed the baboon, making him sacred to Thoth, one of whose characters was the god of letters. It was in Hermopolis, the city of Thoth, that the baboon was particularly sacred, though he is far from being so regarded now.

"The genus Gelada contains a species with oblong head, a maned neck and a short, tufted tail. Its face, hands and callosities are deep black in color; it is between three and four feet long, and lives among the mountains of Abyssinia.

The baboon is often tamed and taught to give service to his master. A troop of them will sometimes act as torch-bearers at a supper party, and you will find them to-day in the streets of Cairo, performing tricks to the music of drums and other instruments."

"Of what species are the visitors we had this evening?"

"The Chacma, which I believe comes from the Hottentot word *t'chackamma*. It is to your credit, Dick, that you made such a good fight with that fellow, for he is stronger than the common English mastiff."

"They appear to travel in families, like the others you have told us about."

"There are large numbers of them in the mountains of the Cape of Good Hope.

THE CHACMA

Those in Table Mountain often cause trouble by coming down in such well-organized droves that the dogs cannot keep them out of the gardens."

"What do they live on?"

"They are fond of bulbous roots, especially the babiana, which is so named by the Dutch colonists because the baboons are so partial to its subterranean stems. You will often come upon heaps of peelings, where the animals have been sitting on the rocks in the sun, stripping them off."

"They don't seem to be very combative," said Dick, "for my customer did not attack me until I first pitched into him."

"No; it isn't likely they would have offered you any harm, if you had not first disturbed them. Sometimes, in climbing the kloofs, or passes of the mountains, travelers will set a troop of baboons scampering before them. If they are fired into, they will retaliate by throwing stones and rolling down boulders on their enemies."

THE GELADA.

"What kind of baboons are met with farther north?" asked Jack.

"The drill and the mandrill belong to the West Coast. Their faces are grooved. The drill is a native of the coast of Guinea, and has an erect, stumpy tail, about two inches long, and covered with short, bristly hair."

"I shouldn't consider that hardly deserving the name of a tail. What is their color?"

"There is a mixture of green in the upper parts, with a light, silvery hue beneath. They wear their whiskers according to the English fashion — that is, brushed backward, and the slight beard on the chin is orange-colored."

"If we catch any of them," said Jack, " I'm going to recommend to Mr. Barnum that he use a dye on their beards, for the color don't seem natural."

"How about their faces?"

"They are naked and black as ink."

"What is the size of the mandrill?"

"About five feet, when fully grown. They are singular-looking creatures, for their cheeks, instead of being black, are of a clear violet-blue, with oblique furrows. Just above the eyes begins a bright red line, and, running down the nose, spreads over the lip. The eyes are small, sparkling, and of a hazel color. The long hair on the side of the head grows upward, ending in a sharp point at the crown. When I add that the long, erect beard is yellowish, and each of the stiff, bristle-like hairs which cover the body has rings of black and yellow, you'll admit that the mandrill is a curiosity well worth seeing. In Borneo is found a long-nosed monkey who is about as frightful-looking a creature as can be imagined."

"I hope we shall be able to capture a mandrill when we go north on our gorilla hunt," remarked Bob Marshall.

"It isn't probable, for they do not frequent the same section of country. But any subject, no matter how interesting at first, becomes tiresome after a time, so we'll drop that of baboons."

It still lacked considerable of daylight, and Jack

THE DRILL

Harvey decided to return to his sleeping-quarters, asking that he should be called if any more visitors put in an appearance before daylight. The director stayed with the boys, and made a tour of the stockade to see that all their prisoners were safe.

So far as they could discover, nothing was amiss. The large giraffe had shown some excitement during the flurry caused by the baboons, but she quieted down on the disappearance of the visitors, and, with that docility which is characteristic of the gentle creatures, seemed to have become quite suited with her novel quarters.

"I don't know," said Mr. Godkin, looking thoughtfully at the dark line of tall grass in the direction of the river, "that it is strange that most of our visitors choose that route. If there is much more of it, I shall move farther back from the stream."

"Pongo told me to-day, or rather yesterday," said Dick, "that he had seen signs of rhinoceroses and hippopotami not far off."

"He was right, for I noticed the same thing. Fact of it is, my glass showed me one of the biggest behemoths I ever looked upon."

THE MANDRILL.

"Where was he?"

"A half mile the other side of the stream. He was standing with his side toward me, so that I had a fair view."

"Why didn't we pay him a visit?"

"He will keep," was the remark of the director; "he isn't the only one in this part of the world. They have been pretty well frightened away from the upper

THE HOWLERS

regions of the Nile, but there are plenty left in Central and South Africa. I have some other work I want to finish before we attack them."

"It will be a job to transport a hippopotamus or rhinoceros to Port Natal."

"Altogether too big a job to move one thither unless he is quite small. We shall have to follow the rule that prevails with other animals — kill the parents and carry off the little ones before they are big enough to cause trouble."

The night continued calm and still, and, after standing on the edge of the camp for a short time, the three friends sauntered back to where the fire had begun to smolder again.

They had sat there but a brief while, when the growing light in the east proved that the eventful night had come to an end, and another day was at hand.

LONG-NOSED MONKEYS.

CHAPTER XLI.

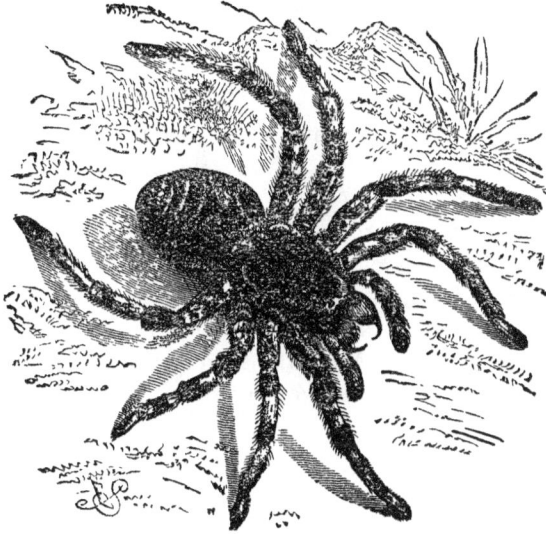

I AM afraid it would be tedious to you if I should give the particulars that attended many of the interesting discoveries of our friends in Southern Africa. They saw some of the wildest and grandest scenery on their way through the Drakenberg Mountains, and encountered storms and tempests almost the equal of the appalling cyclones of our own country. There were times when it seemed impossible to advance farther; but, before the point of despair was reached, some way opened to push on, until we find them at the point where they went into permanent camp, and devoted their entire attention to the capture of curiosities for The Greatest Show on Earth.

It occurs to me that I ought to have mentioned long ago that the procuring of wild animals is not always such a difficult task as would seem. To begin with, I have a resident agent in each of the principal cities of Europe. He is on the lookout for curiosities. Then, all the zoological gardens of Europe are my agents, and I am in constant correspondence with their managers. And finally, I have parties of men who go out on special elephant-hunting expeditions in India and Africa.

At a certain season of the year, our agent, a white man, mounted on a camel, will ride through the country, and the news of his approach will quickly be communicated to the natives in the interior. When he arrives at some well-known point of rendezvous, he will be met by hundreds of the black natives, each member of the party having in charge a camel, a giraffe, a rhinoceros, a party of monkeys, or a group of wild goats, these having been secured by the natives during their hunting expeditions.

The sending of the party into the interior of Southern Africa, under charge of Mr. Carl Godkin, was in the nature of a venture or experiment, and I was persuaded to the attempt by Mr. Godkin, in whom I had unlimited confidence.

No attempt at a history of the enterprise would approach completeness without a description of some of the marvelous exhibitions of insect life that came under the observation of the hunters. Bob and Dick took careful notes and received many suggestions from Mr. Godkin, the result being a record which formed for me one of the most absorbing parts of the narrative of the enterprise.

The termites, or white ants, build nests of different forms. Some are found among the branches of trees, seventy-five feet above the ground; others build a round turret of clay, a couple of feet high, with a projecting roof, so that, as it stands on the earth, it suggests in appearance an enormous mushroom. Within are countless cells, of various forms and sizes.

There are other nests in Africa, more curious than these. They are made of clay, broad, and from twelve to fifteen feet high. It is easy to mistake them for villages, for some of the structures are larger than the huts of the natives themselves.

In building these dwellings, the termites first erect several turrets of clay of the shape of a sugar loaf, and a foot high. These are rapidly added to, increasing in height, until they are joined at the top in one dome, and united into a complete whole by a thick wall of clay. This soon puts on a green coating of grass, so that the resemblance to a haycock is quite complete. When the structure has assumed this shape, the insects remove the clay turrets that have served as supports, and use them in building other dwellings.

Only the lower part of the house is occupied by the inhabitants. The upper portions, being very strong, serve as guards against the weather and enemies, besides preserving the moisture required for the hatching of the ants in the lower part.

In the inhabited part are the apartments for the king and queen, the storehouses for food, and the nurseries for the young.

There must be hundreds of thousands of ants employed in erecting each of these buildings, and it is an amazing fact that every one appears to understand his duty so well that there is never the slightest interference between them as they rush to and fro in their labors.

If each of these ants were as large as a man, and possessed corresponding energy, their houses would be several miles high.

Of course the white ants have their enemies, else they would not take such care in building their houses. The chief of these is the aard-vark, or earth-hog. He has molar teeth, of a cylindrical form, pierced longitudinally with numberless minute tubes. Their surface is quite flat, and fitted for the crushing of insects. Their nails are intended to dig the ground, the head long, the limbs short and strong, and the tongue extensible. The earth-hog lives wholly upon white ants, which it devours wholesale.

The animal makes its home in a burrow a short distance under ground. It keeps out of sight during the day, but at dark comes forth and sets out for the ant-hills. Digging a hole on either side of them, it startles the community, whose members run in all directions, when the long tongue is thrust among them, and they are gathered in without number. The earth-hog has no tusks, its safety depending upon its effective means of concealing itself.

One of the most destructive of flies known in Africa is the tsetse. It is an extraordinary fact that while its sting produces no permanent ill effects upon man or wild beasts, it is sure death to horses and horned cattle. Even the buffalo and zebra, closely allied as they are to the horned cattle and horses, are not harmed by the bite. Fortunately, the tsetse is

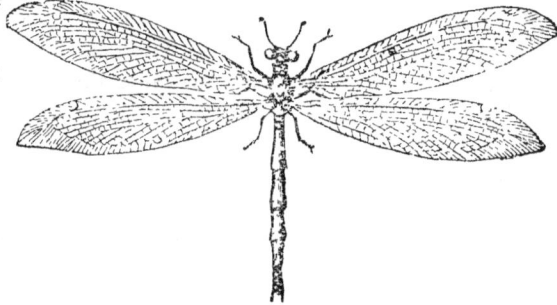

THE ANT-LION.

confined to a distance of only two or three miles from the base of the mountains. Were it otherwise, such a wagon train as mine would never dare venture into the interior. Mr. Godkin's knowledge of the dreadful insect enabled him to avoid its fatal haunts. In the fourth year which Gordon Cumming spent in hunting in Africa, this insect killed all his draught oxen and most of his horses.

There is another fly, with four long wings, which lays its egg on the surface of the ground, or just below, in the loose, sandy soil, where the sun hatches it out, in the form of a caterpillar. You would not think, from its appearance, that it was calculated to catch its prey, for it has a slow pace, and can only move backward, but it plays wild havoc among other insects, especially ants.

This ant-lion, as it is called, begins operations by first tracing a circle in the sand, intended to mark the boundary of its future home. Putting itself inside the circle, it thrusts its rear portion into the sand, using one of its fore-legs as a shovel, and places the load on its flat head and then flings it on the outside of the circle. Moving backward, it keeps this up until it comes around to the point from which it started.

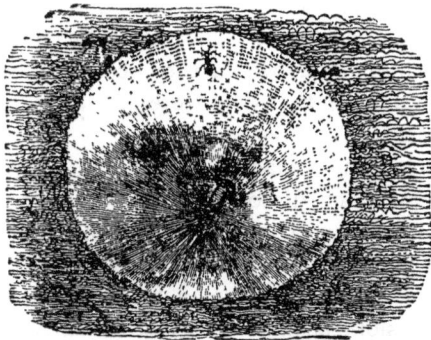

THE ANT-LION'S TRAP.

A second and third circle are traced and filled in the same manner, until it arrives at the center. Then a second series of circles, deeper and of less diameter, are made, ending when the hole has the appearance of an inverted cone.

To avoid fatigue, the insect, after completing one circle, turns around and moves so that it uses the other fore-leg. It snatches out any small stones that may be in its way. If the stone is too heavy to be got rid of in this summary fashion, it balances it on its back, and, carefully carrying it to the top of the boundary line, tumbles it over. If the stone is too large to remove, the ant-lion abandons the spot and builds its abode somewhere else. When completed, the pit is about two inches deep, and the ant buries itself in the bottom, with only its jaws visible. It is now on the watch, and it hasn't long to wait, before some insect, wandering about, stops on the edge of the pit, probably to see what has been going on. The treacherous sand gives way under it, and its struggles only help it to roll down into the jaws waiting to receive it.

Should recent rain hold the particles of sand together, so that the insect can sustain itself, and should it start to crawl to the top before its descent is completed, the ant-lion scrambles out and begins flinging dirt on the head of its prey with such skill, and in such quantities, that it is soon overwhelmed and devoured.

Having sucked the juices from the insect, the shell is flung to a considerable distance beyond the ramparts, so that other insects, passing that way, will not take alarm at the sight.

The ant-lion continues business for two years at the old stand, when it sinks deeper in the sand, spins a silken cocoon, is transformed into a chrysalis, and in three weeks emerges a perfect insect.

There are many wild bees in South Africa. They make their nests in the clefts of rocks, and the natives display a good deal of cunning in hunting them out and extracting the honey, which is carried in leather bags made for the purpose.

A great help to the South African in hunting the bees' nests is the honey-bird. Having found the retreat of the industrious insects, the honey-bird knows better than to disturb them, but looks out for some one to open the way for it. It will fly in front of the first person it sees, uttering sharp screams, and often pausing, as an invitation for him to follow. If he is slow, the bird becomes impatient and cries more excitedly than before.

When the bird has guided the native to the spot, it perches itself on a rock or bush and quietly waits until the store of sweets has been removed. The native does not forget his friend, but leaves the comb with the young bees for its reward, and you may be sure it enjoys a feast.

Bob Marshall and Dick Brownell were so interested in this bird that they offered a liberal price for its capture, but Pongo, Diedrick and the rest of the company were as much opposed as the other friendly natives, whom they occasionally saw, to its capture. They held it in such high esteem that they were unwilling to degrade it by imprisonment.

Among the rocks and stones was found an insect so exactly like them in color, and sometimes in shape, that it never would have been discovered had it not been in motion a moment before. When the birds alight near it in quest of food, the insect, which belongs to the *Gryllus* tribe (including the cricket, grasshopper, locust and the like), remains motionless. The vigilant bird may be but a few inches distant, but, with all its keenness of vision, is unable to distinguish the insect, which is thus saved on the principle of the chameleon, which has the power of accommodating to a certain extent its color to the object upon which it happens to have taken refuge.

The mantis assumes the most grotesque forms, resembling sometimes so closely the plant to which it clings, that only by motion can its real character be ascertained. It lays its eggs upon plants, and covers them with a glutinous substance which hardens and forms a case around the deposit. This is the insect known as "the walking leaf."

CHAPTER XLII.

THE CHAMELEON.

WHILE my task confines me mainly to a description of some of the most striking wonders in the natural history of the Old World, you must not suppose that the New World is lacking in that respect. What more odd-looking objects can be conceived than the belted armadillo of Central and South America, unless it is the ball-shaped armadillo? They are nocturnal in their habits, and can ill stand the glare of sunlight. If detected and shut off from its retreat, it rolls itself up like a ball, tucks its head under its chest, draws in its legs and awaits your pleasure. Its flesh is too strong for our palates, but the natives are quite fond of it.

The tamanoir, or ant-bear, is a native of Brazil and Paraguay as well as of Guinea. The little ant-eater is found among the trees of Central America. It may be said that the ant-bear always carries its umbrella with it, for its plumy tail affords it all the shade it wants, and when sleeping it looks like a bundle of hay flung on the ground.

There is a brown and golden bird in Mexico which has a way of ruffling up its feathers on the top of its head so that its crest resembles a beautiful flower. So perfect is the counterfeit that before long a bee comes buzzing along, and, stopping to sip some honey, is snapped up in a twinkling.

Arizona has a rattlesnake about four feet in length with eyes literally like points of fire. Once a bird catches sight of those eyes, and it is so fascinated that escape is impossible.

In Sinalva are gigantic wasps whose sting not only kills tarantulas, but mummifies and preserves them at the same time. The wasps then drag them off to their holes in the sand-hills, and lay their eggs in them, so that when the young are born, they feed on the tarantula. The blending of the wasp poison with that of the tarantula produces nutritious food for the young wasps.

A centipede builds a cactus fence around him when he lies down to sleep, as a protection against the tarantula, which will never crawl over cactus, but peeps over at the sleeper without daring to disturb him.

Even our plants partake of this amazing ingenuity. In Shasta county, California, grows the pitcher plant. Its pitcher is six inches long, more than an inch through, and with a lid. The sweet-smelling petals inside tempt bugs and insects, and down they go, the lid closing over and shutting them in. The little hair-barbs sticking downward prevent the insects from climbing out, even if it was not for the lid.

Having caught a good supply of insects, the pitcher plant absorbs them into its growth, thus proving that inanimate nature is sometimes able to outwit animate nature.

THE BELTED ARMADILLO

Although Equatorial Africa, Southern Africa and India are the homes of most of the wild beasts, birds and reptiles of the world, I must remind you that only a part of the curiosities of the Greatest Show on Earth come from those countries.

For instance, the odd-looking aye-aye, the sole representative of the *chiromyidæ* family, is a native of Madagascar. In size and shape it bears some resemblance to the domestic cat. Its teeth are large, and consist only of molars and incisors, and, I believe, it makes its nest among the trees.

Chameleons are found principally in the African continent, the common chameleon ranging only as far east as portions of Central Asia and Ceylon, and as far north as Spain. They are all insectivorous, move slowly, and possess the remarkable power of changing the color of their skin. This peculiarity depends partly upon the amount of light to which they are exposed, and partly on the emotions caused by fear or anger.

The martens are so common that I am quite sure you do not need any special description. I may say, however, that the pine-marten is so called because it is generally found in places where pine trees abound. It is shy, but is a little fury when driven at bay. The marten is an inveterate thief and robs every bird's nest in its neighborhood, frequently killing the old ones as well as the young. The impudent rogue often takes possession of the nest of a rook, hawk, crow, magpie, or other bird, and you need not be told that his victims dare not attempt to evict him.

THE BALL-SHAPED ARMADILLO.

Among my curiosities is a musk-ox, of whose peculiarities many people are ignorant. His chosen home is the frozen regions of the North, and you will find mention of him in the accounts of the voyages of the Arctic explorers. He is without a muzzle, rather small in size, low on his legs, and covered with such an immense quantity of wool and dark-brown hair that he appears to be much larger than he is. During the depth of winter this hair almost touches the ground.

There is a grayish-white place on his back called the saddle. His large horns are so flattened at the base that they cover his head like a hat, and sometimes weigh fifty or sixty pounds.

At certain seasons of the year, especially in each spring, the odor of the musk-ox's flesh is so strong that it can be detected on the knives used to cut its flesh. At other seasons the smell is almost absent, and it is excellent eating.

The short legs of the animal are more useful to him than you would suppose. He can run fast, and is as good a mountain climber as the goat. They gather in herds in September, for mutual protection against wolves, which are numerous in their haunts.

When musk-oxen are attacked by hunters they make formidable preparations. The younger animals are put in the center, while all the older ones surround them, and stand with their heads facing outward. They tear up the earth with their hoofs and horns, bellow, and seem eager for the fray.

Then the oldest bull of the herd stations himself at the head, as if about to lead a charge. On the approach of the hunters, he cautiously advances to reconnoiter, closely watching every movement. That duty completed, he saunters back to his fellows and awaits the opening of battle.

You would suppose, from all this flourish, that the

THE TAMANOIR

musk-oxen are among the bravest of quadrupeds. But at the first volley from the hunters the magnificent army of warriors wheel and scamper off in a panic, leaving their dead and wounded to take care of themselves.

However, I have told you enough about the different animals, and it is time I returned to the account of our friends, who had encamped for an indefinite period in Southern Africa. Bob and Dick devoted what leisure they gained to the study of the captives, and to attempt to cultivate their friendship. This was a task which, if not encouraging at all times, was entertaining.

The hartbeest seemed indifferent to their advances. He did not resent their overtures, but showed no appreciation of them, heedless whether they came near or not, so long as they did not allow him to want for food.

The leopard kittens were as frisky as a couple of young domestic cats. They were continually frolicking, tumbling about and playfully using their teeth and claws upon each other. They did not object to a little caressing, but occasionally gave the lads a taste of what they would soon be able to do with the weapons furnished by nature.

Had the juvenile lion been favored with a brother or sister, he would have displayed an equal degree of friskiness, but, though alone, he appeared to be satisfied and comfortable, caring nothing for the loss of his parents, so long as his rations were forthcoming.

THE AYE-AYE

Dick Brownell was sure the little fellow was beginning to learn to recognize and show him affection, but Bob scouted the idea. The creature, he insisted, hadn't enough sense to discriminate, else it would have fixed upon *him* as the object of its friendship.

Bob was willing to admit that the porcupine displayed a partiality for his cousin, and he urged him to take the plaything in his arms and fondle it, with a view of cultivating its lovely disposition.

It was hard to look upon the mother giraffe and its young one without being touched. They showed no fear on the approach of any of their captors, and the parent sometimes reached down its long neck to invite Bob or Dick to pat its forehead. The little one would have followed them about the encampment, had they allowed it freedom. It surely was as contented as if running with its mother over the plains or through the open jungles.

Since there was little expected of the others, our friends were not disappointed.

There was nothing done in the way of hunting on the day succeeding the visit from the baboons. The captured one was so surly that none of the captors attempted any advances, but he was left to sulk alone until he should recover his spirits, if indeed he ever would do so.

But the looks of the heavens presaged a tempest, and, as I have already stated, they are sometimes of the most fearful character in that portion of the Dark Continent.

Extra care was taken in preparing for it. The stockade was examined at every point, and, where there appeared any sign of weakness, it was strength-ened : the wagons were made secure and the horses strongly tethered, the oxen being left to themselves, since, the greater the disturbance, the closer were they likely to cling to camp.

Whatever hopes the hunters may have had that the impending storm would pass by were removed at sunset, when in the northern horizon arose a black cloud, which rapidly climbed and overspread the sky. A cool breeze fanned the faces of all who were watching the coming of the storm, and the animals, as is often the case, showed alarm at the strange appearance of the heavens.

A big fire had been started near the middle of the camp, though it was expected that the storm would drench it out or scatter the brands, like chaff, across the plain.

THE MARTENS

It will be perceived that there never was more need of watchfulness than the present time. The war of the elements would arouse all the wild animals within its area, not a particle of moonlight could find its way through the murky atmosphere, and what light the fire gave was liable to be extinguished from the cause named.

Although Mr. Godkin and Jack Harvey had been on duty a good part of the preceding night, they decided to keep awake until the storm should exhaust itself. They had spent a portion of the afternoon in sleep, and, since they were confident that the tempest would not last more than an hour or two, the task did not promise to be a severe one.

They had as their assistants Bormo, Valmur and Govozy, who were to do their best to keep the fire going, and to prevent any stampede on the part of the animals.

Bob and Dick wanted sleep, and crept into the wagon where they were accustomed to make their beds at night. The canvas over them was so strong that they were confident it would not fail them as a roof; it had been through some of the most violent gales that can be conceived, without suffering damage.

The lads did not withdraw from their friends until the wind was whistling powerfully through the camp, causing some excitement among the animals, captive

"We are Ready"

as well as domestic. The horses whinnied and moved around their circumscribed space, as if seeking for shelter.

It was not any special fear the owners felt of their flight during the night beyond recall, but it was at such times when there was no moon that they were liable to be visited by lions. It was the wish of the hunters to keep all the animals within the area of the camp-fire's illumination, so as to hold them as safe as possible from marauding enemies.

CHAPTER XLIII.

OUT IN THE NIGHT.

AN AFRICAN TEMPEST

THERE is something soothing in the sound of the wind at night, when it moans around your house, and you hear the snow sifting against the window panes, or rustling among the leafless branches. Little possibility of our friends being lulled to sleep by anything in the nature of a snow-storm, though the sudden cooling of the heated air and the violent puffs of wind suggested the thought; but they had not journeyed all the way from Port Natal to learn the nature of an African storm.

"We're going to catch it," said Dick, noticing how rapidly the wind was rising.

"I don't think it will be worse than some of those tempests in the Drakenberg Mountains — *helloa!*"

Without the least warning a vivid flash of lightning clove the sky from horizon to zenith, followed instantly by a crashing peal of thunder that shook the ground as if by an earthquake.

The animals in the camp, young and old, tame and wild, were startled into cries, making a series of discords which deepened the shock, and brought the boys to a sitting posture, causing them to look affrightedly around in the gloom.

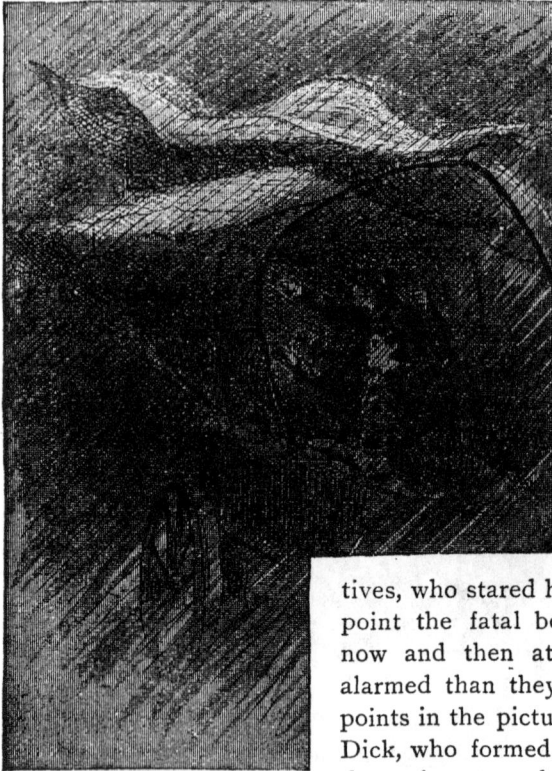

"It Vanished in the Gloom."

The strong canvas cover shut off their view in most directions, but through the opening at the rear they had a view of the camp as shown by the glare of the fire.

The sight was picturesque and striking. The wind, which was blowing more strongly every minute, had fanned the blaze, whose reflection showed almost every member of the camp.

The handsome face of Jack Harvey, as he stood erect, looking around with an inquiring expression, as if to make sure that everything was safe; the pale, thoughtful Mr. Godkin; the sallow countenances of the natives, who stared here and there, uncertain from what point the fatal bolt would come, glancing furtively now and then at the animals, who were no less alarmed than they: these were the most prominent points in the picture which met the eyes of Bob and Dick, who formed no insignificant part of the scene themselves, as they peered out from the canvas-covered wagon.

Naturally, the expectation was that such a prodigious electric explosion would be quickly followed by others, but the exchange between earth and sky seemed to have restored the equilibrium for a time, and the darkness remained unbroken by any blinding flashes.

Suddenly every one was startled by a rattling as of a million bullets. Hailstones of large size came down with such fury that every person ran for shelter, and the animals bellowed and whinnied with terror and pain.

Fortunately, however, the flurry lasted but a few minutes, when the fall of hail-stones ceased as abruptly as it had begun. Mr. Godkin, Jack Harvey and the natives returned to their stations, while the boys crouched in the wagon and wondered what was coming next.

The wind blew strongly, and now and then large drops of rain pattered around them, with a noise like that of the hailstones, which lay in winrows about camp.

"We didn't make preparations for anything like this," said Bob, "and I'm afraid our captives have suffered. If some of the little ones got pelted on the head with those stones, they may have had their brains knocked out."

"How about the baboon?"

"He's too thick-headed to be hurt. I wouldn't care if he did get a rap or two, it might take some of the ugliness out of him."

"I don't wonder that such a flash of lightning — my gracious!"

At that instant, a volley of wind shot under the wagon cover and whipped it from its fastenings. The boys made an instinctive grab for it, but were unable to check its flight. They caught a glimpse of the white sheet, whipping and turning like a sail in a gale, as it vanished in the gloom.

So strong was the wind that, as the canvas struck the earth, it rolled and tumbled and doubled over itself in the oddest way, but all the time skimmed along the ground with a speed hardly less than the wind itself.

"It'll never do to lose that!" exclaimed Dick, leaping out of the wagon and starting on a run after it.

Such was his haste that he never thought of taking his gun along. Fortunately, Bob was more thoughtful, and, as he sprang from the rear of the vehicle, but a few paces behind his cousin, he had his rifle with him.

The whole proceeding was reckless and uncalled-for. Had either Mr. Godkin or Jack Harvey seen it, they would have ordered the boys back again on the instant. The roll of canvas had to go but a short distance to pass beyond sight. It was not likely to be carried far, however, and could be recovered on the morrow.

But you know how impulsive the most sensible boy is at times. It was natural that they should make the attempt to recover the canvas, though Dick had not run far before he felt he had committed a mistake.

The gloom around him was so profound that he was literally unable to see a foot in any direction. The only means of guidance was the glimmer of the camp-fire behind them, which shone over the plain like the eye of some great ogre.

By and by the electricity began to accumulate disproportionately, either in the sky or earth, so disturbing the equilibrium that faint flashes appeared, accompanied by mutterings of thunder.

"The lightning will come," was the thought of Dick, "and then I'll gain a glimpse of what I'm looking for; it can't be far off."

Inasmuch as it was evident that it was only a waste of time to continue forward, the youth came to a halt and waited for the illumination which was to end the wild hunt. Dick was unaware that his cousin had followed him, for his own flight was so hurried that he paid no heed to anything except the skurrying canvas, which he hoped to catch before it went too far.

But Bob was hard after his comrade, though he could see nothing of him, after his leap from the wagon and dash into the darkness. Not doubting that he was close at his heels, Bob kept at a brisk trot until he must have gone several hundred yards, when he stopped.

"Helloa! Dick," he called, "we may as well give it up and wait till morning; don't you think so?"

To his surprise, there was no answer, and he repeated the call in a louder tone, keeping it up until his lungs could stand no more.

It cannot be said that Bob was alarmed, though he was puzzled to understand how they could have got beyond each other's hearing in so short a time. It is improbable that they were far apart at the moment, but the wind was blowing with great force directly across the space between them, and carried his voice away from the ears for which it was intended.

Bob was shrewd enough to understand the most likely cause of his failure to locate his cousin, though even that seemed hardly sufficient, and he thought an additional reason must exist.

Finding he could not make himself heard, he turned about and looked at the camp-fire, which was burning at no great distance. He could see figures moving in front of it, and one of them struck him as being that of his cousin.

"That's it," he said to himself; "Dick has awakened to his blunder and gone back; I'll do the same."

His situation was such that his view of the camp was unobstructed, the stockade being in another direction. It was therefore "clear sailing," as it may be called, and the thought that he would experience any delay did not enter his head.

But Bob had walked only a short distance, when he became convinced that some animal was between him and camp, and that it was moving in the same direction. Now and then it was like a flickering shadow, disappearing so quickly that it was impossible to form any idea of its precise form or nature.

Thrown in relief for the moment against the saffron flames far beyond, its form was of the most shadowy and indistinct character.

"I wonder what it can be," he asked himself a dozen times, while moving softly forward; "I'm mighty glad I brought my gun along, but as it is, I don't want to stumble over it. I'm glad, too, that Dick didn't forget his rifle," he added, with never a suspicion that his friend was abroad in the night unarmed.

The faint flutterings of lightning did little more than make the intense gloom visible. Bob hoped for a flash that would tell him the precise nature of the danger — as he believed it to be — in front of him, and the thought that such an illumination was likely to come every instant caused him to slacken his pace and advance with the utmost caution.

It seemed unwise to him, even though well armed, to follow in the track of the animal, and he, therefore, made a wide circuit to the left, with a view of flanking the beast. He continued until he had gone so far that the stockade threatened to interfere with his vision, when he once more started in a direct line, all his senses on the alert.

In a brief while, the lad feared he had committed a serious blunder, for so long as matters kept the form they had a few minutes before, he held the unknown in front, where he could, to a certain degree, keep it under his eye, but by flanking it, the probabilities were he had given the beast a chance to get behind him, the very situation which a wild animal desires when stealing upon its victim.

Bob's discomfort was increased by a distinct growl which came from some point near at hand, though, for the life of him, he could not make sure of the direction.

As you may suppose, the youth, by this time, was thoroughly scared, for he was in a perilous position indeed. He cocked his Winchester, and braced himself to receive a charge from *some* quarter, the feeling being that horrible one that comes over a man when he is absolutely at a loss to know the point whence a crashing blow is to descend.

Braced thus, Bob glanced around in the impenetrable gloom, hoping that the ear, if not the eye, would give him the knowledge on which his life depended.

Peering in the direction of the camp-fire, he was unable to see anything resembling the outlines of an animal, and he could feel no doubt, therefore, that his enemy was on his flank, or what was more likely, directly behind, and creeping upon him.

CHAPTER XLIV.

PEERING OUT INTO THE GLOOM.

I CANNOT conceive of any situation more trying to the nerves than that of Bob Marshall. Had it been daytime, when he was able to locate his foe, he would have been pleased rather than otherwise, for the spice of danger would have given a pleasant thrill, just as had been the case more than once while on his way to the camp in South Africa. Now, while his dependence was on his sense of hearing, he listened intently for the growl that he had caught a few minutes before. But the warning was not repeated.

I am glad to say that my young friend's nerves were not kept at this painful tension for any length of time, though the period seemed ten-fold greater than it was.

The flickering lightning suddenly spread into one vivid flame, which illumined earth and sky with a distinctness greater than that of midday, while the appalling crash, as before, shook the very earth.

It so happened that at the moment the shock came, Bob had turned half way 'round, and was looking directly behind him. The sight which met his eyes could not have been more terrifying.

Less than fifty feet off, a huge lion was crouching on the earth, and stealthily creeping toward him. A few more seconds, and he would be close enough to make his leap, which would land him upon Bob's shoulders, who would be as helpless as an infant.

There was the single revelation, and then instantly all became profound gloom again. Lion, earth, sky, all were swallowed up in darkness.

The distance to camp was short, and the natural instinct of the young sportsman was to dash thither at full speed; but to do so was fatal, since the lion would have been on him before he could have traveled one-quarter the way.

No; there was but one course to take, and, knowing the value of every second, Bob Marshall did not hesitate.

Although unable to see the king of beasts, he knew precisely where he was, and he was so accustomed to handling his rifle, that he could aim without glancing along the barrel.

It would be too much to say that he was able to fire with anything like the accuracy he would have shown in the daytime, but he was confident of "getting there," all the same.

Up went the gun to his shoulder, and Bob let fly with five shots, as rapidly as he could pump them from his weapon. That number, he felt, ought to be sufficient, and prudence told him to keep a reserve for other contingencies that might arise before he could reach his friends.

Lowering his rifle, Bob quickly retreated several steps, and then listened a full minute, to hear the dying struggles of his foe.

While engaged in firing, he fancied he detected some unusual sounds, and he was sure of catching them again, since the growl that had reached him proved that the wind was in the right direction.

To his astonishment, however, nothing was heard above the gale roaring about his ears.

"Can it be I missed him?" he asked himself with a shudder; "he may have changed his posture; if so, he'll be on me right away."

Once again the lightning came to his aid. The flash was not as overpowering as before, but it was enough to tell him a most gratifying truth.   By one of those strange accidents which now and then come to us in this world, the first bullet fired by Bob Marshall had penetrated the brain of the lion and killed him.   The four balls sent after the first had all found an entrance into the immense head, and any one of them would have been enough to cause death.   So I may say that the youth was guilty of a waste of ammunition.

It was a vast relief, indeed, to him, who was wise enough to improve his chances at once.   There might be other wild beasts near at hand, and it would never do to count on the aid of the lightning, that had just done him such a good turn.

Without glancing in any direction, Bob broke into a run for camp, his feelings quickly changing to a panic as is often the case when we start to flee from some danger.

He almost fell headlong among his friends.

"Where did you come from?" asked the astonished Jack Harvey.

"If you had been going a little faster you wouldn't have been able to stop yet awhile," added the wondering Mr. Godkin.

"I think you would run, too, if you found a lion at your heels," replied the youth, somewhat abashed at the exhibition he had made.

"Was that your gun we heard?"

"Yes; didn't Dick tell you where I was?"

"No; we haven't seen Dick," said Jack; "where is he?"

"I suppose he is in the wagon," remarked the director, his manner showing his uneasiness.

Bob ran thither with little hope of finding his cousin.   Of course he was absent, and Bob came back with the announcement that he had fled, and that his gun had been left behind, there being enough light from the camp-fire to show that disquieting fact.

Jack Harvey was vexed.

"How long before you tenderfeet will gain enough sense to take care of yourselves?"

Bob felt the reproof was deserved, but his whole thoughts now were of his absent friend.   Except for his own experience with the lion, his alarm would have been far less, but the night, as I have shown, was just such a one as was likely to bring out the dreaded beasts against which the hunters had taken every precaution at their command.

The gale had threatened to blow away their fire, but, by heaping on the wood, it roared and crackled with a vigor that threw out a more extended illumination than before.

All the oxen, horses and goats were in sight—a fact which they seemed to appreciate, some of them showing a disposition to crowd still closer, as though well aware that danger was abroad.

The violent tempest had brought each native from his sleeping-quarters, and they were giving their efforts toward the protection of the property of their employers.   Orak was probably the most active, and he made several circuits around the stockade to see that the captives were safe. The inhabitants of the cages, too, seemed to feel there was security in the glow of the fire, and they crowded as near as they could get to it.

"HE ALMOST FELL HEADLONG AMONG HIS FRIENDS"

They formed a singular picture, the older ones showing by their looks their alarm. Those whom a short time before they had viewed as their enemies had been transformed by the elements into friends, to whom they appealed for protection.

The younger ones slept in contentment through the fearful turmoil, but the mother giraffe stood close to the side of her huge cage, her odd head groping along the stakes, as though seeking some opening through which she might force her way closer to her friends.

The baboon shared the alarm, and, though he could not quite rid himself of his surliness, he looked as if he would have welcomed the opportunity to crowd a little nearer to those who had used him so roughly but a short time before.

Mr. Godkin asked Bob several sharp questions, to make sure that no point was lost. He, too, was impatient, that Dick, of whose judgment he had formed such a good opinion, should have forgotten himself in the excitement of the moment.

To him the inexcusable fact was that he had pushed out in the night, when he must have had time to realize his mistake. But he was a philosopher, and he felt that it was not the time to scold, so long as the youth was in danger. He would settle with him when he came back — *provided he ever did come back.*

Now, you will readily understand the bad feature of this business: it lay in the continued absence of Dick Brownell.

If he were unharmed he could not have gone far, without awaking to the absurdity of hunting for an object which it was impossible to locate.

It occurred to his friends that he might have counted on the help of the lightning, which, fortunately, had told Bob Marshall of his danger from the crouching lion, but, if such were the case, it was no credit to Dick's sagacity.

It was that lion that threw his friends into their distressing misgiving.

They reasoned that, since the absent lad had the ligth of the camp-fire to direct his return, as did his cousin, he would have availed himself of that means, had he been in a situation to do so.

That the king of beasts was abroad that night was proven by the experience of Bob Marshall. If *he* had come in collision with one of them, what more probable than that Dick had been threatened by the same danger? Since, too, the former would have perished but for his Winchester, what was likely to be the fate of the other, who was without any fire-arms except his revolver, which was almost useless in such an emergency?

These were the grave questions asked by each of his friends who stood in the light of the camp-fire, discussing the question whether it was in their power to do anything to aid him.

"I'd mount Apache, and ride all the way to the Congo to help that young tenderfoot out of a scrape," said the Texan, "and after I caught him, I would give him a trouncing for playing such a trick."

"There isn't anything that all of us would not try to do to benefit him," quietly added the director, "but that isn't the question; it is whether we have the power to extend him help."

"Can't you think of something?" asked poor Bob, almost beside himself with grief; "I will die if I have to stay here idle."

"You know how foolish it was for you to hope to find that canvas in the darkness; it is ten times more hopeless for us to think of finding Dick."

"But he may not be far off; he may be wounded, and lying on the plain."

"But *where?*" was the terrifying question.

"Ah!" muttered Jack, the exclamation caused by the rain which now began to descend copiously; "*that* isn't going to make it very comfortable for him."

"Nor for us either," added Mr. Godkin.

The three peered out in the gloom, looking, listening, hoping and praying; and that was all they could do, for an emotion akin to despair was in each heart.

CHAPTER XLV.

WHATEVER feeling of resentment or impatience might have been entertained by our friends toward Dick Brownell soon vanished in the anxiety for his welfare. Sleep was out of the question, until toward morning, when Bob sank into an unquiet slumber that lasted until daylight.

During the long, dark hours that silence reigned through the camp, Jack Harvey and Carl Godkin smoked their pipes and discussed what they could do, if anything, for the absent one. So long as night lasted, they must remain idle, the only resource being that of heaping fuel on the fire, so that the light should penetrate the gloom as far as possible, and afford a guide to the youth, if so be it was in his power to struggle toward it.

The course which Jack and Mr. Godkin had decided upon was the natural one that would have suggested itself to any person in their situation. As soon as light came, they would set out to hunt for the absent lad.

The party was to consist of the two gentlemen named, Bob Marshall and Pongo, the Bushman, all of whom would be mounted and fully armed. During their absence the camp was to be left in charge of Diedrick and Abdallah, who were not to go away themselves nor allow any of the other natives to do so.

The director favored leaving Pongo also, but the Texan saw a probable use for him, and fortunately took him along.

It will be observed that the cowboy had now entered upon a duty similar in many respects to that in which he had been thoroughly trained in his own country. The work of capturing wild animals was suspended for the time, while the four engaged in the hunt for a person, just as he had done when on his Indian campaigns in Arizona and New Mexico.

The attempt was to be made, too, in a country of savages who execrated white men. Though these natives widely differed from the American Indians, there was still a resemblance between them: the struggle might take the turn of a contest between the cunning of the white man and that of the black man.

While Mr. Godkin and Bob Marshall believed that Dick's absence was due to wild beasts, and while Jack admitted the probabilities pointed that way, he was still hopeful he had fallen into the hands of a company of natives, from whom he could be regained by strategy or force. His own experience with the savages was the main foundation of this hope. Despite the impatience of Bob, Jack would not allow any departure until all had eaten a substantial breakfast and swallowed a cup of strong coffee apiece. It was a principle with him never to enter upon such an enterprise without a hearty meal, if it was possible to secure one.

The sky was beautifully clear, and the coolness of the air, due to the storm of the night before, rendered the day one of the most delightful they had experienced since their entrance into the country. It would soon become fervid again, but they could not have asked for a more favorable morning for their work.

The first proceeding was to ride to the top of the adjoining elevation, from which they made their survey of the surrounding neighborhood, directly after their arrival.

"What I want you to do," explained Jack, "is to use your eyes. Scan every part of the horizon and tell me whether you see anything of a party of men, or any signs of a camp-fire."

"THE THREE LOOKED LONG AND CLOSELY."

The four engaged in this task, and for a quarter of an hour not a word was spoken by any one. Mr. Godkin had his glass to assist, but at the end of the time, when the Texan asked each in turn, the same answer was received: not the first evidence had been detected of a party of natives in their field of vision.

"You are sure of that?" asked Jack, with an odd expression, addressing himself particularly to the director.

"There can be no doubt of it," he replied, puzzled to understand his full meaning.

"I thought them glasses would help you better, and, as for you, Pongo, I am disappointed."

"That seems to be the situation of all of us," remarked Bob, who was in anything but a hopeful mood.

"I s'pose it's all in a chap's training," was the comment of Jack, who now pointed to the south.

"If you'll follow the way I'm p'inting," he explained, "you'll see a little patch of jungle, covering only a few acres. It isn't far from the stream which winds close to it. Now, all fix your eyes on the sky just above it, and tell me what you observe."

Thus directed, the three looked long and closely, the director once more calling his binocular into use.

"All that I notice," he said, "is the faintest possible appearance of a tiny cloud, seemingly resting on the tree-tops."

"Well," said Jack, "that cloud, that I s'pose you all now see, is what is left of the smoke of a fire that was burning among them trees last night. A party of wild men was there, and may be there still; there's where we must go to look for the youngster." The rest, including Pongo himself, looked admiringly at the Texan, who had discerned that which was beyond their power of vision, and had read its meaning aright.

"I don't see why you didn't take his trail from the camp and follow it," said Bob. But Jack shook his head.

"No living man could have done that, though I s'pose a bloodhound might. It rained so hard after the youngster left that there wasn't the least sign you could have counted on."

There was something in the cool self-confidence of the cowboy which inspired his friends similarly. The Bushman, though he did not speak, showed something of it in the glow of his sallow face and the sparkle of his bright black eye, while Mr. Godkin and Bob did not hesitate to make known their admiration.

But, like those true scouts of the border, Jack Harvey was modest, and the compliments he received rolled from him like water from a duck's back.

Those fellows lose no time in getting down to business. Almost in the same breath that Jack announced his purpose, he had turned the head of his mustang down the slope and was riding, at a swift gallop, toward the patch of jungle, his companions maintaining their places beside him, and asking him many questions, which he willingly answered, though he kept his keen eyes fixed, almost continually, on the wood, as though he suspected some new development would take place before he could reach it.

The dead body of the lion lay where it had fallen, but the horsemen did not go near it, for there was no inducement to do so and time was too valuable. But that glass, as it went from hand to hand, and swept the visible plain, was searching for another body, which the whites dreaded to find, and which, to their inexpressible relief, they did not find.

The theory advanced by Jack Harvey was based on sound sense, though he admitted that it was confronted by some grave objections.

"In the first place," said the Texan, as they rode at their rapid pace, so close together that conversation was easy, "that 'ere young scamp has gone so fur that he passed over that hill right ahead of us."

"What of that? The distance isn't great."

"I'll show you in a minute," replied Jack, who, when they reached the bottom of the slope, on the other side, asked his companions to turn their heads and look at their own camp.

Making the attempt, they found it was not in sight; the hill shut it from view. It followed, therefore, that if they were riding in the footsteps of Dick Brownell, he had reached a point, not far from his friends, where the light of his own camp-fire could serve him no longer as a guide.

A STARTLING DISCOVERY.

"But, if he looked toward them trees right ahead," added Jack, "he would have catched sight of the fire burning there."

"But that was in a course opposite to his own camp," said Bob.

"You know how easy it is for any one to get completely turned 'round, so that he can't get things straight for the life of him."

While this is a truth beyond question, the difficulty lay in the improbability that Dick Brownell, in the first place, would have gone far enough in the darkness to take him to the other side of the hill, and that, having gone that far, with the knowledge that his friends were behind him, he should have formed the belief, almost on the instant, as he must have done, that a camp-fire in the other direction was his real destination.

Jack's explanation, or rather theory, was that the youngster had not held such belief, but, having caught the glimmer of another light than that of his friends, he had been led by his own curiosity to go forward and investigate, and, having done that, he had fallen into the hands of savages.

This presupposed a thoughtlessness on the part of Dick Brownell that was the main obstacle to the theory. Indeed, it could not, in the nature of things, be satisfactory to those who knew him so well, but who of necessity were compelled to hold the supposition until some proof of its falsity should present itself.

Having reached the piece of jungle, it was easy to locate the site of the encampment held there only a few hours before. There were the ashes, bones and remnants, such as always mark the scene of such a halt.

Jack Harvey was out of his saddle before his mustang came to a halt, and, stooping down, scrutinized the ground with a keenness of vision which no one of his company could equal, though Pongo came the nearest to it. He, like Mr. Godkin and Bob, engaged in the same effort, no one speaking, and often glancing slyly at Jack, to see how he was making out.

As at the time when all were investigating the cause of the raft lying against the river bank, he moved entirely around the spot where the fire had been kindled, so that not a square inch of the circuit escaped him.

Almost at the moment he completed this task, which took several minutes, since he walked slowly, in a bent posture, he suddenly straightened up and exclaimed:

"*Dick came to this spot, and was captured by wild men!*"

CHAPTER XLVI.

THE GLIMMER OF A CAMP-FIRE.

MEANWHILE, let us see how Master Dick Brownell made out. I have said several times that he did an almost inexcusable thing in starting to regain the canvas cover that the gale had whisked from over his head.

I am quite sure you will agree with me, and yet I am obliged to say that the young fellow, almost at the moment he reached the same conclusion, was successful in finding the missing article.

Of course it was wholly accidental, but it so came about that while he was moving carefully through the darkness, waiting for a friendly flash of lightning to give its aid, his boot became entangled in something which threw him forward on his face.

In his efforts to scramble to his feet, he knew from the feel of the article that it was the canvas.

"Well, I declare!" he exclaimed, "but that is what I call a piece of luck. I don't think Bob will laugh at me when he sees me coming back bearing the wagon-cover in my arms."

Bending over, he began gathering the awkward bundle together, finding it so much heavier and more cumbersome than he supposed that his exultation was considerably modified.

"It would be safe to leave it here till morning," he thought, "but that would never do — so here goes!"

With no little effort he slung the stuff over his shoulder, and walked some distance without trouble. Then one end began to drag, and, catching under his feet, down he went again, half angry, as was natural.

He now began rolling the canvas into a more compact form, helped thereat by the friendly flash which saved Bob Marshall's life. Of course Dick did not hear the call of his cousin, and the contrary wind carried the reports of the rifle beyond reach of his ears. Thus he was altogether unaware of the solicitude of Bob, who, but for the lion, would have continued his attempts to find him.

Dick tried to keep his bearings, though his annoyance from the awkward bundle caused him several times to forget the danger of going astray. But he had walked only a short distance when his foot plunged into an ant-hole, and he was thrown forward with such violence that he feared for the moment his leg was broken.

"This is a bigger job than I imagined," he said to himself, "but I mean to fight it out on this line if it takes several weeks."

Up to this moment he had thought nothing of the personal peril involved in a venture of this kind. Had he brought his gun with him he would have found it a hard task to carry the weapon and his bundle, but now, after shouldering his load once more, he suddenly recalled what had been said at the camp-fire about the expected visit from lions.

"The best thing I can do," he reflected, "is to get home as soon as I can, for I've wandered some distance from camp."

The thought was still in his mind when he was frightened by the same cause that gave his cousin such a shock, almost at the same moment: it was the unmistakable growl of a wild beast in front of him.

His sense of hearing told him the latter fact, but he was so much farther from the camp than his cousin that his eyes could be of no help at all.

Dick stood still, with the deliberate conviction that of all the mistakes he had ever made the present one was the greatest.

He had his knife and his revolver — weapons which he knew well how to handle in an emergency, but they were not likely to be of much assistance in the impending fight in the dark.

While he was hesitating as to what step he should take, if indeed he could take any, the same streak of lightning which told Bob Marshall the nature of the peril that threatened him, made the same revelation to his cousin.

Still worse, the lion that Dick saw was nigh enough to make his spring and was in the very act of doing so. The youth could not have seen anything more distinctly than he did that appalling sight.

Instead of drawing his pistol, Dick flung up his arms, so as to spread out the canvas, and held it before him as a shield against the impending shock. He knew the lion was coming, and he used the only protection at command.

Now there is nothing so terrifying to a wild animal as a danger which it cannot understand. You have noticed how the appearance of some uncouth object will frighten a horse which is gentle in the presence of danger twice as great.

So long as Dick Brownell remained himself in looks, he was just the kind of a supper to please a large and hungry lion, but when the latter saw him assume the shape of some mysterious creature, with large, white wings, he was scared almost out of his senses. Nothing could induce the king of beasts to attack such a frightful animal, unless he himself were pushed into a corner and forced to fight.

The snarling growl which followed this precaution on the part of Dick apprised him, for the first time, of his singular success; he had succeeded in doing that which seemed impossible: he had frightened the lion.

That certainly was strong reason for satisfaction, but the youth could by no means feel certain the fright would last. The beast, still muttering, trotted several steps, looking back in the gloom, as if he expected pursuit.

Had Dick known it, or rather had he possessed the light to guide him, he could have completed his work by dashing after the lion, swinging and swirling the canvas, and uttering frightful cries. The beast would have fled at the top of his speed, and never halted till a long way off.

But the youth could see nothing of his foe, so long as the Egyptian darkness lasted; and the latter, finding he was not pursued, regained enough courage to stop a short distance, and peering back, as well as his species can in the gloom, he must have wondered that he was spared by the monster.

Possibly some inkling of the truth entered his thick head, for he not only remained motionless several minutes, but turned about to renew his attack. Instead of approaching, however, in a straight line, he circled over the plain, so as to get to the rear of his intended victim — an act that is in accord with the sneaking nature of the king of beasts.

Fortunately, Dick was not unmindful of this peculiar peril, and was guarding, as best he could, against it. The beast emitted no growl, but the lightning, which had done the youth more than one good turn that evening, favored the lad again, by showing his enemy in the very act of flanking him.

"HE CAUGHT THE STAR-LIKE TWINKLE"

Dick now did what he ought to have done before. Spreading out the canvas, so as to make it look as strange as possible, he began flapping his wings, like some immense bird, and, uttering the most dismal cries, headed for the animal that was so anxious to dine upon him. That was altogether more than the lion wanted, and away he scampered.

It was out of Dick's power to learn whither the beast went, but he kept up his pursuit, knowing it was the wisest thing to do, though he was in constant dread of colliding with some object, animate or inanimate. He paused at intervals, and looked and listened, but neither saw nor heard anything.

"I guess it's about time I went back to camp," was his natural conclusion; "I expect I will catch it from Mr. Godkin and Jack, for running off in this way, without my gun."

He was breathing rapidly from his severe exertion, for he had run a long distance. He recalled that part of it had been up and down hill, and it seemed to him that once he had splashed through some water.

Be that as it may, Dick Brownell awoke to the unpleasant fact that he had wandered out of sight of the camp of his friends. He scanned every point of the compass, but in no direction could he catch so much as a glimmer of a light.

As you may suppose, he was in anything but a comfortable state of mind. It was alarming enough to learn that he was lost in an exceedingly dangerous country, with many hours of darkness before him, and without an effective weapon with which to defend himself.

"Well, I have gone and done it," he muttered with a sigh, conscious of a faintness which made him feel like sitting down until it passed over. "This is about the worst scrape of my life. I'll hold on to the cloth anyway, for it has proved too good a friend to cast aside."

It began raining, and he found the canvas was a friend in more than one respect. By gathering the folds around his shoulders, it served as a protection against the wet. The air grew chillier, and, but for it, he would have been in anything but a comfortable state.

This was nothing, however, to compare to his wretchedness over the feeling that he was lost, and that, in all probability, he would not be able to find his way to camp until the rising of the morrow's sun.

What should he do?

He was tempted to lie down, and, wrapping himself as best he could in the canvas, bear it all in grim silence.

But he was not yet rid of his fear of the lion, and, if the beast was not still lurking in the neighborhood, others of his kind or of an equally dangerous species were likely to discover him.

One of the hardest things to do at such times is to sit or stand still, and wait for the minutes to grow into hours. Dick was unable to do that, so he kept trudging on, peering in every direction for the welcome glimmer that would prove a beacon light indeed to him.

The rain soon ceased, but the gloom was, if possible, more profound than ever. He was literally going it blind, and probably he would have come to a stop after a brief while, but for the fact that he found himself ascending quite an elevation.

"This must be the hill I came over when chasing the lion," was his thought; "it hid the camp from my sight and ought to reveal it when I reach the top — helloa!"

With a thrill of pleasure, he caught the star-like twinkle of a point of light, and felt that his troubles were substantially ended.

CHAPTER XLVII.

A CLEVER STRATAGEM.

ALL of Dick Brownell's miseries and sufferings were forgotten the moment he caught the glimmer of the camp-fire through the chilling darkness. He was willing enough to receive the scolding that he knew awaited him, but never was the glow of a beacon light hailed with greater gladness by the storm-tossed mariner than was the twinkle which reached him through the dismal night.

It struck the youth that he must have followed some strange paths after his novel attack on the lion, for he had not gone far before he found himself tramping through a lot of tall grass, apparently of the same kind as that growing along the stream that had sheltered the wild men and baboons.

The possibility of plunging headlong into the river itself caused him some uneasiness, but the listening ear could detect nothing of the roar that would have been present, the gale having entirely died out.

The storm was over. There were faint flickerings of lightning now and then, but not enough to produce the faintest rumbling of thunder. No rain fell, and, through the rifts of black, overhanging clouds, Dick fancied he detected the faint gleam of several stars.

Such storms as I have attempted to describe are violent, but of short duration. They often inflict great damage, but, fortunately, soon expend their fury.

Dick Brownell underwent every degree of imaginable surprise during his hunting expedition in Southern Africa, but he agrees with me that none of them exceeded that which came to him within a half hour after his discovery of the light of the camp-fire, shining across the plain.

The first occurrence that opened the way to the shook of astonishment was the knowledge that, instead of tramping across the open country, as he had been doing all along, he had entered the edge of a jungle.

"What does this mean?" he asked, as the limbs brushed his face.

The puzzling fact was that the light of the camp-fire was still in plain view.

The next shock was when he saw that the reason for this was that he was within a hundred feet of the blaze which had seemed until that moment to be at an indefinite distance. It was in fair view, because it was burning just beyond and close to the margin of the wood, which was open to an unusual extent, so open, indeed, that he had not noticed the few intervening limbs until he looked the second time.

The inevitable corollary of this discovery was that it was not the camp-fire of his friends that he had approached !

All doubt was removed when he observed eight or ten natives, similar in some respects to those described by Jack Harvey, gathered around the blaze, which was burning brightly in a small space. They were naked, except around the loins, had bushy hair, wore huge rings in their ears and noses, carried spears, and were as hideous travesties upon the human form divine as can be imagined.

Since the camp-fire of Dick's friends was out of sight of this group, it was clear that Mr. Godkin and his companions knew nothing of the natives, though it was not so clear that the latter were not aware of the location of the others.

The wild men, as it seems proper to call them, were lolling on the ground and smoking, with the exception of two of their number, who were busily employed in cooking supper. The carcass of some animal was suspended on a strong stick, which, in turn, was supported by forked supports, so far removed from the flames that they were safe against being burned apart.

After the carcass had been exposed to the fire until it was affected by the heat, the two savages turned the stick so as to expose the other side. Inasmuch as the longitudinal support ran through the middle of the body, it was easy to subject every part of it to an equal degree of heat.

In short, the process resembled that which is sometimes seen in our own country when a party of hunters or farmers engage in roasting the carcass of a hog or some big game.

The other wild men, who were lolling on the ground, seemed to find much comfort in smoking their long-stemmed pipes. They showed no impatience for their supper, though, by this time, the hour had become well advanced.

What produced the awful impression that suddenly flashed upon Dick Brownell, it is impossible to say, but, all at once, he asked himself the question whether that body which was being prepared with such thoroughness did not belong to the same race as those that were turning every side of it so regularly to the blaze.

It was a fearful query, indeed, that rose, unbidden, in the mind of the youth, and, for the moment, it almost overcame him. He felt faint and leaned against the nearest tree for support.

It would seem that, with the doubt thus formed, the lad ought to have felt that the last place in the world for him was where he stood. He should have lost no time in taking himself from the neighborhood, no matter whither his footsteps led him.

But there was a horrible fascination in the sight, which, for the time, held him rooted to the spot. Much as he wished to fly, he lacked the power to do so.

"Suppose they discover me," was his thought; "will they not serve me as they are serving *that thing?*"

Suddenly one of the savages, whose duty it was to attend to the turning of the spit, raised his face and looked in the direction of the spectator. The firelight, falling on his countenance, made one of the most hideous pictures it is possible to describe.

Dick asked himself whether it was possible the native had heard or seen anything to awaken his suspicion. The youth was standing well back in the gloom, and was not conscious of having stirred since leaning against the tree. Nevertheless, the fixed stare caused him to shrink farther away, until the trunk of the tree interposed between him and the camp, and he simply peered around the bark.

Still the fixed look of the wild man continued, until there could be no doubt that something in the direction of the youth had caught his eye or ear.

Dick was so alarmed that he was on the point of whirling about and making a break for the depths of the jungle, heedless of what dangers he might encounter in the form of wild beasts or serpents, when the native who had caused this alarm said something in a guttural voice to his companion, who also turned and looked in the same direction.

"By gracious!" thought the youth, "they have found I am here, though I can't imagine how they did it."

But the second wild man made some reply that appeared to satisfy the other, for, withdrawing his gaze, he once more gave his undivided attention to the task before him.

The time had come to turn the food again, and a few minutes after it was done to a turn.

Being removed from its place over the blaze, each of the cooks produced a long knife from the cloth at his waist, and cut enormous slices from the carcass, tossing one in turn to the waiting savages, who ate with the gusto of wild animals.

The same fearful suspicion was in the mind of the lad, who, knowing he was doing wrong in staying, felt that he must wait until some

"HIS ARMS WERE SUDDENLY SEIZED."

turn took place in the extraordinary proceedings. While they were thus engaged, Dick Brownell counted them. There were just ten, and all seemed on an equality —at least, from their appearance and action, it was impossible to pick out one as the chief or leader.

Standing thus a few minutes longer our young friend once more counted them and was astonished to find only nine.

"That's queer," he said to himself; "I was sure I hadn't made a mistake, but certainly there are but nine. What could have become of the other? I don't think they could have eaten him, for I am sure I would have seen it."

Despite the ferocity with which the wild men assailed the food when first handed

to them, they had a way of lingering over their meal which prolonged it indefinitely, until it seemed to the spectator that they must be genuine epicures.

The cooks had helped themselves as well as the rest several times, until but little remained of the original supply.

"Well, I'll be hanged!"

This muttered exclamation was caused by what was certainly an extraordinary discovery: Dick counted the savages once more, and this time there were only eight!

"I haven't seen any of them leave," he thought; "and yet two have vanished since I first looked upon them. I wonder if those cooks are running in their fellows on the others so slyly that no outsider can see it. Will they keep it up till there's only one left, and what then will *he* do?"

Had Dick Brownell possessed the acumen of Jack Harvey he would have seen in this mysterious disappearance of a couple of natives a most significant warning that would have sent him flying, without an instant's delay, from the spot.

It certainly had a meaning which that veteran Indian campaigner would have been quick to penetrate.

With a strange feeling of awe the lad counted them once more.

This time there were eight: the ebb of the tide had probably been reached.

"I would give a good deal to know where those others went without any one—"

At that moment Master Richard Brownell ascertained whither they had gone.

Without the slightest noise his arms were suddenly seized with a power that he could not shake off. Uttering a gasp of terror, he turned his head, and found in the dim light which reached the spot that he was immovably griped by two of the wild men.

The lad was not mistaken in suspecting that, by some means beyond his power to understand, one of the cooks learned of his presence near them. He acquainted the others so quietly that the listener never held a suspicion of the truth.

Then a couple of the warriors, with admirable cleverness, slipped off in the jungle, and, getting behind him, made him prisoner with a deftness and skill that could not have been surpassed by a brace of American Indians.

CHAPTER XLVIII.

THE CAPTIVE AND HIS CAPTORS.

DICK BROWNELL made no resistance, for the reason that it was out of his power to do so, and any attempt in that direction was likely to bring severe punishment upon him.

His captors cleverly relieved him of the canvas that still covered his shoulders, and, at the same time, extracted his revolver and knife from his possession. This was done, indeed, while they were forcing him forward into the fuller light of the camp-fire.

The natives may not have shown much interest in him while he was acting the part of spectator, but they now gathered around, as though he was some wonderful object, on which they had never looked before. They pinched his arms, passed their hands over his face, as if unable to understand why the skin should be so much fairer than their own, felt of his garments, and looked with no little admiration on the boots which encased his shapely feet.

While thus engaged, they expressed their feelings in the oddest clucking sounds, closely resembling the language of the Hottentots, which, as I have said, suggests the noises made by a lot of hens more than anything else I can call to mind.

Dick Brownell stood the ordeal well. Despite the trying situation, he could not help smiling at some of their grotesque actions, while their childish bewilderment would have amused any one.

I suspect that a discovery made by him at this moment had much to do with his improvement of spirits. He gained a good look of the remains of the carcass on which the party had been feasting. He saw that it belonged to some animal, most likely a small antelope. He had done the natives great injustice by suspecting them of cannibalism, and, had he possessed the means of apologizing, I am not sure he would not have done so.

Whatever disposition the captors might make of him, Dick was immeasurably relieved to know that he was not likely to form a meal for them to feast upon.

As if with a view of conciliating him, one of the natives handed his long-stemmed pipe to the lad, who took a few whiffs, through fear of offending them by a refusal, but the tobacco was so strong that he dare not keep it up long.

No little pleasure was displayed over the canvas covering. It consisted of a goodly number of yards, was very strong and had suffered nothing from its rough usage. It was a prize which the wild men knew how to appreciate.

The next proceeding of the latter was to offer Dick some of the meat that had furnished them with their supper. He would have preferred to decline, since he was not hungry, but he ate a few mouthfuls, an act which I need not tell you would have been beyond his power, but for the removal of the harrowing suspicion that had almost caused him to faint a brief while before.

The ever-present thought with him was as to the probable outcome of all this. What did these frightful-looking natives intend to do with him? Would they persist in keeping him prisoner? Would they take him far away to their homes, or, knowing he belonged to a detested race, would they put him to death? If he was retained in their custody for some days, would Jack Harvey and his comrades in camp be able to do anything for his liberation? Was it not possible that they would consent to his departure, and, if not, could he effect his own escape in the darkness?

These and similar questions filled his mind as he sat down on the ground in the midst of his captors, very much after the manner a friendly visitor would have assumed who had called to pay his respects to the natives.

CAPTIVE AND CAPTORS

At the end of an hour, Dick decided to settle the question whether they meant to hold him in custody. Rising to his feet, he made a low salaam, and, without asking for his weapons or the cloth, turned about to walk away.

Whatever hope he had in that direction was dissipated on the instant, by half the warriors leaping to their feet and brandishing their assagais, or javelins, uttering excited words, with such an expression of ferocity that he resumed his seat with more haste than dignity.

It was not the mere failure of the attempt that gave Dick Brownell cause for disquietude. He had shown his captors his eagerness to part company with them, and they were certain to guard him more closely than ever.

It was unfortunate, but really there was no help for it, since common prudence suggested the step.

The next plan of the lad was a natural one, even though it gave little promise of success; he meant to try to throw his captors off their guard, with a view to gaining a chance of escaping in the darkness.

By this time the night was well advanced, and he showed a wish to sleep by stretching out on the ground with the air of one extremely tired. The natives helped to oblige him by tossing the canvas to him. Though it still retained a good deal of its moisture, Dick folded it under his head as a pillow, and acted the part of a sleeper to perfection.

His situation was not what he desired, for the savages were on every side of him, but to have tried to improve it would have awakened the suspicion of the natives, if indeed they were not already awakened.

In due time, the prisoner closed his eyes and breathed slowly and regularly, but, all the same, he was taking sly peeps from the corners of his eyelids, and watching those of the natives whom he could see without turning his head.

The outlook was not encouraging. About half lay down to slumber, but the rest continued smoking their pipes, exchanging their queer-sounding words and showing no more inclination to sleep than if they had done nothing else for a week.

Still Dick did not yield hope, but kept his eyes apparently closed, while he looked between the eyelids for a chance to steal away in the gloom.

What might have been anticipated took place. Without a thought of his liability to do so, the lad fell asleep and never opened his eyes until some one touched his shoulder. Then when he looked around he saw that daylight had come.

The natives were ready to move, and their captive was to bear them company. They evidently considered the meal of the previous evening all-sufficient, for, though enough fragments remained to form quite a repast, they left them lying on the ground. These wild men were without any horses, and, when they started off with the lad, took a southerly course, walking at a moderate pace, which they were capable of continuing many hours.

"I wonder how far we have to go," was the thought of Dick Brownell; "it is cool and delightful now, but the African weather will soon be on us again and I would much rather have my pony."

The ground over which they were traveling was more undulating than that to which he was accustomed, it being nothing more than a succession of hills, some of them wooded, while others were covered with the grassy growth peculiar to the country. Several times the party passed near the river, never quite reaching it, but at a distance of less than two miles from the piece of jungle where they had spent the night, they reached a slight elevation from whose summit Dick Brownell looked down on what proved to be the homes of his captors.

To the unbounded astonishment of the lad, the end of the journey was reached within the succeeding half hour.

The tribe to which these people belonged was the Corannas or Korahs. When the Dutch took possession of Cape Colony, they treated the surrounding natives with great cruelty. The Korahs were so far removed to the northward, that they were beyond convenient reach, and, therefore, were not much disturbed. As a consequence, they lived and did as they pleased.

The Korahs, in their habits, resemble in one respect the Indians of our country. They are migratory, continually shifting their quarters, so that a family that is here to-day, may be found living a hundred miles away a few months later.

They do not care enough for the land to dispute over it. All they want is water and pasturage for their cattle, and they go wherever there is the best chance of finding them.

Dick Brownell, surveying a small, pleasant valley, saw nine native dwellings

HUNTING FOR POISON.

before him. They were cones about six feet high and a little broader in circumference. Each had a single opening that served as a door and for the admission of light. The frameworks of sticks were covered with several folds of matting, formed from rushes and coarse grass.

The water or milk vessels of the Korahs are made of clay, baked in the sun, or of wood, gourds or ostrich eggs. Their property consists of horned cattle, sheep, goats and dogs. They have no vehicles of any kind, and in moving from place to place, pile their possessions, including their women and children, on the backs of their oxen.

The ten Korahs into whose hands Dick Brownell had run, were prospecting for suitable grounds for pasturage and their costumes were scantier than is common among their people, who generally wear the skin-cloaks seen among the Hottentot tribes. The women wear square, ornamented aprons hung from the waist, with copper chains and glass beads around the neck, wrist and ankles. It is believed that these chains are obtained from the Damaras, who live to the northwest, where copper is quite plentiful.

I have referred several times to the deadly poison used by the Bushmen and other tribes on their spears and arrows. I may have spoken of it as a vegetable poison, which is not strictly true, though it contains vegetable elements.

In Southern Africa are some of the deadliest serpents known. A Bushman or Korah will plant his naked foot on a writhing cobra and extract the bursting poison-sac from his mouth and eagerly drink its contents, under the belief that it protects him against the fatal effects of a bite from the reptile, or he will carefully save the horrible stuff for his weapons. This animal venom is too thin and volatile to preserve its power long. It is, therefore, skillfully mixed with vegetable and mineral poisons until it becomes thick and sticky. This compound is applied to the tips of spears and arrows, a single puncture from which is enough to cause death with almost the swiftness of a bite of the dreaded cobra de capello.

CHAPTER XLIX.

AT THE VILLAGE.

JACK HARVEY, having discovered the footprints of Dick Brownell among those made by the barefooted Korahs, thrilled his companions by his announcement of the fact.

The signs, he said, proved that the missing lad, instead of having fallen a prey to wild beasts, was undoubtedly alive, though a captive, and while there was life there was hope.

Immediately after uttering the inspiring words, the Texan bent his head and made another circuit of the camp, with the same care as before. This was with a view to finding how many composed the party of natives. It was beyond the power of even so skillful a scout as Jack Harvey to settle this question, though, as you will observe, he hit it closely when he set down the number as about a dozen.

All the footprints which he saw had been made since the storm of the night before, and nothing could have been easier than to trace them from the back of his mustang. Indeed, had the cowboy been alone, he probably would have done so, while holding his horse at a gallop.

In trailing an enemy, the wise scout does something more than trace his footsteps over the ground. If he keeps his head bent and his eyes fixed on the earth, he is liable to run into the very ambush that may have been set for him. A trained Indian trailer, like Jack Harvey, scans the country through which the footprints lead and never forgets the danger from ambuscades and tricks of the enemy.

Nothing was clearer in the present instance than that no ambuscade threatened, but the veteran of the border often achieves astonishing success by pushing his pursuit on what may be called general principles.

That is, instead of keeping to the trail, he satisfies himself as to the destination of the person he is following. If the tracker understands the country, he is quite sure of some crossing of a stream, some pass in the mountains, or some excellent hiding-place for which his foe is making by a roundabout course, so as to throw his pursuer off the track.

Leaving the trail, therefore, the sagacious scout " cuts across " the country, and probably reaches the goal of the fugitive hours in advance of him.

An old comrade of Kit Carson told me he once rode all night with that fine scout, in pursuit of some thieving Kiowas. Carson was so well satisfied of the point toward which the rascals were aiming, that he left the trail at sunset and took a course almost at right angles. It saved over a dozen miles, provided he was right, as he said would be proven at sunrise, but if wrong, it insured the escape of the marauders.

At sunrise they debouched into the trail again, and, before the forenoon was half gone, overtook the astonished thieves and recovered all the stolen property.

The pursuit of Jack Harvey was somewhat similar, or, more properly, it would have been, had he been able to continue it very long. He glanced over the country in front and asked :

"Carl, where do you s'pose those chaps went ? "

"The trail, so far as I can judge, leads southward."

"But that may be a blind : do you think they crossed the river off there to the left ?"

"I haven't the slightest knowledge upon which to base a guess ; we're in a business now where you are the leader."

"I'm satisfied the party have set out to go to their home, but whether it is on this side of the stream or the other, why, we've got to find out."

"Since they cannot have much the start of us," ventured Bob, "why not keep to the trail and ride fast ? "

"That's sound sense," replied Jack ; "we'll follow the advice."

With his usual promptness, he struck his mustang into a brisk gallop, his companions quickly closing around him, all on the alert for the natives, who they knew could not be far off.

The surprise of the party was as great as that of Dick Brownell, earlier in the morning, for, long before they expected to gain sight of the village, it burst upon their view. There were nine huts, precisely similar to hundreds they had looked upon in Southern Africa, and there were the native Korahs, moving to and fro, with their flocks grazing on the large hills beyond.

"I'll be hanged ! " exclaimed Jack Harvey ; "I didn't expect *this*. I meant to halt and take a look at things before going so far, but they have seen us, and it won't do to show any fear."

In addition to the ten natives whom I have referred to as the captors of Dick Brownell, there was about the same number that remained behind while the party were prospecting through the country.

Little, half-naked children were running to and fro, women occasionally showing themselves, for the Korah, like the red man of our own country, never objects to his better-half performing the greater share of the manual labor.

Near the middle hut, six natives were standing together, evidently discussing some matter. They looked up almost at the moment the four horsemen appeared on the top of the hill, ceased speaking, and walked forward to meet the white men, who had also given rein to their ponies and were coming down the slope in the direction of the huts.

"Pongo," said Jack, "your turn has come to give us a lift : can you make yourself understood with them ? "

"Talk much like Hottentot," said he ; "they Korah — ain't bad man."

"That may be, but I would like to know what they mean by running off with a youngster that belongs to us. Have you ever seen any of this party before ? "

The Bushman shook his head, to signify they were strangers to him, though he was quick to recognize their tribal character.

A few moments later the parties met. Jack Harvey and Pongo were allowed to ride slightly ahead, while Bob and Mr. Godkin fell back, prepared to listen and watch, and, if necessary, take part in the proceedings.

Since the half dozen natives who advanced were members of the party that had captured Dick Brownell, you do not need anything more in the way of description.

But, could you have looked upon them as they met Jack Harvey and Pongo, you would have found it hard to believe, even with such hideously ugly faces, that they had ever done anything cruel or specially bad. So far as it is possible for Korahs to appear innocent, they were the pictures of innocence. Had not the trail of Dick Brownell led directly to this spot, his pursuers would have thought it unjust to suspect them.

THE PARLEY.

Before anything more than a salutation could take place between the parties, the Texan seized one of those opportunities which, slight of themselves, still have an important bearing on impending events.

A large bird was circling overhead, as if waiting a chance to swoop down and secure some of the waste food near the huts. It was sailing, with its wings outspread, at considerable height, but, knowing what he could do, Jack brought his gun to his shoulder, and, taking a quick aim, brought it tumbling to the earth.

His object was to impress the natives with the power of the weapons in the hands of himself and friends. No doubt they had heard of them, but it was well to enlighten their minds.

There could be no doubt of the success of the stratagem, the expressions on the faces of the Africans showing their wonderment and awe too plainly to be mistaken.

"What does he say?" asked Jack of Pongo, who bowed his head in recognition of something just uttered by the leader of the six, upon whom and the white men the women and children of the little settlement were gazing with wondering curiosity.

"He says he is glad to welcome their brothers from over the sea, and hopes they will always live with him."

"That's about the size of the usual lie a civilized person tells, when some one calls that he don't want to see. Well, Pongo, it won't do to slight him by telling a yarn any smaller than his. Say that that's just what we've been dying to do ever since we were born; that we've called to see what arrangements we can make, and that we love all the Korahs here enough to eat them."

The Bushman indulged in a faint smile and shook his head; that kind of a response would not do.

"Well, you know about what should be said; I'll leave it to you."

Thereupon Pongo turned about and exchanged several sentences with his countrymen, who were evidently surprised to see one of their own number, as he might be called, among the visitors.

Turning to the Texan, the Bushman explained that what had passed between him and the Korah leader was of little real significance, consisting mainly of high-flown compliments and protestations of friendship, which deceived neither party.

"I guess we might as well come to the p'int," remarked the Texan, glancing 'round at Mr. Godkin and Bob for their approval; "tell them, Pongo, that we thank them for their kindness to one of us, and we have come to take him back to our camp."

The three whites watched the countenance of the leader as this message was interpreted to him.

A block of stone could not have been more expressionless. Then, when the slow-speaking Bushman had finished what he had to say, the Korah looked up and spoke hastily to the effect that neither he nor any of his people had ever looked upon a white person until that day.

"Tell him he's a liar and I'll prove it!" exclaimed the Texan, losing his temper.

"Go slow, Jack," said Mr. Godkin, soothingly; "we'll be as resolute as necessary, but you know that sort of language is unparliamentary."

"Say to him, then," added Jack, "that we know the young gentleman is here,—that he is in one of those huts over yonder, and that if he isn't produced p. d. q. —I mean within five minutes—we'll clean out this whole shebang."

The substance of which was duly translated to the spokesman of the Korahs.

CHAPTER L.

LIVELY TIMES.

DESPITE the eagerness of Jack Harvey, and in the face of the impression he had made by the display of marksmanship, the Korah spokesman continued to parry his verbal ruses, with a temerity that surprised Bob and Mr. Godkin.

The Texan was the owner of a fiery temper when aroused, and more than once he was at the exploding point. When he rested his right hand on one of his revolvers, the temptation to snatch it out and put a bullet through the impudent native was almost irresistible.

It would have been in keeping with the old hilarious times, had he, holding a pistol in each hand, galloped back and forth among the huts, firing at a head wherever it appeared, and "cleaning out" the African town in genuine American border style.

But his fear of the consequences to Dick restrained him. Convinced that his young friend was somewhere in that little hamlet, he was yet unable to locate him, and any sudden dash on his part might precipitate a calamity that would have been beyond remedy.

While Pongo was interpreting the utterances that were rapidly growing heated, Mr. Godkin and Bob Marshall allowed not a syllable to escape them. More than that, the young man was searching through the hamlet with his eyes for some clue that would tell him the news he was so anxious to learn.

"Mr. Godkin," he suddenly said in a lower voice, "I believe I know where Dick is."

"What do you mean?" asked the director.

"Did you notice that hut in front of which these six wretches were standing when we rode to the top of the hill?"

"I did."

"They've got Dick in there."

"What's your reason for thinking so?"

"Jack says there were a dozen in the party; here are only half a dozen; where are the rest?"

"I do not see that the answer to that question involves anything, since other natives are in sight and they may be among them."

"But there are several in that same hut, where these were standing. They are inside and are trying to keep out of view. I have seen their faces several times at the door, which is the only opening; I believe Dick is in there and they are holding him prisoner, so that he dare not show himself."

This was only a startling assertion, but the director more than half believed Bob was right.

"I can't understand it," he said; "those people have the reputation, so far as I have heard, of being on fairly friendly terms with white people."

"But Jack saw a party of them that were torturing a prisoner to death, and he shot the leader."

"I don't believe they were Korahs, though they corresponded to the description. As it was, it was not a white man they meant to kill."

"But it was a white man who shot their leader ——"

"Hark!" interrupted Mr. Godkin, referring to the words that Jack Harvey was instructing Pongo to translate to the Korah chieftain. The fact was that the Texan could control himself no longer. His manner and loud tones proved it.

"I SAW HIM! I SAW HIM!" EXCLAIMED BOB

"Tell the old scoundrel that I know the young man is in one of the huts, and if he isn't produced, we'll open fire right off." And he handled his Winchester in a most suggestive manner. At that moment an exciting incident took place.

Bob Marshall still had his eyes on the hut, at whose door he saw the swarthy faces of more than one native appear and vanish, as though they were trying to keep watch of the visitors without being seen. Suddenly a pale countenance was thrust forward, and withdrawn so quickly that, had not Bob been looking at the exact spot, he would not have caught the glimpse of the face.

"*I saw him! I saw him!*" exclaimed Bob.

"Where?" demanded Jack, turning sharply upon him.

"Yonder, in that hut! He looked out, and they drew him back again," replied the youth, pointing at the structure which he had been watching for several minutes.

Without waiting for further questioning, Jack Harvey wheeled the head of Apache toward the building, and speaking a single word, sent him flying at headlong speed straight for the prison of Dick Brownell.

"We're in for it now!" exclaimed Mr. Godkin; "come on and look out for their poisoned spears."

The two, accompanied by Pongo, tore away at a furious rate after their leader. The time for words had passed and that for hurricane action had come.

A victory is often gained by promptness and vigor, when a moment's hesitation would be fatal.

The half dozen Korahs in front of Jack Harvey were stupefied for the moment by the impetuous rush of the horsemen, but quickly regained their senses, and started after them on a full run, brandishing their assagais and uttering cries of rage.

The rush of the mounted men carried them beyond reach of their pursuers for the moment, but directly in front of those crowded into the hut.

Bob Marshall was right; Dick Brownell *was* in the structure, and, despite the fearful risk he ran, he managed to catch sight of his friends. Not only that, but, with a daring dash, he fought his way to the door and reached the outside.

Prompted by some whim which cannot be fully understood, the Korahs had returned the lad his weapons after placing him within the hut under a guard, where they impressed upon him by gesture that it would be certain death to try to escape, or even to allow his friends to see him.

But before handing the revolver back to him, the captors had rendered it harmless by removing the charges. Then, as he dared not attempt to reload it in their presence, they may have wanted to show him how they despised any demonstration on his part, by placing his weapons in his possession again.

Dick jammed the pistol in place, and, grasping only his knife, fought his way to the outside, and ran with might and main to meet the galloping horsemen.

But his situation was desperate. The Korahs were not the ones to stand idle and allow a prisoner to escape in that manner.

Despite the fact that the four horsemen were thundering down upon the hut, three of the guards started in hot pursuit of the boy, thereby running straight toward the white men, who would soon be upon them.

One of them was fully a rod in advance of the others — nigh enough to raise his javelin to hurl with unerring aim at the fugitive, who, in his haste, could not take time to glance over his shoulder.

But everything in this direction was under the eyes of the rescuers. Jack Harvey was expecting something of the kind, and, at the moment the savage lifted his right arm with the assagai, he threw up his rifle.

He needed but a second to make his aim sure. Before the Korah could launch his poisoned missile, he plunged forward on his face with a rasping screech, as the weapon left his hand, the point sticking in the ground a few feet in front of him.

LIVELY TIMES.

By this time Dick was among his friends. Reaching downward, Bob seized his hand, and with one leap the athletic fellow vaulted upon the back of the pony in front of his cousin.

"Off with you!" cried Jack Harvey, who saw the maneuver and shouted before it was fairly completed; "don't wait a single minute."

The boys would have preferred to stay and help their fearless friend, but, when he spoke in such tones, no one dared disobey him.

Bob wheeled his pony, and, heading for the point which seemed most free of enemies, put the animal to a dead run, he and Dick leaning as far over on his neck as possible, to avoid the fatal missiles which were expected to descend in a shower. But, as you know, none of the Korahs were mounted, and a brief minute or two was sufficient to carry the cousins beyond reach of the fleetest-footed pursuer

They did not pause, however, until more than safe, when Bob drew the rein and turned about to learn how went the battle.

With the flight of the boys, all occasion for the men to linger was gone, though Jack Harvey longed to open on the savages and fight them single-handed.

It was such a vivid reminder of old times with Geronimo, Naiche and their Apaches, that the impulse was well-nigh resistless.

But Mr. Godkin kept cool and devoted all his energies to extricating his friend from a situation wherein it looked as if death was inevitable.

"Get away, Jack!" he shouted, he and Pongo being a considerable distance behind him; "they will fill you full of their poisoned assagais."

The Texan's headlong impetuosity drew the whole attention of the Korahs, for the moment, upon him. Mr. Godkin and the Bushman were safe. All they had to do was to wheel and follow the lads. But they could not desert their brave friend in his extremity.

At the moment when despair was in the heart of the director, and while Pongo was balancing one of his boomerangs, uncertain at which particular foe to launch it, they saw Jack go forward on his horse.

"He is killed! he is killed!" moaned Mr. Godkin.

"No; ain't hurt—see!—look!" said the Bushman, forgetting, in his excitement, to make use of his novel weapon.

The Texan had wheeled his mustang to one side at the instant he threw himself forward, and, before even his friends suspected his purpose, he seized a Korah child and raised it in front of his body as a shield.

The chief uttered a cry of anguish; it was his own daughter, and he read the meaning of the action.

At that cry, every uniformed arm was lowered, and the assagais that were about to be hurled at the body of the brave white man were suspended motionless.

Jack spoke to his horse, which turned in the direction of his friends, and broke into a gallop. The intrepid rider leaned over, but held the child with a grip of iron, so that any javelin launched at him was certain to bury itself in the little one's body.

A brief ride, and the safety point was reached. Then Jack slackened the pace of his mustang and gently placed the unharmed child on the ground. A minute later he joined his friends.

"Dick," said he, sharply, "where is that wagon-cover?"

"I left it in the hut," was the reply.

"I'll be hanged if I don't get it!"

And before any one could prevent him, he wheeled about and dashed back toward the native village.

CHAPTER LI.

THE RHINOCEROS HUNTERS.

THE blood of the Texan was roused, and, heedless of the fearful risk he ran, he wheeled his mustang and sped toward the native village on a dead run. The distance was short, and the yell which he sent out as he thundered down the slope was the same that had rung through the mountain gorges of Arizona when charging upon the dusky marauders of the border.

The Korahs had not yet recovered from the panic caused by the rescue of the lad, and the sight of the white man, swinging his Winchester over his head, must have made them think the whole party had returned to attack them. They scattered as if from before a smoking bombshell.

Jack headed for the hut from which Dick Brownell had dashed a few minutes before. He supposed several of his captors were still there, but they had all hurried forth in pursuit, and were still out of doors.

A native woman and two children were within, and when the white man, leaping from his saddle, bounded through the small door, they were transfixed with terror.

Jack saw the canvas where it had been spread in one corner, probably to serve as a bed for some of the inmates. In a twinkling, he had snatched it up, ran out, and was in the saddle again.

The intelligent mustang needed no guidance. Hardly was his master on his back, when he whirled about and went up the slope like a whirlwind.

There really was no peril involved in the act, for not a spear or arrow was sent after the Texan, who swung the fluttering canvas aloft, and uttered a shout to which his waiting friends replied with a delight no less than his own.

The exploit was begun and ended so quickly, that it was over before the bewildered natives could interfere. But for the stirring events immediately preceding, the charge of the Texan would have led him to as certain death as if he had plunged over a precipice a thousand feet high.

Dick Brownell expected a rasping like the scraping of a lion's tongue over the naked hand, for the part he had played in the business, but not one of his companions uttered a word of reproof. The feeling of impatience on the part of Jack Harvey and Mr. Godkin had vanished long before, and they were too grateful for the outcome to utter any words except those of gratulation.

Then, too, Dick could not be made to regret more keenly his remissness than he now lamented it, and the most that was done in the way of rebuke was a smile and shake of the director's head, when the lad, relating his story at the request of his friends, told how he had persisted in hunting for the missing canvas until by mere accident he came upon it.

Dick said that, while his captors offered him no violence, they showed an ugly disposition after reaching the little cluster of huts, which caused him much misgiving. The whole proceeding was such a daring one on their part that our friends believed they meant to hold the lad for ransom. They thought the white hunters wealthy, for, indeed, they had considerable possessions with them, and if it had proven impossible to arrange a ransom, it is likely they would have put their prisoner to death.

The first thing done by the party on reaching camp was to restore the canvas cover to its proper place over the wagon. It had been the cause of some lively work on the part of the hunters, and more than once it had looked as if it would involve them in serious difficulty, but, thank Providence, all had come out well.

Diedrick and his friends took good care of the camp during the absence of the white men, but the anxiety of the Hottentot for the recapture and return of the missing youth led him to venture to the top of the nearest elevation, where he carefully surveyed all the country in his field of vision.

The horsemen were not in sight, but he observed them soon after, on their return, and was quick to discover that one of the ponies bore two riders. That was enough, and it may safely be said that none rejoiced more heartily over the rescue of Dick Brownell than did his African friend.

But, while the native was scanning the country on all sides, he made a discovery which turned the excitement of his employers into a new channel. He caught sight of an animal, at no great distance, in the tall grass along the river, which he believed was a rhinoceros, and, since Mr. Godkin had announced, but a short time before, that he was ready to give his attention to that species of game, the expectation was that it would now be done without further delay.

Rhinoceros hunting is attended not only with great danger, but is so delicate and difficult that many a failure has been made by veteran hunters who have bagged all other kinds of game. Before telling you about the perilous adventures in which our friends became involved on the afternoon of Dick Brownell's return from captivity, I must give you some idea of the work they undertook.

In the first place, there are four varieties of rhinoceros found in South Africa. They are known as the *borele*, or black rhinoceros, the *keitloa*, or two-horned black species, the *mochocho*, or ordinary white rhinoceros, and the *kobaoba*, or long-horned white rhinoceros. The black species is smaller than the others, but is ten-fold fiercer and more dangerous.

The Asiatic rhinoceros is smaller than the African, has his hide in looser folds, and two of the species have but a single horn.

The square-nosed white rhinoceros is the largest known. He is not white in color, but shows a dirty resemblance to that hue. They have been found eighteen feet in length, and I have known them to be with a circumference still greater.

Set not in the bone, but in the skin of its blunt nose, is the horn, sharp, hard, curved, and more than a yard long. Just behind this is a smaller horn, but equally sharp and hard.

The eyes of the beast are very small, its ears are long, and tipped with scrubby bristles, and its sense of hearing and smell is so acute that it is almost useless for a hunter to approach him from the windward. Besides this, despite its enormous bulk (the rhinoceros ranks next to the elephant in size), he is so swift of foot that it takes an unusually good steed to overtake him.

The long-horned white rhinoceros is the rarer of the two and is found far in the interior and mainly to the eastward of the Limpopo. Many of them have horns four feet in length, curving forward, while the horn of the *mochoeho* bends backward and is rarely more than two-thirds the length of the other. A survey of the head and front of one of these creatures will satisfy you that he holds the championship for ugliness in the way of looks.

THE JAVANESE RHINOCEROS.

The Javanese rhinoceros is not so bulky as the Indian species, and has longer legs. It is mischievous, but less dangerous than those I have named.

When I add that the rhinoceros is nocturnal in his habits, that he is a terrible fighter when aroused, and that he has one of the most alert of small birds to warn him of danger, you will admit there are many obstacles to success in hunting him.

The point where Pongo and Diedrick had located the game was fully a mile to the northward of the camp, and at no great distance, therefore, from the elevation which was used as an observatory on the first arrival of our friends in this section

They had not seen the beast distinctly, but it seemed to have been aroused by thirst and was pushing its way through the tall grass from the river to its resting-place during the day-time.

There was enough uneasiness over the Korahs to make Mr. Godkin unwilling to leave the camp without full protection. The natives might feel revengeful enough to watch for some chance for stealthy work, while afraid to attack openly.

The director, therefore, decided that he and Pongo would stay behind, leaving the cousins and Jack Harvey to prosecute the hunt with only Diedrick as their companion. These four knew enough of the nature of the animals to render unnecessary any instructions or hints. Mr. Godkin said he would accompany them on the morrow, leaving the inference that he had no faith in their meeting with success before that time.

The preparations for the hunt were quickly completed. The air had grown quite warm, but enough coolness remained from the storm of the night before to render the day one of the finest experienced since entering that section.

Jack Harvey, I need not say, carried his lasso with him, though there was little probability of any chance for its use. Bob Marshall had borrowed the glass of Mr. Godkin, for that was likely to do them service.

The first proceeding was to ride to the elevation from which the two natives had seen what they believed was the rhinoceros. Diedrick remembered the exact spot and at once turned his keen eyes in that direction.

He was gazing toward a portion of the broad stream which swept by the camp, and between him and the water was a growth of grass, taller and denser than that which had sheltered the baboons, and spread over a much greater area of territory.

It was near the middle of this that the natives discerned some large animal moving, which they believed was a rhinoceros, though the view was too indistinct for them to be certain.

Every eye followed the course Diedrick pointed out, and the glass was freely used, but nothing could be discovered of the animal, though, as a matter of course, there were many places where a score of such beasts might have been concealed beyond detection. It was the fact that the brute was in motion which had revealed it to the African, who happened to look at the point when not scanning the plain for his absent friends.

"There's only one thing to do," said Dick Brownell. "We have set out to hunt for a rhinoceros, and we have got to hunt him. We haven't reason to believe he means to hunt *us.*"

"I don't suppose he is a great way from where he was seen," remarked Bob, "for he won't move around much until night-time."

"Come ahead," said Jack Harvey, giving rein to his horse; "we'll go straight for the spot, and we'll know inside of half an hour whether the critter is there or not."

CHAPTER LII.

THE BUPHAGA AFRICANA.

THE well-mounted hunters had but a comparatively short distance to ride, when they dashed into the tall grass, amid which grew a great deal of the native rice, of which the hippopotamus, as well as the rhinoceros, is so fond. The ponies, of necessity, slackened their pace, for, knowing how quick the big game is to detect danger, the time had come for the exercise of extreme caution.

Conscious that the proceedings had now reached a stage in which the Hottentot was the most competent director, Jack Harvey fell to the rear with the boys, all preserving silence, and the three keeping sharp watch of their native leader.

All at once, Diedrick raised his hand as a signal for the others to halt. Although they saw nothing, there could be no doubt that he had detected something important.

Just in front, the grass, which was five or six feet in height, became more dense and abundant. The party could see but a short distance, and, of course, it was beyond the power of the native to discern anything that was not manifest to his friends.

Several minutes passed, during which all were silent and listening. Diedrick then turned and explained that, while he saw nothing, he was of the belief that more than one of the animals was close to them. A gentle wind was blowing from that point, which was fortunate for the hunters, since, were the direction different, the sagacious beast would be quick to scent his danger.

Diedrick proposed that he and one of the boys should make a circuit, which would take them around to a point a half mile away. Then, if any rhinoceros was between the parties, he would discover his danger and make off toward those in waiting, who, if they used ordinary discretion, would gain a chance of bringing down some of the gigantic game.

This understanding was scarcely reached when a small bird suddenly rose from the grass at a distance of less than a hundred yards, and, darting straight up in the air, gave utterance to a sharp peculiar note, that could be heard a long way off.

The Hottentot muttered impatiently in his own language as he faced about to explain the cause of his anger.

The bird, which had just risen, was the *buphaga africana*, or rhinoceros bird, the most devoted and faithful friend of the rhinoceros. It constantly attends the beast, feeding on the insects which infest its muddy hide. While thus employed, it is on the lookout for enemies of the animal. The instant it detects the approach of the hunter, it flies above the beast, uttering the sharp cries which he understands at once.

Many hunters claim that if the rhinoceros happens to be asleep when danger appears, the little friend will peck the inside of his ears until he awakens.

"HE CAUGHT SIGHT OF THE VAST BEAST."

In the present instance the party had come almost upon one of the animals without suspecting it. Indeed, the advance was so cautious that the vigilant bird did not discover them until it was almost too late; but it made up for its remissness. It did not rise more than fifty feet from the ground, when it descended and circled about in great excitement, all the time emitting the cries of warning. The horsemen could not see the rhinoceros, but he was plainly heard as he went crashing through the grass with a speed which the best steed would find it hard to surpass when impeded by the luxuriant vegetation.

"Let's dash into the grass and charge upon him," proposed Dick, when told that they were so close to the brute. But the Texan shook his head.

"The fellow can travel faster than we, and that bird will keep him warned all the while, so we won't get within gun-shot of him."

"Then we might as well turn back and give up," said Bob; and I should like to know what warrant we had, in the first place, to expect any success in hunting rhinoceroses?"

"Others have brought them down; therefore we may succeed. It isn't every rhinoceros that is furnished with such a bird to give warning when danger threatens. Let us hear what Diedrick has to propose."

The Hottentot made known that he and the parties whom he conducted through the grass and jungles had often been baffled in the same manner by the vigilance of the little bird, but, where the hunters numbered three or four, he had succeeded in outwitting the feathered sentinel by a simple device.

What he suggested, as I have said, was that while two of the company stayed where they were, the others should carefully work around to the opposite side of the game, and thus induce it to flee toward those in waiting.

This appeared to promise success, though it was apparent to all that nothing of the kind could be assured, since it was not likely to be an easy task to reach the point without alarming the beast, and, furthermore, it would be hard to drive him toward the hunters in waiting. The whole scheme, it may be said, was based on very uncertain conditions, but, as it was the best that presented itself, it was adopted at once.

The arrangement was that Diedrick and Bob Marshall should attempt the difficult task of reaching a point on the other side of the rhinoceros, while Jack and Dick should stay where they were, with the expectation, or rather hope, that the game would thus be forced within reach of their guns.

Accordingly the two friends named turned their horses' heads to the right and began the long circuit, which sober second thought, as it struck Bob, convinced him was more likely to fail than to succeed.

The grass continued abundant, and in some places it was no light work for the animals to force their way through. Diedrick rode a short distance in advance, leaning forward and peering right and left, like an Indian trying to steal his way through an enemy's lines.

The route taken by the Hottentot was considerably more than half a mile. The sameness of their surroundings prevented Bob from keeping the points of the compass clear, but the slight breeze blowing enabled him to tell when the final turn was made, and they were advancing straight toward their friends whom they had left behind.

As I have already said, there were uncertain conditions involved in the problem which the two, or rather the native himself, had undertaken to solve. It was likely that the rhinoceros, when he was warned by the bird, plunged through the grass to the right or left, so that he was not between the divisions of the party.

But Diedrick was hopeful that, if he was not there, others were, which would answer as well. After penetrating a short distance, he suggested to the boy that they separate for a brief space, inasmuch as they would be more likely to drive out the game.

This was done, and the success was surprising and speedy. All at once the *buphaga africana* uttered its piercing note, fluttered excitedly to view, gyrating about as though caught in a whirlwind, and proving, beyond question, that the enormous game was at hand.

As it was immediately in front of Bob that the bird rose, he knew he was near one of the beasts. He spurred his horse forward and stood up in the stirrups so as to gain, if possible, a view of the quadruped.

He could see the swaying grass, and a second later he caught sight of the vast back, like a shoal of dried mud, as it swung ponderously through the vegetation. The legs of the rhinoceros are so short that a tall man can stand beside him and look over his back, and it is curious how such a bulky mass can attain so great speed.

Nothing inspires a sportsman with courage so much as the sight of his fleeing game, and Bob urged his horse to do his best. The steed did not need spurring, but, with a snort of excitement, galloped forward.

When the lad caught sight of the huge animal again, he could hardly restrain his excitement.

"We've got him!" he called out; "let's shoot him ourselves! the others can wait; we have earned the best right to the fellow. Ride fast and he won't get away from us!"

Bob ceased his appeals, for, in looking about, he failed to see the Hottentot from whom he had separated only a few minutes before. He wondered how it was he had disappeared so quickly, but it was no time to inquire, and he kept his horse at his best pace, fired by the thrilling thought that it might be his good fortune to bring down the royal game without the help of any one.

Diedrick had vanished, and it was a long run before the beast would pass within range of the other party, if, indeed, he did so at all. Bob let the reins lie loose on his horse's neck, while he held his rifle ready to fire whenever the proper moment should come.

The conduct of the little bird was not without interest. Having got its bulky friend on the run, it ascended still higher in air, and ceased its cries, as though content to view the chase from that elevation. When, however, the rhinoceros held up for a few moments, as if to take its bearings, the bird shot downward again, uttering such piercing warnings that the beast plunged forward with renewed speed.

About this time Bob, even when in the flush of his newly-formed ambition, became aware of the unpleasant fact that he was not gaining upon the game. The rhinoceros, perhaps on account of its vastly superior weight, crushed through the obstructions with greater speed than did the lighter and more graceful horse.

The sight of the laboring beast kept hope alive in the breast of Bob, who did not spare his animal, but, strive as he might, he could not lessen the space between them.

"You shan't get away without receiving something to remember me!" exclaimed the disappointed boy, bringing his rifle to his shoulder.

He had learned to fire from the back of his horse when on a gallop, and he was confident his aim was true at the moment he pulled trigger. Most probably he struck the rhinoceros, but, if so, the animal gave no evidence of it. Like a locomotive, he seemed to have gotten up steam, and he went crashing and plunging onward, as though he would bear down a tree or any obstruction in his path.

"I don't know whether he has taken the right course or not," muttered Bob, drawing his horse down to a walk, and then checking him altogether; "but, if he has, and runs into Jack and Dick, he will conclude he made a mistake in not staying here and having it out with me."

For a minute or two longer he could hear the animal tearing through the grass, though nothing could be seen of him, nor could the eye follow his course. Even the alarm-bird was not visible, and Bob could not help suspecting that the little sentinel had settled down to rest, under the belief that no danger threatened its gigantic friend.

CHAPTER LIII.

BOB MARSHALL was a sorely disappointed boy, though it must be admitted that youngsters in that state are found in every part of the world. His chagrin was that of the lad who sees a prize slip from his grasp at the moment he is closing his fingers upon it.

There was a brief space of time when he was sure he was going to bring down the rhinoceros without the assistance of any one ; and, had he succeeded in doing so, it would have been an exploit of which he could have boasted for the rest of his life. But he was too much of a philosopher to lament over that which could not be helped.

"I wonder whether the old fellow won't find out that a party is waiting in ambush for him, and turn about and come back for me : if he does, I'll get a chance after all. But I suppose the bird will see the danger and will go to chattering and screaming again. He will think it is I, and will take a header right in among them. What can have become of Diedrick !— helloa ! what's the matter with my horse ? — my gracious !

There were few times in the life of Bob that he received such a shock as he did at that moment. Hearing a movement in the grass behind him, he turned his head, just as his horse began to show restlessness, and saw a second rhinoceros fully as large as the other, and not twenty yards distant.

It was certainly extraordinary that he could have ridden so close to the game without its being detected, either by his steed or himself, but such was the fact, partly due, no doubt, to the concentration of the attention of boy and animal on the fleeing beast.

The rhinoceros that had just introduced himself was of prodigious size, and seemed of a milk-white color, though its hue was mainly due to the coating of dried clay that covered its entire body. Inasmuch as no *buphaga africana* was seen or heard giving warning to the beast of impending peril, it is to be presumed that the second specimen was not furnished with such a valuable body-guard.

Another striking difference between the two creatures was that the second did not show any of the timidity displayed by the first. Though he saw the horse and rider, and in his dim, instinctive fashion must have comprehended that they meant business of the most serious character, yet he made no attempt to flee or get beyond rifle-shot.

When Bob faced about, the beast was standing motionless, looking at him and his horse as if to ask them their errand. The boy could not help wondering at the enormous bulk of the rhinoceros, which resembled an immense hogshead supported

300

on four short posts.   As for its head, with the two curving horns over its nose, it was ugly beyond description.   Its very repulsiveness was enough to make one run. But Bob felt the old thrill, when he ran his eyes over the monster, and realized that the very chance he coveted was his.

Here was the rhinoceros, and with no one in sight to rob him of the glory of "bagging" him.

Although the horse was naturally alarmed when confronted by such a frightful-looking enemy, he did not break away in a panic, as an untrained

A SUDDEN ATTACK.

animal would have done. He maintained his ground, though his rider felt him trembling like an aspen. So long as the rhinoceros approached no closer, he would not flee, but at the first advance of the terrible beast the steed would become ungovernable.

The two enemies stared at each other probably for less than a single minute, when the young hunter felt it incumbent to do something. He could ask no better opportunity, as he thought, and, raising his gun, sighted at the aggregation of ugliness in front of him, and let fly.

He struck the rhinoceros in the head, though it may be doubted whether the beast was aware of the fact. He would have aimed at the eye could he have identified the little orbs clearly. Just as he fired, a cold chill ran down his back. He recalled that Diedrick, in talking of these animals, had cautioned his friends against shooting at their heads, since it was almost impossible to inflict a fatal wound. The proper course was to fire into the side, say back of the foreleg, where the skin is thin and a vital portion can be reached.

Almost at the same instant that the gun broke the stillness, the rhinoceros uttered a pig-like grunt, and charged. It would have been beyond the power of the youth to restrain his animal had he wished to do so; but he had no such desire. He and his steed had become the hunted instead of the hunters, and the only duty before them was to leave that particular section with all possible haste.

The horse made a terrific leap and bounded off at the highest bent of speed; it was by no means certain that even that would save him.

A colder shiver than before swept over the youthful rider when he recalled the alarming fact that the first rhinoceros had made his way more swiftly through the tall grass than his horse was able to do. Bob had forced the animal to his very best pace, and yet the game had drawn away from him without trouble.

Why could not the second beast do equally well? Aye, why not? A few minutes must decide.

And so they did. Bob continually glanced behind him, and, with a fear that cannot be described, he saw that the mountainous brute, which was bearing savagely down upon him, was steadily gaining ground.

The Hottentot was not in sight: the rest of the party were too far off to render assistance, and matters certainly wore a serious look.

It was useless to shout to or urge the horse: he was inspired by the most powerful of all motives — a mortal fear of the peril that was bearing down upon him. He could do no more than he was already doing, and alas! for the noble animal, that was insufficient to save him.

Had Bob Marshall been on the open plain, he might have escaped, for there are few animals which in fleetness can equal a well-trained horse, but his pony was unaccustomed to the grass, which was scarcely any obstruction to the massive rhinoceros. It was hard, too, for the lad to know that, although he held a most excellent magazine rifle in his hands, it was practically useless. His pursuer presented no vulnerable point, while charging upon him with such speed, unless it was his eye; and though, as I have said, the lad could fire quite well from the back of his steed, he was incapable of such marksmanship as was now required.

He made several flying shots, but, it may be doubted whether he did more that graze the brute, if he succeeded even in doing that.

A short distance only was ridden, when Bob saw that his pony was doomed. The rhinoceros was not only gaining, but was gaining rapidly, and in a few minutes would overtake the steed.

"My horse must go," he thought, "and it looks pretty rough for me ; where the mischief can Diedrick be ? "

A few minutes later the pursuer overhauled the fugitive.

The infuriated rhinoceros ran his snout under the belly of the horse, and Bob, feeling something strike his foot, glanced down. The point of the terrible horn had passed entirely through the body of his steed and touched his foot. Freeing his feet from the stirrups, the lad made a flying leap, landing in the grass and falling upon his side with a violence that stunned him for a few seconds.

During that time he heard the brief but furious struggle of his horse, which speedily became still. He was quickly killed by his savage antagonist, which turned about to look for the missing rider.

The rhinoceros was much closer to the lad than was pleasant for the latter, but there was a chance that the youth would not be seen. He was lying in the grass, his gun a rod distant, and praying that he might escape discovery.

The beast, having finished his dreadful work, stood still, listening for some sound that would tell where the presumptuous youth was that had dared to fire a gun at him. Had Bob made the least noise the rhinoceros would have swept down upon him like an avalanche. From where he lay he could see the long, clay-coated body of the monster close to the ground, looking like a locomotive boiler partly hoisted in position. The short, beam-like legs were invisible, but the massive head was uplifted so that it was on a line with the back. The ears seemed to be tremulous with the desire to catch the coveted sound that should betray his victim.

" HE SEES ME "

It need not be said that Bob made no noise. He had shifted his position slightly, so that he was lying on his face, his hat off, his body flattened close to the earth, while his eyes were fixed upon his dreaded enemy.

The rhinoceros stood in an attitude of intense attention for several seconds Then the ponderous head slowly moved part way to the left, coming gradually back again, so as to describe a semicircle. He was so close to Bob while making this movement that the youth saw distinctly the ugly-looking red lining of the upper lip, which overhung with a sharp point the lower jaw, and the dark, muddy skin running along under the head and between the forelegs.

When the enormous bulk swung around so that the two sword-like horns towered directly above the boy, the mass settled to rest as though the piggish eyes, up above, had detected something suspicious.

"He sees me," was the thought of Bob, softly drawing in his feet so that he would be ready to spring up and dart off.

But, if the rhinoceros observed the lad, he ought to have lowered his head, so as to bring his eyes in position. The fact that he did not do so led the youth to hope that his presence remained undetected.

Finally, when the head had described its partial circle and settled back to rest, the point of the hideous snout was lowered as though the owner believed his game had escaped. He made no further search, but, with a grunting sniff, moved off through the grass.

The course which he took brought him still nearer Bob, who scarcely breathed until the beast lumbered past and vanished in the vegetation, his crashing tread being audible for several minutes afterward.

Bob dared not stir until sure his enemy was gone. Then he rose to his feet, and hurriedly recovered his rifle. That finished, he walked over to where his poor horse lay.

Tears came to his eyes as he gazed on the noble animal, or rather, on what had been such a noble animal, for there was no breath left in his body. A hunter always forms a strong attachment to his horse or dog, and cannot look upon his death without a pang.

When Bob had stood several minutes in silence, he stooped over and removed the bridle and saddle.

"We have spare horses, but alas, my faithful pony, none of them is you," he muttered; "I'll take these with me."

His situation was not the most pleasant in the world, for he did not know where his friends were, and was afraid of making any outcry or signal lest he should bring down the enraged rhinoceros from which he had barely escaped with his life.

The direction of the wind enabled him to form a general idea of the proper course to reach Jack and Dick. He tramped through the tall grass, reflecting on the contrast between hunting wild game and being hunted yourself by the wild game.

As the Frenchman observed, "It iz veree fine to hunt ze tigare, but, when ze tigare hunts you, it is not so fine."

"I would like to get another shot at that fellow," he said, half tempted to turn about and hunt for him; "but there don't seem much use of pumping bullets into him unless you reach the right spot. Hope the rest of the folks will have better luck than I."

CHAPTER LIV.

A LOST HOTTENTOT.

EANWHILE, Jack Harvey and Dick Brownell impatiently awaited the appearance of the royal game which Bob and Diedrick expected to drive toward them.

"I don't think I'll try my lasso on him," remarked the Texan, after they had sat some minutes in silence.

"No; he is one of the few animals that is too powerful to be checked by the strongest horse. I think it would be hard work for any one to bring him to a halt. But the greatest obstacle in the way of success, it seems to me is that plaguey little bird that is always on guard."

"There's one way of fixing that."

"How?"

"Shoot the thing, if it won't keep its clatter still. After we get it out of the way, we shall have some chance. I've known sportsmen to do that when hunting the rhinoceros."

Dick shook his head.

"That strikes me as wrong. I cannot see any justification for killing a little bird simply because it warns an animal of danger."

"Is it any more wrong than shooting the animal itself?" was the pertinent query of Jack; "we are apt to forget — helloa! I hear something!"

The horses became restless, but they were so well trained that they kept their places and were speedily soothed. The rhinoceros that was first observed had indeed taken the back trail, and was heading for the horsemen. The intervening grass prevented him catching sight of the men until quite close, so there was every chance of gaining a good shot at the beast.

He was yet some distance off, pounding through the vegetation, when the little bird, which had perched itself again on his back, made the alarming discovery that its gigantic patron was plunging directly into the danger from which he supposed he was fleeing. Instantly the bird shot up in the air, circling, uttering its wildest cries, and straining every nerve to apprise the rhinoceros of his peril.

But the situation was an unfortunate one for the endangered party. He knew, of course, that his enemies were near, but, as he last saw them directly behind him, he must have supposed they were advancing from that point.

Accepting the warning of his diminutive friend, therefore, as a call to increase his speed, he crashed forward until he found himself in front of the party from which he supposed he was fleeing. Observing the horsemen, he stopped, wheeled and started off in the opposite direction; but this was what the hunters were waiting for. Jack Harvey knew the proper and, indeed, the only manner in which the beast should be shot, and he and Dick fired together.

Struck under such circumstances, the animal could not fail to be hit hard. He emitted his whiffing, pig-like grunt, and drove furiously through the grass for a few steps, when he lunged forward, plowing up the earth with his horned nose, and rolling upon his side. Then the mountainous mass lay still.

"He is dead!" exclaimed Dick, in no little excitement, spurring his horse toward him.

"Be careful!" admonished Jack, scarcely behind him; "the animal sometimes pretends he is dead, like the 'possum, and he may rip up your horse if you ride too close."

Thus warned, the lad sprang to the ground and advanced toward the carcass, his friend doing the same. A brief scrutiny convinced them that the game was lifeless, and they stepped forward to make a closer examination.

"That is curious," remarked Dick, after inspecting every part of the body; "I can't find a wound upon it."

"No," replied the Texan, "there is none to be seen, unless it's on the other side; and the only way to decide that is to dig a pit under him, for he's too big to roll over."

"But you and I fired from his left side, and he is lying on his right, so it would seem we ought to see the wounds."

Jack laughed as he added:

"Each hit him fairly."

"Where, then, are the marks?"

"Though you may see no signs of them, they have done their execution all the same. If the carcass was turned over you would not see any hurt on the other side. The reason is that the skin is so thick and flabby that, when a bullet passes through it into his body, the skin slides over and covers up the wound. No blood shows itself, even though the beast is mortally wounded, for he bleeds to death inwardly."

Dick laughed, for he had forgotten a fact that had once been familiar to him.

"I ought to have remembered that," he said, adding: "Well, we have brought down our game, and from the sounds of the guns, I shouldn't be surprised to learn that Diedrick and Bob have been equally fortunate."

At that moment a familiar voice was heard calling:

"Helloa, fellows! where are you?"

"This way, Bob! What's up?"

"I'm all right," was the reply, "but I have lost my horse."

"Lost his horse," replied the astonished Dick; "how could that have happened?"

"Maybe it run away from him," suggested Jack, who raised his voice and shouted: "How came you to lose him, Bob?"

"A rhinoceros killed him."

There was no mistaking that answer, and once more the two looked at each other with something like consternation.

The loss of a horse was a grievous one, but considerably less so than the loss of the owner of the horse would have been.

"Where is Diedrick?" shouted Dick. "I've lost him, too."

Before his friends could ask the meaning of this alarming declaration, Bob explained that they had become separated, and he did not know where to look for the Hottentot.

It followed that it was hard work for Bob to pick his way through the grass, which offered such obstruction to the animals, and the party rode toward him. The youths frequently called to each other, and in this way approached in a direct line. In the course of fifteen or twenty minutes the figure of the lad was discerned laboring forward under the burden of his heavy rifle and the saddle and bridle of his dead horse.

All were so glad to see him alive and well that the loss of his steed seemed a small matter, since they had extra animals.

Bob told his thrilling story, and Dick gave an account of what had befallen them since the separation. It was then arranged that the saddle and bridle should be secured upon the horse of Jack — that is, merely for the purpose of being carried as a part of the luggage of the party, while Bob himself should mount behind Dick.

It need not be said that his seat was lacking in comfort, but he could support himself very well by throwing one arm about his friend, who sat securely in the saddle, besides which the cousins could exchange situations whenever they chose.

The question now was as to the whereabouts of the Hottentot. He had vanished so suddenly, and kept out of sight so persistently, that the boys were afraid some accident had befallen him. The Texan, however, felt little anxiety on his account.

"He understands the country and himself well enough to pull through any scrape he is likely to run into," said the Texan.

The boys wished they could share the faith of Jack Harvey, but were unable to do so.

CHAPTER LV.

DIEDRICK'S VICISSITUDES.

THE afternoon was wearing away, and the three friends were in doubt whether to wait in the hope of being joined by Diedrick, or return to camp and leave him to take care of himself.

Bob and Dick were opposed to anything like a desertion of their friend, who might really be in need of help. The question was still undecided, when the three heard the report of a rifle from the direction of the grass beyond them.

"That's his gun!" exclaimed Bob; "he's all right."

"I hope he is," said Dick, "but I don't know as there is any noticeable difference between the noise made by guns: that weapon may belong to some one else."

There was much comfort in the fact that the sound reached them from the right point of the compass. More than likely the weapon had been fired by the Hottentot: at any rate his friends would believe such to be the fact until the contrary should be proved. The horsemen were on the northern side of a gentle slope that intervened between them and the grassy tract in which they had finished up their rhinoceros hunting, so they rode to the top and looked down over the plain spread out before them. For a while they could see nothing, but suddenly, to their amazement, they observed Diedrick himself approaching. He was on foot, and the elevated position of the horsemen enabled them to see him distinctly.

"He has no horse," called out Dick.

The Hottentot caught sight of the party on the crest, and waved his hand in salute. His friends were so pleased to see that he was well and safe that they waved their hats in return, and bade him hurry up and join them.

The conclusion was unanimous that his horse had been slain in some encounter with a savage beast, when the spectators were astounded to catch sight of the animal himself. He was some two hundred yards behind his master, and was walking in the same direction, the intervening grass probably shutting them out from sight of each other.

"What can that mean?" was the natural query of Bob Marshall.

"He has lost his horse—his horse has lost him," said Jack; "he has wearied of looking after the horse, and now the horse has begun to look for him."

It really appeared as if such was the fact, though the truth could not be learned until the arrival of Diedrick, who was making good progress in the direction of his waiting companions.

As he continued advancing his pony did the same. His friends, suspecting that he was unaware of the peculiar position, refrained from doing or saying anything that could give him a clew to the truth.

"Where is your horse?" shouted Jack Harvey, as the panting fellow hurried up the slope.

"Me lose him — he gone — run off — neber see — break my heart ——"

At that moment the Hottentot heard the sound of hoofs, and turned to look behind him. When his eyes rested on his own animal, the expression of his face

TWO-HORNED RHINOCEROS.

and his whole manner were amusing beyond description. His under jaw fell, his eyes protruded, his legs bent forward at the knees as though about to give way, his gun dropped from his grasp, and his fingers spread apart as though each repelled the other. He appeared to be in a collapse of amazement and chagrin.

The three, who were seated on their horses, laughed merrily, for the sight was the most amusing on which they had gazed for many a day.

It looked, indeed, as if the returning steed shared in the general hilarity, for the trot was accompanied by a whinny, as he dropped down to a walk and came to a halt within arm's reach of his master.

By this time Diedrick had recovered himself, and, seizing the bridle, he bounded upon the back of the animal. Then the native appeared to boil with indignation because of the ridiculous light in which he had been placed by his steed. He began beating his ribs with his feet, as though he meant to stave them in. But it must not be thought that the Hottentot's broad, flat heels inflicted any particular hurt. He was unable to punish the pony in that fashion, and it was not until he had kept it up for some minutes, accompanying it by all sorts of calumny on the brute's ancestors, that the horse broke into a gallop.

When Diedrick thought he had chastised him enough (and about that time the latter was beginning to enjoy the sport), he gradually sheered him 'round and headed back toward the waiting party, which he joined in the course of the next few minutes.

The experience of Diedrick had been hardly less thrilling than that of his young friend, from whom he had separated for the purpose of driving the rhinoceroses toward the horsemen that were waiting on the other side of the tall grass. Since two persons can cover twice as much ground when apart as when together, the plan was a good one, provided the conditions did not change.

The first rhinoceros started up, as you will recall, headed, after a time, toward the waiting hunters, tramped heavily, progressed steadily, and went down surely. But the second displayed a fierceness altogether unexpected in his charge upon Bob Marshall.

It seemed to be a good day for that species of ungulate mammals, for the native had not gone far when the fright of his animal showed that something in the way of game was close at hand. He became so restless that he refused to advance farther, and the native lost his temper. As he had pursued a different direction from that taken by Bob, the two were a considerable distance apart, and the only notice that reached the ear of the native of anything special being under way was the report of the lad's rifle. That did not cause him uneasiness, and just then his own hands were full of business.

Diedrick dismounted to learn the cause of his horse's fright, advancing in a straight line, and in doing so he committed an unfortunate error. The particular animal that had frightened his horse was not where he supposed, but was in an unusually thick mass of grass to the right.

The Hottentot had gone but a short distance, when he heard a whiffing grunt that he recognized. He wheeled just in time to see a black rhinoceros charge from the matted grass in a paroxysm of fury because he was intruded upon by a horse and his rider.

Fortunately for the latter, however, the animal paid no heed to him, but concentrated his rage upon the steed, and proceeded to "go for him" with a vigor that could not be surpassed. No animal possessing the power of locomotion will stand still before such an attack. The steed bounded off and dashed through the grass on a dead run.

In this case the horse could travel slightly faster than the one ridden by Bob Marshall, while the rhinoceros, being smaller, could not go as rapidly as the pursuer of the youth. Thus it happened that the fugitive was able to outrun the vicious rhinoceros, though the difference in speed was so slight that the huge creature was encouraged to keep up the pur-

suit for a considerable time. The Hottentot did not wish to lose his horse, and he had some desire to capture the rhinoceros; so he ran after the beast with all the speed of which he was master.

Thus a sort of double chase was set on foot: while the rhinoceros pursued the horse, the Hottentot

A DOUBLE CHASE.

chased the rhinoceros, the front and rear of the procession being on the best of terms, while the middle portion was arrayed against both.

In this novel competition Diedrick was at a great disadvantage, the others being much more fleet than he. They rapidly drew away and disappeared from sight;

but, as he could not afford to lose his horse, the Hottentot continued the chase. He grew more savage every minute. The animal was beyond hearing, and was doubtless increasing the space at a rapid rate. Diedrick soon had little breath left, while the prospect of losing the steed was fast resolving itself into a certainty.

By-and-by the native was compelled to drop down to a slow walk, tramping heavily and wearily, and speculating as to which animal he felt the fiercest resentment against. He was angry toward the rhinoceros, as a matter of course, but he expected much better things of his intelligent horse.

He was in no special fear of the former, for he had killed more than one of his kind, and was confident that with his loaded gun he was a master of any he might encounter.

His belief was that the pursuit of the horse by the rhinoceros could not last long, for the pursuer must soon lose sight of him in the grass and see that the chase was hopeless.

Diedrick expected to come up with his pony in a brief while, but to his dismay he learned, when he examined the ground at his feet, that he was off the trail altogether.

For a few minutes succeeding this discovery, he was the best specimen of a Hottentot "mad clear through" that can be imagined. Convinced, finally, that it was useless to follow him, he turned to rejoin his friends. What followed has already been told.

CHAPTER LVI.

A WHOLE ARMFUL.

THE story of Diedrick, as it was gradually drawn from him, was of the highest interest to his listeners, but in the course of the narration he made a statement which threw the three into a flutter of excitement.

The rhinoceros that had given him such a sharp brush was a female, and at the moment she had rushed from her resting-place upon the intruder, he had seen a little one lying in the grass. It must have been quite young, for it made no attempt to follow its mother.

"That's lucky!" exclaimed Dick Brownell; "there's just the best chance in the world to secure the very prize we want."

"That's what we are here for," was the characteristic remark of Jack (since he was a Texan); "though we have had plenty of fun, the trip will be a failure if we don't scoop in a young one to take back with us."

"And you'll gain a chance to use that lasso of yours," laughed Bob Marshall; "I know you must have felt bad to sit here and have so little part in the fun."

The afternoon was so far along that there was no time to spare. Mounted in the manner described, the four hunters on their three steeds plunged into the grass. Diedrick took the lead, feeling quite willing for another encounter with the savage female because of the trick she had served him.

Although matters had not gone very satisfactorily up to this time, yet our friends seemed now to have reached what may be called the turn in the tide. Diedrick had not penetrated two hundred yards in the grass from which he had emerged a short time before on foot, when he almost ran his horse against the very female for which he was searching.

But for the alertness and vigilance of the pony, he would have been impaled on the frightful horn of the brute. The first thing that his friends observed was the sudden wheeling about of the startled horse and his plunge, as though he was about to run over them.

Dick Brownell had just time to turn his pony to one side and Jack Harvey to the other, when the native shot between them, with the rhinoceros in hot pursuit. This "arrangement" gave the very chance the hunters wanted, since the beast, paying no attention to them, exposed her broadside as she lumbered past.

Jack, Bob and Dick let drive at the proper moment, and it may be safely said that no animal of that species was ever killed with greater suddenness. The vast bulk sagged forward and downward, swinging over on one side, and the animal died without a struggle. As before, the wounds were hardly visible, the victim bleeding to death inwardly.

"That's well enough," remarked Jack Harvey, after taking a hasty survey of the carcass, "but where's the youngster?"

It seemed curious that the mother should have come to this spot, and abandoned her offspring, when the latter was so very young, for the rhinoceros and her progeny display a strong affection for each other. Our friends believed the little one could not be far off, the mother probably having been on her way to it when she discovered the approach of the hunters, and stopped to give them battle.

PONDEROUS GAME.

"I wish it was earlier in the day," said Jack, who was riding slowly around in a circle, and peering among the grass in the hope of catching sight of the youngster.

"We can come back in the morning."

"But there's no telling what may happen between now and then."

"It would be cruel to leave the little one without any attendance," said Dick, "and it will make a hole in our supply of milk — I say, Bob," he suddenly added in a whisper; "there's something moving through the grass right ahead of us."

Diedrick had caught sight of the object and hastened toward it. The next instant he called out that the young rhinoceros was found, and the party closed around the prize.

It was one of the funniest sights you can imagine. About the size of a large, chunky dog, it was so ugly-looking that no one could view it without laughing, as it came waddling through the grass, poking its comical snout here and there in quest of its mother. It paid no attention to the horsemen and would have pushed its way straight to the inanimate parent, had they not interposed their animals across its path.

"Well, I'll be hanged!" exclaimed Jack Harvey, with a laugh; "I've seen a good many homely-looking things in my life, but that beats them all."

The youngster, finding its way blocked, raised its head and looked up at the hunters as if to inquire what it all meant. Its body was pig-shaped, its legs short, round and unsymmetrical, and its head bore some resemblance to that of a calf swollen much out of shape. Just above its blunt nose was a hump, the beginning of the horn, which does not acquire its full growth for eight or ten years.

Mingled with the feeling of amusement was that of pity for the little one that was looking for its parent, which had been shot only a few minutes before. A young rhinoceros is so attached to its mother that it will fight with great fury in her defense. The youngster had not yet seen its parent, though her body lay but a short distance off, and the hunters were desirous of preventing the discovery.

Without a moment's hesitation, Jack Harvey sprang from his mustang, and, gathering the pumpkin-like object in his arm, clambered back into the saddle. It required all his strength to do so, and when he was seated once more on his steed, he found he had his hands full indeed, for it weighed a good many pounds and was as awkward to handle as a prize watermelon.

Had it offered any resistance, the task would have been impossible, but the prize was unexpectedly docile, lying as motionlesss in its novel resting-place as a tired lamb reposes in the arms of its shepherd.

Turning about, the party lost no time in forcing its way out of the grass into the plain on the higher ground. Night had now descended, but they were in high spirits over their success. They had had a sharp brush with the huge animals, and secured the prize they were anxious to get.

The hunters had gone but a short distance when they caught the twinkle of the encampment, which was at no great distance, and they moved forward at an easy pace.

Bob and Dick would not have been themselves had they not indulged in many quirps and jests at the expense of Jack Harvey, who was so pleased over his success that he took everything with the best nature. He carried the plump fellow as though it were a baby, changing its head from one arm to the other, and endeavoring to make its position as well as

A TROUBLESOME CAPTURE.

his own comfortable. The ungainly chunk never protested except once, when the nurse, in shifting it about, accidentally got it wrong end upward. The infant lay still a minute, as if waiting for its attendant to correct his error, but, finding he did not do so, kicked so vigorously that Jack made haste to re-invert the captive, which now bears the name of "Mungo."

After that everything went well, and the camp was reached without mishap. Carl Godkin was delighted. He took the pumpkin-like creature in his arms and carried it to a part of the inclosure reserved for extra company. It was furnished with a supply of goats' milk, and disposed of such a quantity that it almost caused consternation among the natives when they reflected that the demand was sure to increase rapidly instead of diminish.

"Do you know," said the director later in the evening, after supper, and when he and the Texan had relighted their pipes, "that our work is almost finished?"

"How is that?" asked Bob and Dick together.

"We have done exceedingly well; there is but one more animal for us to capture."

"What's that?"

"A hippopotamus; as soon as we get one or two of them, I shall pull up stakes and start for Port Natal."

"And what *then?*" asked Jack, the boys listening anxiously for the answer.

"I shall find letters there from Mr. Barnum, and our future movements will depend on his wishes. We are in his employ, and whatever he directs, of course, must be done."

"What about the gorilla country?" asked Bob.

"I have no doubt that a journey will be made there, but I cannot speak positively until after reaching Port Natal. I will say that if it is in my power to arrange it I shall do so." This certainly was all the boys could ask, and their eyes sparkled as they thanked the director for his promise.

"As for the hippopotami," added Mr. Godkin, "they are around us; while you were off on your hunt, Pongo and I took the best observation we could without the aid of the glass, and we saw a couple over on the other side of the river. To-morrow, as soon as we can make a start, we will be off on the hunt. If we succeed, I shall begin preparations for the journey to the coast without delay."

"Who will compose the party?" asked Dick.

"We'll take Pongo and Diedrick along; they are natives of the country and know a good deal about its animals."

"Will it be safe to leave the camp in charge of the natives alone?"

"I think so; I kept a sharp watch to-day, but haven't detected the first sign of wild men; I am quite sure, therefore, they won't trouble us."

"I suppose we'll make use of the raft to cross the stream."

"Yes; we must cross to the other shore, for the indications point to the animals being there. We had a stroke of luck this afternoon," added the director, "for, while I was along the bank of the river, hunting for signs, a dug-out drifted by so close, that with little work I secured and brought it ashore."

"It strikes me that that's suspicious," said Jack Harvey; "leastways we would believe so in our part of the world."

"No; I don't think there's anything to cause alarm, for the wild men have been so thoroughly trounced that they ain't likely to bother us any more——"

"What noise is that?" interrupted the Texan.

CHAPTER LVII.

THE BEHEMOTH.

THE night was unusually still, the hunters being so far removed from the jungle that most of the noises which are never silent failed to reach their ears, or did so with such subdued power that they only served to render the silence more impressive.

Everything had been put in good shape for the night, Abdallah taking charge of his countrymen, with the exception of Pongo and Diedrick, who were gathered with the white men around the fire.

Abdallah, Govozy and Wart were to act as sentinels for the first half of the night, while Adz, Bormo, Valmur and Gooboo, under the direction of Orak (who considered himself fully recovered), were to perform the duty for the remaining hours of darkness.

This placed the responsibility on the most insignificant members of the expedition, but Mr. Godkin wished to give himself and friends abundant rest, so they would be in good form for the morrow.

The sound which caused the interruption on the part of Jack Harvey was a heavy, wheezing snort, from the direction of the river. The director suspected its nature, but, without speaking, sprang to his feet, and looked toward the point whence it came.

At the same moment Pongo came running toward them.

"River-horse in grass," he said, "out there — me see him."

This was news indeeed.

"Well, I'll be hanged!" exclaimed Jack; "why not go on the hunt to-night, Carl?"

"We will," was the reply; "come on, Pongo and Diedrick and the rest of you. Jack, you don't want your lasso, but each of you make sure you have a weapon. Pongo, leave your boomerangs behind and fetch one of the shot-guns."

The directions were quickly obeyed, and a few minutes later the party, numbering six, on foot, were hurrying toward the river, whence had come the suspicious sound, and where the Bushman had seen the mountainous behemoth.

It was not in sight, but a heavy splashing on the other side of the stream left no doubt that the animal had crossed the river, and was making its way along the opposite bank.

"We must follow," said Mr. Godkin, "for we may not have as good a chance to-morrow."

There were the raft and dug-out ready for use, and it need not be said they were appropriated without delay. The boat, although quite large, was barely able to hold three persons, while the other structure was somewhat more buoyant: it was, therefore, necessary to employ both means of ferriage.

Pongo, Mr. Godkin and Jack Harvey took their places in the dug-out, thereby taxing it to the utmost. The boys and Diedrick stepped upon the raft, the Hottentot taking up the long pole. Pongo was an adept in handling the slender paddle, and, since the men were eager to reach the other shore, in order to keep track, if possible, of the hippopotamus, Pongo plied the implement with a skill that took him rapidly away from his friends. He promised, however, that on landing the gentlemen, he would come back to meet his young friends.

There was no moon in the sky, though it was clear, and the stars shone with a brilliancy almost unknown in the Northern hemisphere. Pongo reached land ere the more cumbersome craft was half way across.

They had disembarked, when Mr. Godkin, whose sense of hearing was unusually acute, instantly stepped back in the boat, where, standing erect, he brought his gun to his shoulder and fired at some object out in the river.

The director had seen an immense female hippopotamus, swimming toward the other shore with its young one on its back. He aimed at the mother and struck her, for she instantly sank out of sight, all except her huge snout, and the nose of the little one, which still clung to its support. Before any measures could be taken to follow her, she vanished in the gloom.

The fact that she was heading for the other shore, and that she had received a shot that must have thrown her into a rage, caused some misgiving for Diedrick and the boys that were approaching on the raft.

Pongo was directed to take the dug-out and push off as fast as he could go. On reaching the raft he was to take off the two boys and hurry back.

Jack Harvey called out in a guarded voice the explanation of the rifle shot that had just been fired, and cautioned the youths to keep quiet. Instantly their voices were hushed, while the Hottentot plied the pole with such skill that it caused hardly a ripple. A brief row brought Pongo to the side of the raft, where he invited the boys to step in. Bob obeyed, but Dick drew back.

"I don't see why," he said in a whisper, "one place isn't as good as another; I'll keep company with Diedrick."

The keen eyes that peered through the surrounding gloom failed to catch sight of the monster. The fact that she had a young one with her seemed to be in favor of a neutrality on her part until she could place it in some safe place, that would leave her free to attack the hunters.

Pongo kept the dug-out close to the raft, with a view of giving what help he could in the event of attack. He believed the shot of Mr. Godkin was a mistake, since the wounding of the mother would throw her into rage and lead her to attack the hunters before they were in the best situation to dispose of her.

He expressed the belief that she would deposit her little one in shallow water, among the grass, and then turn about and assail the sportsmen wherever she could reach them.

While our friends are pushing their way across the stream, suppose I take a few minutes to tell you something about the hippopotamus (*hippopotamidæ*), which is undoubtedly the behemoth of the Bible.

The animal is believed to inhabit nearly all the great rivers of Africa. Formerly

THE HIPPOPOTAMUS

it was met with as far north as Egypt, but its limit in that direction is now Abyssinia. Away back in the remote ages of antiquity, it was common to Europe and Asia, but in its wild state it lives alone in the Dark Continent.

The period during which the hippopotamus can remain under water has never been satisfactorily settled, but it is believed to be about ten minutes. The full-grown animal is a dozen feet in length and as much in circumference. Its legs are so short that, where the ground is uneven, the belly touches the earth when the monster walks, so that it resembles a huge hogshead mounted on four billets of wood. Its nostrils and ears are on the same plane, its ears small, sharp and stiff, and its hide, of a dirty chocolate color, is an inch and a half thick. I can conceive of no more repulsive sight than that of its mouth when fully open.

The teeth of the hippopotamus are very formidable, their number, form and situation varying with its years. The canines are immense tusks, resembling a chisel, and help to form a fitting apparatus for grinding the supply for a stomach which is capable of containing six bushels of food.

Both the jaws are movable and constitute a terrible engine for crushing its prey, whether seated in a boat or unprotected in the water.

Although many claim that the hippopotamus is more stupid than the pig, yet in some respects he shows remarkable cunning. It is almost impossible to ensnare him, for, no matter how carefully the contrivance is hidden, the huge beast seems to suspect something is wrong, and, after pausing a minute or two, will deliberately walk around the trap upon which the native has set such hopes.

As a rule, hippopotami are found in families of a dozen or a score, though sometimes the single members are detached for a greater or less time.

The nostrils are so placed that they are the first part of the animal to appear when he rises to the surface, and, like those of the seal, they are closed, while he takes a promenade along the bed of his river home.

The eyes at first sight appear to have an unusual protuberance, but this is a wise provision of nature, as seen in the eagle and some other birds of prey, where the muscles and horny rings constitute a telescopic apparatus which allows the organs to be protruded or withdrawn at will.

I once heard a mischievous lad express the wish that his eyes were constructed on the same principle, so as to permit him to look behind him without moving his head. Thus he would be enabled to detect his teacher or any frolicsome playmate trying to steal upon him.

I have referred to the voice of the hippopotamus, but it is of a nature that is hard to describe. One hunter speaks of it as a loud and short, harsh note, uttered four or five times quickly and suggesting the snort of a horse, ending with an explosive sound like a bark.

An excellent authority represents the sounds by the letters *"heurah hurh hesh-heoh!"* the first two combinations being uttered in a hoarse, sharp, tremulous tone, like the grunting of animals, while the compound word is shot forth and resembles the neigh of a horse.

However, if it is ever your fortune to hear the cry of the beast, you will admit that it is difficult to describe.

Recalling the situation of our friends, Mr. Godkin and Jack Harvey were standing, rifles in hand, on the farther side of the river, on the watch for the appearance of the river-horse, while the raft and dug-out were pushing toward them, Pongo and Bob being in the latter and Diedrick and Dick on the former.

All dreaded the appearance of the animal, for their situation placed them at a disadvantage, and she was known to be in a furious mood because of the wound received from the rifle of Mr. Godkin.

CHAPTER LVIII.

THE CRASH OF SPLINTERING WOOD.

IT was natural that all the party should feel more or less uneasiness from the fact that no one could say where the hippopotamus was. The probabilities were that she had left the neighborhood, but for the present there could be no certainty on that point. All appreciated the necessity of stillness, for a loud word or a careless splash with pole or paddle might draw the beast directly upon them. She was probably so enraged because of her wound, that nothing like fear would restrain her from rushing headlong at anything which might present itself.

It will be understood that the main danger lay in the inevitable noise of the pole or paddle while propelling the craft across the river. Water is a much better conductor of sound than air, and no little skill was required to handle those implements.

As the raft and dug-out kept so nigh each other, it was an easy matter to exchange words in low tones, without increasing the danger of detection by their giant enemy.

The stars were dazzling in their brilliancy, and the constellations shone with a splendor surpassing anything they had ever seen. Nothing could equal the beauty of the Southern Cross, on which both Bob and Dick gazed more than once while crossing the stream.

But the increasing sense of danger brought back their attention to the sphere on which they lived, and, when they found they were near the middle of the river, they thought of nothing else.

"I wonder where she can be," said Bob, in a guarded undertone, from his perch in the stern of the dug-out, to his cousin, who was standing erect on the raft less than a dozen feet away.

"I cannot think there is any likelihood of our stirring her up," said Dick, in reply. "It seems impossible that we should run against her when we traverse such a narrow path"

"It isn't impossible, but we ought to be able to go very close to the hippopotamus without disturbing her. Can you hear the ripple of Pongo's paddle?"

The two were silent a moment, during which they could scarcely distinguish the soft rustling of the implement which the Bushman plied with such skill. He kept the dug-out in motion by using it first on one side of the boat and then on the other, but his extreme care prevented him going very fast.

It was the same with the Hottentot, who handled the long pole. He did not raise the lower end above the surface, for it was not necessary to do so, but he was obliged continually to withdraw the point from the muddy bottom, and a slight

disturbance of the current was unavoidable; but, had it been less, it
would have been silence itself.

All at once the two natives
stopped propelling, and, leaning
forward, peered intently through
the gloom. They had caught a
sound, the nature of which neither
understood, but no one thought of
anything else except the hippopotamus.

Observing the alarm of their
guides, as they may be termed, the
boys held their peace,
and used eyes and
ears to the utmost.

A RESISTLESS ATTACK

The whole four heard distinctly the moving of some body in the water near
them   It was not such a ripple as would have been made by a natural obstruction
in the current, but it was irregular and spasmodic, proving that it was caused by
some fish or animal.

Diedrick and Dick were standing erect on the raft, peering forward in the darkness, the Hottentot holding the long pole half out of water and firmly grasped with
both hands.   His gun lay near the middle of the raft, but the lad not only clung to
his weapon, but he kept it ready for the river-horse if she should attack them.

Bob remained seated in the stern, but he was equally prepared with his effective weapon in case of need.

As I have stated, the Bushman, in propelling the dug-out, faced the front, thus increasing the similarity of his action to that of an American Indian approaching a hostile camp by night in his canoe. He was accustomed to using his eyes in the gloom, and yet his vision was not equal to that of the Hottentot, for it was the latter who first caught sight of the cause of the disturbance in front.

"'Tis the beast we dread!" was his startling exclamation, uttered in a whisper which all heard.

Pongo had now also detected it, and whispered:

"Speak not — no noise make!"

No one stirred a muscle, for the action of the hippopotamus led them to hope she had not observed them. The boys dimly saw the outlines of a vast square snout gliding down stream, at right angles to the course the craft were pursuing. She was not approaching, but it was the slight onward motion of the craft themselves that was taking them closer to her.

How every one wished that the boat and raft would stop, but they dared not put forth the necessary effort, for that would have attracted the notice of their enemy and precipitated the attack she was eager to make upon any animate thing.

Just at the moment the enormous head was vanishing in the gloom, a slight splash was heard, and it sank out of sight.

It was impossible to tell what this movement meant, for the hippopotamus, like all animals, is often controlled by whims, and she may have been tired of swimming. If such was the fact, she could walk a while on the muddy bottom until compelled to come to the surface for air.

Not one of the four moved or spoke. Everything was so dependent upon absolute stillness that the utmost precaution was taken by all. The Bushman sat crouched in the front of the dug-out with his paddle in air, ready to drive the boat forward or backward, as the exigency might demand. Half of the pole in the hand of Diedrick was submerged, and, as that and the raft were floating with the current, not the slightest ripple was produced.

All of us know how slowly time drags when we are waiting, and to the anxious group the minutes seemed ten-fold their real duration. But with each passing moment hope increased, for it lessened the chances of the behemoth rising anywhere near them.

It seemed to all that fully a half hour had elapsed, when in reality no more than a third of that period had gone by, a space during which the river-horse can stay under water without inconvenience.

Suddenly a faint splash broke the stillness. It was in the direction of the shore toward which they were laboring, and was so far off that it was impossible to tell what produced it.

"It is the hippopotamus," said Dick; "lucky indeed it was that she swam by without seeing us."

"It was the closest call we ever had," observed Bob, with a sigh of relief; "I'm sure that for a minute or two we were in the greatest possible danger."

"What says Pongo?" asked Diedrick, still holding the pole motionless.

"We safe — go on — fast!"

He obeyed his own suggestion by dipping his paddle deep in the current, and the Hottentot, scarcely a second later, pressed the pole into the muddy bottom of the river, his body almost horizontal from the strenuousness of his effort.

At this instant came a sound as of rushing waters, and the head of the hippopotamus rose to the surface directly between the raft and the dug-out. It was so close, indeed, that the paddle in the hand of the Bushman struck the grotesque bulk and slipped off as if from a wet log.

This involuntary act of Pongo drew the fury of the beast upon the smaller craft. The enormous head, with the hideous jaws distended, shot forward and caught the end of the dug-out between them. Then they came together with resistless force, crushing the hollowed log as though it were made of card-board.

The crash of the splintering wood, the furious grunt of the behemoth and the flying spray, all seemed to come simultaneously, and before the first step could be taken to drive off the monster or to escape her fury.

A wild cry, such as a man utters in mortal terror, came from the lips of the Bushman, who dropped his paddle, caught up his gun and made a tremendous leap far out into the river. He could swim like a water-fowl, and the instant he struck, he went under until his feet touched the velvety bottom.

He still clung to his gun, for, in his eyes, its value was scarcely less than his own life, and, swimming as far beneath the surface as possible, he came up only long enough to inhale what air was needed, when down he went again. He kept his wits about him, and, instead of swimming aimlessly, worked toward the shore which was the destination of the party.

When he rose the second time, he glanced over his shoulder to learn whether his foe was pursuing him. Nothing was to be seen of her, and, believing he now held his fate in his own hands, he swam more leisurely; but he was continually haunted by the dread that, after all, the hippopotamus was walking over the river floor and keeping pace with him, with the purpose of rising when she was ready and crushing him to nothingness in her prodigious jaws.

Not until the feet of Pongo reached bottom and he scrambled out among the reeds and grass, did he breathe freely. Then he uttered an exclamation of thankfulness and a prayer that his friends on the river might be equally fortunate.

It will be understood that at the moment the hippopotamus crushed the boat between her jaws, the situation of Bob Marshall was scarcely less dangerous than that of the Hottentot. In one respect it was not so bad, for he was seated in the stern, while it was the front portion which collapsed like an egg-shell in the terrific vise. Indeed, had Pongo been a whit less spry, his body would surely have been crushed to a jelly.

What Bob did will scarcely be believed when told; nevertheless it is strictly true and was witnessed by his cousin and Diedrick. The youth insists (doubtless with truth), that the act was in obedience to the instinctive impulse that comes over man and animal alike in the crisis of extreme danger.

He sprang to his feet at the moment the stern of the dug-out went down, because the front was raised by the jaws of the hippopotamus, with the intention of leaping to the raft; but that was too far off to be reached at a single bound, and he naturally dreaded to enter the water when the monster was so near.

Just as the under jaw of the behemoth met the upper one, Bob sprang forward and placed one foot upon her back.

It was only for an instant that his weight rested on that extraordinary foot-stool, when he made a flying leap, which carried him to the raft, his momentum almost precipitating him into the water on the other side, despite the hand which Diedrick threw out to check him.

The hippopotamus has never been accused of possessing unusual intelligence, and it is not to be supposed that the particular one of which I am speaking ever knew that her head, for a brief space of time, bore the weight of an exceedingly frightened youth. Could the creature have foreseen the act, no doubt she would have opened her capacious jaws and taken him in.

It followed, also, that in the wild confusion of the moment the monster was slightly bewildered. She did not follow the Bushman when he made his desperate leap, as I have already shown, nor for a minute or so did she comprehend that the major portion of the party upon whom she had charged were still within her reach.

There was no possible means of escaping the hippopotamus by flight, and Diedrick was too wise to attempt it.

"Shoot her! shoot her!" he called out, flinging down his pole on the raft and catching up his gun.

The excited words were yet in his mouth when Bob, taking the best aim he could in the gloom, lodged a ball in the skull of the beast. Dick almost touched the head when he too pulled trigger, and the Hottentot was equally prompt in discharging his weapon.

Thus, in the briefest possible time, two bullets and a charge of shot were fired into the hippopotamus, not one of them failing to "reach home."

But, even with such wounds, the beast would have been able to inflict fatal injuries upon all three of her enemies but for the fact that the ball fired by Bob was providentially directed. It went plumb into the right eye, and thus ploughed its way to her brain.

The other two shots did scarcely less damage, though they could not have been so instant in their effects. As it was, she was rendered furious and partially blind. She emitted a rasping grunt and charged upon the ruins of the dug-out. Her impetuosity carried her almost over the crushed log, and, instead of grasping it in her distended jaws, her forequarters bore it under the surface and out of sight.

At that juncture she seemed to gain some idea of the true state of affairs, and, making a circle with such a rush that the water foamed away from her head as it does from a rapidly driven boat, she plunged toward the raft on which our three friends were standing.

She acted as though she comprehended her mistake and was determined to correct it before it was too late.

CHAPTER LIX.

A STROKE OF FORTUNE.

THERE was the golden opportunity for the repeating rifles with which the boys were furnished. Diedrick had emptied the shot-gun into the head of the beast, but he made no attempt to use the weapon further, leaving his companions to complete the work so well begun.

"What are you doing?" called Jack Harvey from the shore; "why don't you fill her full of lead?"

And that is precisely what Bob and Dick proceeded to do in the most approved fashion. The shot that the former sent into the eye of the animal bewildered her so that the charge which she made upon the raft miscarried, she ploughing by it in the most grotesque manner.

Realizing her failure, she turned again, but by this time her fearful wounds produced their inevitable effect, and becoming suddenly motionless, she disappeared beneath the surface like the sinking of an enormous diving-bell.

The behemoth was dead and was seen no more.

During this flurry, our two friends on the shore were in what may be called a state of mind. They had set out with the expectation of taking charge of the hippopotamus business, and yet, through the rush of circumstances, it had passed wholly out of their hands and was pushed to an issue by the boys and natives.

"I think, Carl," said the Texan, stamping back and forth, half exasperated from his enforced idleness, "that there must be more of those critters 'round here, since they herd together, and I don't propose to let the folks out there have all the fun."

"It was that shot of mine that played the mischief," replied the director, "but things are so lively out on the stream, that I'm afraid something may have gone wrong with the boys."

"Have no fear," was the reassuring response of the Texan, who, as he afterward stated, was without the least concern for his young friends: "they have their guns, and, from the way things sound, they are using them to advantage."

"There is no telling how things may turn out — helloa! what's this?"

The exclamation of Mr. Godkin was caused by the appearance of a man's head on the surface of the water rapidly approaching.

"Is that you, Pongo?" asked the director, stepping to the edge of the stream and peering out in the gloom.

"It me — Pongo," was the answer, and the next minute the Bushman rose to his feet and walked ashore.

"Why didn't you come in the dug-out?" was the query of Jack Harvey, who suspected what had taken place.

"How come in dug-out when ain't any dug-out come in — eh?"

"What's become of it?"

"River-horse chaw him up."

"Ah," laughed Mr. Godkin, "that makes another matter of it; your explanation is accepted; how are the boys getting along?"

"Get 'long like thunder," was the rather startling reply of the Bushman, who did not enjoy the bath he was compelled to take because of the attack of the behemoth.

Meanwhile the men kept up communication with the young gentlemen on the raft, who announced about this time that their assailant was killed and Diedrick was hard at work pushing the support toward them.

A few minutes later the awkward craft and the three figures loomed to view through the darkness, and soon all parties were shaking hands and congratulating each other on the fortunate issue of the hunt.

But, as you will recall, the real business that had brought them thither remained unaccomplished. They had slain the mother hippopotamus, but had not captured her young, nor could any one tell where it was to be found.

The dug-out would have been a most convenient help in searching for it, but the boat had been destroyed, and all that remained was the raft. When our friends came to step upon this it would not sustain them.

"Me swim," said Pongo, springing into the water and striking out for the other shore. Inasmuch as he had already had a souse, there was no hardship in this act. Diedrick would have imitated him had there been necessity for doing so, but the structure was found just buoyant enough to bear the three men and two boys, while the Hottentot was serviceable in using the pole.

The progress of the raft could not equal that of the Bushman, who swam with a powerful, easy stroke that would have delighted a professional. The current seemed to cause him no trouble, while the structure drifted considerably down stream before it made the other bank.

At the very moment that it entered the tall grass a great splashing was heard some way above, and the well-known voice of Pongo rang out:

"Come help — me got him — fight hard!"

Every one on the raft leaped off and dashed through the water and vegetation to the spot where the native was struggling with *something*.

Pongo had no thought of anything of the kind, but was swimming leisurely, and finding he could reach bottom with his feet, stopped floating and began walking out on land.

He had reached a point where the water came only to his knees, when he was startled by some queer-looking creature rushing from the grass and impetuously attacking him.

It was on him before he could retreat, but, fortunately, its capacity for inflicting injury was less than its will, and the nose which it banged against the legs of the Bushman did no harm, though it came nigh knocking him over.

Pongo recognized it at this moment, and, knowing the anxiety of his employers to obtain a young hippopotamus, he resolutely grappled with it and shouted for help.

Notwithstanding its youth, the little pumpkin-bellied creature fought and floundered with such vigor that it required the united exertions of Pongo, Mr. Godkin and Jack Harvey to overcome and get it out on dry land, where it still rolled, rooted, butted and grunted like a pig with the colic.

Had they been a little farther from camp, they would have sent thither for conveniences to help carry it, for the little one was so bulky that it was too big a load for a single person to transport far without help. As it was, however, the distance was brief, and it was brought in after considerable difficulty and lodged in its quarters, which, I may say, was all the room that remained at the disposal of the hunters, though, of course, more could have been arranged.

"*That* winds up our work of catching animals in South Africa," said Mr. Godkin, once more resuming his seat around the camp-fire; "to-morrow we begin to make preparations for the journey to Port Natal."

"But," said Dick Brownell, "the largest animal of all has not been caught."

"You mean the elephant? I did intend to try to secure one or two of them, but Mr. Barnum said he needed them less than any other curiosities. He has a large number with his show, and if he needs more he will meet no trouble in buying them. He told me not to put myself out to secure them, though if a good opportunity presented, I might gather some in. We may gain a chance on the way."

True to what he said, the preparations were made at an early hour the next day to start for the sea-coast. It was a big job, and the journey was necessarily long, tedious and excessively trying.

They had a goodly number of captives which required constant and careful attention. There were the two young leopards, the hartbeest, the eland, the young lion, two oryxes, mother and young giraffe, mother and young zebra, por-

"COME, HELP!"

cupine, secretary-bird, baboon, and the young rhinoceros and hippopotamus. These of themselves formed a goodly menagerie, and my friends could count themselves fortunate if they succeeded in reaching Port Natal without the loss of more than three or four.

Mr. Godkin's experience in the business fitted him better than any man that could have been selected for the delicate and difficult work. There seemed no possible contingency of which he did not think and for which he did not provide.

But he assured me that of all the tasks he ever undertook, that of conducting the train and the animals through the long stretch of desert and mountainous country, from a point west of the center of Southern Africa to Port Natal, was the hardest. He suffered three attacks from wild men in which Valmur and Gooboo were killed, and Orak was again wounded,—this time so severely that he will never fully recover from it. In the second fight Pongo distinguished himself by instantly killing one of the assailants with a boomerang, decapitating him as neatly as it could have been done by the sword of a Crusader.

Govozy, another native, fell sick when in the Orange Free State, and, despite everything that could be done, died and was buried in one of the wildest glens in the mountains.

Both Bob Marshall and Dick Brownell became ill with some fever peculiar to the country, but fortunately they pulled through, and expressed themselves as being stronger than ever.

It was about this time that the baboon managed to break his way out of the cage in which he was confined, but, before he was fairly started on the highway to freedom, Jack Harvey's lasso yanked him back again.

The rhinoceros and hippopotamus developed such amazing appetites that they threatened to raise a famine in the expedition. Three of the oxen, two of the goats and one of the horses perished on the way, but when, at last, the far-off destination was reached, and the wearied party looked out on the flashing waters of the Indian Ocean, not a single one of the captives was missing, and all were in excellent condition.

It was an exploit of which any person might feel proud, and the handsome gold watch and chain which Mr. Carl Godkin now wears was sent to him as a token of my appreciation of his skill and devotion.

At Port Natal, the remaining natives were paid liberally for their services, with the promise that when my agents went that way again, they would be sought out and re-engaged, for they had rendered most excellent service, and Pongo and Diedrick especially had proven themselves beyond value. I have met other travelers in South Africa who have employed them, and they all speak in the highest terms of their faithfulness and skill.

When I add that the captive birds and animals, which were shipped from Port Natal to England, and thence to America, made the long voyage in safety, with the exception of one of the leopard kittens and an oryx, you will agree with me that the expedition which I sent into South Africa was brilliantly successful in every respect.

CHAPTER LX.

R. CARL GODKIN, my director, was not disappointed in his expectation of receiving a communication from me on his arrival at Port Natal. In fact, he found several awaiting him, for his return had been delayed far beyond the period I had anticipated. I knew he would be in need of funds, and I made sure that he did not lack in that essential respect.

But he acquainted his friends with the contents of one letter, which interested them beyond measure. I ordered Mr. Godkin to divide his forces, and, since I wished to leave no room for discussion, I gave minute directions as to what should be done.

Mr. Godkin and Dick Brownell were to go to India and devote several months to the capture of wild animals peculiar to that country, while Jack Harvey and Bob Marshall were to find their way up the west coast of Africa to the Gaboon country, where they were to do their utmost to buy or capture a couple of gorillas, the same number of chimpanzees, and any other curiosities worth securing. They were told to let no expense stand in the way of their success either in India or Western Africa.

You would suppose that Dick Brownell would have been much disappointed in finding himself shut out from the expedition on which he had set his heart, but I am happy to say that it was otherwise. The taste that he had had of sickness and the sufferings he had undergone from the African climate resulted in lessening his enthusiasm for that country, and I have no doubt that he wrote me the truth when he said that if I had given him his choice between Africa and India he would have selected the latter.

Since Bob Marshall was equally positive that he would have fixed upon Equatorial Africa as the scene of his hunting experiences, I really think I was fortunate enough to make the best possible arrangement all around.

Inasmuch as Jack Harvey, who was also pleased with his appointed task, and Bob were left to their own devices to reach their destination, they decided to take ship to Cape Town, where they were confident they would not have to wait long before finding passage to the western coast.

With the good luck which seemed always to attend him, Mr. Godkin had no difficulty in arranging for the transport of his animals to England. He was obliged to spend several days in Port Natal, for which all were glad, since it deferred for a short time the hour of separation that no one could not say would be final.

It was on one of the pleasant evenings that our friends spent in each other's company that they fell to discussing the countries which were their respective destinations.

Mr. Godkin had little to say about Equatorial Africa, for he had never visited the section, but when they spoke of Hindostan he was at home, for the greater part of his life had been spent in that remarkable region, which, though a dependency of England, contains more than four times its population.

Bob and Dick reminded their friend that he had promised to tell them about his singular experience in India many years before, and that there could be no time more favorable for the telling than the present. The gentleman seemed loth to relate the story, but, since he had given his promise, he could not refuse, and you may be sure he had attentive listeners to his narrative, which I think is interesting enough to insert in this place.

"I believe I told you," said he, after lighting his pipe, "that when I first went to India for Mr. Barnum, it was before either of you young gentlemen was born. In fact, I reached the country in the year 1857, just in time to be caught in the swirl of the Sepoy mutiny, which horrified the whole civilized world, and I can say that among all the strange adventures which befell the foreign residents enveloped in that lurid tragedy, I don't think any one had a more extraordinary experience than I.

"I had a cousin, who was a missionary, living with his wife and three children two miles south of Dacca. I was but a youth, when, fulfilling a promise, I reached their pleasant home in the latter part of June, 1857, which, as you know, was the month succeeding the first outbreak at Meerut, where the troops mutinied on Sunday, May 10th. In the same month the Mogul Empire was proclaimed at Delhi.

"I had a pretty rough time on the road to Dacca, for there were signs of the upheaval all around me, though I, like most of the Europeans, was inclined to believe that it would amount to little and would soon be suppressed.

"I had sent no notice to cousin Fred of my coming, knowing I would be welcome at any time, and the result was, when I arrived at his home, I found that he and his family had left several weeks before, and were probably at that very hour in Calcutta, safe under the guns of Fort William.

"But Fred's house was open and in charge of a single native servant, Kush-awa, a converted Hindoo, of whom he had often written me. The native was as devoted as a Newfoundland dog, so Fred wrote, and he declared he would unhesitatingly place his life in his hands; but I distrusted the fellow from the first.

"He spoke English well, and, when I made known my identity, he told me that his master had often spoken of me, and with such affection that he (the native) loved me before he saw me. He was tall, thin, muscular and reserved, scarcely ever speaking unless first addressed by me.

"At that season the weather in India is like sheol, and much as I wanted to get out and follow Fred to Calcutta, before the road thither was closed by the mutineers, I hesitated to start on account of the frightful temperature. I still hoped that the skies would clear and that affairs would speedily settle down as before.

"One characteristic of Kush-awa deepened my distrust of him. He had a habit of moving about with such silent stealth that he reminded me of a cobra. Often, when stretched in a hammock reading or smoking, I instinctively felt that some danger was near, and, looking about suddenly, found him standing a few paces off, watching me with strange intensity. The moment he saw he was discovered, he would move away with the same noiselessness, only to fix his stare upon me from some other point where he fancied he was invisible.

"One Sunday morning Kush-awa asked permission to be absent until nightfall, and I willingly granted it, for, to tell the truth, I felt that it would be a vast relief to be rid of the fellow, even for a day. You see, I had made myself at home in cousin Fred's house, for that was just what he would have wanted me to do had he known I was there.

"So Kush-awa took his departure and I settled down to enjoy, or rather to worry through the day as best I could.

"Whew! wasn't it hot? I had eaten lightly of fruit in the morning, had taken a draught of goat's milk, and would not need another mouthful of food before night. I did little but loll in one of the hammocks, smoking cheroots and reading. I dawdled over a novel until the letters ran together, the thread of the story melted into nothingness, and I sank into sleep.

"When I awoke, the afternoon was well along and I felt disgusted and sticky. A species of green-winged fly was boring into my nostrils, and several millions, more or less, of red-legged ants were crawling down my back. Sitting upright, I sniffed vigorously, slapped spitefully and brushed furiously, anathematizing, meanwhile, the oven-like climate that caused all this suffering.

"My hammock was swung between two trees in front of the house. To my left wound the road to Dacca, there being a dense wood on both sides of the highway, so that it may be said the bamboo house stood in a sort of clearing in the Indian forest. Still, the shade was so plentiful that hardly a ray of sunlight forced its way through the exuberant vegetation. But to me the heat seemed all the more oppressive on that account.

"Looking to the wood or jungle on the left, I suddenly became aware that it contained a number of men, approaching with such stealth that there could be no doubt they meant to surround the house, or perhaps to rush upon me before I could take refuge within doors.

"It flashed upon me at once that these natives, of whom I caught glimpses, were Sepoys whom Kush-awa had brought from Dacca to kill me. He had gone to town that morning for the express purpose of guiding them thither, and had I not opened my eyes when I did, I never would have opened them in this world.

"Now, it was a custom with me, when stretching out in the hammock, to lean my rifle against the nearest tree. Like all new-comers in India, I had magnified ideas of the perils which impended, though it may seem that that was impossible, since the Sepoy mutiny was fairly under way.

"The instant I discovered the swarthy figures moving among the trees like so many Indians, I sprang up, seized my gun, took a quick aim at the nearest wretch and pulled trigger.

"I PULLED TRIGGER."

"The screech which followed showed that there was one less mutineer left to raise the mischief in India, and I made a dash into the house, accompanied by several shots which whistled all about me.

"Hastily shutting the doors, I prepared to die with my boots, or rather slippers, on. The house had never been intended to serve as a fort, and though Fred had left his loaded rifle within, and I had my fully charged revolver at command, there was no prospect of my being able to hold out long.

"Wheeling about, I observed a dozen dusky miscreants running across the highway, brandishing their knives, shrieking and fairly leaping with joy at the prospect of the treat before them in putting me to a cruel death.

"In that fearful moment, while I stood by the side of a window, with Jack's loaded rifle in hand, I held my fire a moment, while I anxiously looked for Kush-awa, the treacherous villain that had brought this upon me. I wanted to bore a hole through *his* bronzed skull before I succumbed.

"But he was invisible, and I let drive at the nearest fiend, who went down with a howl that fairly made the leaves tremble.

"This acted as a temporary check of the ardent Sepoys, who instantly scattered to cover.

"But I knew they would not remain quiet long, and. when they made a united charge, even though I defended myself with the utmost desperation, nothing could save me.

"It was at this critical juncture, when the natives were like so many tigers gathering themselves for a spring, that I heard distinctly the boom of a gun, followed by another and another in quick succession, just as if a cannonade was going on only a few hundred yards to the south.

"Before I could form the faintest idea of what it meant, I caught the terrified cry·

"'*The Feringhees are coming! fly! fly!*'

"It was uttered by one of the natives in Hindustanee, and instantly the whole party of Sepoys skurried away, vanishing from sight with incredible quickness.

"The booming continued, though it did not approach, and, while I stood wondering what it could mean, and speculating as to what I ought to do, if, indeed, I could do anything, Kush-awa dashed forward, calling out in an excited undertone:

"'*Run, sahib! quick, sahib! they will soon be back!*'

"It was taking desperate chances, but, yielding to an instinct which I did not understand, I followed him within the jungle, and a couple of hours later, under his pilotage, reached Dacca. From that point, with the help of trusty friends, I succeeded finally in entering the British lines, and was never again in serious danger from the mutineers.

"Now, as to the explanation: Kush-awa was going to Dacca when he met the Sepoys on their way to the missionary's house to destroy him and his family. Kush-awa told them the people were gone, but one of them knew of my presence, and they were determined to slay me. Kush-awa did not dare pretend the friendship he felt, and he accompanied them back, hoping a chance would offer to give me warning of my danger.

"The booming, cannon-like sounds unexpectedly presented an opportunity of which he took instant advantage, and, before the Sepoys could recover from their astonishment and panic, I was beyond their reach."

"But what were those sounds that saved you?" asked the wondering youths.

"*The guns of Burrisaul*, which, although never fully explained, will doubtless be understood before long. One of the stations in the Sunderbunds of India is Burrisaul, and it has given its name to certain singular noises which are sometimes noticed in that region during the rainy season. There seems to be no reason why the sounds should be specially connected with Burrisaul, for they are heard at Backerjung and even at Dacca. The explosions, which resemble the booming of cannon, vary in frequency. They are only heard during the rainy season; they proceed from the south, are audible one hundred miles inland, they still come from the south even on the sea-coast, and are very slightly, if any, louder in one place than in another."

As Mr. Godkin said, the phenomenon known as *the guns of Burrisaul* has not yet been sufficiently investigated to be understood. The cause is evidently atmospheric and, no doubt, we shall learn all about it in time. To quote an authority, explained or unexplained, as surely as July comes round, far out in the tropic Sunderbunds, through the long darkness, in hushes of the splashing rain, and amid the hum of myriads of insects, to wakeful and feverish ears throb the strange discharges of this mysterious artillery, and startled sleepers sink back relieved, exclaiming, "'Tis but the guns of Burrisaul!'"

CHAPTER LXI.

THE time has now arrived when I must take up the history of my friends, and, for awhile, pursue them separately.

A thrilling experience fell to the lot of both parties, and I propose to give the narratives in full, leaving the account of Jack Harvey and Bob Marshall's adventures in Equatorial Africa, in search of the gorilla, chimpanzee, and other curiosities, for the close of this volume. Having seen them started on their way to that pestilential region, by way of Cape Town, we will follow Mr. Godkin and Dick Brownell to India, where I am sure you will find their experiences worth reading.

I have not time nor the space, nor would you care to have me give the particulars of the voyage to Calcutta and up the Ganges to Lucknow, famous for the massacre and siege during the Sepoy mutiny of which Mr. Godkin had given an entertaining incident.

Let us open the story after the arrival of our friends in that neighborhood, fully prepared for the prosecution of their search for natural curiosities for The Greatest Show on Earth.

A mishap occurred on the very threshold of the enterprise. While completing their arrangements in Lucknow, some conscienceless thief stole both their repeating rifles. The help of the police was secured, but no trace of the weapons could be found, and, unwilling to lose any more valuable time, and unable to obtain Winchesters, Mr. Godkin secured a couple of the well-known English Express pattern, with twenty-two inch barrel, single shot breech-loaders. They set out on their hunt with some misgiving, but consoled themselves with the thought that their fire-arms were of the kind popular with English sportsmen, and they had figured in some of the most stirring adventures in the jungles of India.

Dick Brownell was a young man who kept his eyes and ears open, and strove to acquaint himself with everything worth learning. I cannot pretend to give one-half of the entertaining contents of his letters, but I recall that he said he was specially interested in two animals of which he saw numerous specimens before engaging in hunting in India.

One of these was the domestic beast known as the zebu, which has a curious fatty hump projecting from the withers, and a heavy dewlap falling in thick folds from the throat. The zebu is a quiet, intelligent animal, and is used in drawing either carriages or plows.

One of the most familiar varieties is the famous Brahmin bull, which, being stamped with the sacred mark of Siva, is allowed to wander about and do just as it pleases, no one venturing to disturb or offend him in the slightest degree.

The gayal abounds among the hills forming the eastern boundary of Bengal. It is truly a valuable animal, its milk being very rich, while its flesh is extremely palatable. The gayal is easily domesticated, and, as you will observe from the illustration, is quite attractive in appearance.

The party of hunters included, beside Mr. Godkin and Dick, three experienced natives, all of whom were old acquaintances of my agent, who had visited that section more than once before.

The Americans were mounted on fine, tough little ponies common to the country, but the natives preferred to do their work on foot.

SACRED COW.

There was some talk of engaging in a tiger hunt, which, if carried out, would be upon the backs of trained elephants, in accordance with the fashion of India.

It was about ten o'clock that night that Dick stretched out to sleep until the morrow.

The natives had gone to rest in the home of one of their friends, while the boy and Mr. Godkin occupied a bamboo structure that hardly deserved the name of a house.

It consisted of one room, without any upper story, and with no floor, but the ground had been worn smooth and hard by the feet of the former occupants.

Dick spread his blanket in one corner, and flung himself upon it, the warmth of the night preventing him from throwing the covering over his body.   Mr. Godkin sat in front of the structure for a long time with his hookah, or native pipe, while Dick, with his rugged health unimpaired, soon sank into a sweet, refreshing slumber.

This sleep of the boy lasted, probably, until midnight, when, without any apparent cause so far as he could tell, he opened his eyes in the full possession of his senses.

He was lying partly on his left side, with his face toward the single opening in the bamboos, which served as a door.   There being really no door, of course the opening was always there, so that it may be said that the name bungalow sometimes given to the building, was altogether undeserved.

The moon was shining with unusual brightness, even for that country, where the light of the orb sometimes turns night into day.   It seemed to Dick that when he looked through the opening on the other side that the sun was really out, though a moment's thought convinced him it would be a number of hours before it rose.

Probably one half of the interior was illuminated by a flood of moonlight, which showed the form of Mr. Godkin lying on his blanket and sound asleep, as was proven by his deep, heavy breathing.   He was on the right-hand side of the lad, there being a space of but a foot or two between them.

"I wonder what made me wake?" was the thought that came to Dick, after he had looked around the apartment and then noticed the form of his friend; "it must be the climate is so hot in this part of the world that a person unaccustomed to it finds it hard to sleep as he does in his own home."

He recalled that just before falling asleep, he had drawn a portion of the blanket, not over his body, but across his lower limbs, which were covered to the knees. This act was in obedience to a habit, for, as I have shown, the temperature was such that the thinnest clothing was a burden.

He now noticed that the fold of the blanket, resting on the lower part of his legs, felt strangely heavy.   Mr. Godkin had related an incident to him the night before, of one of his friends who had awoke in the night and found a hideous cobra coiled over his breast.   This incident instantly came to the mind of Dick, and fortunately prevented him from kicking his limbs free of the covering, as was his first inclination to do.

"It would be strange if one of those reptiles had located himself on my blanket," reflected the boy, adding, the next instant: "I notice that smell like the odor of raw potatoes, which the cobra gives out — my gracious! *it is a cobra!*"

The feet of the youth were turned toward the door, so that, looking through the opening at the moonlit world beyond, his gaze was in a line with his own body. Furthermore, the rays of the moon entered the bamboo building far enough to strike the ground within a few inches of where his feet rested.

Dick was looking intently at the irregular fold of the blanket and fancying that he dimly saw something else mixed with the cloth, when an object slowly rose to view between him and the door. and from the blanket across his ankles.

Rearing itself aloft, against the background of moonlight, it had the appearance of being stamped in ink on a fleecy curtain: the outlines could not have been more distinct had the sun been in the zenith

One glance was enough. it was a cobra de capello, the most dreaded serpent of all India, whose venom has a malignancy that approaches the miraculous. A bite

THE GAYAL

from this reptile is the death-warrant of the victim, as assuredly as if he were smitten by a bolt from heaven.

The serpent had undoubtedly been attracted by the warmth of the lad's body, and had coiled on the blanket which lay over his lower limbs while he was asleep, and, of course, after Mr. Godkin had also lain down and lost consciousness.

Although the lad was not aware that he had stirred, there must have been a slight, involuntary twitching of his legs which disturbed the cobra, and caused him to raise his head threateningly. This species is easily alarmed, and the least movement on the part of the boy would have brought the fangs into some part of his body with the quickness of the lightning's flash.

Dick knew better than to stir, but all the same *something must be done!*

He could not lie still for hours with that horrible thing coiled at his feet, and holding itself ready to strike. Human nature was unequal to the fearful test, especially when the truth was also apparent, that if he were able to remain motionless until daylight, there was no certainty that that would bring safety.

Dick's first thought was that, without stirring a muscle, he would call the name of Mr. Godkin; but he dared not do so, through fear that the sound would irritate the cobra to the point of striking, while, if his friend was a little tardy in grasping the situation, he might by some indiscretion bring the blow upon himself.

"No; I've got to manage the snake myself," was Dick's conclusion, "and I wish some one would tell me what to do, for I'm sure I don't know."

CHAPTER LXII.

BANG! BANG! BANG! BANG! BANG!

THE hardest thing for Dick Brownell was to resist an inclination which, it obeyed, would have been fatal.

It seemed to him that by a sudden kick of one of his feet he could fling a part of his blanket over the cobra, and, imprisoning the reptile in the folds, smother him before he could strike, or, at any rate, so entangle him that he could be killed within the cloth.

But if the first kick should fail to catch the upraised head!

It was most likely to do so, in which case the spectacled front, with the erect hood, would shoot forward from the blanket, and inject the fatal poison before the lad could make another move.

No; the risk was too great.

His rifle was lying so near him that he could almost reach it without moving, but it might as well have been a hundred miles distant for all the good it could do him

His revolver was in his hip pocket, and as he lay on his left side, the weapon being on his right, he hoped that he could draw it forth, and, carefully aiming, send a bullet through the upper part of the serpent's body.

As slowly as the minute hand glides over the face of the clock the lad began reaching for the pistol, but at the very first essay the frightful head commenced swaying from side to side in such a threatening manner that he desisted.

If such a slight movement alarmed the reptile, the act of drawing forth the weapon and pulling the trigger would be sure to excite him to action. No; *that* would not do.

All at once a strange idea entered Dick's head. He had seen the serpent-charmers of India, and had witnessed the wonderful manner in which they governed the serpents by their monotonous reed music; could he not do something in the same line?

So faintly that his voice scarcely broke the oppressive stillness, he began a low humming, which, at first, was like the soft music of the wind-harp. He attempted no tune, but merely hummed, his voice rising and sinking no more than a note or two of the scale.

The first result was not calculated to soothe the nerves of the youth. The head of the serpent swayed more and more, from side to side and back and forth, as though the noise irritated him; but the youth persevered, imparting a certain swing to the music, if it may be termed such, and slightly increasing its volume.

The first encouragement was when he perceived that the cobra, in its rude way, was oscillating its head in accord with the swing of his humming sounds. The music was producing its effect and he was "keeping time."

Dick sang a little louder; the hooded head rose higher and the serpent moved from the blanket out upon the smooth ground.

A cold chill ran through the lad at the fear that the reptile was about to approach his head. He was sure he could not stand any advance of that nature.

But, fortunately, instead of doing so, it slowly crept away from him, until it was in plain sight in the moonlight which poured through the door. It did not leave the hut, but coiling and uncoiling, raising and lowering its head, it showed that it was pleased by the low, monotonous music which came from between the lips of the boy whose eyes were fixed upon his strange visitor.

Once more the latter began moving his right hand toward his hip pocket. The snake offered no objection, seemingly now wholly occupied with his enjoyment of the strange entertainment. The latter continued unchanged, except perhaps there was a slight addition of vigor, when the lad's hand grasped the butt of his revolver and he began slowly drawing it forth. Still the singing went on as the lad brought the weapon to a level and carefully sighted at the reptile.

"I think I can pink you," was Dick's thought, as he pointed with an arm as rigid as iron at the hooded head, and held it thus until he could make his aim sure; "at any rate, if I miss the first time, I'll give you the contents of all the chambers, and you may think, if hurt, that it is a part of the

Music's Charms.

music." The humming continued, and the head gently undulated in time, the snake coiling and uncoiling in a curious fashion, once going so near the door that the lad was sure he meant to leave, possibly because he could not stand any more of his music.   But, no; when near the door, he moved back again, until he reached the same spot on the blanket he was occupying when discovered, where he paused a moment, rearing his head higher than before.

At that instant — *Bang! bang! bang! bang! bang!*

Five reports rang out in quick succession, and the mischief was to pay.

The first bullet from the revolver went straight through the neck of the cobra, close to the head, and two of the remaining ones perforated the body lower down.

There was fierce threshing of the ground, the snake twisting and untwisting with furious quickness during the few seconds that his death-struggles lasted.

Fortunately, its throes carried it toward the opening of the hut, out of which it went as if kicked by an indignant foot, and came to rest just beyond the door, as dead as Julius Cæsar.

"What under the sun is up?" asked Mr. Godkin, raising his head from his blanket on hearing the reports and peering into the gloom, with a feeling that something dreadful must have caused the deafening shots of the revolver.

"I found that big cobra in the room," replied Dick, springing from his couch, "and I have been practicing a little on him with my pistol."

"You're mighty lucky if he didn't practice on you," said his friend, who instantly saw the snake and was only a second in rising to his feet; "didn't he bite you?"

"Not that I am aware of," replied Dick, who stepped to the door of the hut and looked at the limp, rope-like mass; "in my opinion, that cobra de capello, considered strictly as a cobra de capello, is of no further account." And then he related the incident which I have told you.

"You were fortunate indeed," said Mr. Godkin, "for the slightest motion on your part, when you awoke, would have caused him to bury his fangs in you, and then that would have been the last of Master Richard Brownell, from America."

The nervous shock produced by the visit of the serpent drove away all disposition to sleep on the part of Mr. Godkin and Dick.

They knew, too, that if they lay down again, they were liable to a visit from the mate, or another of the hideous

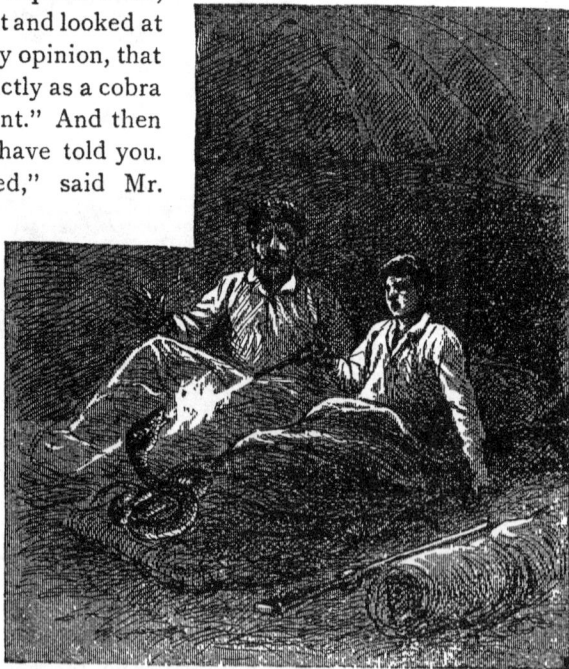

"FIVE REPORTS RANG OUT"

reptiles, for there was no way of shutting them out. So the man filled and lit his hookah, and sat down outside the hut, Dick joining him and recharging his revolver.

The night was a beautiful one, the moon having reached a high point in the heavens, while the sky was without a single cloud to interfere with its light.

Some distance off a dark line rose against the clear sky, stretching farther to the right and left than the eye could follow. It marked the jungle, those enormous reaches of forest in India which abound with multifarious forms of animal life, and which are so choked with undergrowth, vines and the dense vegetation that it is impossible to force one's way through many portions, except by following the paths that have been opened.

"There's enough game in there," remarked Mr. Godkin, knocking the ashes from his pipe, "to keep an army of hunters busy."

"Yes; and I would be glad if it would stay there and wait for us to go after it."

"What do you mean?" asked his friend, turning suddenly toward him with an expression of anxiety; "have you seen anything?"

"I am not sure, but once or twice I fancied there was something moving along in front of the jungle, keeping most of the time within the line of shadow."

"Since I fancied the same thing I am quite sure that it is no fancy at all. Now that the moon has crept much higher we shall be likely to gain a better view of the object."

"Have you a suspicion, Mr. Godkin, of what it is?"

"I have," he replied, compressing his lips and nodding his head; "but I hope I am mistaken."

"What do you fear?"

"One of the most fearful animals in the world. You know what *that* is."

"A royal Bengal tiger."

"That's it. This little bamboo structure would be no more protection against a tiger of the kind I have in mind than so much tissue paper, not even if we had a second story to which we could retreat."

"I have read fearful stories about the tigers of this country, and supposed some of them were exaggerated."

"Probably they were, but the truth is bad enough. The only way to hunt the creature is with a large party, so that if he turns they can give him a volley. Since it is out of our power to do that, we can only hope that we may not be troubled by one of them just at present."

"But if there should be a tiger prowling along the edge of the jungle out there, Mr. Godkin, we ought to be ready for him."

"The suggestion is a good one," remarked his friend, rising to his feet, and passing within the hut. Dick did the same, and the next minute the two emerged, each bearing his loaded rifle. They seated themselves, as before, on the ground, with their backs against the bamboos.

The moon being so near overhead, the line of deep shadow along the jungle was so thin that any animal venturing out was quite certain to be detected.

A Whole Family.

"There he is!" whispered Dick.

"I see him!" said Mr. Godkin; "don't stir!"

The eyes of both were fixed on the long stretch of jungle when they observed a beast that was undoubtedly a tiger, moving in a direction parallel to the wood. He walked slowly, and stopped after going about a dozen yards.

He acted as if he was not quite satisfied with the looks of things, and was reconnoitering the bamboo hut before venturing to pay it closer attention.

"I think we had better go inside," added Mr. Godkin, in the same guarded undertone.

The precaution was wise, and the youth made no objection, for it seemed reasonable to believe that their presence was likely to tempt the beast to attack them.

"Now," added the man, "if he will be considerate enough to let us alone we will reciprocate."

"I don't understand why he has held off so long," replied Dick, who, standing back out of the moonlight, kept his eyes on the beast in such plain sight.

"They are very cunning at times. He is suspicious, too, and, I suppose, he doesn't exactly understand how things are here."

"*Good gracious!*"

A SERPENT CHARMER

There was cause for the latter exclamation, for the tiger acted as though all misgiving on his part had vanished. Having stood motionless for two or three minutes he began stealthily approaching the hut, as if he hesitated no longer about making an assault.

"We musn't lie idle while he does *that*," said Dick, raising his gun.

"The time hasn't come to fire"

"I know that, but it is time to be ready."

"No matter what happens, don't shoot until you get the word from me; I'm afraid you will be too rash. Now is the time, my boy, for coolness and presence of mind."

"Absence of body would be much better," thought Dick, though he said nothing.

It was an impressive sight when the royal Bengal tiger advanced directly toward the hut, his terrible head aloft, and his tail vibrating gently from side to side. He emitted no growl, and, since the two in the hut were silent, the stillness was oppressive to a degree.

"He will stop before he reaches us," whispered Mr. Godkin, who had also raiseu the hammer of his heavy rifle.

This surmise was correct, for the words were yet in his mouth when the brute paused. He was too cunning to venture into what might prove an ingeniously laid trap.

At this moment he was standing about fifty feet from the door of the hut, and formed a striking picture indeed, the very embodiment as he was of prodigious strength, cat-like activity and irrestrainable ferocity.

No better target could have been desired could the hunters **have** been in a secure spot. As it was, Mr. Godkin was more tempted than he would have admitted at the time, to send a bullet into the neck, just below the head, where, if rightly aimed, the messenger would bore its way through the seat of life.

But the critical moment had not yet come. The tiger might change his mind and go away. If he did, so much the better.

If he decided to attack he must approach still nearer, and there was a better chance of making the aim fatal, though it was hardly to be expected that he would halt again in such a favorable position.

So plainly was the beast seen that a slight turning of his head — no more than an inch or two each way — was observed. His own posture threw the moon slightly behind him, so that his front was partly in shadow, which fact added ten-fold to his terrible appearance.

Dick had read of "blazing eye-balls," "flaming orbs," and that sort of thing, but never saw anything of the kind until the Bengal tiger struck an attitude before him.

You know that the eyes of the cat species have a peculiar greenish, phosphorescent glow, and there was a glitter about those of the tiger which justified the seemingly extravagant expressions that are so often used in describing them.

If the beast withdrew, well: if he advanced, to say the least, it would not be well.

But the animal had no intention of holding the attitude he had taken, and again he moved.

Dick Brownell's heart almost stopped beating when he observed that, instead of retreating or turning to one side, the creature was once more walking with his stealthy tread directly toward the door of the hut.

"He is coming for us *this* time sure," whispered the lad.

"It looks so. but hold on; the time has not yet come to shoot."

"It is very near though."

But at the very moment the lad had decided to bring his gun to his shoulder, and not to await the command of his unduly cautious friend, the tiger once more hesitated.

He was so close now, however, that it looked as if he was about to gather himself for a terrific leap upon the hut and its inmates.

At Home.

CHAPTER LXIII.

BUILDING BETTER THAN HE KNEW

The crisis seemed to be at hand. Both Mr. Godkin and Dick raised their rifles and leveled them at the terrible tiger, which stood only a few paces off, apparently on the point of making a bound directly at the little bamboo structure, which, as the man had asserted, could have offered no more resistance to his fury than so much card board. Before leaping, the beast, like all of his kind, would squat on his legs, so as to gather his muscles for the terrific effort that would bring him upon the defenders.

This premonitory movement was all they were waiting for. The instant the long, graceful body should sink toward the ground, the two would fire, trusting that Heaven would direct one of the bullets, at least, through the center of life and stay the beast, on the threshold, as may be said, of his assault.

But the tiger did not lower his body. Like many a great enterprise, this one was checked by an insignificant cause. His sharp eyes caught sight of the mangled cobra doubled up on the ground in front of him. He knew its nature, but did not know it was dead. That strange intuition which we call instinct warned him of the fatal result of a darting blow from that fearful reptile, and he drew back with a suddenness which, under other circumstances, would have been ludicrous. Not only that, but he turned directly about and trotted back to the jungle, where he disappeared.

"Well, if that doesn't beat anything I ever saw!" exclaimed Dick.

"You know what frightened him off?"

"A dead snake."

"Yes; when you shot the reptile, you builded better than you knew."

"I builded well enough to save my life."

"Truly; not once, but twice; but for it, the tiger assuredly would have attacked us, and I need not tell you how slight our chance of escape would have

350

IN A TIGHT PLACE

been ; but, since the royal Bengal has taken a little shy at us, we will give him a tussle to-morrow."

"Do you really mean *that?*" asked Dick, with sparkling eyes, for one of the most coveted treats he counted upon enjoying in India was a tiger hunt. He was aware of the peril attending such a venture, but you can understand how it was that the very danger was its chief attraction.

"Yes ; we will arrange a party to hunt him to-morrow in true style. We can get a couple of well-trained elephants at the village, and we will take along Jim, and Jack, and Jo."

India is the home of the tiger (*felis tigris*). In some respects he is the most dangerous wild animal that lives. Scientific investigation has proven him to be one-fifth stronger than the lion, while in courage, activity and ferocity he is far his superior.

The range of the tiger is much less than that of the lion, being unknown in every country except Asia, and flourishing only in the southern and eastern portions of that continent. Certain sections of India are overrun with this dreaded beast.

While the ship which bore Dick Brownell and Mr. Godkin from Port Natal, lay anchored inside the Hooghly River, one of the many estuaries of the Ganges, the gentleman made known two interesting facts. A few miles up that broad stream is a beach, outwardly calm, but whose bottom is a shifting quicksand which is almost certain destruction to any steamer that touches it. The sands suck in ships as leeches suck in blood, and always are hungry for more. Skillful pilotage and day-light are necessary to escape the treacherous peril.

On a low island to the eastward the tigers are more numerous than in any other part of the globe. The keepers of the signal station live within high brick walls and dare not venture a hundred yards beyond them. Refuge houses are built along the coast on high piles, close to the water. Canned food, four hundred gallons of water, a chart with full directions how to find a port and a boat are at each. Large placards are hung up, warning the shipwrecked man to beware of the tigers, and not to attempt to get off except by day, and at no time to venture into the jungle. The islands and surrounding mainland are swampy, and swarm with tigers and crocodiles.

"I think it is the most fearful place in the world," said Mr. Godkin. "When I first came to India, I was foolish enough to venture into that section on a wager made by a party of English sportsmen."

"I suppose you looked upon some strange sights," suggested Dick.

"More than I ever want to see again," he replied with a shudder ; "how I got back alive is more than I can understand. I was there but a short time, during which I saw a tiger fighting with a crocodile, while its mate stood in the grass alongshore, calmly watching the combat, as if she had no misgivings about the success of her lord. He seemed to me, however, to be in a tight place, since his head was between the jaws of the crocodile, and the powerful paw didn't appear to do much execution on the iron front of the reptile. I didn't stay to see the result of the fight.

While stealing out of the jungle, I caught a glimpse of two other tigers that were peering out from their lair at a group of deer just beyond, and evidently considering whether they should kill every one, or spare a few for their neighbors.

"I made a circuit that took me around that dangerous section, but before I could get out of the place, I narrowly missed running upon two others. I paused long enough to notice that one was licking his paw, while the other was raising a howl, as if impatient that I was so long in delaying their supper.

"Even when I thought I was fairly clear of the appalling section, I saw a tiger that had leaped on the neck of a buffalo as he was drinking from the water, and was tearing the poor fellow to pieces.

"How I got out with my life, as I said, is a mystery, but I wouldn't repeat the attempt for the Kohinoor itself."

The three individuals who, Mr. Godkin said, would accompany them on the tiger hunt, were the natives whom he had hired to go with them on the expedition.

They were all Hindoos, and their right names were Buktar Sing, Budao, and Kassi Roy. You see how awkward they sound on the lips of an American, and so, merely for convenience, our friends gave them the handy appellations named.

I have already said that they were experienced hunters, who received such liberal pay from Mr. Godkin that they were anxious to serve him in every way possible.

The friend with whom they were spending the night lived on the borders of the village, less than a mile distant; and, since elephants are so common in India, my agent knew he would have no trouble in securing any number of them whenever he desired.

The events of the night, as you will admit, were enough to shake the nerves of the strongest man, and neither Mr. Godkin nor Dick Brownell felt the least disposition to lie down for more sleep. Convinced that the tiger had taken his departure for good, they once more came outdoors. Each held his loaded gun in hand, for in such a country as India it is wise to be prepared at all times for a hostile visit.

The couple had been seated but a few minutes in conversation, when Mr. Godkin directed his companion's attention to the growing light in the East.

"Daylight is at hand," he added, "and you are as glad as I."

"Indeed I am; it is one of the longest nights I ever spent. I looked at my watch a few minutes ago, and saw that the sun would soon rise."

They stayed where they were a short time longer, and then, rising to their feet, flung their blankets over their arms and set out in the direction of the village where they had left their horses in charge of Jim, Jack and Jo.

Before our friends had gone half way to the village, day dawned, and all the signs indicated another trying spell of heat.

Turning a bend in the highway, Mr. Godkin and Dick found themselves within a short distance of the village. The instant they were seen, a crowd of men, women and children came running toward them, uttering the most dismal wailing and cries.

23

"What does this mean?" asked the wondering Dick.

"Some calamity has befallen them during the night. there is Jo — he will inform us."

Jo, who was the leading servant, spoke English almost as well as a European. Seeing his masters, he ran forward to meet them.

"Oh, sahib!" said he, making an elaborate salaam, "great sorrow has come upon the village."

"What is the trouble?"

"The tiger, the tiger! He entered the village last night, sahib. and seized a child right before its father and mother. We ran after the beast, shouting and throwing torches at him, but he heeded us not, he is gone with the child, and great is the grief of our friends over their loss, sahib."

Mr. Godkin turned to Dick.

"You may depend upon it that was the animal that paid us a visit last night."

"It must have been after he carried off the child."

"Likely it was the same beast."

"And, sahib," continued Jo, "a snake bit one of the villagers, and he died."

"That wasn't the same serpent that visited us last night," remarked Dick.

"But it was the same species. I don't know that we would have been any safer in the village than in the bamboo hut."

"Where are the ichneumons that are sure death to all cobras?" asked the youth.

"It would seem that these people ought to be supplied with those valuable creatures, which have saved many a life from serpents."

The villagers continued their lamentations, and besought Mr. Godkin and Dick who they saw were fully armed, to slay the dreaded tiger, which would give them no peace now that he had had a taste of one of their number.

By this time Jim and Jack came up, and they added their lamentations to those of their friends. With some trouble, my agent secured an account of what had taken place during the night.

The native who had died of the cobra's bite had been stricken early in the evening, but the appearance of the tiger had been so recent that Dick saw he was mistaken in believing that it was before he visited them. He must have come directly from the hut and seized his victim.

There could be no doubt that it was the same beast, for two of them rarely work so near each other in the manner named.

"Be calm." called Mr Godkin, forgetting that only three or four of those who heard him could understand his words; "we shall rid this district of the man-eater; we have come to slay him."

TIGER AND BUFFALO.

CHAPTER LXIV.

THE TIGER-HUNTERS.

THE announcement that the two hunters had determined to kill the dreaded tiger caused such joy among the hearers — who quickly gathered the meaning from those who understood the words — that they seemed to forget the recent visit of the man-eater.

Even the father and mother of the captured child flung their hands aloft and expressed their pleasure at learning that the neighborhood was to be rid of the scourge.

This course being settled upon, Mr. Godkin went about the task with the prompt thoroughness which marked everything he did.

The first step was for him and Dick to secure their morning meal, a very easy task as they were situated.

Little meat is eaten during the hot season in India, because of its heating nature, though at other times enormous quantities of beef, mutton and game are consumed.

In one of the natives' huts the expenditure of live annas — about fifteen cents — procured all the goat's milk and fruit they needed.

The villager was so delighted over the presence of two such mighty hunters that had come to slay the fearful pest that he was unwilling to take payment, and would have been only too glad to provide his friends with all they wanted for nothing; but Mr. Godkin had made the wise rule of never accepting favors of that kind.

By the time our friends had finished their morning meal (the custom in most tropical countries, as you know, is to eat but two meals a day, the second being late in the afternoon), the servants had brought the two elephants in front of the hut, where they awaited their riders.

Both the animals were small, that of Dick being a female, and not much larger than a good-sized ox. Mr. Godkin's was somewhat taller, but both were so low that each person, with a little help, was able to climb upon the neck and enter the howdah, or box-like saddle, which is used in riding the beasts.

The arrangement was that Jo should accompany Dick, while Jim was to ride with Mr. Godkin. Jack had already mounted the pony of the gentleman, and, placing himself at the head, seemed disposed to assume the part of leader of the expedition. Each assistant carried a spear, though it would seem fire-arms would have been more appropriate.

A half dozen natives begged the privilege of accompanying the party on foot, though they were likely to prove more of an impediment than a help in the perilous business.

Such was the company that set out to hunt down the man-eater which had thrown the whole village into a state of consternation which nothing but the death of the animal could remove.

Leaving the little town, they headed to the westward, which was toward that part of the jungle where the beast had been seen the evening before. Fully two score men, women and children accompanied the party some distance out on the road, but they turned back before coming in sight of the bamboo hut, and the company was left with the members already mentioned.

" If the tiger is gone very far into the jungle," said Mr. Godkin, whose elephant was walking so close to Dick's that they could readily converse, " I doubt whether we shall be able to force our animals after him."

" What then shall be done ? "

" We must get the people to drive him out, or, if they refuse, we shall have to dismount and do it ourselves."

" I don't fancy that part of the sport."

" More than likely we shall find him along the edge of the jungle, in the tall grass which skirts it, though he may take a notion to dart in among the trees."

" How about the beasts we are riding ? "

" They have been in the business before, and behaved themselves admirably, though an elephant will sometimes turn tail to a tiger and give him a wide berth."

" I wouldn't be surprised if mine did that, for she isn't much bigger than a tiger herself, and can't be any kind of a match for the one we are hunting."

" You see how thoroughly Jo understands her. She is a very intelligent creature."

" And there is the trouble — her intelligence may tell her that the wisest thing she can do is to locate herself beyond reach of the game."

" It is not impossible, but I am hopeful that both will acquit themselves creditably. The conduct of an elephant, however, does not depend on his size, and one three times as large as mine is as likely to run as a smaller one."

During the brief ride along the highway on the back of the little elephant, Dick formed quite a fondness for her. She showed a frolicsome disposition that would have made her a pet with children at once.

She would trot a few paces in a way that shook the howdah dreadfully. She knew it, and that was the reason she did it.

Jo affected great indignation, and would whack the brute over the head, or prick her ears with the point of his spear. Then she became as meek as a child, and stopped so suddenly that the lad received several vigorous bumps against the front of the howdah before he could prepare himself for the shock.

A favorite trick of hers was to reach as far around and over her back as she could with her trunk, as if she wished to fondle her riders. But Jo met all such demonstrations with a blow from his spear, which caused the pendulous snout to seek its proper place.

The female gave one exhibition of playfulness which was relished by all save the victim.

One of the natives was trotting by the roadside, looking attentively ahead, for they were nearing the spot where it was wise to increase their vigilance, when the beast moved up behind and seized him around the waist.

The terrified fellow began yelling and kicking with might and main, while Jo banged his spear on the head of the creature and ordered her to release the man at once; but the blows did not amount to anything, and the elephant was bound to have her fun.

She raised the native as high in the air as she could, his head pointing toward the ground and his feet toward the sky. No wonder he was frightened, and his legs beat the air like a couple of drumsticks, while he swung his arms and called out to Jo to save him from death.

Holding her victim thus for a few seconds, the female lowered him as gently as a feather, and deposited him on his feet again, without a hair of his head being harmed Then she resumed her advance as seriously as though she had never thought of molesting any one in the world.

Both Mr. Godkin and Dick laughed, for the incident was most amusing.

" I wonder whether she will handle the tiger in that style if she gets the chance ? " said the lad.

"No fear of *that*, for the tiger will not permit it; but she is in capital spirits this morning, and is bound to have her fun in spite of Jo and his spear-thrusts However, there is the hut on one side and the jungle on the other, and the time for serious business has arrived "

CHAPTER LXV.

THE TIGER

THE party now halted within a few rods of the bamboo hut that had been the scene of the adventures already described. By this time the courage of several of the natives had oozed away and they quietly slunk off, so that when our friends looked around they found there was but a single one left beside the three servants, two of whom were mounted on the elephants, while the third was riding the pony of Mr. Godkin.

The anxious glances which all cast around failed to reveal anything of the tiger for which they were hunting; but, nevertheless, the belief was general that he was not far off.

"Nothing can be done," said Mr Godkin, "by sitting idle. Jo, Jim, Jack and the other fellow there will enter the jungle with a view of driving out the game into the open plain where we can get a shot at him."

"But he may be hiding in the grass beyond," suggested Dick.

As the boy spoke he pointed to some grass that extended out, perhaps, a hundred yards from the front of the jungle, and ran parallel with it for five or six times that distance. It did not begin opposite the bamboo structure, but farther to the west — that is, in the direction leading away from the village.

This grass was several feet high, quite dense, and parched by the sun to a reddish-brown. It would hardly be supposed that a wild beast would ensconce himself among this, unless he wished to lie in wait for his prey passing along the highway. The audacity of the tiger gave probability to the theory that he was really waiting there, even though he had indulged in such a frightful feast but a short time before.

"We'll examine the grass," said Mr. Godkin, after surveying it from the back of the elephant. The elevation, however, was so slight that it gave little facility in the way of observation.

After a brief consultation it was agreed that Jack, who was mounted on my agent's horse, should enter the grass at a point nearest to them, and, keeping close to the jungle, advance with extreme caution.

This was deemed prudent, for if it should prove that the beast was there, it was believed he would be seen soon enough for the pony to carry himself and rider out of danger. He was a well-trained animal, very agile, and had been in several scrimmages with tigers, so that considerable reliance was placed on his intelligence.

If one of the natives should go forward on foot he could not escape a direct attack from the tiger, even though the others hurried to his assistance. Two or three prodigious leaps of the animal would be sufficient to overtake the fleetest of men

You can imagine the intense interest with which the others watched the movements of Jack.

The native who was on foot climbed upon the back of Mr. Godkin's elephant, so that none was unmounted.

Jack had not ridden twenty paces into the tall grass when all were startled by seeing him rein up his horse with a suddenness which proved that he had made an important discovery.

"It can't be the tiger," remarked Mr. Godkin, without removing his gaze from the man.

"No, there's something on the ground close to his pony's head," replied Dick.

Jack spent but a minute or two in scrutiny, when, without dismounting, he galloped back to his friends.

He explained his ghastly discovery.

Observing that the grass appeared to have been trampled near where he halted, he examined it closely, and saw several bones lying on the ground, their appearance showing that the flesh had been gnawed from them very recently.

A brief scrutiny left no doubt in the mind of the native that they were a part of the remains of the poor girl who had been carried off by the tiger only a few hours before.

"Depend upon it, he isn't far away," said Mr. Godkin, when the dreadful incident was told.

"Do you think he is in the grass?"

"Very likely."

Jack once more turned the pony about and entered the parched tract, while the others edged their beasts a little closer behind him: the fellow was braver than most of his race, or he would not have done this. Dick saw no signs of trepidation on his part, but there could be no doubt that he appreciated the peril into which he was entering.

This time he rode a couple of rods in advance of where he had halted on his first entry. His pony stepped very deliberately, with his head high in air, and his ears thrown forward, as if he fully understood his danger.

All at once he stopped again, and then it was that Dick Brownell and Carl Godkin witnessed one of the most striking tableaux on which they had ever gazed.

From a point only a few yards in advance of the horseman a gigantic tiger rose from the grass, so that his whole body was in plain sight, and, facing the native, looked straight at him.

He did not growl nor sway his tail, but stood in the attitude of curiosity or inquiry, as if seeking to learn the meaning of the disturbance. The pony held precisely the same attitude. Instead of whirling about and dashing off, as would have been natural, he braced himself as rigidly as a bronze statue, with his front hoofs planted close together, his head aloft, and his eyes staring at the terror in front of him.

Whether or not the rider was transfixed by fear cannot be said, but he also played the part of a motionless spectator — the tableau being the most impressive that can be imagined.

For a few moments the hunters were equally stationary. and then the first evidence of fright came from the quarter where it was least expected.

Among the quadrupeds, there was one which, realizing the delicate situation, made up his mind that the time had come for disappearing: that was the elephant on which Mr. Godkin and

two of the natives were perched.

Throwing aloft his trunk, he trumpeted loudly, and then deliberately swung his heavy body around and started off.

In vain the natives belabored him with spears. Jim jabbed him sharply, calling him the worst names he could summon, while Mr. Godkin was angry enough to shoot

A STRIKING TABLEAU.

the poltroon. It was the more provoking because in the previous tiger hunts in which he had been engaged he had never been known to misbehave himself.

But all in vain. You have seen a yoke of oxen make a break for water, and have noticed that no driver could check or turn them aside. So it was with the elephant. Pointing his nose toward the village, he swung into his ungainly trot, and not all the efforts of his three riders could restrain him, though they exerted themselves to the point of desperation.

Dick Brownell laughed over the discomfiture of his friend, especially as it had been believed that, if either of the elephants showed any panic, it would be the female ridden by him; but there was too serious business before the party for the youth to spend any time in looking at the group that were making such good time toward the village.

The break of the cowardly brute seemed to be the signal for the drama to open.

The tiger could not have failed to see that the whole party were intruders, and that a good chance was presented for teaching them a needed lesson, as well as for procuring a grander feast than he had ever yet enjoyed.

Holding himself erect, he now began walking straight toward the horseman with that soft, cat-like tread that adds to the terror inspired by his presence. The distance was too great for him to leap, and he was merely seeking to shorten the space enough to make it an easy task.

You may be sure that the pony finished his attitudinizing about that time. He spun around like a top, and dashed off at the height of his speed, which was much greater than that of the tiger.

The latter broke into a gallop, keeping in a direct line with the horse, which shot by the elephant at a distance of no more than a dozen feet. Thus the pursuer was brought near the animal on which Dick was perched and who bravely held her ground

Seeing that it was useless to follow the horseman, and finding himself close to the two hunters, the tiger seemed to conclude

"You'll do just as well."

At any rate, without the least hesitation, he veered in his course and made straight for Dick and Jim!

CHAPTER LXVI.

A FORTUNATE SHOT.

IT is a brave hunter who keeps his head in such a crisis as now came upon Dick, and it is no discredit to him to say that he was flustered for a brief while.

He held his rifle ready, knowing that he would fire the next moment ; but when the native, Jo, saw the tiger following the skurrying horseman at a gallop, and knew that he would pass quite close to him, it proved too much for his nerves.

He was not sitting in the howdah, but had perched himself astride the elephant's neck, the better to control her.

With a whoop of terror he described a back somersault, landing on his feet, and dashed after the fleeing pony at a gait that almost equaled his.

At the same moment, the female veered so as to present her front to the approaching tiger, and flung her trunk aloft.

This wonderful organ, composed of tens of thousands of muscles, as perhaps you know, is extremely sensitive, and the owners take the utmost care to protect it from injury. That is the reason why, in passing through a forest, they often hold it aloft and out of the way.

The flight of Jo and the action of the elephant took place at the moment that Dick brought his rifle to his shoulder and was pressing the trigger. The confusion caused him to hold his fire, and, before he could aim again, the tiger attacked.

Rising in air, he shot across the intervening space, and landed on the haunch of the female, which uttered a cry of pain, and turned around in the vain effort to reach him with her trunk.

But the rending of the elephant's thick hide was all by the way ; the assailant was not after *her*, but after the white-faced boy crouching in the howdah on her back

The tiger held his position, and began creeping over the brown haunch, his short ears pressed flat on his head, his eyes glaring, his sharp teeth showing while he growled savagely and whipped the side of the larger brute with his thumping tail. He was the embodiment of ferocity as he steadily climbed toward the perch of the youth, who had been almost within his reach from the first.

The frenzied swaying of the elephant bothered Dick for a moment, but he quickly regained his self-possession.

Unable to keep his feet as steadily as he desired, he placed one knee on the seat of the howdah, and, resting the barrel of his rifle on the back, leveled the weapon at his foe.

The latter was so close that the muzzle of the gun was almost against his nose.

At so slight a distance a miss was out of the question, and, aiming at a point directly between the eyes of the beast, Dick let fly.

For one moment the appalled lad believed he had failed, for the tiger gave no evidence of being hurt. But, glancing through the thin wreath of smoke rising from the muzzle of his gun, he saw the round hole made by the bullet.

It was red and clean at first, without any blood, but the crimson fluid began quickly to pour from the opening.

The eyes glared with the same burning fierceness, and the outstretched claws were still buried in the thick hide of the elephant, piercing the tender flesh beneath and causing agonizing pain.

"What can it mean?" asked Dick; "is it impossible to kill one of those brutes with a single bullet?"

WARM WORK

Just then he observed a convulsive shudder pass through the fore legs and front; beyond question the tiger was hit hard; indeed, he was fatally wounded, but it did seem as if death itself could not loosen the grip of his needle-like claws.

At that instant Dick saw that the tiger was sinking toward the earth, but his grasp was not relaxed, and the elephant was going with him.

Rendered wild by her suffering the huge beast theew herself on the ground with the intention of crushing her foe by rolling upon him.

Dick made a bound from the howdah, which was smashed to splinters the next moment under the weight of the elephant, whose trunk and beam-like legs were pointed toward the sky and waddling in the air overhead. The tiger missed being caught in the general wreck and ruin, but he was almost dead before the ground was reached.

His final struggle at last released his hold, and he rolled away from the elephant at the moment he would have been crushed had he hung fast. He came to rest on his back, with his legs also pointing upward. They gave a few twitches, and then it was all over.

So the tiger was killed by a single bullet fired by Dick Brownell.

Meanwhile, Mr. Godkin, finding it impossible to check the headlong flight of his huge steed, took a rather dangerous leap to the ground, his servant, Jim, doing the same, while the other remained in his seat and soon after reached the village without harm.

Mr. Godkin was impelled to this step by his solicitude for Dick, whom he had left behind, within reach of the infuriated tiger. On his way back he met the terrified Jack, who assured him that Jo and the young man had been killed.

A short distance farther Jo was encountered, fleeing also for his life, and carrying the tidings that Dick was entirely swallowed and in process of digestion by that time.

Mr. Godkin might have felt frightened had he not been near enough to the scene of the conflict to see that his young friend, the report of whose weapon he had heard, was alive and standing on his feet beside the prostrate tiger and the elephant, which was in the act of climbing to an upright posture again.

By this time the natives began to flock back, the news having been carried to the crowds, who had not yet reached the village, that a fight was going on with the tiger which they might be able to look upon from a safe distance.

It did not take them long to find out the beast had been killed by the youngest member of the party, and it was then that Dick Brownell experienced a taste of the annoyances of popularity. Some of the natives seemed to suspect he was above the range of ordinary mortals, and they gathered around him as if to satisfy their doubts.

The three servants, Jo, Jack and Jim, were among the most enthusiastic ; and I am afraid that Mr. Godkin mischievously added to the adulation of the party by relating some mythical exploits of his young friend on the other side of the great water.

CHAPTER LXVII.

A FRIGHTFUL OCCURRENCE,

AMONG the natives who crowded admiringly around the tiger-hunters was one whose unusual intelligence attracted their notice. He was mounted on a pony similar to theirs, and seemed such a desirable companion that Mr. Godkin asked him to form one of their company, offering him liberal pay for his services.

The new recruit, who was immediately christened Jed, accepted the offer at once. He possessed considerable experience of the kind needed by our friends, and it was a wise proceeding on the part of Mr. Godkin thus to engage him.

"It would have been a fine thing," remarked Dick, "if we could have captured that tiger for Mr. Barnum, instead of killing him."

"That was out of the question," replied Mr. Godkin. "Can you help us, Jed, to get one or two tiger kittens?"

"Yes, sahib," was the prompt response.

Jed then explained that, while riding rapidly along the road, and when hardly a mile distant, he was descending a long hill and was near a small stream which crossed the highway, when he was terrified almost out of his senses by seeing an enormous tiger emerge from the jungle on his right, and trot across the road in front, less than a hundred feet distant.

Jed's horse stopped short, and the rider was on the point of wheeling about and dashing back to Lucknow, when he observed that the animal was a female, and was carrying a kitten in her mouth.

The mother tiger is very affectionate, and she was so engaged in her task that she paid no heed to anything else.

Reaching the side of the dusty highway, she bounded into the jungle on the other side and disappeared.

Jed spurred his horse forward and passed the spot like a whirlwind. Looking back, after going a considerable distance, he saw precisely the same thing repeated. The tiger was trotting across the road again with a second kitten in her mouth. Jed, feeling quite safe, halted his horse and waited several minutes, but nothing more was observed of the beast. The conclusion of this narrative was that the tiger had two young at least, the usual number being from three to five. She was undoubtedly the mate of the tiger that had been killed, and the coveted opportunity of obtaining her offspring was presented.

"But I tell you it's mighty dangerous business," said Mr. Godkin, compressing his lips and shaking his head; "you would not think a fiercer brute than the one we have just shot could exist, but wait till you see a tiger mother defending her young."

" I don't intend to creep up and try to take them away from her; but we've got to steal them when she's off hunting for food. Come, Mr. Godkin, I'm ready if you are."

Ordinarily it would have been hard, if not impossible, to hire a number of natives to take part in such a desperate enterprise; but the exploit of Dick Brownell, in slaying the terrible scourge, gave them such boundless faith in his bravery and skill that they were ready to follow him anywhere.

As a consequence the four signified their readiness to join in the hunt for the tiger kittens.

The preparations for the desperate venture were simple and soon made. It was arranged that Jed, Dick and Mr. Godkin should ride cautiously forward, the three servants following them at a short distance. Since they were afoot, and armed with only their primitive weapons, it was prudent that they should keep well to the rear, so as to escape any sudden onslaught of the savage beast.

Jed was to point out the spot where she had entered the jungle, and it then remained for our friends to locate the home of the animal and to await her departure, if she was still with her young, before attempting to steal them.

Jed displayed more bravery than would have been expected, for he insisted on keeping several rods in advance of the other horsemen. He seemed to think, and not without reason, that his greater experience in hunting all kinds of wild animals would enable him to detect the proximity of the beast before the Americans. Jo, Jack and Jim were nearly two hundred yards to the rear of the proprietors, as they may be called, of the enterprise.

It will be remembered that the point where Jed had seen the female crossing the highway with her young was at the bottom of a long hill, consequently the exact spot could not be distinguished until the head of the slope was reached, so as to permit the horsemen to look downward in front at the small stream which crossed the highway.

Jed was yet some distance off, his pony proceeding on a walk, when he was observed to check his animal, turn his head, and motion with his hand for his friends to halt.

They obeyed, wondering what it meant.

" Hark !" whispered Dick; " do you hear that ? "

Listening intently, the faint, regular tinkling of a small bell was heard coming from a point beyond the hill and not far from the spot our friends were approaching.

While Dick and Mr. Godkin were looking they observed the figure of a native descending the opposite slope and coming toward them. He was nearly naked, except for a voluminous turban and a light muslin skirt around his middle. He was advancing on a loping trot, bearing on his shoulder a slim pole, to one end of which was attached a small bell that gave out the tinkling which arrested the attention of the party.

This fellow was one of the native postmen of India, who carry the mail in that fashion. Unmindful of the sweltering weather, one of those tough runners will trot five or ten miles along the dusty highway, bearing a bundle of letters and papers. The small bell which he carries suspended to the stick is to give notice of his coming, just as the postman in this country apprises us of his approach by blowing his whistle.

DEATH OF THE POSTMAN.

The native trots the entire distance until he meets another postman to whom he delivers the mail, and, while the second takes up the trot, the first turns about and goes back at a more leisurely pace.

"I'm afraid that fellow is running into more danger than he suspects," remarked Mr. Godkin; "I have often wondered why they persist in proclaiming their coming in that way, for the sound of the bell often serves to guide the tiger lying in wait for his victim."

"Ought we not to warn him of his peril?" asked Dick, feeling that the poor fellow's life was worth more than a thousand tiger kittens.

"By all means," replied his companion.

The two started their animals at the same moment, and galloped to where the wondering Jed awaited their approach. They quickly explained their wishes, but he shook his head.

"Too late—mebbe no tiger there!"

"Listen!" broke in Dick, with a start of terror.

The hearts of the two almost stopped beating as they heard frenzied shrieks and screams, just such as a strong man makes when caught in the grip of some power that is tearing him to death.

"Come on!" called Dick, spurring his horse into such a gallop that he quickly placed himself at the head of the others, who followed close behind.

Meanwhile, the rest of the servants, seeing that something was amiss, took good care to linger in the background.

A sharp ride brought the three horsemen to the top of the hill, but, brief as was the gallop, the cries of the poor native were hushed before our friends could gaze down the long stretch in front of them.

The sight they saw was enough to startle the bravest man.

It is more than probable that the postman had met his death by the means Mr. Godkin referred to. The tiger most likely was nursing her young at some distance from the roadside, when she caught the tintinnabulation, whose meaning she knew. Leaving her kittens in their new bed, she crept noiselessly out to the side of the highway and awaited the coming of the man with the tinkling bell.

Then followed the long, fearful leap, and the native was borne to the earth, and so frightfully torn that his sufferings were mercifully ended almost as soon as they began.

Looking down the hill, the spectators saw the tiger holding the body of the man in her mouth, just as she would have carried one of her kittens. She had crushed him down in the middle of the highway, and, lifting his body so that only his bare heels touched the ground, she trotted from the road into the jungle with no more apparent effort than if carrying one of her tiny young.

This proof of the prodigious strength of the tiger was not needed by our friends, but they were so impressed by what they saw, that for a few minutes they looked in each other's face without speaking.

"What a pity we did not arrive sooner," was the remark of Dick, made in a low voice, as if afraid of attracting the attention of their terrible enemy.

"Yes; and the fact that that man lost his life through his own shortsightedness cannot lessen our pity for him. I tell you, Dick, I think Mr. Barnum will excuse you from capturing one or two young tigers."

"But I will not excuse myself," was the sturdy response. "I am more resolved than ever to rob that merciless beast of her offspring."

"All right; I am with you; but it strikes me that since she has secured a good day's meal, she will not be apt to leave her young for some time, and we are likely to have a tedious wait of it."

"I am afraid so, but I was thinking that if it was her husband which we shot, she may set out to hunt him up, if he stays out too late."

Mr. Godkin looked inquiringly at Jed, who nodded his head.

"Mebbe so — don't know — wait — see."

"Where shall we wait?" was the important question which Dick proposed for joint consideration.

By this time Jo, Jack and Jim had gained enough courage to move forward and join the horsemen, when they quickly learned all that had taken place.

The reasonable conclusion was formed by all that the tiger would be likely to indulge in her siesta during the afternoon, breaking it only at long intervals to go to the brook near at hand to quench her thirst. Toward night she would probably set out to look for her mate, or perhaps to seek more game, though after such a feast she could conveniently go several days without any food.

The decision was to ride silently down the hill and up the opposite one. Jed informed them that a native hut stood but a small distance beyond. There they would leave their animals, and carefully make their way back to the spot, approaching as near as they dared. They would then hide themselves in the dense jungle,

24

and watch and wait, with no encouraging prospect of success, as must be con-
fessed.   The duty of passing directly over the spot where a man had been killed but a
few minutes before was anything but pleasant, even to such brave persons as Dick
and Mr. Godkin, but it seemed necessary, since there was no way of going around
the place, and it was too far to ride to the native village.

Mr. Godkin told those on foot that if they feared to make the venture, they
need not do so; but, when they saw the horsemen start, and probably, too, when
they recalled the wonderful bravery and marksmanship of the young man, they
showed no hesitation in following.

All instinctively held their peace as they slowly descended the hill, but you
may be sure that Mr. Godkin and Dick were certain their rifles were ready for the
emergency, and they glanced from right to left like a couple of Indian warriors
approaching a hostile camp.

The youth half wished the tiger would show herself, though he would have been
sorry indeed to see any member of the party lose his life; but if the mother could
be put out of the way, the task of securing the kittens would be much simplified.

CHAPTER LXVIII.

CAUGHT IN THE ACT.

IN absolute silence the three horsemen rode down the long hill. The horses, as if in sympathy with their riders, seemed to plant their hoofs more guardedly in the soft dust of the highway, while they flung their ears forward and glanced to the right and left like creatures who scent danger in the air.

Dick was allowed to keep a few steps in front of Jed, while Mr. Godkin was abreast of the latter, the footmen walking behind in Indian file. I must remind you that there was no fence on either side of the highway, and the little stream, which was only a few inches in depth, had to be waded by all who passed that way. The jungle came close to the road on either side, and was so dense that when Dick glanced at it, he could not help muttering to himself: "What finer place could a tiger want for hiding——" The question was not finished when the tiger appeared.

It may have been that she was in an unusually wrathful mood, because she thought her enemies were seeking to disturb her before she could complete her feast, for she hardly waited until the foremost horseman was opposite to where she was crouching when she made her attack.

While looking at the dense jungle on his right, Dick observed a slight agitation of the vegetation, and before he could tell what it meant, the body of the tiger shot outward and upward as if propelled from a catapult.

The figure of the immense beast, brilliant, ferocious and frightfully beautiful as she seemed suspended for a single instant in mid-air, was a sight which, once seen, must remain vivid forever.

Those who stood in the background saw the horrid front, the half-contracted limbs, the drooping tail, as the lithe, sinewy form curved over toward the apparently doomed lad.

The latter observed the frightful head with the flaming eyes, the ears flattened back, the wide-open jaws with their long, white, gleaming teeth and blood-red mouth, as the beast seemed rushing through space like a comet directly at him.

The intelligent animal that Dick bestrode had detected the peril before his rider, and made one tremendous bound forward. Thus it happened that when the assaulting beast landed, it was on the ground several paces behind its intended victim.

It would have been an easy matter for her to leap upon the pony of Dick, or to wheel and attack either of the other horsemen that were at hand; but you may not know that it is a peculiarity of the tiger that, when it misses seizing its prey at the first leap, it generally refrains from repeating it, turning about and dashing off as if ashamed of its failure.

The female did so in this case, and, although Dick and Mr. Godkin fired at her as she darted into the jungle, and were sure they struck her, she showed no signs of receiving any injury.

"Now is our time to hurry by," called out Mr. Godkin to the servants behind them; "she won't hurt us if we make haste."

The ponies were forced into a sharp gallop, which they maintained all the way to the top of the long hill in front, Jo, Jack and Jim skurrying after them with such swiftness that they were but a very little way behind.

Dick and his friend could afford to laugh at their singular experience with the tiger, and the lad did not fail to give full credit to his sagacious beast, which had snatched him from under the descending monster, who, had she alighted where she intended, would have made as short work with the plucky boy as she had done with the unfortunate postman a short time before.

CAUGHT IN THE ACT

As the party hastened from the spot they saw the shocking evidences of the tragedy. Blood and the torn turhan were on the ground, while the long pole with its bell and fragments of paper were scattered about.

"I am going to have one or both of those tiger kittens, or die in the attempt," said Dick, when they reined up shortly after in front of the native's hut by the wayside. "I propose that we shall leave all the rest here, while you and I steal back along the highway and see what we can see."

"I like the suggestion, for I don't believe we can all hide from her, and the natives are really of no account in the task we have undertaken, or rather, are about to undertake."

This proposition, as may be supposed, was not objected to by the others, and it was about the middle of the afternoon when Dick and Mr. Godkin set out on foot to return to the little stream which had been the scene of so many stirring occurrences of the day.

They met no persons, either riding or on foot, and reached a point about half way down the hill before they stopped. Deeming it unwise to go farther, they softly crept into the jungle to wait, with little prospect of success, as any one must admit who studies the situation.

But that which they wished to come to pass did so sooner than they dared hope.

They had no more than comfortably established themselves in the thick vegetation, so close to the highway that, by parting the bushes in front, they could look down to the bottom of the hill and see the gleam of the water in the small stream that wound its way across the road, when Mr. Godkin exclaimed, in an excited whisper:

"By gracious! there she is now!"

Sure enough, as Dick peered forth he discerned the identical beast, which had emerged from the same point in the jungle where she had vanished, and approached the water. She was in the middle of the highway, and was walking slowly, swinging her tail from side to side, and looking straight ahead. She was so near that she was seen to be licking her bloody jaws.

"A tiger often stops to drink while eating," whispered Mr. Godkin, "and that is what she is after."

Such proved to be the fact. Arriving on the edge of the stream, the tiger lowered her head and lapped the cool current, just as the cat species do when taking a drink.

She quickly slaked her thirst, and then, raising her head, looked around, as if to say:

"If there are any more of you folks that would like to pay me a visit, I'd be glad to welcome you."

"It can't be she sees us," said Dick, "but why does she look so long in this direction?"

"There she goes!"

The tiger turned about and walked back with the same deliberate tread until, opposite the point where she had emerged from the jungle, when she made a leap into it and disappeared.

But she did so on the opposite side of the highway.

"That's lucky!" exclaimed Dick, "she's gone off to hunt her mate. Now's our time!"

"You may be right, but it will be awfully awkward if she happens to come back before we can get away."

"Come on; every minute counts."

It was just like the lad to push his way through the jungle into the road, and to go down the hill almost on a run, Mr. Godkin finding it hard to keep up with him.

Dick did half expect the mother to return, but he believed that, after the two bullets sent into her body, he and his companion could make short work of her with their weapons.

You will suspect that his success earlier in the day gave him more self-assurance than he should have felt, and I have no doubt such was the fact.

"Her home can't be far off," remarked Dick, recalling how close the animal was to the highway when she made her desperate effort to leap upon his horse.

"I shall soon find out," he added, boldly entering the vegetation. "Helloa! this is luck."

It was less than fifty feet from the road that a faint purring sound fell upon his ear, and the next minute he came upon a couple of beautiful tiger kittens, playing and tumbling over each other like two puppies.

"Here, hold my gun!" whispered the excited Dick, running back a few steps, and handing his weapon to Mr. Godkin; "stay where you are till I return."

The man was half dazed as he accepted the rifle, by the audacity of the youth, who, without giving him time to protest, ran forward again, and, paying no heed to the mangled remains of the poor postman, seized each kitten by the nape of the neck, lifted them clear of the ground and started off.

The little ones thus unceremoniously disturbed struggled hard, but he had no difficulty in holding them fast, and, with a heart beating high with exultation, he started back to rejoin his companion, awaiting his return on the edge of the jungle.

But before he could catch sight of him a muttering growl caused him to turn his head like a flash.

There stood the infuriated mother, less than twenty feet distant, with her blazing eyes fixed upon him.

Her attitude seemed to say:

"Young man, I've returned! Drop that property of mine and say your prayers."

CHAPTER LXIX.

TWO CURIOSITIES.

NOTHING could surpass the audacity of Dick Brownell in entering the tiger's lair for the purpose of stealing her young.

The most experienced hunter that would dare do such a thing would be declared reckless beyond excuse. The only thing that I can say about the exploit was that it was characteristic of the lad.

It was a strange sight when the youth, picking his way through the jungle toward the highway, holding a plump, squirming kitten in each hand, stopped short, face to face with the terrible mother.

The latter, instead of going off for an hour or two, had made a circuit through the jungle on the other side of the highway, recrossed it farther up at the moment the two friends were entering the undergrowth, and approached her lair by a circuitous course.

Just as Dick darted back to his friend, with the request that he should hold his gun for a minute or two, it occurred to Mr. Godkin that the true place for him was on the edge of the jungle, where he could watch the road and detect the tiger should she return before they could get away.

Had the gentleman been one minute sooner in taking his post, he would have discovered the danger in time to warn his companion, and to prepare for the reception of the mother; but the movements of the beast were silent and lightning-like.

Dick was "caught foul," as the expression goes.

There he stood in front of the beast, transfixed, and holding her beloved offspring by the napes of their necks, clear proof that he was engaged in stealing her progeny.

What punishment was too great for the outraged mother to inflict upon such a miscreant?

According to Dick's account he was absolutely paralyzed for the moment. He did not think it possible the mother would return so soon, though he was prepared for a fight with her before getting off with his prizes.

Then, knowing how strong the attachment of the tiger is for her young, he gave such a vigorous fling to each of the kittens that they went over her head and fell among the bushes behind her, or rather one of them did so.

It was at this extraordinary juncture that the beast gave a striking and singular exhibition of her dexterity.

The second kitten was going through the air like a big dumpling, when the mother threw up her head and caught it fairly between her jaws, doing so with a skill that prevented any harm to her offspring, and with a deftness that would have been a strong recommendation for a position in the champion base-ball nine of the country.

The instant the kittens left the hands of Dick, he whirled about and dashed for the highway, shouting :

"Look out, Mr. Godkin!   The mother has arrived !'

Before the gentleman could rush into the jungle to the help of his young friend, the latter was at his side.

"Here ! let me have my gun !" he added, reaching for the weapon ; "it's getting too warm for me in there !"

"There couldn't be a better time for making a change of base," was the comment of the elder, who leaped almost into the middle of the highway ; "depend upon it, she will come for us."

Mr. Godkin was right.   Evidently the tiger tarried only long enough to make sure her children were unharmed, and to place them back in their bed, when she burst through the jungle, aflame with fury and with the intent of visiting awful vengeance upon those who had dared to lay hands on her offspring.

Her charge could not have been better timed — that is, for those who had to receive it.

They were on the other side of the highway with guns at their shoulder and ready for the raging beast.

She looked around for an instant, as if to locate her victims, and then she squatted to gather her muscles for the leap that was to be the death-signal of the hunters.

But at the very moment she was leaving the ground the two rifles were discharged — so nearly together that the reports were like that of a single gun.   The aim was accurate, both bullets entering the brain of the tiger, who made an odd, twisting jump almost straight upward, and, falling on her back, lay a moment pawing the air, and then became still.

"I wonder if she's dead ?" said Dick, reloading his gun, but with one eye fixed on the motionless brute.

"As dead as dead can be," was the reply of Mr. Godkin, who proved his faith in his own words by walking forward and giving the body a kick.

"Those two bullets that we plumped into her body awhile ago and that didn't seem to do any hurt, produced their good effect after all," added the elder, "though we had such a fair aim that I think either of our shots would have finished her."

"Like her mate, she deserved death," remarked Dick, "but only think !" he exclaimed, slapping the shoulder of Mr. Godkin, "that gives us the prizes we're after."

"And there they are !"

The two kittens (as they will often do when with their mother) had left their bed, and appeared on the edge of the jungle, blinking, winking and tumbling about as though curious to learn the cause of all the excitement.

They were pretty, plump creatures, though even in their playful gambols their claws and teeth gave evidence of the fearful weapons they were sure to become in the course of time.

"Poor things!" said Dick, with mock sympathy; "only think, they are orphans now, and entitled to our care; so I'll take charge of them." Passing his rifle once more to his friend, he picked up the kittens as before, and started up the hill with

IN THE NICK OF TIME

them. They did not weigh more than a dozen pounds apiece, and for a brief time were quite docile. Supported by the loose skin at the back of the neck, it is not likely that at first they felt any special discomfort; but, before the top of the hill was reached, they were squirming about with a vigor that compelled attention. It was now arranged that each of the hunters should carry a young one in his arms. This had its disadvantages, and both Mr. Godkin and Dick received some scratches; but, by humoring the little terrors, they managed to get them to the wayside hut, where, as may be supposed, their arrival produced a stir amounting almost to consternation.

In this simple dwelling dwelt an old man and his daughter, a middle-aged woman, who were sure that the mother of the kittens would follow the kidnapers to the spot, and slay every one of the party.

Jed and the other natives were of the same opinion, until assured that the mother had departed this life.

Mr. Godkin was waggish enough to try to make the rest believe that Dick had fired the shot that killed the second tiger, as he had fired the one that slew the first; but, inasmuch as it was all he could do to persuade them that the second had really been killed, he stuck to the facts.

It could not be denied that our friends had done an inestimable service to the neighborhood by ridding it of two such dreaded man-eaters, and when the natives should come to learn the glad tidings there would be hardly anything that they would not willingly do to prove their gratitude.

The owner of the hut knew the postman who had been killed by the tiger, and gave his name to Jed, who promised to inform his relatives living in Lucknow. As for the destroyed mail, that would have to be left to other parties to look after.

"But we've got the kittens," said Dick, exultingly, "and what shall we do with them."

"Send them to Lucknow by Jed; I will give him the name of our friend there, with whom I made arrangements the other day, and he will take good care of anything we may forward, until we are ready to ship them to Calcutta, and thence to England and home." The suggestion was a wise one, and it was carried out.

With the help of the native at whose hut they were stopping, a bamboo cage was constructed, large enough to hold the tiger kittens, while, at the same time, it could be carried without inconvenience on the horse in front of the rider.

Lucknow was so nigh that it was but a moderate ride thither, and Jed gladly undertook the duty of delivering the prizes to the gentleman named by Mr. Godkin, and who was well known.

It was so late in the day, however, that the entire party spent the night in and around the hut of their host, who received liberal payment for his food and some-what primitive accommodations.

Early the next day Jed left with his prizes, promising to come back and join his new friends in their hunt for other curiosities.

On the same day that witnessed the departure of the native Jed with the two tiger kittens, our friends moved their quarters several miles to the southwest. This took them somewhat farther from Lucknow, which, however, may be said to have been within easy reach.

The surrounding country offered admirable facilities for hunting, and they were on the edge of another jungle, not so extensive as that in which took place the adventures with the tiger, but large enough to shelter the fiercest animals found in India.

The forenoon passed without special incident, though the spoor of a herd of elephants was observed. It was the opinion of Mr. Godkin that it was not worth while to attempt to capture any of them, since there are always so many tame ones to be had at a fair price, and that is the most practical way of securing them.

Dick Brownell, however, thought that it would be a fine thing to make prisoners of some of the huge beasts, and more than once he declared that he meant to make the attempt when a favorable opportunity presented.

It was yet early in the afternoon when the party sought a place to rest until the fervid heat of the day should subside so as to render action upon their part less trying and oppressive. As before, the two horses were allowed to move at will along the edge of the jungle, while the owners and the three natives stretched themselves in the shade, where the air was so suffocating that it would be an error to speak of it as cool, or in any sense pleasant.

CHAPTER LXX.

ATTACKED IN FRONT AND REAR.

THE temperature continued so high during the afternoon that Mr Godkin decided to defer anything in the nature of a systematic hunt for curiosities. He had such faith in Jed's ability that he wished his presence if possible during the most important efforts of himself and Dick.

The latter found the idleness so irksome, that he ventured off on a little tour of his own, leaving the natives asleep and the director smoking his hookah and about ready to follow them into the land of dreams.

When young Brownell was alone in

the Aisatic jungle, he was not surprised to find his self-confidence considerably lessened. His experience in South Africa had taught him that the most skillful hunter is always in peril, and that that sportsman is unwise who, however well armed, ventures far into a wild country without companions.

It was because of his previous experience and the fact that he held a good knowledge of the perils of the hunt in East India, that he did not extend his wanderings far. He saw innumerable birds, some with brilliantly-beautiful plumage, including parrots, paroquets, cockatoos, macaws. He caught a glimpse of a panther, and descried a serpent a dozen feet in length, coiled around a limb above his head. The reptile seemed to be watching him with such an attentive expression, that he made a circuit that carried him out of sight of it. Returning to camp as the day was drawing to a close, Dick joined his friends at the evening meal, consisting of some well-cooked goat's meat and fruit.

Now, you need not be reminded that no company of men would dare lie down in a jungle with the purpose of sleeping through the night without any guard. While the fire of itself always serves as a wall against the too near approach of the fierce creatures that throng those dense forests, yet, as the hours pass, the flames smoulder, until, long before morning, nothing more than a few embers are left, for which no wild animal would care a straw.

Since many of the denizens about which I am telling you are nocturnal in their habits, a most tempting opportunity would present itself to them,— too tempting indeed for any pru-

THE COCKATOO

dent person to take the risk. Besides, the horses are also exposed to the same peril and are too valuable to the hunters to be lost in that way.

"I have had a good deal of sleep this afternoon," said Mr. Godkin, "and will act as sentinel until midnight, when, if you choose, you may take my place."

"That will suit me," replied Dick, "for I had a good long sleep last night, and

a few hours more will be all I can need for some time to come, though," he added with a laugh, looking at the others, " Jack and Jim and Jo ought to be able to keep their eyes open for a week to come."

The natives were always ready to obey orders, and they expressed a wish to go on guard, but Dick thanked them and said he would wait until the next night, when he would probably give them all they wanted of that business.

The horses were brought so near that they were in plain sight and within the circle of light thrown out by the fire that was kept burning vigorously. Before the natives sank in slumber, they gathered enough wood to last until daylight,—a comparatively easy task, since there was an abundance of fuel all around them.

The warmth of the night was such that the heat of the flames added nothing to the comfort of our friends, who would have found it much more pleasant to stretch themselves on the bare ground, but for the danger to which I have referred.

The glare of the fire brought innumerable insects from the jungle, and they swarmed about the flames, thousands of them falling victims, like so many moths, to their own recklessness. Now and then, the cry of some wild animal resounded among the trees, but the party were so accustomed to such noises that they caused them no disturbance and interfered not the least with their slumber. Dick lay as near the fire as he could with comfort, his back being turned toward it. He was tired from the exertions of the day, which, you will agree, were enough in their way to furnish a veteran hunter with material for an indefinite number of reminiscences.

But fortunately we are so constituted that we can become used to almost anything, and the youth saw nothing in what had befallen him since coming to India that was remarkable, except in the one fact that he had been extremely fortunate and a kind heaven seemed to have had him in its kindly keeping. Dick, like the manly fellow that he was, realized that fact and did not fail always to give thanks to the beneficent Power that had shielded him from all harm.

FAN-CRESTED PARROT.

"What time is it, Mr. Godkin?" inquired Dick Brownell, stretching his limbs.

"Just one o'clock," replied the director, replacing his watch.

"You ought to have called me before."

"I wouldn't have waked you before daylight."

"Just like you," was the grateful
remark of Dick, as he rose to a sitting posture, and, rubbing his eyes,
looked up in the smiling face of his
friend, and then blinked at the bright
fire until his vision became accustomed to
the glare.

"Have you noticed anything?" asked
the lad, glancing at the lock of his rifle
before rising to his feet.

"Nothing special, though I am quite
sure there is more than one animal prowling among the trees out there; but they
won't be apt to trouble you, so long as you
keep the fire burning, and there is plenty of
fuel for *that*."

"I'll not forget it, you may be sure."

Mr. Godkin drew an ember from the
flames, and, lighting his pipe, sat down with
his back against a tree.

"I'll keep you company for a while," he
remarked, beginning to puff the vapor with
the enjoyment of an old devotee of the weed.

"It looks," said Dick. "as if you had
spent all your time pacing back and forth:
the ground is pretty well worn for some
distance."

"That is the only safe thing to do, when
you want to keep awake, as you learned in
Africa. You know what an insidious enemy
sleep is, and, just so sure as you sit down
on the ground, you are gone."

THE HYACINTH ARARA

"I would not do that," said the youth, "but I expected to maintain a standing position; by the way," added Dick, "are we likely to
obtain any antelopes like those which furnished us such good food in
South Africa?"

"Hardly; though India has its supply of the beautiful creatures.
For instance, there is the goral of the Western Himalayas; the steppe
antelope, from beyond, with its queer bulging forehead; the nylghau,
belonging to the thickly wooded districts of India; Falconer's goat,
living in the highest portions of the Thibetan Himalayas; the panda

of the Himalayas, hunted for its pelt and flesh, though the latter has a strong musky odor, and a species of goat antelope which is a sacred animal among the Hindoos."

"What about the maned sheep?"

"He is a strange-looking animal, indeed, but his home is in the Atlas Mountains and about the headwaters of the Nile. He is known as the aoudad. However, if you want to keep faithful ward and watch, while we sleep, follow my advice and maintain a regular pacing to and fro."

GORAL ANTELOPE.

This was good sense, and Dick was wise enough to follow it, but, so long as his friend remained awake, he took his place near him, the two talking in low tones, their conversation hardly worth the recording.

Finally Dick asked a question and received no answer. Looking at Mr. Godkin, he saw he was asleep. The director's hookah had fallen from his mouth, his hat had dropped to the ground, and his head had drooped over on his shoulder, while his heavy breathing showed that he was unconscious.

"He was too generous to awaken me at twelve o'clock, as he ought to have done," thought Dick. "I can see how he is trying to conduct this whole business, so as to give me most of the glory that ought to belong to him. Well, now I have the safety of this whole company in my hands, and it won't do to shut my eyes again. No fear of it, for I never felt more wide-awake in my life."

The natives looked like so many logs lying near the fire, their swarthy faces glistening as though they were oiled; but they were accustomed to heat and felt no discomfort in a temperature which a white man would have found intolerable.

The ponies were tethered just beyond them, the two having lain down, so that they were also unconscious, though they were likely to be the first to awaken on the approach of danger.

THE STEPPE ANTELOPE

"I don't believe I would run the least risk in leaning against the tree here," reflected Dick, "but I will do as Mr. Godkin advised."

The firelight showed a path some twenty paces in length made by the gentleman in walking back and forth pausing only at long intervals to fling wood on the flames.

"If this fire were burning on the bank of the Ganges, or some other stream, it would bring thousands of fish close to the shore, and I am quite sure Mr. Godkin was right in saying that wild animals are prowling near us."

The scene was weird and impressive.

25

The brightly-burning fire, the tall, column-like trees, with the dense vegetation below, the running vines, resembling long serpents, winding in and out among the limbs; the unconscious figures stretched near the fire, the two horses close by, the strange, shrill cries that now and then trembled from the depths of the jungle, the myriads of insects fluttering in the smoke over the flames, and occasionally a soft rustling of the leaves and undergrowth, which showed that some beast was moving stealthily about the camp and seeking an opening through which to leap upon the

THE NYLGHAU.

unconscious ones — all these helped to make up a picture which, once seen, could never be forgotten.

Dick paced back and forth with the monotonous regularity of a military sentinel on duty, until he observed that the fire was beginning to subside. Then he leaned his rifle against the tree that supported the back of the sleeping Mr. Godkin, and, taking up several armfuls from the pile of branches, threw them on the burning sticks. Withdrawing a few paces, he watched the crackling flames, which blazed up so high that the area of illumination was doubled. It struck him, while viewing the fire, that there was a singular agitation in the upper part, among the last sticks that he had flung upon it. One of the branches appeared to be twisting fiercely, but only for a second or two, when it shriveled into nothingness, losing its individuality in a twinkling.

"I never suspected *that*," said Dick to himself, as he recognized in the strange-looking stick a serpent that had lain among the last pieces of wood he had tossed

FALCONER'S GOAT

on the flames, "but there is no telling when you run against those creatures in this part of the world."

The snake, which was no more than a couple of feet in length, could not have been in the pile of wood when the natives gathered the fuel, since it would have made its presence known; but it had probably crawled there to enjoy the heat of the camp-fire, just as the cobra some nights before had sought the warmth of Dick's body.

"It's a wonder he didn't bite me when I picked up the wood, but he is out of the calculation *now*."

Looking straight across the camp-fire, and through the thin smoke, the lad caught a momentary gleam of something which vanished before he could gain more than a glimpse of it.

But he was shrewd enough to read its meaning aright. The glare was that of two circular objects, seemingly a couple of inches in diameter and separated from each other by about three times of space.

Such an exhibition could have been made only by the glowing eye-balls of some wild animal that had whisked out of sight before the youth could see anything more.

THE PANDA OF THE HIMALAYAS.

"I thought it was about time for something like that, and likely enough there are more of them."

Sure enough, the thought was hardly formed, when not only the same sight presented itself, but a similar one was observed a short distance to the right. Furthermore, several well defined growls struck Dick's ear.

The second pair of optics that appeared were quite near one of the horses, for whom the youth was more apprehensive than for any one of the company.

The latter were so near the fire that it was not to be believed that the most daring wild beast would molest them; but the animals of necessity were tethered a little farther off, though it was believed that they were also close enough to share in the protection thus afforded the rest.

Neither of the ponies had awakened, but they were likely to do so at any

IN AMBUSH

389

moment. With a view of guarding them, Dick now left his beat and walked around the fire, stepping very lightly, so as not to disturb them.

At the first step, the wild animals vanished, as suddenly as if each had taken a backward leap of twenty feet.

"They'll show themselves again," said Dick to himself, "and then I'll take a whack at one of them."

He had not long to wait, when the phosphorescent eye-balls were seen once more. This time they remained fixed so steadily upon the youth that he could not

THE AOUDAD

have asked for a better target, since the illumination on his gun was all that he needed.

"I wonder where the other one is."

Strange that the bright lad did not think of the probability of the second wild beast being *behind him* instead of in front!

Yet such was the fact, and, the moment he brought his gun to his shoulder and sighted at the first beast, the other was creeping noiselessly and swiftly upon him from the rear.

CHAPTER LXXI.

JUMBO AND TOUNG TALOUNG.

AS I said, Dick could not have asked for a better target than was given by the glimpse of the glaring eye-balls on the other side of the camp-fire, for the organs themselves were not only in sight, but he plainly saw the outlines of the wild beast, which he suspected was a cheetah or hunting leopard, an animal rarely found out of India.

This brute is not so large nor fine-looking as the leopard, and its name is due to the fact that it can be tamed and trained to assist the hunter in bringing down deer. It is lighter than the panther and lives much in the lower branches of large trees, where the female brings forth its young. In its wild state it is stealthy and treacherous like all of its kind.

At the very moment Dick pulled the trigger, the stillness around him was such that he caught the faint rustle made by the second animal stealing upon him from the rear.

The bullet had hardly left the barrel, when the lad whirled about like a flash and confronted the danger behind him.

He was not an instant too soon.

The second cheetah, which was much larger than the first, was no more than a dozen feet distant, crouching low and gathering himself for his deadly spring.

Since Dick's gun was discharged, it will be seen that his situation was extremely dangerous, inasmuch as the animal was quite sure to attack before he could reload his weapon.

But Mr. Godkin's long experience had taught him not only to awaken from a sound slumber with all his senses at command, but to know that when thus awakened by the report of a gun, his services were almost certain to be in immediate need.

Before the other members of the party were fairly aroused, and before the youth's situation had become hopelessly desperate, the director's weapon was fired, and the second cheetah perished almost as quickly as the first.

Meanwhile, the reports of the rifles had brought the others to their feet. The horses had been aroused, too, but they merely opened their eyes without rising.

A few seconds were enough to understand what had taken place, the dead bodies of the cheetahs near the camp-fire bearing witness to the accuracy of the aim of Dick and Mr. Godkin.

"I believe they have been hanging around the camp ever since the fire was kindled," said Mr. Godkin, "and since there may be more of them, I will bear you company until daylight, which is not far off."

Dick protested that this was unnecessary, for he was abundantly able to take care of himself; but his friend insisted that he had had enough slumber to last him twenty-four hours, so he re-filled and lit his hookah, while the natives, seeing their services were not wanted, lay down again, and were soon unconscious.

With two intelligent sentinels on duty, it would have been strange if the party had not been safe. The fire was kept up, and while Dick resumed his pacing back and forth, he maintained a pleasant conversation with his friend, who puffed away at his pipe and entertained him with stories of his experiences, not only in

THE SACRED ANTELOPE.

India, but in other parts of the world, while engaged in my service. Dick expected that his friend would drop off into sleep again, but he did not, and remained fully awake during the remaining hours of darkness.

The rustling among the leaves which they heard now and then proved that other wild animals were prowling near, and doubtless looking for a chance to get at the men or horses, but the glare of the fire, and perhaps a suspicion of what the reports of the rifles had to do with the inanimate forms lying near, kept them from venturing too close.

"Those creatures are more often found in the groves and large forests than in the jungles," said Mr. Godkin, "and I hardly expected when the report of your gun awakened me that it was a cheetah you had shot."

"I tell you, Mr. Godkin, a fellow has got to keep his wits about him in this part of the world."

A FAMILY OF ELKS.

"It does look that way; and, in fact, I don't know any part of this sphere where it is safe to do otherwise."

"This is a good enough country to hunt and spend a few months in, but after I have gathered all the curiosities I can — with your help, of course — I shall be glad to get back to the United States, the most *blessed and glorious place in the* wide world."

You may be sure that the hunters would not remain idle long. The morning meal was hardly finished when the sharp-eared Jack, who had applied his ear to the ground, said that he heard the sounds made by some heavy animals moving at no great distance, and a few minutes later he declared they were elephant's.

"We may as well have a look at them," added Mr. Godkin. "This is your first hunting jaunt in India, Dick, and you can't afford to lose anything."

The servants were told to remain where they were, and since that suited them, they stretched out on the ground, ready for any duty their masters might require.

FALLOW DEER

"Do you mean to shoot an elephant?" asked Dick, as the two began picking their way through the jungle.

"That depends upon circumstances; since you will be able to tell about the Bengal tiger you brought down, the addition of an elephant or two to your game bag will be a small matter."

"If they are of the usual size, I suspect it will be a rather large matter," was the reply of the youth, who kept close to the heels of his companion.

JUMBO ON HIS TRAVELS.

The noise made by the passage of a herd of elephants was now plainly audible, so there was no difficulty in follow·ng the right course.

The couple had penetrated less than a hundred yards, when they caught sight of the rear of the drove, swinging through the dense jungle as though it could offer no impediment to their progress.

There were seven, proceeding in irregular order, crashing through the under-growth, tearing off the branches above their heads, occasionally trumpeting and evidently disposed to have considerable sport with each other.

Though these huge beasts, when their suspicions are aroused, are wonderfully quick of ear and eye, they showed no knowledge of their enemies, so near at hand. The latter kept at a respectful distance, for they did not wish to alarm them. Had they done so, more than likely the whole herd would have broken away, and, trav-eling rapidly, would pass out of sight of the hunters, and keep it up for eight or ten miles — much too far for Dick and Mr. Godkin to follow.

"They are going to the water," said the gentleman, who prevented the youth from walking too fast; "there is a pool or stream not far off."

"If we were no more particular than they, we might enjoy a bath also," replied Dick, greatly interested in the sight.

The seven animals were of great size, one of them, as Mr. Godkin afterward informed me, being fully ten feet high.

This is an unusual height, and right here, since I am anxious you should gain knowledge as well as entertainment from what I am relating, I will give you some interesting information.

There isn't a boy or girl in England or America who has not seen or read about Jumbo, the largest elephant ever known. You have learned of his affecting death by a railway accident, and perhaps have seen his mounted skeleton, now with my show. I had him mounted by Professor Henry A. Ward, of Rochester, New York, who made careful measurements, which he reported to me, as follows, which I believe are now published for the first time:

Circumference (6 inches back of the eye), 10 feet 4 inches.
Largest diameter of the ear, 5 feet 5 inches. (Jumbo was an African elephant.)
Circumference of tusk at the base, 1 foot 6 inches.
Circumference of trunk at base, 3 feet 5 inches.
Length of trunk from base of tusk, 5 feet 11 inches.
Body circumference, just back of shoulders, 16 feet 4 inches.
Body circumference at middle, 18 feet.
Body circumference at point in front of hind legs, 17 feet.
Length of tail, 4 feet 6 inches.
Fore legs: circumference of foot, 5 feet 3 inches.
Circumference of leg (3 feet above sole of foot), 3 feet 10 inches.
Hind legs: circumference of foot, 4 feet.
Circumference of leg (2 feet above sole of foot), 3 feet.
Circumference of leg (4 feet above sole of foot), 4 feet 8 inches

Height, measuring from sole of foot to a point between shoulder-blades, about 12 feet.

Entire length of animal, 14 feet.

The heart weighed 46 pounds.

When alive Jumbo weighed 7 tons, and the weight of the mounted skeleton is about 3 tons.

Since Jumbo was the most wonderful elephant that ever lived, I may as well give you all that is known about him.

He was twenty-three years old when he died, and as elephants cease growing only when they attain the age of thirty, we began to have great fears as to how we should get him through the numerous railroad tunnels of the country. He was within five or six inches of the height of an ordinary railroad tunnel when he died.

Originally, Jumbo was a small African elephant. He was brought across the deserts by Arabs, and was fed on camel's milk. He was consigned to the *Jardin des Plantes*, in Paris, and when he arrived there he was a funny little animal that attracted no particular notice. In an exchange of some animals with the Zoological Garden in London, the managers of the *Jardin des Plantes* sent this little elephant among the rest, not considering him of much account.

After he had been for a few months at the Zoological Garden, he and his keeper, Mr. Scott, were one day photographed, and in the picture it is shown that the keeper stood a breast higher than Jumbo. All at once, however, a sudden spurt of growing came over him, just as ordinary-sized boys in a family suddenly grow up into giants; and Jumbo grew, and grew, and grew, until he got to be twelve feet high, fourteen feet long, eighteen feet around the middle of his body, and reached the very respectable aldermanic-elephantine weight of seven tons.

During my visits to London I had often seen the famous big elephant, and had ridden on him, but it never entered my head that I could buy him. I eventually told my agent to approach Mr. Bartlett, the Superintendent of the Gardens, on the subject. He conferred with the Council of the Gardens, and they accepted my offer of $10,000 for the animal.

In view of the results of this enterprise, it seems a little singular, but the fact is, my partner, Mr. Hutchinson, was strongly opposed to buying Jumbo.

"What is the difference," he would say, "between an elephant seven feet high and another eleven or twelve feet high? — an elephant is an elephant."

I insisted that this was the greatest beast in the world, and urged that, being such, Barnum's Circus couldn't afford to be without him. Finally the objections of my partner were overruled and we sent over the money to pay for Jumbo.

When the English people got information that Jumbo was to be taken out of the country, they were fairly wild with excitement. Many newspapers looked upon it as an outrage, and blamed the Superintendent of the Gardens, the Council, and every one who had had anything to do with the affair. The great art critic John Ruskin took part in the discussion, and said that England was not accustomed to sell her pets.

There was so much dissatisfaction expressed, that the Zoological Garden people tried to induce my agent to rescind the sale, but I told them I could not; I had announced the purchase of the elephant and I could not afford to disappoint the American people.

TOUNG TALOUNG, MY FAMOUS WHITE ELEPHANT

The stockholders of the Zoological Garden held a meeting. They insisted that the Council had no right to sell without their consent, and got out an injunction on us, which, by some legal hocus-pocus which it would require too much space here to explain, came up in the Court of Chancery.

The editor of the London *Telegraph*, Mr. Lesarge, sent me a telegram in which he stated that all the British children were distressed at the elephant's departure: on what terms would I return Jumbo? "Answer, prepaid, unlimited."

When I read the last three words of this dispatch, I am afraid that the spirit of practical joking took possession of me for the moment. I took the Englishman at his word and answered "unlimited." I told him that a hundred thousand pounds would not induce me to cancel my purchase, and then I gave him a pretty full description of my circus, commencing, "My largest tent seats 20,000 persons," etc., etc., and ended with "wishing long life and prosperity to the British nation, the *Telegraph* and Jumbo." This dispatch was published in the *Telegraph* the next morning, and was republished on the following day in the principal newspapers throughout Great Britain. It did its part in keeping up the excitement.

Jumbo had never been out of the Garden since the day he had entered it, twenty years before. When my agents attempted to get him out he would not stir; he seemed to know instinctively that something extraordinary was going to happen. My agent cabled me: "Jumbo is lying in the Garden and will not stir. What shall we do?" I replied: "Let him lie there as long as he wants to." All this, it will be observed, kept up public interest.

Then we built a cage on wheels, and sank the wheels into the ground, leaving both ends of the cage open. It was many days before he could be induced to walk through. We let him get used to going through for several days and finally shut him in. It took a score of horses to pull the cage out of the earth, after we had dug around the wheels, and we dragged the cage down to the wharf. There Jumbo met a whole crowd of his admirers, including such fashionable people as Lady Burdett-Coutts, who brought him cakes and dainties. One enthusiast testified his affection by sending some champagne and oysters. On the vessel we had to cut away a part of the deck above his lodgings to make his apartment large enough.

The original price of Jumbo was $10,000; his final cost was $30,000. He paid for himself the first ten days after his arrival.

Toung Taloung, the famous white elephant, which I brought from Burmah, cost me $200,000. Like the public, I was greatly disappointed in him. He was as genuine a white elephant as ever existed, but, in fact, there was never such an animal known. The white spots are simply diseased blotches.

My white elephant was burned to death at Bridgeport in November, 1887, and I can't say that I grieved much over his loss.

Among the elephants on which Mr. Godkin and Dick Brownell were gazing was a mother with a young one, of which all seemed extremely fond. This was shown conclusively at the time the herd was crossing an open space some distance from where they had entered the jungle.

Without the least warning a large tiger dashed out from cover and made for the little one, which just then was standing with its head in the other direction, caressing its mother. The female saw the tiger, but showed no excitement, knowing she had brave friends around her.

Before the tiger could get anywhere near the young one, the bull interposed his prodigious form, and, rearing on his hind legs, aimed a blow at the assailant with his tusks and fore feet which required all of the animal's dexterity to avoid. By this time the rest of the herd had taken the alarm, and the tiger was wise enough to give up his intention of making a meal from a young elephant.

26   A BATTLE IN THE JUNGLE.

CHAPTER LXXII.

AN INTERLOPER.

WHEN Mr. Godkin pronounced the bull elephant only two feet less in height than Jumbo you may be sure that the animal was a remarkable one. The first thought of the excellent gentleman was that of the value of such a prize to me.

The suspicion that the herd were on their way to water was confirmed, for it reached a pool before going a quarter of a mile.

It was just such a place as delights those animals, being about an acre in extent, fed by a little stream, and with a similar outlet. The pond was shallow at the sides, but quite deep in the middle.

The bulky beasts waded slowly in, brandishing their trunks over their heads and trumpeting with pleasure, for the contact of the comparatively cool water must have been delightful. Indeed, Dick envied them, and felt as though, had he known of the pool so near, he would have been tempted to take a plunge himself.

He had noticed on his way thither that a couple of the beasts followed a well-marked path, the rest crashing through the jungle on both sides of it. This showed that other animals were in the habit of visiting the place, as the hunters would have known had they come upon the trail anywhere in the jungle.

The bull, who took the post of honor at the head of his family, walked slowly out into the pond, his enormous body gradually sinking lower, like the submerging of some wreck, until he was half covered. Then he paused and swung his head around to see how the rest were making out.

Mr. Godkin and Dick had taken positions where they could watch everything without exposing themselves to detection.

The six members of his family were not holding back, but pushed into the water with more eagerness than the old bull had shown. As if he desired to impress more becoming dignity upon them, he filled his trunk with water, and, aiming at the front of the nearest elephant, let fly.

The aim was accurate, and the brute was in the condition of an innocent spectator at a fire, who has the hose suddenly turned in his face. The water struck his massive forehead with a splash and force that sent the spray flying in every direction.

But he liked it and had his own remedy. Drawing in several gallons of the fluid, he dispatched it in the direction of their lord and master, hitting him squarely in the eyes and compelling him to scatter his own supply of moisture impartially over the pool. The fun became fast and furious. Dick and Mr. Godkin, in their hiding-place, laughed like a couple of school-boys at the sight of what suggested to them the antics of the same number of American lads just let out for play.

HUGE SPORT.

In a trice all the elephants were sending the water over each other, the hose-like streams going up in the air, cut among the vegetation and against the flabby sides of the monsters, with a promiscuousness and vigor that could not have been improved. Once a poorly-aimed hydraulic bomb, which the bull dispatched at the head of a lady near the side of the pool, missed its mark, and went so far over into the jungle that it came near finding the two spectators.

"My gracious!" whispered Dick, who plainly felt the mist, "wouldn't they give us a ducking if they knew we were here!"

"They might do more than that," replied Mr. Godkin, "for those elephants are wild, and have intelligence enough to understand that all bipeds are their enemies. Take care that they do not get sight of you."

The huge beasts now began to vary the fun, showing an ingenuity that was as surprising as it was amusing to the small but select body of spectators.

Near one end of the pond stood the most diminutive member of the party. She was in just far enough to cover her legs, her entire body being above the surface. Standing thus, she filled her trunk and sent the water and spray flying far out among the rest. The distance was twenty feet or more, and the curving stream went not only high in the air, but spread out more like a fan the farther it reached, often falling in spray and mist.

She aimed at no particular one, but was impartial in her attentions, dispatching the deluge wherever the best target offered. The others seemed to pay no attention to her, but, before long, the watchful Mr. Godkin directed Dick's notice to the action of the bull and two of his family.

"There's mischief afoot," he whispered; "they are hatching a plot against that lady who is having such fine sport on the edge of the pond."

The bull was gradually working his way out of the water, as though he had had enough of it. He did not seem to observe the presence of the one that was dousing him, but, all the same, he emerged from the pool at a point quite close to her.

The female gave him a blast at the moment he swung from the pond, sending a deluge straight in his face, like the stream with which a steam fire engine breaks in the windows of a burning building. Indeed, it was so terrific that the old fellow threw up his trunk and head as if to protest.

Two others kept edging closer to this female, but managed it so deftly that she did not suspect anything was on foot. In fact, she was so happy that Dick afterward declared he saw the corners of her mouth draw up, just as if she was indulging in a grin over the discomfiture of the head of the household.

But really my young friend must have been mistaken, though there can be no question that those huge animals find the keenest enjoyment in such sport.

Suddenly, and without the least warning, the bull made a plunge along the edge of the pool, which placed him in the rear of the young lady that was having such a good time. At the same moment, the two that had been cautiously edging along made a dash for her.

She saw what was coming and tried to get away; but it was too late. In short, she was between two fires, and escape was out of the question.

She had time to take only a couple of steps in the direction of the shore, when the bull placed his head against her side and gave her such a prodigious push that she went over, like a house tumbling off the wharf. Instantly the other two began pelting her with water until it looked as if she must be drowned. She floundered and struggled, while the bull, allowing her to get half way to her feet, regularly pressed her over again.

This seemed to be the very acme of enjoyment for all the elephants except the victim, and there is reason to believe that she herself found a certain relish in the rough bath to which she was being subjected.

The water became muddy from its violent stirring, but that made no difference to the participants, who tramped back and forth, lay down in it until only the tops of their heads were visible, sent it spurting everywhere in fountains, and reveled in delight.

From where the hunters carefully screened themselves in the jungle it would have been the easiest matter in the world to kill one or two of the animals, but to break in upon such a scene of innocent fun with the crack of the heavy rifles would have been inexcusable. It gives me pleasure to say that neither Mr. Godkin nor Dick felt the least disposition to do anything of the kind.

Our friends were still watching the uncouth gambols of the huge creatures, when a disturbance among the undergrowth near at hand caused them to look around.

To their astonishment, they perceived another bull elephant, almost as large as the one that lorded it over the herd in the pool. He was moving slowly, and evidently with great care, as if to prevent the others from discovering him. His attention was fixed so closely upon them that he failed to notice the hunters crouching not far off.

An Intruder.

The action of the animal was so peculiar that Dick was puzzled, though his friend suspected the truth.

"I wonder whether he is the leader of another herd," said the lad, in a low voice.

"No; he is alone."

"But what does he mean by acting that way?"

"Keep still and watch him; I will explain when we have a better opportunity for talking. He must not see us."

The behavior of the strange elephant was for all the world like a prowling enemy looking for a chance to do his foes some evil.

After observing the sportive beasts for a few minutes, the interloper resumed his advance, though with less care than before. He must have known that he would soon be detected.

Such was the case. All at once the elephants ceased their pranks, and turned their huge heads in the direction of the new arrival, as if to inquire what he wanted. He threw up his trunk and emitted his own peculiar call, probably meaning it for a friendly salutation.

But if such was its purport, it was received in anything but a spirit of comity. With one accord, the herd, headed by the gigantic bull, charged upon the stranger. There could be no mistaking their fury, and the interloper was too wise to stand his ground.

The flight and pursuit of the intruder brought the whole party so close to our friends that discovery was sure. Dick and Mr. Godkin hugged the ground as close as they could, but the charging bull saw them, and, trumpeting the alarm, made a wide detour, followed by all that came after him.

The opportunity for a shot as they lumbered past was excellent, but neither fired, content to leave the animals alone, so long as it was not necessary to shoot in self-defense.

It is hardly to be supposed that the pursuers overtook the fugitive, judging from the exhibition he gave, but the chase quickly carried all beyond sight of our friends, who rose to their feet and started back to camp, where the horses and servants had been left.

"That interloper," explained Mr. Godkin, "is what is known as a 'goondah,' or 'sawn,' or 'rogue elephant.' In Ceylon he is called a 'hora.'"

Dick's inquiring looks showed that this was something of which he was ignorant, having come across nothing referring to such a ceature in all his reading of natural history.

"You have seen," continued the elder, glad to give such a bright lad information, "that the elephants generally herd together, the companies sometimes numbering a dozen or a score, though they are more generally of the dimensions of the bathers. It now and then happens that one belonging to a herd becomes separated from the rest and is unable to find them again. He may hunt long and patiently, but the chances are against his success.

"If that proves the case, he becomes an outcast, for no other herd will suffer him to join them. He may attempt it, but the rest reject all his overtures and drive him off. If he insists on staying, the others will attack, and most likely kill him. Henceforth, he is a 'goondah,' or 'rogue.'"

"And why that?"

"His expatriation, if we may call it such, makes him vicious. He seems to conclude that, since his own species have turned against him, he will become an Ishmaelite and make a general nuisance of himself. I have known a 'rogue' in

Ceylon to prowl around a planter's house at night, tearing down his fences and killing his stock out of pure wantonness. If he is interfered with, he becomes ugly and displays considerable bravery in attacking hunters."

"Suppose that the 'goondah' had seen us?"

"It isn't likely he would have disturbed us, for his whole interest lay in the herd, to which, as you saw for yourself, he made advances looking to affiliation; but had he come upon us when none of his kind was in sight, there would have been trouble."

"But he ought to receive the greater share, since we are both loaded for elephant," replied Dick.

"That is true, but there is no guarding against accidents. You observed in what spirit his overtures were received?"

"Elephants seem very much like human beings," was the truthful observation of my young friend Dick Brownell.

CHAPTER LXXIII.

A FLYING SHOT OR TWO.

THE hunters picked their way at their leisure through the jungle. Keeping to the path which they had struck while following the herd of elephants, the walking was found quite easy and pleasant.

You need not be told that, though the friends were conversing with the carelessness they would have shown had they been grouped in one of the native huts, they keep their eyes and ears wide open. There could be no doubt that the trail was used by many animals in going to and from the pool in which the herd of elephants had disported themselves, and the hunters, therefore, were liable to encounter some of them.

Mr. Godkin was walking a few paces in front of the youth, who left to him the principal duty of looking out for danger in that direction, while he occasionally cast a furtive glance over his own shoulder to make sure that no enemy stole upon him unawares.

Sure enough, they had walked but a short distance when the leader suddenly halted with the exclamation:

"Something is coming!"

Both sprang aside and held their guns ready for instant use, for the chances were that a fight impended. The next moment, however, a half-suppressed exclamation of amazement escaped both, as they recognized an enormous wild boar.

He was not trotting, but walking along the trail from the direction of the plain, and no doubt was on his way to the pool of water beyond our friends. Having made a good dinner, he probably wanted a drink, after which he would take a siesta, as many animals are accustomed to do in that warm country.

Mr. Godkin and Dick were standing only a pace or two from the path, and the boar must have seen them, though nothing in his manner betrayed it, since he did not retreat nor change his pace.

"If he attacks, we will each give him a shot," said the elder, "but, since we spared the elephants, we will do the same with him, provided he behaves himself."

"I am willing," replied Dick, who nevertheless felt some misgiving, as he recalled the vigorous style in which the animal in Africa had handled Pongo and his pony. I am confident you have not forgotten the stirring experience of the Bushman with the wild boar which he encountered with Mr. Godkin along the edge of the South African jungle. Dick had seen nothing of that affray, but he had been interested in the account, and had expressed his regrets so often that he had not been thus favored that the director promised to secure him a taste of what may truly be called royal sport.

On reaching camp, Jed, who had meanwhile returned from Lucknow, told them that he had seen the same boar, as he believed, eating some nuts which grew in a grove of trees not far off, and, though he had gone to the pool for water, he was quite sure to return to his former feeding-place.

You may be sure Dick was eager for the sport, especially as he was well aware not only of the amazing strength and courage of the animal, but of the chivalry that he often displays toward a fallen enemy.

Mr. Godkin was inclined at first to arm himself and companion with the spears which the natives used, but they were so long and slender, and his young friend was so unaccustomed to handling them, that he decided it would be wiser to rely on their own weapons.

Furthermore, he thought the chances about even of seeing the brute again. Those creatures, as they grow older, do not associate with herds of their kind, but are fond of browsing by themselves. If Dick should be fortunate enough to catch sight of one, his intention was to ride as closely as possible and take a shot at him. If the bullet was well aimed, he might bring down his game, though he was more likely to fail than succeed.

Leaving the natives in camp, our friends, a couple of hours later, rode out to the edge of the grassy plain, where Mr. Godkin glanced over the tract with the observing eye of a true sportsman.

"Yonder," said he, "is the clump of trees that Jed told us about. I recognize them as bearing the fruit to which the boar is so partial, and if the one we saw does not return, we may catch sight of another."

"If I am not mistaken," replied Dick, speaking slowly and with his gaze fixed on the clump of trees, "I see something moving in the grass on the farther side; tell me what *you* make of it."

"It is the boar, as you live!" exclaimed Mr. Godkin; "we're in luck to-day."

"How shall we proceed?"

"You may ride toward the trees, while I will take a course parallel with the trend of the jungle."

"What is the reason for that?"

"I am going to let you have the first chance, and if necessary, I will give you help in the final disposition of the boar — provided," added the gentleman with a laugh, "the boar doesn't first dispose of *us*."

Dick was thankful for the consideration of his friend, and he felt no misgiving about any mishap befalling him.

It seemed to him that if he drove the animal from beneath the trees, he would dart into the jungle, where it would be impossible to follow him on horseback or on foot with any prospect of overtaking him.

But a few minutes would decide.

The youth had ridden only a little way when he saw that the boar was really under the trees, poking his snout over the ground, among the grass, in quest of the nuts he liked so well.

It was not until the hunter was within three or four rods that the animal became aware of his approach and raised his head.

He was a formidable creature, and Dick checked his pony and surveyed him several minutes with wonder, not unmixed with admiration. Then with a grunt the brute started off on a trot, not entering the jungle, but taking a course parallel to it.

It appeared to Dick, as he rode after him, that the boar was as tall as a cow, very gaunt, and with such long limbs that at first glance he half suspected he was some other animal; but watching him, as he leisurely trotted away, he noticed his enormous tusks, curling up in front of his eyes, and he was convinced he was pursuing as magnificent a specimen of the wild boar as could be found in all India.

The brute was going easily, but Dick was surprised to observe that his pony, which was on a gallop, was not gaining upon him. He, therefore, pushed him to a sharper pace.

Finally the young hunter thought he had reached about the right distance, and, bringing his gun to his shoulder, he aimed at the neck of the boar and let fly.

Probably he hit the target, though, if such was the case, the brute gave no evidence of it, but continued the same trot, neither faster nor slower. Most likely the ball had struck some part of the snout or head and glanced off without causing the recipient any inconvenience.

"If you can get in fifteen or twenty more shots like that!" shouted Mr. Godkin, who was having his own fun, "you will make him take some notice of you."

Dick laughed to himself, for he was too sensible to mind the badinage of his friend, and began recharging his weapon, which, being a breech-loader, did not require much time or bother. The cartridge was quickly in place, and he was prepared for another shot.

But, during the brief spell required to get his weapon ready, the pony had slackened his pace slightly, and, as a consequence, the boar was farther off than before: it was necessary to be as near as then, and, in the hope of making the second shot effectual, Dick determined to decrease the distance still more.

He observed a disturbing fact: the grassy plain over which all parties were hastening terminated not very far off, the jungle sweeping around in front, so that, unless the game was bagged before the boundary was reached, he was likely to get away altogether.

Our young friend, therefore, devoted a few seconds to bringing himself closer to the animal. The pony, in accordance with a habit he had formed, had lessened his speed and showed a disposition to draw off after his rider fired.

This probably was on the theory that the youth required only a single shot to bring down his game — a faith undoubtedly complimentary to the hunter himself, but not without its disadvantages.

The horse was also quick to comprehend his duty, and, now that he was headed toward the boar once more, he did his level best, gradually but surely lessening the space separating the youth from the swiftly-fleeing game.

"Don't aim at his hind leg this time!" shouted Mr. Godkin, "for he can go on three legs as well as four."

Dick made no answer, for he could think of none that promised to hush his friend: it was enough to attend to the game that was likely to escape him before he could be checked.

Despite all the pony was able to do, it was not until the boar was on the farther edge of the plain that Dick felt himself close enough to risk another attempt to bring him down. The intervening space was only a trifle less than before, when he leveled his rifle and fired his second shot.

To his mortification the pony at that instant half stumbled over some obstruction in his path, so disturbing the aim of the rider that he knew, without looking, he had missed entirely.

"Well done!" called his tormentor, whose laugh rang across the plain; "that shot didn't go more than ten feet above his head. Can't we manage to get the fellow to stand still a minute while you poke the muzzle into his ear?"

"It's too late now" replied Dick, checking his horse, as he saw that the boar was close to the end of the plain; "your gun is loaded; suppose *you* show me how to do it."

Dick was looking at Mr. Godkin, who instantly began making excited gestures.

"It isn't too late either!" he called. "Load quick! you've got a better chance now than ever."

Dick turned, and saw to his amazement that the boar, instead of taking refuge in the jungle, had turned squarely about and was returning over the same route he had just followed.

But the boy's gun was unloaded and his horse had come to a full halt. He could do nothing until a new cartridge was in place, and he set about repairing his forgetfulness.

This compelled him to withdraw his attention for the moment from the animal. Short as was the time required to recharge his weapon, he had not yet finished doing so when Mr. Godkin, who was riding toward him, called:

"Look out! the boar is coming for you!"

The lad glanced up and saw that his friend spoke the truth. The boar had wheeled about, not with the purpose of keeping up his flight, but to punish the parties who had presumed to molest him while peacefully groping for dinner.

Running along the side of the jungle until opposite the point where Dick had halted, he turned sharply to the right, and, with his head lowered, charged upon the horseman at full speed, coming with such a hurricane rush that he was upon the terrified pony before the latter could gather himself for flight.

CHAPTER LXXIV.

A STRANGE EXPERIENCE.

LEST you may think I am romancing, I beg to assure you that the incident which I am describing is true in every particular; and I may add that the experience of Dick Brownell was similar to that of one other hunter, as I know from my personal knowledge.

The infuriated wild boar charged so swiftly upon the youth that, as I have said, he reached the pony before the latter could comprehend his peril and gather himself for flight.

In accordance with his instincts, the boar ran his head directly beneath the horse, with the intention of disemboweling him by an upward flirt of those terrible tusks; but, in his rage, he drove his snout beyond the steed, so that, when it was flung aloft, it missed the body of his victim, and the blade-like ivories clove empty air instead of flesh and bone.

But the swing of the head lifted the pony entirely off his feet, and he fell broadside across the neck of the boar, kicking and striving desperately to free himself from the brute beneath him.

Dick had dropped his gun and strove to leap from the back of his horse; but, before he could do so, the latter had fallen, and the boy's foot was inextricably caught in the stirrup.

Thus it was that the boar supported on his neck, not only the full weight of the pony, but that of his rider also; and, holding them there, he resumed his swift trot, as though unincumbered with anything of the kind.

It was a strange sight that Mr. Godkin saw, the kicking pony on his side across the neck of the animal, with the rider entangled also, while the boar himself resumed his trot toward the edge of the jungle, which he had nearly reached when he wheeled about to charge his tormentors.

This distance, at the very least, was a hundred yards, and, incredible as the statement may seem, the boar trotted it all, carrying the pony and Dick Brownell the entire distance.

Mr. Godkin was terrified lest the youth should be killed. Springing from the back of his horse, he ran forward with the intention of planting a bullet back of the boar's fore leg, but the risk of hitting either the pony or his rider was so great that he dared not fire.

The natives, from their place on the edge of the plain, saw that something serious was amiss, and came running to the help of their friends, shouting, brandishing their spears aloft, and eager to do what they could to help the young but mighty hunter.

412

But they were so far off that they could not possibly arrive in time to do any-thing. To Mr. Godkin it looked as if Dick's chief danger was from the hoofs of the pony, which were flying about in such a frantic way that they were liable to shatter his skull.

But at the edge of the plain the steed fought himself free and fell to the ground, Dick going with him. The boar paid no further attention to either, but, without increasing or diminishing his speed, trotted into the jungle and vanished.

While the pony was clambering to his feet, Mr. Godkin hurried up and bent over his young friend who lay still.

"Are you hurt, Dick?" he asked, observing that his eyes were open.

"I'm bruised a little, but I don't think any bones are broken," he replied, rising slowly to his feet with the help of his companion.

He had dropped his gun and hat, and his clothes presented a sorry appearance; but it was just like the boy, after shaking himself together and finding that he was free from fractured bones, to ask in a quizzical voice:

"How is the boar?"

"He seemed to be in the enjoyment of his usual health, when I saw him last."

The next question, which ought to have preceded the other, was as to how the pony had come out of his rough experience.

It was evident that he was not too badly injured to climb to his feet. Looking around, Dick and Mr. Godkin saw him skurrying across the plain, hair, mane, bridle and stirrups flying, while he snorted with fright. Surely, if ever a horse was warranted in yielding to panic, the pony was that one.

But he was heading toward the three natives, running to the help of their masters. Seeing him coming, they spread out over the plain, and, as he was a well-trained steed, he suffered himself to be caught by Jim, who found him so weak and trembling that he could hardly stand. When, however, the native undertook to lead him back to his owner, he refused to move. He had had enough hard handling in that direction to make him anxious to shun the spot forever after.

So Jim stayed with him, while his companions hurried forward.

"Well," laughed Mr. Godkin, unspeakably relieved to find that Dick had not been seriously hurt, "what do you think of the wild boar as game to be hunted?"

"I know of *one* specimen that is able to hold his own against *me* at least."

"Yes: and against a half a dozen. I am surprised that he failed to kill your pony."

"He doesn't seem to have hurt him at all," remarked Dick some minutes later, when they had reached the spot where the trembling beast stood, with Jim holding him.

"It was his very eagerness to kill him that prevented," remarked Mr. Godkin, attentively examining the steed; "he has scratched him somewhat, and no doubt the pony has been as well shaken up as his master, but the boar drove his head so far forward that he undershot the mark."

"But he had only to draw back a step or two to out the poor horse fatally."

"I wonder that he didn't, but, having got you both on his neck, he wanted to give you a free ride."

"It's the sort of ride that I wouldn't take again for all the wealth of India," remarked Dick with a shudder, as he began patting the neck of his steed. "No one can imagine my feelings during those two or three minutes when the boar was under me and the pony on top."

"I thought he would kick your brains out."

"He must have come very near it; I can't understand why he did not. My foot was caught in such a way that I couldn't possibly get it out of the stirrup. Although I did not have his whole weight on me, I felt as if my breast was crushed in by the mountain pressing me down. I fought and kicked, too, but I couldn't see anything plainly, and all was a blind struggle for life."

"But you *did* get your foot loose."

"When the pony toppled off he must have twisted the stirrup in such a way that my foot drew out, By that time everything looked dark, and you saw I was a little dazed when you came up."

"It was most providential that you were not killed outright."

"I feel that, and I shall thank Heaven as long as I live for preserving me, not only from this peril, but from the others by which I have been threatened. I can now appreciate Pongo's escape from the wild boar in Africa."

"It is better to be born lucky than rich, and best of all to be born plucky," was the truthful comment of Mr. Godkin. "I judge we have all had enough hunting for to-day."

It was some time before our friends recovered from the flurry caused by

"ROYAL SPORT, INDEED."

the encounter with the wild boar, which in some respects was similar to the Bushman's experience with one of the animals in South Africa. Dick's pony showed a formidable disposition to regard more than one inanimate object as another of the beasts in disguise, awaiting the chance to charge upon him again, while his rider found he had been so severely shaken up that he was likely to feel the effects for several days.

Before reaching camp, Mr. Godkin had noticed the absence of Jack. Jim explained that he had set out to call on a friend living hardly a third of a mile distant. The migratory life of the Hindoos precludes all our ideas of home, and Jack meant to stay with him for only a short time. He expected to procure some food, and it was his intention to return before the set of sun.

This course of the native would have been considered presumptuous by many, since Jed had also gone on a short visit, but Mr. Godkin expressed no objection. He was a kind master and allowed his servants great latitude in their actions. He related the interesting sight he and Dick had witnessed by the pool.

It would be supposed that Jim and Jo would have felt the most interest in the incident in which they had just taken a slight part, but they seemed to think more about the "rogue" elephant than anything else. Both had encountered the animals and knew all about their ugly disposition, though, for that matter, the most tractable of them have moods when they are extremely dangerous.

"Glad he no see you," said Jim, speaking slowly, so as to make the best showing with his English.

"I don't know that it would have made any difference," replied Mr. Godkin, unable to share the apprehension of his servant. "I have killed a good many elephants, and would rather have a fight with half a dozen than encounter a tiger."

"Hora bad — he ugly — he kill," added Jim, who must have had some reason of his own for holding the animal in such dread.

"That may all be, but a man can be ugly without being dangerous, and if we meet the 'rogue' I shall not hesitate to let him have the contents of my gun."

How often, when inclined to boast, we are taught a lesson that should close our lips forever to that manner of speaking! It is hardly just, however, to charge my friend Carl Godkin with boasting, for I never knew a man freer from the objectionable habit than he; but he could not share the fear that his servant expressed of the vagabond elephant, which possibly he treated with too much contempt.

But it was less than an hour later, when the conversation was growing languid and Dick Brownell was beginning to think his bruises were getting better, that a fearful interruption of the conference took place.

The absent Jack reappeared, but in what manner?

Instead of coming across the plain, as he had walked away, he burst into sight from the path in the jungle over which Mr. Godkin and Dick had passed a short time before.

He was on a dead run and in the extremity of terror. Catching sight of his friends, he screeched: "The 'goondah'! 'goondah'! save me!"

Hardly had he dashed into view, when the identical "rogue" elephant that had been driven away by the herd swung after him. He was so close, too, that his trunk was extended and almost reached the fugitive.

Jack had lost his spear in some way, but, had he possessed it, it could have done him no service. Realizing that death was literally at his heels, the appalled native made a short turn in his wild flight and precipitated himself headlong among his friends. The latter were eager to do their utmost to save the poor fellow, but they were taken at fearful disadvantage. The panic, for an instant, seized all, and they flew apart, in the extremity of terror.

BY A HAIR'S BREADTH

Having started for Jack, the enraged monster could not be diverted, and, sad to say, in the flurry that prevailed for a few seconds, he was only too successful.

The fall of the native on his hands and knees gave the brute his opportunity. With incredible quickness, he coiled his trunk about the dusky waist, and, swinging the poor fellow aloft, hurled him with such awful violence against the trunk of the nearest tree, that it must have shattered nearly every bone in his body.

Then he flung the limp mass out upon the plain and gave his attention to the rest of the party. Dick Brownell was the first to recover from the panic. He comprehended that it must be a fight to the death, and that unless the beast was brought low, he would slay every one of them.

The other two natives had dashed into the jungle to save themselves; Mr. God-kin, in the first bound that he made, forgot to catch up his rifle, and he ran twenty paces before he awoke to his forgetfulness. Even then, he would not have ventured to return had he not seen that his young friend was standing his ground, and that the whole fury of the mad elephant was turned upon him.

It occurred to Mr. Godkin, too, at that moment, that no flight could save all the members of the party, since poor Jack had already been sacrificed, and their furious pursuer would be sure to overtake some of the party before they could run or climb beyond his reach.

Dick stood coolly in front of the elephant and not more than two rods distant. He knew the location of that small spot, just above the trunk, into which, if the tiniest bullet can be driven, the monster is doomed as certainly as if smitten by a bolt from heaven.

Aiming directly at that spot, Dick let the "goondah" take several steps before he pressed the trigger.

To his consternation, his piece missed fire.

CHAPTER LXXV.

ANOTHER "CLOSE CALL."

DURING his stay in India Dick Brownell was involved in many perilous adventures, in most of which he was saved by his own intrepidity and coolness; but among all his thrilling experiences, I have no knowledge of any in which he displayed such marvelous presence of mind as in his encounter with the "rogue" elephant in the district of Oude.

When barely two rods separated him from the furious brute that was charging down upon him, Dick brought his rifle to his shoulder, aimed quickly at the fatal spot in the front of the beast, and pulled trigger, only to have his weapon miss fire.

It was useless to turn and flee, for he could not go twenty steps before being seized, by the trunk that was already extended to grasp him. The cartridge which he had placed in the breech of his gun was defective, and it must be removed and another put in its place before there was any possibility of helping himself.

The lad proceeded to do this with wonderful self-possession. The worthless shell was withdrawn and another inserted. Then he hastily adjusted the breech, and attempted to bring the gun to his shoulder.

But it was too late.

The outstretched trunk caught him about the waist just as he turned to dart aside, and he was held immovable.

Meanwhile Mr. Godkin had not been idle. Catching up his gun, he leveled it at the furious brute, but unfortunately his position at that instant was such that he could not select a fatal spot into which to drive the bullet, and there was not a second to wait. As the best and only thing he could do, he aimed at the head and pulled trigger.

There was no miss, and the ball crashed its way into the huge skull, inflicting a wound which, perhaps, was mortal, though not immediately so, and Dick must be saved at once if at all.

The smoke had not yet cleared from the muzzle, and the enormous beast gave no evidence of being hurt, except by an irritated flirt of the head, when the horrified Mr. Godkin saw the lad lifted in air, his arms and legs flying in the desperate effort to release himself from the terrible grip of the "goondah."

"Where is your gun?" shouted his friend, running forward; "quick! and I'll give him another shot!"

The words were yet in his mouth when Dick pointed to the weapon at the feet of Mr. Godkin. Even in that awful moment the lad did not lose his wits.

When the man stooped to pick it up the elephant lowered his trunk and placed the youth on the ground in front of him.

Instead of dashing him to death, as he had done with the wretched native, he laid him down, with the intention of kneeling upon him, that being one of the animal's favorite methods of killing its victim.

You need not be told that no living creature can withstand the crush of so many tons. Many an elephant by such means has mashed a squirming tiger to pulp. Dick knew the purpose of the beast, and maintained his presence of mind. The moment the trunk relaxed its grip, and he found himself free, with the huge beam-like knee slowly descending upon him, he rolled slightly to one side, so that the knee just missed him, coming down upon the earth instead.

Then, with inimitable dexterity, he leaped to his feet, and, as the disappointed elephant groped for him again with his trunk, half turning his head to see what had become of him, the boy dashed between his hind legs.

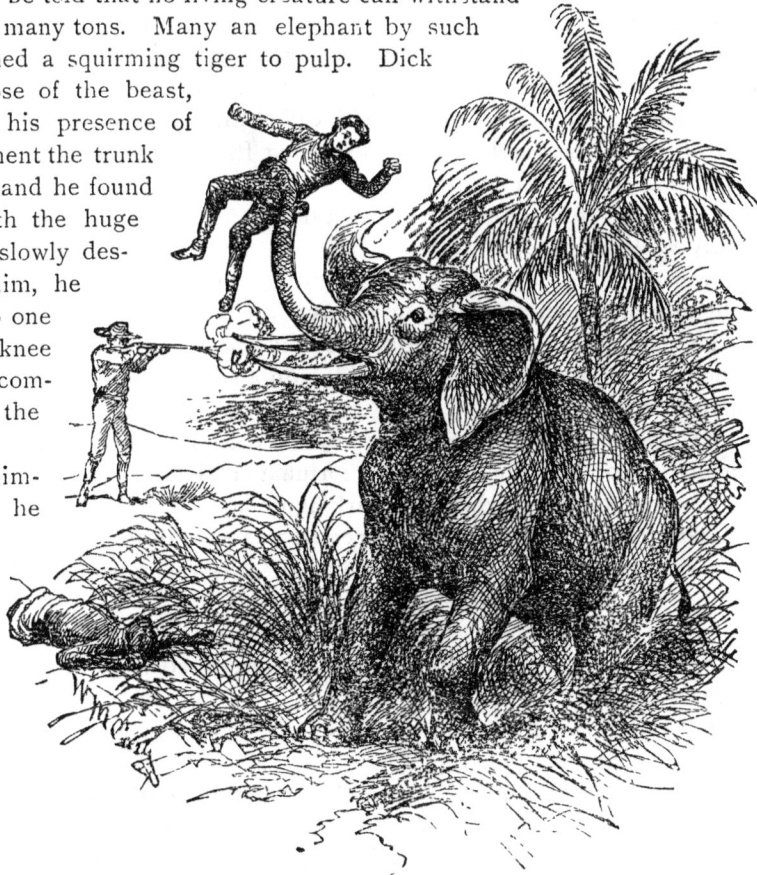

"But it was too late"

Even that amazing achievement would not have saved him but for the intervention of Mr. Godkin.

The latter, as he caught up the rifle of the youth, was placed exactly in front of the "rogue," and, as the beast inclined his head forward and downward to replace his victim in position for crushing, he exposed the most vulnerable joint in his "armor."

Not Gordon Cumming himself knew more accurately the location of the fatally weak spot in the most gigantic creature that walks the earth, and no fairer target could have been presented.

It was when the brute was turning his head to see what had become of the boy, that Mr. Godkin pulled the trigger. *That* did the business.

The ball tore its way through the thin sheathing of bone which at that point covers the brain, and extinguished life as effectually as if the animal had been struck by a cannon ball.

The great beast stood motionless a moment, with his head partly turned to one side, as though dumb. Then a shudder passed through the enormous mass, and down he went like a falling house, splintering one of his tusks at the base, and emitting his death cry, in one single whinnying snort which was his last.

"Hello, Dick! how do you feel?" called the happy man, running around to the rear of the carcass, and meeting his young friend, who had clambered to his feet, his face as white as a sheet.

"A little better than when I was a dozen feet in air," was the reply, "but I am pretty well shaken up."

And then the reaction from his frightful experience made him faint, and he was obliged to lie down on the ground to recover himself.

Mr. Godkin ran to him, but the boy did not swoon, though he was on the verge of doing so. He quickly rallied, and, with a smile at his own weakness, once more climbed to his feet.

"It was a narrow escape," he said, and then, recalling the fate of the native, he added: "Poor Jack! he was not so fortunate as I."

The two walked to where the dark figure lay and saw that not a semblance of life was left. The handling he had received was enough to kill a dozen men.

"We can only give him decent burial," was the remark of Mr. Godkin, as the two bent over the inanimate form.

"How grateful I feel," was the fervent remark of Dick, "that God was again so merciful to me. More than once has He interfered when there seemed no chance of my escape."

"Did not the elephant injure you at all?" asked his friend, feeling some misgiving at his continued paleness.

"I think not, though I felt when he first took me off my feet, as though he were crushing me to death, and you see I am all of a tremble."

"That will soon pass off, though I hope you won't have any more such shakings as that How did you manage to elude him when he fixed you in position for crushing?"

"I would have been a fool not to have taken advantage of the single chance he gave me. If he had held me still with his trunk until he got one of his knees on me, that would have been the end, but he released me for an instant, and it was enough."

"I held my breath," said Mr. Godkin, shuddering at the recollection, "for I thought it was all up with you."

"So did I, though, as they say, while there's life there's hope, and the slight roll to one side saved me. Before he could locate me again I was on my feet and darted between his legs. Then came your shot, and it was good-by, Mr. Goondah"

"I never saw a 'rogue' elephant that was so vicious; he must have had one of his worst spells, and it was intensified by the treatment he received from that herd which he wished to join when they were bathing in the pool."

"Well," added Dick with a sigh, "he has run his course; I wonder whether Jim and Jo will put in an appearance again."

It was not long, however, before the natives, finding all danger past, showed themselves once more. No one could blame them for their flight, for they would only have endangered themselves by staying, without being able to help their doomed companion.

Jed returning shortly afterward, it was decided by the party to make their way to the village, where the assistants had plenty of acquaintances, and secure their help in putting the body away in its last resting-place.

The sad duty was completed in a respectful and impressive manner, no one of the natives mourning the loss of Jack more sincerely than did Mr. Godkin and Dick Brownell.

Returning to the hut by the wayside, which had become a sort of headquarters for our friends, they remained over night. The director and his young friend sat for a long time discussing their future course.

Dick was in favor of an attempt to secure the big elephant which had aroused their admiration at the pool where he and his family were bathing.

Mr. Godkin thought there was a poor prospect of finding the herd again, the members having probably moved their quarters to some point miles distant. If such should prove the case, there was no means of following them, and the hunt would have to be abandoned. It seemed to Dick that such a prize as this enormous Asiatic elephant would be a fitting termination to their enterprise in India, and Mr. Godkin consented to make the effort with him.

An indispensable necessity of the hunt, as laid out, was an India rubber rope, which, fortunately, was in the

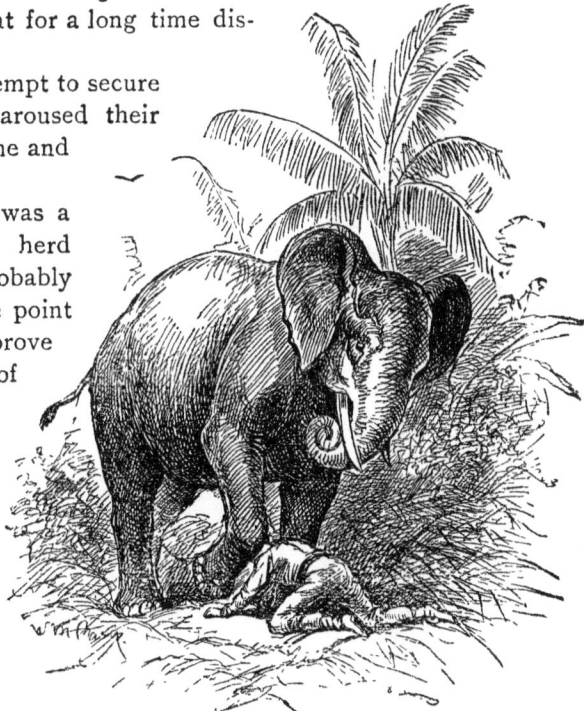

"HE LAID HIM DOWN"

possession of their host, who gladly placed it at their disposal. The plan of campaign, as it may be called, rendered unnecessary the company of the natives, and it was decided to leave them behind.

The next morning, therefore, bright and early, the two mounted their horses and rode off at a brisk pace, in the direction of the grassy plain and jungle which had been the scene of so many stirring adventures to both parties.

You will recall that it was there that our friends had caught their first sight of the herd, as they swung over the trail to the pool of water where they had had such a jolly time. The supposition was that the elephants would be likely to make another visit to the pool, and that vicinity, therefore, was the right one in which to look for them.

Accordingly the friends lost no time in riding directly to the spot, where most unexpected good fortune awaited them.

CHAPTER LXXVI.

DICK BROWNELL'S LAST EXPLOIT IN INDIA.

THE bulky body of the "rogue" elephant, which had killed the poor native, Jack, and had in turn been shot by Mr. Godkin, still lay where it had fallen near the edge of the jungle. The sight of the carcass was so striking that seven spectators were grouped around, surveying it with emotions of inquiring wonder.

Those seven spectators were the elephants that our friends had seen bathing in the pool. They formed a unique picture, indeed, their interest manifestly as deep as any person's could have been.

The ponies were sweeping along on a sharp gallop, when the bull elephant uttered that peculiar *"phut!"* by which he apprised the other members of his family, not only of danger, but located it by extending his trunk toward the horsemen.

"By George! there they are!" was the excited exclamation of Dick, forgetting his bruises in his delight at catching sight of the very herd for which they were searching. The brutes seemed to be frightened at the appearance of the hunters, and started tumultuously into the jungle, taking the same path they had previously followed when going to the pool to bathe.

"Now is our time," added Mr. Godkin, hardly less excited than his companion; "let's hurry after them."

The ponies required no attention, since they were sure to await the return of their masters. The latter took their rifles, and Dick carried the indispensable rubber rope, the two making straight for the spoor, over which they passed at a run.

As they neared the pool they slackened their pace, and when they caught sight of

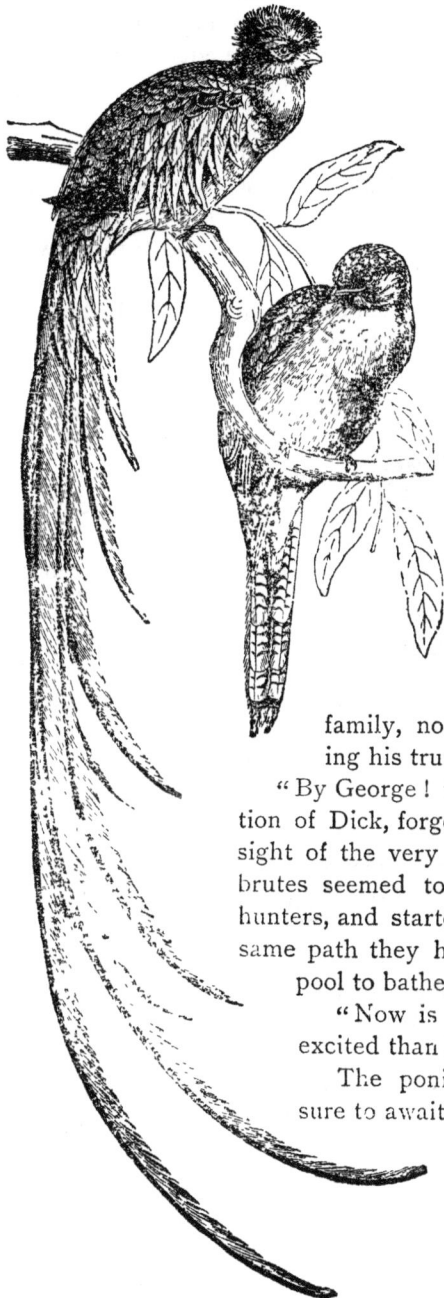

GOLDEN TROGONS.

423

one of the herd came to a halt for a brief consultation. While the members of the bull's family seemed to believe their short run had taken them beyond all danger, the head of the household was not satisfied. He stood on the edge of the water, looking doubtfully at the others, including the baby elephant, that were sporting in the same frolicsome fashion as before.

THE CRITICAL MOMENT.

"We couldn't have a better chance," whispered Dick, leaning his gun against a tree and stealing carefully forward.

The head of the gigantic bull was turned away, and, provided he maintained that posture, it was clear that the golden opportunity which the hunters coveted was at their command. It was necessary to approach the animal from the rear, and, above all things, it must be done without detection.

Dick Brownell's ardor was the only thing to be feared, and his companion cautioned him several times.

The bull, however, did not remain motionless. He showed his suspicious mood, while standing with his face toward the pool, by occasionally turning his head as if to guard against the very peril that now threatened him. Dick kept his eyes fixed on the fellow, while stealing toward him in a crouching position, and, whenever the head moved, the lad not only stopped, but sank down on his face, to wait until the huge front swung away again.

For one instant both he and Mr. Godkin thought it was all up. The bull turned partly round, and stared so long over the back trail that they were sure he had discovered them.

Mr. Godkin held his rifle ready, for he did not mean to be caught at a disadvantage if their prize turned upon them, as he was likely to do in case of discovery.

But the head went back, and once more the hunters resumed their stealthy advance.

Ten minutes later Dick had "crossed the Rubicon,"—that is, he had gone so far as to be unable to withdraw without discovery.

Mr. Godkin stopped his own advance a couple of rods away, for there was no call for him to go farther: everything now depended on the lad.

But the gentleman had one end of the rubber rope in his hand. Setting down his gun, he deftly fastened it around a tree, fully two feet in diameter. Then, picking up his weapon again, he stationed himself behind the trunk, ready to fire on an instant's warning.

He was resolved to take no more chances than possible. Much as he desired to capture the valuable beast, he was determined that the plucky boy's life should be placed in no greater peril than was unavoidable.

If the bull should detect the lad at his feet, he would be certain to turn upon him, and, to do so, would have to swing his head completely around.

The instant he brought his skull into fair range, Mr. Godkin intended to drive

THE SATIN BOWER BIRD.

the bullet between the eye and ear or into the same fatally weak spot that had admitted the ball into the skull of the " goondah."

The six elephants in the pool were so occupied with their own fun, that they paid no heed to the bull standing on shore, hesitating whether or not to march in and join them.

Had they bestowed a glance on the respected head of the family, they could not have failed to observe the crouching form at his hind feet and they would have been sure to utter a warning that would have apprised him of his danger.

The moment Dick reached the bull he was ready for business.

As you have doubtless suspected, his plan was to slip a noose of the rubber rope

over one of the feet, where any motion of the brute would draw it taut.   But. to do
this, it was necessary that the intended victim should first lift one of his feet —
which he was not likely to do of his own accord.

THE SOCIABLE WEAVER BIRD

The elephant hunters, however, have an easy way of overcoming *that* difficulty.
With the fingers of his right hand, Dick scratched the left hind leg of the bull.
Despite the thickness of the elephant's skin, it is extremely sensitive, and the action

THE PARADISE WHIDAH BIRD

caused a tickling sensation which led the monster to lift the foot in the effort to free it of the irritation.

This was the critical time.

The loop at the end of the rubber rope lay close to the foot on the ground, its circumference being like that of a barrel-hoop.

The instant the foot was lifted a few inches, Dick slipped the coil over it, gave a quick jerk which tightened the rope, and then, knowing he had done all that was possible, wheeled and ran in the direction of the waiting and intensely anxious Mr. Godkin. He had hardly started, when the elephant made for him with uplifted trunk.

You know that Dick was fleet of foot, and need I tell you that he never ran faster in all his life than when the wrathful bull elephant was trumpeting at his heels?

Mr. Godkin had gone back over the trail, so as to place himself beyond reach of the brute, provided the rubber rope did not break. There he stood, with his breech-loader at his shoulder, leveled at the front of the savage beast, charging down upon him like a runaway locomotive.

He knew the point the rope would permit him to reach; it was within a dozen feet of where he was standing. If he should come any farther, it would show that

THE LYRE BIRD

THE AFRICAN BARBET.

the rubber was unequal to the tension and had parted.

The instant that took place, the leveled rifle would be fired and the valuable prize would be snuffed out in a twinkling.

The bull gained rapidly on Dick, despite the lad's remarkable swiftness. Of necessity the thrilling race could last but a few seconds.

At the moment when it seemed the boy was doomed, and when Mr. Godkin's finger was pressing the trigger, the bull uttered a cry of terror and pain and fell on his side.

The rope was equal to the terrific strain, and, being extended to its utmost limit, jerked the monster backward with such violence that he was flung on his side, where he lay trumpeting with pain and fury, while his imprisoned leg was drawn straight out behind him by the elastic rope.

This occurrence instantly created the wildest panic among the other elephants. They rushed out of the pool, plunged around in a circle, tramped into the water again, then hurried toward the bull, then back once more, and finally made off into the jungle as if fleeing from a mortal peril. The faithless family had deserted its head and master.

By and by, the latter, still trumpeting and lashing furiously, struggled to his feet and stumbled and worked his way back toward the water, until the tension was so relaxed that he was able to stand without difficulty.

Catching sight of the two hunters in the path, his rage burst forth again, and he charged a second time, coming so near that Mr. Godkin

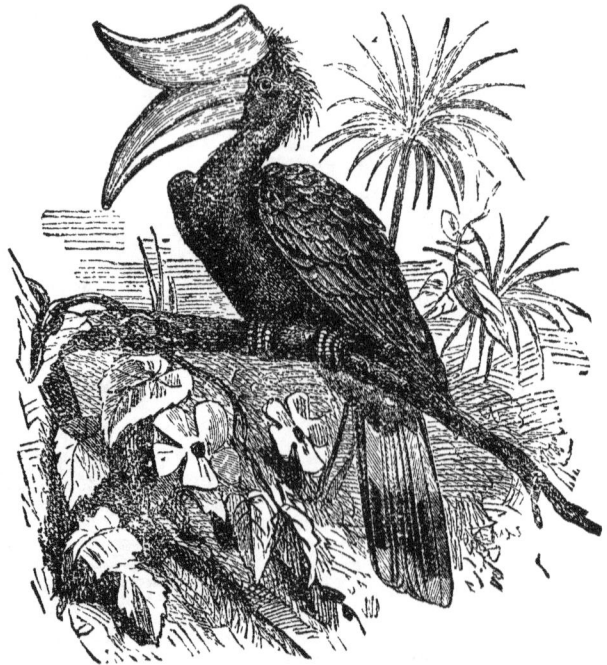

THE HORNBILL.

raised his gun as before. But precisely the same discomfiture was repeated. He went down broadside with such violence that it must have made every nerve in his body quiver, while the tremendous pull upon his leg caused him to scream with agony. Floundering to his feet, he stumbled backward until once more the strain was loosened and he became comparatively free from pain.

"He must be conquered," remarked Mr. Godkin, "and that will take consider-

THE TAILOR BIRD

able time, for he is a savage fellow. We will leave him where he is until to-morrow morning, when he will be ready to give up, unless I am much mistaken."

It was cruel to leave the beast alone, but really that was the best thing to do.

Accordingly, our friends turned their backs upon him and deliberately walked to the plain, remounted their ponies and rode to the wayside hut, in which they had spent the preceding night   They were by no means free from misgiving, for the continual tugging at the rope was likely to wear it out at last, while there was fear that the other elephants might come back and find some way of releasing the captive.

But they could only wait and hope.

THE OVEN BIRD

The next morning, Mr. Godkin and Dick, accompanied by Jim, Jo and Jed, made their way to the pool, wondering what they would find.

On their way thither, Jed, who had made a detour and discovered a female panthe
with several young ones, rushed back in great excitement with the news. But My
Godkin remarked that they were "loaded for elephant," and had no time to bothe

THE STORMY PETREL

with such small game as panthers. The animals were therefore left undisturbed,
and our friends pushed on. To their inexpressible delight, they found a completely
conquered elephant, of most unusual size.

PANTHER AND HER YOUNG.—Page 431.

THE LAUGHING
KINGFISHER.

Long before their arrival, the intelligent brute had reached a realizing sense of his helplessness. He knew he was at the mercy of those who had captured him, and the moment they came in sight he trumpeted his unconditional surrender. Evidently his family had reached the conclusion that a lord who was held immovably fast was of no further account to them, and they basely abandoned him to his fate.

Becoming fully satisfied of his conquest, the bull was released. No vicious stallion, under the manipulation of Rarey himself, was meeker than this monarch elephant, who allowed the three natives to clamber upon his back, and who obediently moved through the jungle and across the plain to the hut by the wayside, Mr. Godkin and Dick riding their ponies by his side.

Halting at the hut only long enough to pay the host for his kindness and to bid him good-by, the company took up their march to Lucknow, which was reached without incident worth mentioning. There they found their agent had bestowed most excellent care on the precious curiosities sent to him.

It was an easy matter to arrange for their shipment down the Ganges to Calcutta, which was reached in the course of the following week. They were reshipped thence on an English vessel to London, from which point they arrived at New York in good condition.

Dick Brownell and Mr. Godkin arrived on the same vessel that brought the curiosities, in whose capture I trust you have felt some interest, and in the telling of which I hope you have received not only entertainment but instruction.

You will understand that the work of my friends in Africa and India was mainly the capture of wild animals, but my record of their doings would not be satisfactory without a reference to some of the interesting birds which they brought home. It would not have been worth

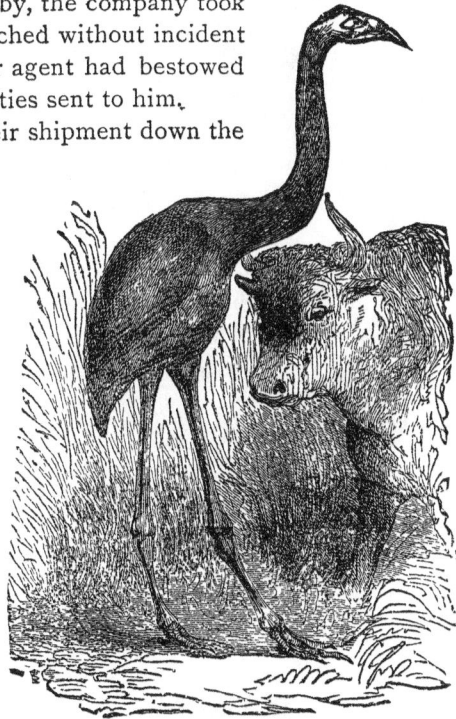

THE DINORNIS.

28

their while to entrap these feathered beauties, and in many cases it would have been impossible, since a number came from parts of the world distant from those visited by them. Such were readily obtained from parties who make a business

THE BRUSH TURKEY OF AUSTRALIA.

of rearing and selling them to those who are willing to pay the prices charged. One of the most interesting specimens is the great bird of paradise, the largest of its species known, being about eighteen inches from the beak to the tip of the

THE APTERYX.

tail, which, with the body and wings, is of a rich coffee-brown, deepening on the breast to a blackish violet or purple brown. The top of the head and neck is of a delicate straw-yellow, the feathers short and close set, resembling plush and velvet; the lower part of the throat to the eye is an emerald green, the feathers scaly, with a metallic gloss. Velvety plumes of deeper green extend across the forehead and chin to the eye, which is a clear yellow.

Nature seems to have run riot in coloring this wonderful bird. The beak is a pale lead-blue, and the feet a pale pink. The two middle feathers of the tail are without webs, except a tiny one at the base and tip, forming wire-like cirri, spreading out in a splendid double curve, almost three feet long. From each side of the body below the wings projects a dense tuft of dainty plumes, two feet long, of a dazzling, glossy golden-orange color, changing, toward the tips, to a pale brown. The bird can elevate and spread this tuft at pleasure, so as to hide its body.

Remember that I am describing the male bird, the female, in accordance with the rule, being plain and not specially attractive. The paradise birds are confined to New Guinea, the Papuan Islands and portions of Australia.

The satin bower bird is a native of Eastern Australia. The interesting fact connected with them is their practice of building bowers, evidently with no purpose except that of affording places of frolic

THE GREAT BIRD OF PARADISE.

THE PELICAN

and sport. At least no other object has yet been discovered. The birds decorate the bowers around the entrance with the most brilliantly-colored objects they can gather.

The sociable weaver bird's chief claim to distinction rests upon the size of its dwelling-house, which is generally placed in large, lofty trees. The structure being completed, as shown in the illustration, each pair builds its nest underneath the huge umbrella-like root which is large enough to permit two or three-hundred nests. The bird is native in South Africa.

The paradise whidah bird belongs to Western Africa, from Senegal to Angola. It seems never to be at res, but is continually flitting among the branches, stopping now and then for a second or two, evidently to admire itself.

Look at the lyre bird and notice the appropriateness of its name. It is a native of Australia, where the beautiful curved tail feathers can be bought in pairs in the shops of Sydney. They are of a pearly color beneath, with several crescent-shaped spaces of a rich rufous or black color.

The African barbets are plump, gaudy-colored birds, chiefly met with in Western Africa and tropical America.

A very interesting bird is the golden trogon, rivaling the bird of paradise in the richness of its plumage. The golden trogon has the greater portion of its plumage apparently composed of burnished gold.

The tailor bird is remarkable for its curious nest. This bird literally sews together two leaves, sometimes the edges of one large leaf, at the extremity of a slender twig, and, with soft, cottony down, constructs a habitation as comfortable as it is ingenious. The bill of the bird serves as a needle, and vegetable fibers are used as thread. The nest of the tailor bird is always hung at the extremity of the

THE SCISSORS BILL.

THE EAGLE OWL

twigs in order to keep it, as far as possible, out of the way of monkeys, snakes and other enemies.

A very picturesque bird is the eagle owl, which dwells among the deep recesses of vast forests in Norway, Sweden and Russia, and sometimes in the clefts of rocks or the desolate ruins of ancient towers. It is found also at the Cape of Good Hope.

The oven bird is so called because it constructs its earthen nest in the form of an oven, and this habitation, although of considerable size, is often completed by a pair of these birds in about two days, both male and female engaging in the task. The nest is made of earth and is six inches and a half in diameter, the walls being one inch thick, and the interior is divided into two chambers by a partition beginning at the entrance and carried circularly backward.

THE EARED GREBE.

I cannot refrain in this place from telling you something about the stormy petrels, familiarly known as Mother Cary's chickens, which are seen in every part of the ocean skimming over the surface of a heavy-rolling sea. They flock under the wake of ships before a storm, and superstitious sailors look upon them as prophets of evil. "But," says an eminent naturalist, "as well might they curse the midnight light-house that, star-like, guides them on their watery way, or the buoy that warns them of the sunken rocks below, as this harmless wanderer, whose

THE ADJUTANT BIRD.

manner informs them of the approach of the storm, and enables them to prepare for it." The illustration on page 431 represents the Fulmar petrel, which is especially abundant in the Arctic seas.

The laughing king fisher of Australia is an exquisitely beautiful bird, and one of the largest species. It is as fond of reptiles as of fish.

What a queer-looking bird is the hornbill! The male is addicted to the extraordinary practice of plastering up the female with her egg and feeding her during the whole period of incubation, or till the young one is fledged.

There is reason to believe that the dinornis is found in New Zealand. It towers aloft like a giraffe, but is very rare, and my friends were unable to obtain a specimen.

The brush turkey, of Australia, New Guinea and the chain of islands in the South Pacific Ocean, is a remarkable bird. In the months of August and September, when there is scarcely any rain, they come down in pairs from the interior, and scratch holes three or four feet deep, just above high-water mark, where the female deposits her single egg. Covering this with a foot of sand, she goes back to the forest. Ten or twelve days later she makes another visit and lays a second egg, continuing until six or eight are deposited. The male bird gives his help in digging the hole and covering the egg, the two birds closely resembling each other in appearance. Several females lay in the same hole. The natives come many miles to plunder the nests, the eggs when fresh being very delicious, and they are of large size. The parent bird gives no further attention to them after covering them up in the sand. The young, on breaking the shell, take to the woods at once, and are able to fly a few hours after hatching.

The scissors-bill is noted for its long and compressed beak, the under mandible being much larger than the upper, and closing into it like a knife-blade into the handle. Skimming swiftly over the water, and close to the surface, its sharp bill cuts the water, gathering up crustaceans, fish and mollusks, on which it feeds. Running along the beach, it skillfully inserts its beak in the bivalves, and, striking the shells against the stones, breaks them and devours the contents.

I wish I could procure a specimen of the apteryx of New Zealand, called "kiwi" by the natives, who are fond of its flesh. It keeps out of sight in the deep recesses of the forest until night, when the birds come forth in couples to search for food, which is readily seen in the darkness.

The natives capture it by imitating its whistling cry. They say the bird buries its eggs in the sand, and hatches them by sitting beneath, instead of over them. This is doubtful, since those at the London Zoological Garden hatch them in the usual fashion. It lays one egg at a time and breeds twice a year.

The pelican is found in North Africa, and in the south and east of Europe. I believe it is the largest of the swimming birds, and you have noticed their immense pouches, some of which can be dilated enough to hold two gallons of water.

The eared grebe is a rare British bird. It is a fine swimmer, very active in the water, and is able to stay a long time under the surface, where it swims swiftly with the aid of its wings and feet.

The adjutant bird belongs to India, and attains a height of six feet, its extended wings measuring nearly three times as much, from tip to tip. Its head and neck

THE COMMON OCTOPUS 441

are almost bare, a sausage-like pouch hanging from the under part of its neck, while its bill is enormous. It has been known less than twenty-five years to naturalists. The upper part of its thighs furnishes plumes more beautiful and valuable than those of the ostrich, and its voracity is almost as great.

I must tell you something here about the octopus, which may be called the gorilla of the ocean. It grows to an immense size along some coasts, and is justly dreaded by the most experienced fishermen.

Its usual resting-place is under a huge stone, or in the broad cleft of a rock, where it can squeeze itself as flat as a sandal. When moving about it uses its eight arms as paddles, working them alternately, while the central disc may be regarded as a boat. You would think this an awkward means of locomotion, but the octopus travels easily and swiftly over the sandy bottoms, climbs the slippery ledges, or, attaching its numerous suckers to the face of rocks, moves at will in any direction.

Besides the amazing strength of the creature, and the fact that lopping off several of its huge arms or feelers does not affect its aggressiveness, it has the power of numbing its victim. The deep contains many hideous creatures, but I can conceive of none more dreadful than the octopus.

And now we must turn our attention to Jack Harvey and Bob Marshall's adventures in the land of the gorilla.

CHAPTER LXXVII.

IN THE LAND OF THE GORILLA.

JACK HARVEY and Bob Marshall tarried at Port Natal several days after the departure of Mr. Godkin and Dick Brownell for India. Finally they secured passage to Cape Town. where, after another tedious wait, they shipped in a Portuguese vessel, bound for the Gold Coast, the captain of which, for a generous consideration, agreed to run into the Gaboon and land his four passengers; for our friends had picked up a couple of hunters bound on the same errand as themselves.

I should have told you that Jack and Bob, having become satisfied that their ponies would be valueless in the gorilla country, left them in safe hands at Cape Town. The Texan would not part with Apache at any price, and Bob had formed so strong an attachment for his own steed that he was glad of the prospect of seeing him again.

If the result of their visit to Equatorial Africa should render it unnecessary to return to the Cape of Good Hope, it would be a simple matter to send for the horses and have them shipped home.

The two acquaintances formed on the ship were Englishmen just from India. where they had spent a couple of months in hunting, and proposed to wind up their sport under the Equator.

The opening experience of the party in the Gaboon country was enough to dampen the ardor of the most enthusiastic of sportsmen.

The Gaboon was found to resemble an arm of the sea, with its strong salt tides and sluggish current. On the right bank was the French fort, somewhat beyond a village of English factories, and behind these, on a hill clothed in bright green vegetation, was the American mission, including church, school and houses.

On the left bank rose the town of King William, sometimes called Roi Denis. It is built of bamboo and is the metropolis of Gaboon. Here the four gorilla-hunters landed to arrange their hunt in the adjoining jungles for that extraordinary creature which has never yet been seen on this side of the Atlantic.

When the party came ashore, three of them were so ill that they were compelled to take to their beds at once. The section of the Dark Continent visited by them is one of the most pestilential regions of the globe. The very ground exhales disease, and sea captains have told me that the sickening odor of the malarious swamps can be noticed while scores of miles from land.

Jack Harvey was the only one that was entirely well. The Texan seemed to be climate-proof, though his naturally vigorous constitution, his active life and his freedom from bad habits doubtless had much to do with his immunity, and besides he had taken the precaution to dose himself and his companions with a preparation of quinine before leaving ship.

The American missionary at King William was the good Samaritan to those who needed his kind offices. He insisted on the folks taking up their quarters at his house, and he and his wife could not have been kinder to their own children than they were to the comparative strangers.

But the utmost they could do was not enough to save the Englishmen. Both succumbed, after having braved all other forms of danger, and were buried in that far-off land, thousands of miles from the dear ones at home, victims to the deadly climate that has claimed its hundreds of thousands.

For days and nights Bob Marshall hovered on the verge of death; but, thanks to Providence and good nursing, he pulled through, and, to the delight of Jack, finally became his old, lively, high-spirited self again.

Supposing his ardor had departed, the Texan offered to send him home and prosecute the task without him. But, as you may suppose, the young man would not hear of such a thing.

"I came here to hunt gorillas," was his characteristic reply, "and I'll do it or die."

"I don't think you'll die after what you've stood. You ain't a tenderfoot any longer."

"All I ask is that you will get me a chance."

The friends made their preparations as thorough as possible, and within the following week attended one of those singular ceremonies known in that country as a gorilla dance.

It was at a village on the borders of the immense jungle into which they intended to plunge in quest of the marvelous animal for which I stand ready to-day to pay almost any sum ot money.

The two natives whom Jack engaged to accompany him were known respectively as Gyp and Hargo. They were in middle life, dusky, wrinkled, homely, half naked, but lithe and muscular. Gyp, the elder, bore a number of frightful scars on his thigh and shoulder, and seemed quite proud to tell his employers that they were gained in his encounters with *njinas*, as the gorillas are often called.

Gyp and Hargo had heard the cry of one of the animals, and were confident of being able to kill him on the morrow, so confident, indeed, that they and their friends arranged to anticipate the exploit by a gorilla dance.

HEAD OF THE GORILLA.

It was in the structure assigned to the slaves of a large plantation that the dance took place. Two men played a rude drum and a one-stringed harp, while Gyp exhibited the grotesque movements of the gorilla.

The imitation of the action of the animal when alarmed, when attacking its prey, when climbing a tree, or listening, running, leaping or eating, was so perfect, that it startled the spectators, who learned a great deal of the habits and peculiarities of the terrible creature which they expected soon to meet in its native wilds.

And now before telling you about the hunt, let me give you some information concerning this interesting inhabitant of the Dark Continent.

The *troglodytes gorilla* is the largest of apes, a full-grown male sometimes reaching the height of six feet. It is found in the same geographical area as the chimpanzee, but within narrower limits, on or near the Equator. Its skin is jet black, but this is shown only on the face, chest and the palms of the paws, which are devoid of the iron-gray hair that covers the rest of the body.

The hair is two inches long, growing downward on the main arm and upward on the fore-arm. The males always have their heads covered with short and reddish-brown hair, the females not gaining this ornamental crown-piece until fully grown.

The hide is thick and tough, except under the arms and near the hips. Both sexes have the breast bare, and some of the older ones have the hair worn off along the spine from frequent sitting on the ground with their backs against the tree trunks.

The eyes are deeply sunken and restless, overhung by a bony ridge which gives the face a most forbidding appearance and a perpetual scowl. The nose is more prominent than in the chimpanzee or orang-outan. The mouth is enormous, the lips large and of uniform thickness, and the chin short and receding. The canine teeth in the male resemble tusks, and the ears, which are shaped like our own, are much smaller than in the chimpanzee.

The upper limbs seem disproportionately large, but this is due to the shortness of the lower ones, which have no calves and increase in size from the knee to the ankle.

Strangely enough, the main arm of the gorilla is longer than the fore-arm, and the thumb extends beyond the first joint of the forefinger, while in the chimpanzee and ape it does not reach that joint.

The hand is broad, thick, and with a long palm, the fingers short, tapering quickly at the ends to the nails, which are about the size of our own. The back of the hand is hairy to the finger divisions, the palm bare and callous, and the thumb hardly as thick as the forefinger.

The chimpanzee and other apes make less use of the sole of the foot in walking than the gorilla, and the great toe of the gorilla is stronger than in those animals, standing out like a large thumb from the rest of the foot.

The gorilla is a strict vegetarian. He has a shuffling gait, never upright like ours, but bent forward. His arms being longer than those of the chimpanzee, he does not stoop as much in walking, but, like that creature, advances by pushing his arms forward, resting the hands on the ground and then giving the body a motion which is partly a jump and partly a swing. In doing this he does not bend his fingers, but uses the hand as a fulcrum.

If you should come upon the trail of a gorilla running on all fours, you would not see any trace of the marks of the hind feet. Only the ball of the foot and the great toe appear to touch, and the fingers of the fore-arm are lightly marked on the earth.

The power of the gorilla is prodigious. Those tremendous jaws can crush an ordinary gun-barrel, and the arms will bend the weapon as though it were putty. When enraged, the thin, black lips shrink so that all his teeth are visible, gleaming unnaturally white in the vast mouth, which is as red as blood.

The shoulders are broad, and the hideous head is placed upon them without the intervention of a neck. The abdomen is very large and rounding at the sides. You may gain some idea of the capacity of the immense hand when told that the middle finger has been found in some gorillas to be more than six inches in circumference at the first joint.

Strange stories were told by the early navigators of a fearful object seen on the west coast of Africa, whose description leaves little doubt that he was the animal since known as the gorilla. In 1847, Rev. J. L. Wilson, senior missionary of the American Board of Foreign Missions to West Africa, obtained from some of the natives on Gaboon River a number of skulls of a monkey-like creature, noted for its size and ferocity. These were turned over to Dr. Thomas S. Savage, a member of the Boston Society of Natural History, and were minutely described by Dr. Wyman, Professor of Anatomy in Harvard University.

When the male is first seen he utters a frightful yell that resounds through the forest something like "*kh-ah! kh-ah!*" His huge jaws are wide open, his under lip hangs over his chin, and his hairy ridge and scalp are contracted upon the brow, giving his front an appearance of indescribable ferocity.

The gorillas generally live in bands, the females outnumbering the males. Their dwellings hardly merit the name, consisting of a few sticks and leafy branches, supported by the limbs of trees. The natives say the gorilla is a fool, for, though he lives where the annual rain-fall is great, he doesn't know enough to place a roof on his house.

There is a bird in Equatorial Africa which, if it chose, could give him many points on how to construct a comfortable home; for, after making a large nest with a tight roof, it daubs it with mud on the inside, and, unfolding its wings, whirls round and round until every crevice is filled and the inside is as smoothly plastered as your own house.

CHAPTER LXXVIII.

ON THE EDGE OF THE POOL.

IN the gloomiest depths of the pestilential jungles of Equatorial Africa, where eternal twilight

DISCOURAGED.

reigns, and the intolerable rays of the flaming sun can never penetrate, the gorilla-hunters halted one forenoon, and, sitting down on a fallen tree, almost hidden from sight by suffocating vines. discussed the business that had brought them thither, far beyond all human habitations. The ardor with which the sportsmen had entered upon the task was somewhat dampened by hope deferred, for this was the second day of the hunt, and, in the face of the promises of Gyp and Hargo, they had not yet caught sight of the first gorilla.

This was the more trying since they had approached nigh enough several times to hear the animals, and to detect unmistakable signs of their presence very near them. They saw the spoor of a large male, and came upon a spot which, it may be said, was still warm from the recent visit of a female and her young, that had been engaged in eating a species of berry growing close to the ground and of which the creature is extremely fond.

The knowledge that they were close to the animals, I think, must have made the hunters so eager to get a shot that they failed to exercise the precaution indispensable in approaching them. The gorilla is wonderfully alert, and many a skillful hunter has been baffled again and again until compelled to give up in despair.

The natives, being experienced in hunting the animals, were armed the same as Jack and Bob. That is to say, they were provided with guns, though of the old-fashioned pattern, being single-barreled muzzle-loaders, carrying large balls and capable of doing effective execution when rightly handled. The Texan would have been glad to furnish them with repeating rifles, but that was impossible, and the blacks were contented with their own fire-arms, in which their faith was as unbounded as that of the whites in their magazine weapons.

Gyp and Hargo had been associated with Europeans long enough to speak the English language tolerably well, though they were little inclined to conversation. They sat on the log, silent and glum, while Bob and Jack did about all the talking.

The natives appeared to feel the disappointment as much as their employers, and, though they may have seen that the failure was due to the ardor of the gentlemen, they were too thoughtful to say so. Probably they were convinced that Jack and Bob suspected it themselves and would remedy the fault.

The Texan was armed as when careering over the pampas of Bechuana Land, on the back of his fleet-footed Apache, carrying not only his Winchester, two revolvers and a knife, but his valued lasso as well. It was slung over his left shoulder, and, accustomed as he was to riding his mustang, he found the task of tramping through the dense jungle laborious, but he clung to the rawhide, confident that he would find use for it before his return.

Gyp was provided with a strong net, extremely useful in flinging over the heads of young animals when they proved vigorous enough to use their teeth and claws. He declared that it had been employed in capturing snakes and gorillas, though the Texan believed the fellow was addicted to drawing the long bow in the story line.

Through the interstices of the dense vegetation by which they were enveloped, could be seen the shimmer of water. It was a large, stagnant pool, covering several acres, and while more than one tiny stream wound its way into it, it was with-

29

out any outlet, so far as the hunters could discover.   It may have been that in such a smothering climate the evaporation prevented all overflow, and rendered any outlet unnecessary.   It was on the banks of this pool that the party had seen proof of the recent presence of gorillas.   The hunters made its entire circuit, climbing over rotting trees that lay half imbedded in the mud and water, with rank vegetation growing around them, slimy serpents hardly caring enough for the intruders to crawl out of their path, and with here and there some gaunt, long-legged bird of brilliant plumage, standing in the edge of the lake, lazily waiting for its victim to come nigh enough to be gobbled into its capacious maw, which never seemed to be filled.

"I don't understand," said Bob Marshall, "how it is that such a formidable animal as the gorilla, and one that is said to be afraid of no living creature, shows such timidity about meeting us."

"I don't know of any game that will not avoid man," replied Jack, "but we know some of them will fight like all creation when they meet us face to face."

"Mr. Godkin said that the tiger of India will often hunt those who are not hunting him," said Bob, "but then we don't find tigers in Africa."

"So will the Apache," added the Texan with a grim smile, "but, as a rule, the biggest kind of game prefers to give us a wide berth."

"There's one thing certain ; we are in the heart of the gorilla country, and there is no reason why we shouldn't run against plenty of them."

"I've been thinking," added Jack, after smoking his pipe a minute or two in silence, "whether it wouldn't be a good plan to do as we sometimes did down in South Africa."

"How is that ? "

"Separate ; you take one course, I another, while Gyp and Hargo keep together."

"I was on the point of proposing it when we first sat down on the log," said Bob, "but I was afraid you would think it too dangerous."

"Dangerous for what ?   The game ? "

"No ; for us."

"I suppose there would be a little more risk, but then, you ain't afraid to try it, are you ? "

"Nothing will suit me better."

"Then it shall be done.   Howsumever, the only thing that I fear is that we may get lost from each other.   This is a confounded country, without any roads, paths, openings, houses or anything that can serve as landmarks."

"We had enough experience in South Africa to know how to avoid such a blunder.   Besides, we can signal to each other, either by firing our guns or whistling."

Bob's urgency removed whatever misgivings the Texan may have had in mind, and it was agreed that, after a brief rest, the proposal should be adopted.   It was explained to Gyp, who exercised some kind of authority over Hargo, and he nodded his head, though it was impossible to tell from his manner whether he favored the plan or not.

CROCODILE AND ITS YOUNG.

"The understanding had better be," added Jack, "that whenever any one of us hears a gun go off, he is to make all haste to that point; not because help may be needed to escape danger, but to gather in the beast, whatever it may be."

"That is, if I run against a big male gorilla and shoot him, you will know that you and the natives are wanted at once."

"Of course; we can't capture one of those six-foot chaps any more than we could capture an African buffalo or an East India tiger; but, wherever we may find the male, the female is pretty apt to be in the neighborhood, and, if she has a young one with her, the job of managing the two will be too big for any one of us."

"You are talking sense; let us be sure that Gyp and Hargo catch on."

It was easy to make them comprehend, and, since the two tired ones were pretty well rested by this time, Bob suggested that the hunt be resumed.

But, at the moment he moved to rise from the fallen tree, Gyp held up his hand and uttered a warning "Sh!" which caused the others to look silently at him and listen.

Without speaking, the native pointed with his finger to the left of the pool, which, you will remember, was partly in view of the hunters.

It was at this juncture that all caught a faint rustling of the undergrowth, such as might have been made by the stealthy passage of a bird among the vegetation. Faint as it was, the hunters were able to locate it without the guidance of the dusky finger, which continued for several seconds to point at the spot.

Suddenly every heart stood still, for they saw dimly, through the enveloping bushes, vines and leaves, a gigantic figure moving toward the pool. Its back was bent forward and its short legs doubled under the immense hairy body, while the long, dusky arms reached to the ground, the hands being partly used to help in locomotion.

"It's a gorilla, sure enough!" whispered Bob, turning pale with excitement.

Jack raised his hand warningly, but did not speak.

As the six-foot terror approached the pool, he came into plainer view and was so nigh that the least noise on the part of any one of the party would have alarmed him. Bob made a motion as if to raise his rifle and looked inquiringly at Jack. The Texan shook his head: the time had not arrived for shooting. He wished to wait and see whether the mother and perhaps her offspring did not show themselves.

At the moment the gorilla reached the edge of the water, the hunters became aware of a fact unknown till then.

On the edge of the pool lay an enormous crocodile, with his long, corrugated head and snout resting on the bank and his body in the stagnant water. His size was revealed by several protuberances of his spine, showing here and there above the surface, while, seemingly twenty feet beyond, the water was agitated by an occasional motion of his tail.

It was evident that the two had seen each other while some distance separated them. Indeed, it looked as if the gorilla had come forth with the purpose of raising a rumpus with the saurian.

The sportsmen were so anxious to witness this impending battle, that they rose to their feet, and silently took positions behind the nearest trees, from which they peeped forth with the stealth of so many Indians.

Had not the gorilla been exclusively interested in the crocodile, it is more than likely he would have detected the hunters near him, but he looked neither to the right nor left, keeping his small black eyes fixed on the reptile, which was one of the largest of its species.

It was clear that neither of the combatants, so different in every respect, felt the slighest fear of the other, though their mutual respect led each to maneuver with great caution.

The gorilla stopped about a rod distant and looked at the crocodile as if to ask him his intentions. The latter did not move, except to shift his tail slightly.

This clearly was done with a view of holding it in readiness to deliver one of those blows which are tremendous enough to smash the ribs of an elephant, though the jaws of the reptile are often the most fearful weapons that can be employed in battle.

CHAPTER LXXIX.

A STRANGE BATTLE.

THE crocodile and gorilla are two of the most ferocious members of the animal kingdom. Both stand low on the plane of intelligence, but each possesses a certain cunning which enables him to use his prodigious strength to the best possible advantage. Had they been endowed with the brains of the elephant, they could not have made a better fight than they did.

Bending slightly forward, the gorilla indulged in some odd grimacing motions, much like those of the ordinary monkey, and which were meant to tantalize the crocodile into coming forth and assailing him.

But the huge reptile knew better than to do that, though it is hard to see wherein it would have added to its danger. He preferred the water and mud, where he could use his peculiar means of fighting better than on land.

The gorilla kept up his taunts for a minute or two, and then walked lightly toward the crocodile, as if he intended to attack in front. The reptile did not stir, but you may be sure he kept his gaze on his enemy.

If the animal opened the battle in the style he seemed to intend, the jaws of the defender would bring it to a quick conclusion.

Uttering his cry in a half-suppressed voice, the gorilla made a leap forward, as if to alight on the snout of the other. Instantly those jaws opened like a vast steel trap, and, had the gorilla made the bound that he really appeared to have started upon, he would have been caught in a vise from which ten times his power would not have extricated him.

But, with inimitable dexterity, the animal turned himself to one side and leaped backward, eluding the mouth, which snapped shut with a sound that startled the spectators.

Hardly had the gorilla jumped when the crocodile doubled himself sideways, and his great tail made a terrific sweep, like that of a scythe in the hands of a giant. It whizzed over the ground where the gorilla was standing, but did not hit him.

He bounded into the air with a nimbleness that could not have been surpassed, and the next moment did a thing so incredible that the hunters could hardly believe their eyes.

The crocodile knew he was going to miss before his furious blow was delivered, and, with astonishing agility, he wheeled with open jaws to seize the exasperating enemy ; but the same dexterity that had saved the latter an instant before did not fail him now. He darted like a flash to the left, then sprang directly upon the back of the saurian, and, bending over, grasped his forelegs.

One was seized in either hand,
and, summoning his Samson-like
strength, he leaned backward and
jerked with might and main.

The spectators heard the bones
crack, and they knew that both the
crocodile's legs were broken like a
couple of pipe-stems.

The reptile struggled fiercely,
lashing his tail, contorting his body
and snapping his jaws in a way that
seemed impossible in one so griev-
ously wounded. But his struggles

were those of blind fury, and the useless dangling forelimbs interfered fatally with anything like successful fighting.

"By gracious! he's got him!" exclaimed Bob Marshall, stepping from behind the tree in his excitement.

"What do you mean?" asked Jack, hardly less agitated.

"I mean the crocodile has got the gorilla."

"How do you make that out?"

HEAD OF THE CHIMPANZEE

"Didn't you see him fall on the other side of him? The crocodile has him under his body and is hammering the life out of him?"

"No—no—no—not so," said Gyp, as he and Hargo ran forward with the others, for he had seen what escaped their eyes.

Dashing as close to the floundering reptile as was safe, Bob and Jack looked for the bruised gorilla weakly struggling under the threshing body; but he was not visible.

"He must have him down in the mud and water out of sight," remarked the puzzled lad.

At that instant came the frightful "*kh—ah! kh—ah!*" from the other side of

CHIMPANZEES

the pool, and the amazed sportsmen looked up in time to catch sight of the gorilla as he vanished in the jungle.

Our friends stared at each other in astonishment.

"Well, I'll be hanged!" muttered the Texan, who was the first to recover his voice.

"He has given us the slip again," was the disappointed response of Bob; "how did he do it?"

Gyp was the only one that could explain it.

No doubt that at the moment the gorilla broke the legs of the crocodile, he discovered the presence of the hunters in the wood near him. But for that, he would have kept up the fight with his antagonist, but, with a cunning natural to the creature, he flung himself on the farther side of the saurian, and, using his shield as a screen, darted behind the nearest bushes on the edge of the pool. Along the water he skurried swiftly, his body being invisible until he rose erect on the farther side, emitted his resounding cry and disappeared.

Gyp suspected the meaning of the creature's sudden leap behind the body of the reptile, but it was executed with such extraordinary deftness that it could not be frustrated.

Out of mercy for the wounded reptile, Jack Harvey brought his gun to his shoulder and sent a bullet into one of the eyes, following it the next instant with another just back of the foreleg. Five minutes later the crocodile was dead.

It was an exasperating disappointment to the hunters, when they had had the immense gorilla at their mercy, but they were too philosophical to waste any time in useless laments.

"I don't believe we shall ever see him again; he has had a good sight of us, and will be sure to keep his family out of the way," said Jack.

"What good, then, would it have done to shoot him?"

"It might have brought the mother from the wood with her young, and it would have been easy enough to dispose of *her* and capture her offspring, if it wasn't too big."

"There's another fact against us," said Bob; "the gorilla is such a big eater that he cannot subsist long in one place, and this fellow would have been likely to change his quarters, even if he hadn't seen us."

"Where is Gyp?" suddenly asked Jack, looking around.

"He go—soon be back—he look," replied Hargo, with a number of grimaces and gestures.

A minute later the well-known whistle of the African was heard from the other side of the pool and near the spot where the gorilla was last seen. As his friends looked, Gyp appeared and beckoned them to approach.

"I wonder what's up now," said Bob, as the three hurriedly tramped through the jungle to where their servant was awaiting them.

"Have you found him?" eagerly asked the youth, in an undertone, the instant they joined the other.

Gyp motioned them to follow him silently, adding, in a whisper:

"Don't talk—walk slow—keep eyes open."

It seemed incredible that Gyp by any possible means should have gained sight of the gorilla or any member of his family, for there could be no question that the animal had discovered the hunters, and it was contrary to his nature to remain in the vicinity or allow any of his relatives to do so.

It was not the gorilla that Gyp had detected, but a creature almost as interesting.

The genus *troglodytes* contains only two species — that upon which our friends had just looked, and the chimpanzee, which is the *troglodytes niger*. The adult male of the latter is about five feet in height, and is much less powerful than the gorilla, with which it lives at peace in the jungle.

HEAD OF THE GORILLA, FRONT VIEW.

The skin is of a yellowish white tint, scantily covered with long black hair in front and more behind. The hair on the head is rather thin, being thickest on the forehead, with a few stiff hairs on the eyebrows and with a scanty eyelash. The face is naked and the skin whitish and wrinkled.

The ears are exactly like those of a man, but very prominent and much larger proportionately than the gorilla's. The nose doesn't amount to anything, appearing to be more of a depression than a projection. The nostrils open upward and the jaws protrude excessively. The mouth is wide, the lips thin and lacking that recurvation that gives so much expression to our countenances. The spread of the shoulders is plainly seen, the body decreasing rapidly from the lower limbs to the loins. The thumb is the smallest of the fingers, and the foot closely resembles the human hand.

I am quite sure that many of my readers have seen a chimpanzee, as I have had them for years in my show. It is of one of these that I am now giving the history. Thousands of visitors to Central Park, New York City, have been interested in the two chim- panzees there. The male was christened "Mr. Crowley," and the female "Miss Kitty." They are very cunning and amusing. "Crow- ley" was taken down with pneu- monia (to which the chimpanzee ap- pears to be peculiarly subject) during the past winter (1887-8), and for several days his life was despaired of. I took a look at him while he lay motionless and suffering, and saw that there was little hope for the poor fellow; but he had the best of nursing, and in this

"Nip" and "Tuck."

month of April, 1888, is as frolicsome and bright as ever. I have always had strange feelings when looking into the bright, human-like eyes of the chimpanzee, for there seems to be something there which is visible in no other being except those belonging to our own species. Some of their performances, too, display so much intelligence and such a close resemblance to our own actions as to be startling.

The chimpanzee prefers a hilly country with intervening valleys. The edible fruits are abundant, and they gather the pine-apple, banana, and a species of plant- ain, and the papaw, of which they are extremely fond.

You should bear in mind that it takes the chimpanzee eight or ten years to at-

tain his full height, so that those that you have seen and studied with so much interest were, no doubt, still growing.

The first chimpanzees ever brought to Europe alive were "Nip" and "Tuck,"
exhibited at the Aquarium in London.

The stories of this interesting animal are almost as numerous and extravagant
as those of the gorilla. Living in the same country, belonging to the same genus,
sharing some of the most marked characteristics with him, it was only natural that
the accounts brought back by explorers should be as devoid of truth in many
respects, when applied to the chimpanzee, as were those related of his gigantic
brother, the gorilla.

CHAPTER LXXX.

A BATTLE OF GIANTS.

YP explained that a female chimpanzee with a single young one was eating a species of berry a short distance off among the undergrowth. He had caught only a glimpse of them, but they were unaware of his presence, and he believed that, by using care, they could capture the little one. It was probable that the male was not far off, though the native had not seen him.

The plan of the hunters was simple. They were to separate and surround the animals before showing themselves. Gyp would take station behind a tree, while his companions started the couple toward him. Then he would have to exercise his skill in flinging the net over the intended victim.

Pausing only long enough to make sure the scheme was understood by all, the hunters immediately parted company, each falling back so far that he was sure of being out of sight of the chimpanzees until he should begin closing in upon them.

This movement was pressed with so much care, that a half hour passed before our friends commenced to draw in their lines. Unable to see each other, their actions were governed by signals, so skillfully emitted that no ears except those for which they were intended read their meaning.

Bob Marshall was the first to catch sight of the creatures, and his heart gave a throb of pleasure when he saw the comical mother plucking the small, crimson berries, while her offspring frolicked around her like a kitten. Some of the antics of the latter were so comical that Bob could not help smiling. While the mother was gathering the fruit her offspring would jump upon her back, skurry up her shoulders, and hop from her crown before she could give it a cuff with her paw.

Catching the signal, the youth stepped forward with a rustling that caused the mother instantly to stop eating and look up. Seeing the strange figure, she uttered a sharp, warning cry and scampered off in an opposite direction, taking care, however, that her pace was so graduated that she did not pass beyond her progeny.

Unfortunately for the couple, their course led them straight for the tree where fate in the form of Gyp was awaiting them. The situations of Hargo and Jack Harvey gave them a view of what was going on, but they did not expose themselves, since the creatures were going right, and it would have been imprudent to interfere.

Bob followed at such a leisurely pace that in a minute or two he had fallen almost out of sight of the game. The mother continued hopping and running until she had placed herself a long way in front. Then, as if to learn whether she was still pursued, she stopped and looked around, chattering and frightened. Her little one, too young to understand their peril, frisked about like a puppy so full of life that it cannot keep still.

It so happened that at this moment they were within ten feet of the tree behind which the black-eyed native was furtively watching their movements. Hardly
was the halt made when Gyp leaped noiselessly from his hiding-place, and, flinging
the net with the skill of Jack Harvey, landed it directly over the head and
shoulders of the little one. The latter
uttered a series of odd squeaks and
squeals, and struggled like a wild cat;
but it was fast, and every effort only rendered its entanglement more certain.

The mother's affection gave her a
courage which she never could have
possessed at any other time. She flew
fiercely at the African, but he expected
it, and, paying no heed to her frantic
attack until sure the little one
was secure, he whirled about,
and with a quick sweep of his
long knife ended her career.

At this moment the other
hunters ran forward, and gathered around the captive in no
little excitement.

"Look out for the male,"
said Bob, the most flurried of
all; "he's an uglier customer
than the mother."

It was singular that the head
of the family did not show him-

THE CAPTURE

self, for he ought to have been near at hand. Perhaps he did take a sly peep at the scene from some
safe hiding-place, and was wise enough to know it
would be fatal for him to interfere. Be that as it may, nothing was seen of
him from first to last.

The captive proved less troublesome than would be supposed. It was a male,
several months old, possessed of considerable activity, and for a time he made a
brave fight, biting at the hands which persisted in keeping the netting over his
head and about his body, and uttering his odd cries of distress.

Before long, however, he exhausted himself and became quiescent. His captors
managed to prevent the little one seeing the inanimate mother, quickly removing
him from the spot. He was too young to realize his loss, and, though he doubtless
meant many of his cries for the ears of his dead parent, yet he gave little exhibition
of grief or distress over his loss.

The net having been made secure about the young chimpanzee, he was suspended

from a pole, carried on the shoulders of Gyp and Hargo, and the party set out for the camp, which was only a short distance off. Since the hunters were in an Equatorial country, and engaged upon a specific errand, their camp was quite primitive, comprising nothing more than a small open space, near a stream which was neither clear nor cool, and where at night a fire was kept burning, for protection against animals, and because of the cheerfulness it afforded.

The stream was in reality a sluggish river, winding its course through that malarious section, and showing signs on its bank of being frequented by some of the most formidable animals of the Dark Continent. Had our friends been prepared

"MIGHT IS RIGHT."

they could have secured rhinoceroses, hippopotami or elephants, for these animals were fully as plentiful as in South Africa.

"We've made a good capture, or rather you have," said Jack Harvey to Gyp; "and you must take him down the river at once to King William."

The Texan had arranged with his friend, the missionary, to assume charge of such young animals as were sent him until the return of the hunters from the jungle. The good man was an excellent naturalist and accepted the trust with pleasure. A portion of his premises were fitted up for such purposes, and he had already sent a number of valuable specimens across the ocean.

A Tropical Tea Party

465

Jack did not intend to withdraw from the jungle until he had secured a gorilla, and, understanding the nature of the animal as well as he did, he resolved that the hands of the party should be unhampered when the golden opportunity came, if come it should.

A short distance down the river, which was a tributary of the Gaboon, lay the small boat that had brought the party almost to the camp. By entering this at once, and making good use of their time, the natives ought to deliver the young chimpanzee into the hands of the missionary before night, and return to their camp by noon of the following day.

Warning them against undue haste or carelessness, Jack and Bob bade the natives good-by, and they quickly disappeared in the jungle, bearing their precious burden between them.

Although Jack and Bob felt the need of the presence of the natives, they did not mean to loiter until their return. They were competent to the task of hunting any game, and they set out to do so before Gyp and Hargo had been gone ten minutes.

Their prime purpose, however, being the capture of a gorilla, they gave little thought to anything else; but, before they had gone far upon their renewed hunt, they came upon a scene which, for the time, drove everything else from their minds.

It seemed that a party of elephants were returning from a bath in the muddy river, when they encountered three rhinoceroses on their way after the same luxury. The meeting took place in a sort of rough path in the jungle, not far from the camp of our friends.

Two of the rhinoceroses turned out for the elephants, but the third, a huge, ugly fellow, refused to give an inch. Thereupon the dozen or more elephants sensibly yielded the path to him.

All excepting one, a huge bull, who was in just as ugly a mood as the rhinoceros. Within less than two minutes of their meeting these monarchs of the jungle came together like a couple of animated mountains.

The rhinoceros ran across the front of the elephant, and flung up his two horns with the purpose of tearing him asunder, but the elephant threw his left foreleg over the huge, flabby neck of the mailed rhinoceros, and, partly holding him motionless, bore down upon him with such awful power that one of his tusks was driven clean through the victim's body, just back of his shoulders. As the fearful ivory sword was withdrawn it was crimsoned with blood, which streamed down its length and dripped to the ground, while the rhinoceros collapsed like so much mud, killed as utterly as if a thousand tons of rock had crushed him.

"The only law of the road in Africa is might," said Bob, after the elephant, having contemplated his work for a moment, swung off to join the herd, which viewed the battle from a point some distance away.

"That rhinoceros was a fool," remarked Jack; "he was too stubborn to turn out, but preferred to fight, and as a consequence he was knocked out in the first round."

"A rhinoceros doesn't always make such a failure. Mr. Godkin told me they

A Fight to the Death

sometimes wound and drive off the elephant, but this bull is an unusually large fellow, and he made a better fight than usual. But, I say, Jack, we seem to have struck the latitude for all sorts of wild beasts and reptiles."

"How can that be," asked the Texan, "when the spot we are in has no latitude at all, being under the Equator?"

"You are right on that point, but look at the monkeys off yonder, along the edge of the jungle. They seem to be feeding without any fear of us, who are in plain sight."

More than a score of the animals with which our friends had, long since, become familiar, were playing along the edge of the forest. Some were plucking a species of banana-like fruit, others seemed to be shaking hands and sporting with each other, giving utterance now and then to their peculiar cries, and paying no heed to the two hunters who were within gun-shot.

"We are after more valuable game than you," said Bob, having watched them some minutes; "you must know you are of little account, or you wouldn't tempt us in that style."

Had the hunters ventured nearer, the creatures would have scampered off, but, as the youth had intimated, they were in no danger, for the "game wasn't worth the candle."

CHAPTER LXXXI.

A CAMP-FIRE VISITOR.

BUT for the recollection of their good fortune in the easy capture of the chimpanzee, I am afraid Jack Harvey and Bob Marshall would have lost their patience before the close of the afternoon, for, though they hunted with a persistency that ought to have been rewarded, they were baffled in their efforts to catch sight of the most famed denizen of the African jungle.

This was the more trying, since, as in former instances, they knew they were often close to the animal. They even heard its peculiar cry, and caught the sound of one of them skurrying among the vegetation a short distance in front, but in no case was it possible to secure the coveted shot.

There was no lack of other game. They could have bagged a score of the huge-eared elephants, which they saw bathing with several hippopotami on the other side of the river, and an enormous water-serpent that boldly swam out in the stream tempted a shot from Jack Harvey, who sent the bullet so accurately that the enormous reptile never saw land again.

Turning from the teeming life of the sluggish Equatorial river, they plunged into the jungle, where they observed so many strange, brilliantly-colored birds that they were inclined more than once to make strong efforts to secure them, but they gave it over, determined not to be drawn aside from their real business.

The plan of parting company was tried, but with no better success than when they hunted together. At last the hot, suffocating day drew to a close, and the two met at the camp, where they ate their evening meal of fruit, growing so abundantly around them. You know the craving for meat is much less in warm weather than in cold or temperate, and our friends had, long since, adopted the wise plan of eating only twice a day, and then chiefly of fruit, and drinking as little water as it was possible to get along with. They were convinced, and I agree with them, that the chief danger to explorers and hunters lies in their carelessness about their drink and diet.

"We can understand how it is that we don't see any of those plaguey critters in our own country," remarked Jack Harvey, who, having lighted his pipe, lolled on the earth with the full enjoyment of the rest which comes to one worn out and tired.

"What do you take to be the reason?" asked Bob, who also felt the delight of stretching his limbs on the ground. It was not yet dark and no attention was given the fire.

"Why, 'cause you can't catch 'em."

"That is hardly the reason," said Bob, "it's the difficulty the gorillas find of standing any climate except this horrible one."

"Why is it the chimpanzees live in England and America?"

"It must be because the chimpanzee can stand the change of latitude better than his bigger and stronger brother. Yet a good many of the chimpanzees die, in spite of all the care taken of them. Mr. Barnum described to me a gorilla that he saw in London, but I believe it died soon afterward, and you know they have never had a live one in America."

"I suppose if they could send over a dozen or so, some of them would become used to our country, and after a time thrive in it."

"It will be done after awhile, no doubt, just as the flying machine will. Mr. Barnum believes in the flying machine, and he insists that if he doesn't live to see it, his descendants will be able to travel through the air, just as readily as they pass from one point to another over the land."

"I would like to get another chimpanzee, but if we can manage to gather in a young gorilla, I shall be satisfied to start for home with the two prizes."

CONTENTMENT.

"And if we succeed in landing both there, Mr. Barnum will consider the expense repaid ten-fold."

"Well," said the Texan, puffing away at his pipe, "I shall never up give till we succeed."

BULKY BATHERS.

"And I'm with you; there's no doubt to my mind that Dick and Mr. Godkin will secure plenty of valuable curiosities in India, and we mustn't go back empty-handed. That reminds me," said Bob eagerly, "that we ought to christen the young chimpanzee: what shall it be?"

The Texan smoked awhile in silence, and then looked up with a smile:

"Call him 'Dick.'"

"Why?"

"There's a good deal about him that reminds me of Dick; he is lively and frisky, and, when he gets into a tight place, will fight like the mischief."

"Then 'Dick' it shall be," replied Bob with a laugh, and so the young chimpanzee was named for the bright young fellow who just then was having such stirring times with Mr. Godkin in the wilds of India, the particulars of which have already been told you.

"We must have a name also for the gorilla," added Jack.

"We haven't caught him yet."

"But we shall do so. I think it will be well to name him 'Bob'—that is, if it should be a *him*."

"Is there anything about *me* to remind you of a gorilla?" asked the youth with feigned indignation.

"Well — I hope you won't insist on my answering," replied Jack with a twinkle of his fine dark eyes; "I wouldn't mind your calling him Jocko or Jack, but the name is too common with monkeys."

"Yes," remarked Bob meaningly, "I know several instances where monkeys bear the name of Jack, and it fits them well, but one or two more wouldn't make much difference. I've no objection, however, and I will be so delighted if we capture a gorilla, that I will be proud to have him bear my name."

"If it should prove a female,— well, we will be able to find some sweet name that will fit her. I guess we had better start the fire," added the Texan, rising to his feet; "it's beginning to grow dark, and I hear animals prowling around in the jungle."

Gyp and Hargo had gathered so much wood the evening before, that nothing was required except to kindle the flames, which were soon going at a merry rate.

With such surroundings it would never do for both our friends to sleep at the same time. They were so tired that it would have been exceedingly pleasant, but the peril forbade such indulgence.

The gleam of the fire was sure to attract the attention of some of the fiercest animals known to any part of the world. Indeed, they had been seen near at hand, and the glare of more than one threatening pair of eyes was caught in startling proximity to the camp.

All animals have a dread of fire, and, so long as the hunters kept theirs burning brightly, they were in little danger, provided they maintained their usual vigilance at the same time. The tiger, as you know, will sometimes steal fearfully close to the flames for the purpose of seizing his sleeping victim, and, should the sportsman sink into unconsciousness, the smouldering embers are sure to tempt some beast to a venture he would not make were the man awake.

"I will put myself in your care," said Jack, "for half the night, provided you are sure to keep your eyes open."

"I understand the situation too well to give way," replied the youth, "you know we both had a good long sleep last night, and I shall keep in motion all the time."

"That settles it; if you will stick to that there's no danger of closing your eyes."

It was yet early in the evening, but since each expected to pass half the night awake, Jack prudently decided to gain all the slumber he could while the opportunity was his.

He therefore knocked the ashes from his pipe, saluted Bob, sent up a prayer to Heaven, and five minutes later was sleeping as sweetly as an infant.

"It would be a good deal pleasanter to sit here on the ground," reflected Bob, "but I know what the result would be. Dick and I found that out down in South Africa. I've often tried to remember the instant I dropped off to sleep, but could no more do it than I could keep awake all night when sleepy and sitting still. I wonder where Dick and Mr. Godkin are," he added, with that quick transition of thought peculiar to youth, as he rose to his feet, and, loaded rifle in hand, began pacing back and forth near the camp-fire. "They have had plenty of time to reach India and get well into their work. What a fine thing it would be if Dick and I had telephonic communication and could keep each other posted. Wouldn't we have some interesting stories to tell?"

The youth smiled at his own conceit, and did not forget to maintain a sharp watch on the dismal jungle which closed in on every hand.

The stream was just far enough off to be invisible in the gloom, though a splashing of the water now and then apprised him that some of its inhabitants were in motion. Many of the animals of India and Africa are nocturnal in their habits, and, though our friends had come in collision with them during the day-time, yet they were far more active and dangerous when darkness shrouded the earth and men were asleep.

Less than an hour had passed of Bob's watch when he became convinced that some large beast was prowling perilously near. He caught shadowy glimpses of him as he came to the very edge of the circle of illumination, and then, when the sentinel stopped to gain a better view of the intruder, he glided noiselessly back like a shadow and was swallowed up in the gloom.

No doubt the beast had his heart set on the youth, who could tell from his movements that himself, and not the sleeping friend, was the object of attention.

"I'll settle *you*," muttered Bob, "just as soon as I can get the chance."

The situation was anything but a comfortable one, and the youth had a constant fear that the brute was about to make a sudden leap from the gloom and land on his shoulders before he could give him a shot. Three separate times he brought his rifle to his shoulder, but the beast acted as though he suspected the meaning of the movement and instantly darted out of range.

The most terrifying feeling was when some slight rustling directly behind the lad warned him that, in spite of all his care, his unknown enemy had got in the rear.

The youth suspected it was a lion or leopard that was so persistent, and he finally resolved to force matters to an issue.

Stopping in his walk, with his back to the fire, he held his gun ready. Almost the same instant he caught the glimpse he wanted, and, bringing his weapon to his shoulder, let fly, sending in three shots in quick succession.

" Did you hit him ? " asked Jack, sleepily, as he raised his head on his elbow.

" Yes — each time."

" All right — then I'll go to sleep again ; call me when it's my turn, but try not to disturb me before then."

CHAPTER LXXXII.

THE KING OF THE JUNGLE.

PROMPTLY at midnight Bob Marshall awakened his friend Jack, and the latter assumed his place as sentinel. He did not take the trouble to learn the nature of the animal shot some time before, since, as he said, it would " keep" until morning.

The shot had produced a salutary effect upon the other marauders that may have contemplated a venture of the kind, for, though there were a number of them in the vicinity, none approached nigh enough to draw a shot from the Texan.

With the coming of daylight, the visitor that had paid such a dear price for his temerity was found to be a large leopard, resembling in appearance the cheetah or famed hunting leopard of India. Our friends bestowed little attention on him, for they had seen too many of his kind to feel any special interest in the brute.

Following the plan agreed upon the previous day, Jack Harvey and Bob Marshall, after their simple morning meal, separated. They had fixed quite clearly in their minds the course to pursue, it being one which, if adhered to, would hold them within easy signaling distance of each other.

It fell to the lot of one speedily to come upon an interesting scene, and to the other to be involved in a most stirring experience.

It need not be said that, after the two days' vain hunt for the gorilla, our friends used all the care possible. No veterans of the jungle could have stolen through the tangled vegetation with more noiselessness than they.

Thus it was that Jack had not gone far, when he caught sight of an animal which with all its extreme watchfulness had no suspicion of his proximity.

On the massive branch of a fallen tree sat a female leopard, calmly gazing at some point in the jungle. Since it was not in the direction of the hunter, the latter knew he was undiscovered.

With the same skill he had shown from the first, the Texan crept closer until he observed that the leopard was the mother of a litter of kittens that were in a partial cavity just below the limb on which she was sitting.

There were three pretty spotted creatures. One was holding another down with playful vigor, while the third lay near, apparently looking up at its parent with an affection that was fully reciprocated.

It would have been the easiest thing in the world for Jack to shoot the mother, sitting so proudly on the old bough above, but, even had he no fear of alarming the gorillas in the neighborhood, he would not have done so. They had obtained a couple of young leopards weeks before in South Africa, and there was no call to burden themselves with more. So the hunter stole away as cautiously as he had

A Happy Mother.

476

approached the spot, and that mother never knew her narrow escape from death. If she had been able to understand it, it isn't likely she would have felt any gratitude therefor.

"I shouldn't wonder if it was your mate that Bob picked off last night," thought Jack, "but it was his own fault, and I've no such excuse for shooting *you*."

Meanwhile Bob Marshall, almost at the same moment, detected a handsome female leopard a short distance in front of him, whose actions showed she had her attention fixed upon something so far in advance that it was invisible to him. Little did he suspect its nature.

The head of the animal was directly away from the youth, and she was moving so guardedly that Bob would not have seen her had she not suddenly paused and risen to her feet, precisely as a brute does when seeking to make sure its prey is where it suspects it to be.

Bob also stopped, and, crouching down, stole to the nearest tree and sheltered himself behind it, while he watched the actions of the leopard with absorbing interest. He was still wondering what her intended victim could be, when he saw something stirring in the undergrowth just beyond. He could not distinguish it clearly and was still trying to do so, when his blood was set tingling by a wild, resounding "*kh — ah! kh — ah!*" the well-known cry of the gorilla. At the same moment, the dimly-seen object in advance of the leopard resolved itself into a female of that species, which dashed off among the limbs, fallen trees and running vines, with her young one held to her breast, as a mother clasps her baby.

In this instance the head of the family was on hand, as the leopard discovered without a second's delay.

The latter had hardly time to rise to her feet with the purpose of dashing after the female gorilla and her young, when the male, a gigantic fellow, fully six feet tall, burst through the vegetation, and assailed her with inconceivable ferocity.

The astounded Bob saw the beam-like arms make a terrific sweep through the air, and in an instant the leopard was grasped and flung on its side. One of the gorilla's enormous arms gripped his prey under the throat, while the other, passing over her shoulders, seized the left paw and held it as immovable as if it were the arm of an infant.

This brought the leopard's head under the chin of the terrible creature, which opened its vast jaws until they inclosed half the leopard's neck between them. Then the teeth met, and the victim had barely time to give one frenzied screech, when her life went out like a flash of lightning, and that, too, before she was able to inflict so much as a scratch upon her fearful assailant.

The gorilla kept his jaws shut for a full half minute in the back of the leopard's neck, never releasing the grip of his right hand from her throat, nor that of the left from her paw. It looked as if he was holding his victim stationary while he felt for her pulse to learn whether she was alive or not.

If such was the fact, the result must have satisfied him.

Suddenly he flung up his head, half straightened his body, and gave the carcass

THE KING OF THE JUNGLE.

a flirt which sent it flying, end over end, among the branches to a point fifty feet away. The male stood motionless, watching the flight of the body until it fell, when he wheeled to join his mate, who, with her young one still clasped to her breast, was watching him from her perch, no doubt with proud admiration of his prowess, and both utterly unconscious of the presence of more formidable enemies than the one which had just been vanquished.

At the instant of turning, the male uttered an appalling, human-like screech and went over backward, flinging his arms aloft, as man sometimes does when mortally stricken. He was dead, instantly killed by a bullet from Bob Marshall's rifle, which had pierced through his iron skull as he stood with his front to ward the youth,

A LITTLE FURY.

the shot being so effective that no second one was required. There must have been a dim perception in the mind of the female that some overwhelming calamity had overtaken her lord, for, with a strange cry, she scampered down from her low perch, and, still holding her young one to her breast, ran toward the body.

She never reached it. Hardly half the distance was passed when she bounded forward, uttered a wild shriek, and fell dead, with her young one so tightly clasped that it was thrown beneath her body.

The same fate which her burly mate had met overtook her before she could realize the presence of the death-dealing hunter.

Bob Marshall had understood from the first what was necessary, and he executed his design with a promptness and success that would have delighted any ranger of the jungles.

Thrilled by what he had accomplished, he dashed from behind the tree and ran to where the little one was still desperately struggling to free itself from the dead weight upon it.

As he did so, he almost stepped upon the body of the huge male, which lay stretched on its back, so fearful-looking, even in death, that the boy involuntarily checked himself and grasped his rifle, half expecting the monstrous animal to spring at him. But the king of the jungle was past anything like *that*.

At the moment Bob reached the female, the young one succeeded in working itself loose, and now confronted him with an expression of such ferocious venom that he involuntarily recoiled and placed his hand on his revolver.

The youngster seemed to feel that the strange creature which it now beheld had done it an irreparable wrong, and it was ready to assail him with the fury, if not the strength, with which its father had annihilated the leopard but a few minutes before.

Of course, Bob had no fear of the little one, which was a male, after disposing of his mother in such summary fashion, and nothing short of necessity could have tempted him to put a bullet through the young spitfire.

Bob afterward said that during the brief seconds he and the infant gorilla confronted each other it seemed to him that the hideous beast represented a million of dollars, and he pictured the delight I would feel when he presented him to me, on this side of the Atlantic.

But the youngster, after snarling and showing his teeth, seemed to expect the youth would attack him, and it was that for which he was waiting.

Joyously as Bob would have thrown his arms around the creature and held him fast, he was too prudent to attempt it. The infant was too strong for him, and he felt that, unless he had help very soon, the young one would escape, if he chose to leave the vicinity of his dead parents.

But luck was once more with our friends on that hot day. Bob was standing, undecided what to do, when his heart was delighted by a whistle which he recognized as the signal of Gyp. The native and his companion must have returned from their voyage down the river sooner than any one anticipated.

The reports of the youth's Winchester had guided Gyp to the locality, and a few minutes later he appeared among the trees.

A glance told him the situation, and he hurried to the spot. The fiery young gorilla was no more frightened by the appearance of two hunters than by a single one, and he confronted them with the same defiance that he had shown when opposed by the single sportsman.

The contract, however, was too extensive for the young fury, and, kicking, scratching, biting and fighting with a fierceness that was amazing, he was finally obliged to succumb to the entanglements of the same net that had served so well in making captive the chimpanzee.

CHAPTER LXXXIII.

HOME AGAIN.

THE natives, Gyp and Hargo, had pushed matters with such vigor that they returned from King William several hours sooner than they had expected at the time of starting thither with the captive chimpanzee. The missionary was pleased to take charge of the little creature, and promised it the best of care. He had had others in his keeping before, and understood them so well that no one could have done better.

The servants had reached camp only a short time after the departure of Jack Harvey and Bob Marshall on their gorilla hunt. It was not an easy matter to follow them through the jungle, but they set out to do so, and were thus engaged when the report of Bob's Winchester fell on their ears.

The sound showed that he was not far off, and Gyp at once started to join him. Hargo decided to stay where he was and to pursue his hunt of the animals alone unless summoned by signal from his master.

This, you will perceive, was in keeping with Jack Harvey's policy of separating the hunters, and the act of the native was at the suggestion of Gyp himself.

Hargo had not been left alone ten minutes, when his trained ear told him that he was in the neighborhood of one of the creatures for which they had hunted so long in vain. Like his friend Gyp, he had been in the business before, and was confident he fully understood all the requirements.

The native stood still and looked carefully around, half suspecting he had already been discovered by the terrific game.

Such, indeed, was the fact, for he had hardly had time to take a quick survey when he descried a female skurrying off among the trees. As is generally the case, she was the first to discover the danger, and announced it to her mate, who was feeding near at hand. The female had no young one with her, so far as Hargo could see, but, all the same, she turned over to the head of the family the duty of attending to intruders.

The gorilla that rose on his hind feet and advanced toward the African was fully as large as the one shot by Bob Marshall. Indeed Hargo had never seen such a formidable creature, which, instead of fleeing, appeared to be eager for a fight.

Walking forward, he stopped a rod away, struck his tremendous breast with his paw, sending out a sound like a bass drum, and, opening his vast crimson mouth to its full extent, emitted a roar that was enough to test the nerves of the bravest man. Then he commenced walking slowly forward, with his wicked black eyes fixed on the native and the hair over his skull twitching with rage.

It would not do to miss hitting this monster at the first fire, for, as you will recall, Hargo's gun was a single-barrel. He knew his peril, and, with the coolness of a veteran, stood his ground, calmly awaiting the moment when the gorilla should be so close that a failure of aim was out of the question.

It would seem that that point was reached when he was within twenty paces, but Hargo held his fire until half that distance separated them, when he brought his gun to his shoulder, took aim at the point over the heart of the animal, and, with the muzzle of his weapon almost within reach of his paw, pulled trigger.

Alas! the piece missed fire, and the instant it did so the African knew he was

JUST TOO LATE

doomed. Hastily clubbing his gun, he made a sweeping blow at the monster, who bounded forward with the fury of his brother assailing the leopard.

The blow landed, but produced no more effect than if it had struck the side of a tree. In an instant the weapon was wrenched from his grasp by a single paw of the gorilla, who smote the man with his other, the blow crushing his skull as though it had been card-board, and striking him to the earth, dead almost before he fell.

Standing over the prostrate figure, the gorilla stared around in the jungle, uttering his resonant roar, as if to say that if there were any more human beings who wished to dispute his sovereignty of the jungle he was ready for them.

He did not have to wait long, for it so happened that Jack Harvey was pushing his way among the trees, drawn thither by the cry of the gorilla, which was quite near him.

As he came in sight he saw the creature standing over the motionless figure, and he needed nothing more to tell him that poor Hargo was beyond all suffering.

The beast still held the gun, and, as if in the pure wantonness of strength, he bent it over in a half circle, apparently with no more effort than if it were a thin pipe of lead.

The Texan stopped while fifty feet distant, and leveled his Winchester at the gorilla, which began advancing toward him. Jack did not wait for him to lessen the space, but let fly the instant he was sure of his aim, and with such accuracy that the first ball bored its way through the heart of the monster, who went to the earth very much as the victims of Bob Marshall's marksmanship had done a brief time before.

The hunter ran forward and stooped over the figure of Hargo. He knew before doing so that he was past help, and he was stirred with sorrow for the unfortunate victim of the animal's ferocity.

In order to protect the body from wild beasts, Jack decided to stay by it until it could be removed. He uttered the signal agreed upon, and had to wait only a short time when, to his astonishment, Gyp and Bob appeared, carrying the captive gorilla between them, suspended in the net supported on a pole, with the little one as savage and defiant in its way as its parent had been.

Gyp and Bob were shocked by the fate of their attendant, but he was killed beyond remedy, and all that remained was to carry his body to the boat and thence down the river to King William.

It was a difficult task, but it was accomplished at last, the party reaching the town the following day with the remains and the young gorilla in good condition. Bob and Jack distributed a liberal sum of money among Hargo's nearest relatives, whose gratitude seemed to be more pronounced than their grief for the loss of their friend.

The two hunters decided that their work in Equatorial Africa was finished, and they now desired to leave the country with the least possible delay. They were hopeful of finding some vessel bound across the Atlantic to America ; but they were disappointed, and, after waiting several days, took ship to the Cape of Good Hope. There they secured passage by way of Calcutta for England.

At Cape Town, the horses which they had left were taken on board, and the run up the Indian Ocean was begun in the highest spirits on the part of both. "Dick," the chimpanzee, and "Bob," the gorilla, were in excellent condition, and their captors were hopeful of landing both in America in the best of health and vigor.

The gorilla seems to be absolutely untamable. My old friend Du Chaillu tells me he made repeated attempts to win the regard of the young ones he was fortunate enough to capture, but was never able to awaken the first spark of affection in them.

Bob Marshall's experience with "Dick" was quite similar. Jack Harvey became so disgusted with the spitfire that he gave up the task and left him to himself. Many a time Bob felt like doing the same, but some slight indication, as he thought, of an appreciation of his efforts, induced him to persevere in his attempts to make friends with the little one.

He spoke to it in the most soothing language, proffered it delicacies, and spent hours in trying to win its regard, but all in vain; and, when Calcutta was reached, he was compelled to admit to Jack that the animal was just as fierce and wild as when the net was thrown over its head in the Gaboon country.

"If there

DICK

is any difference," added Bob, "I think he is worse, for he has grown rapidly and is a good deal stronger. If he could get the chance I believe he would throttle us both."

"There's no doubt of it; I daren't trust myself to fool with him, for if he should bite me I'm afraid I would knock his plagued head off before I could restrain myself."

"He is too valuable to take any such risks," said Bob, with a laugh, "for you know gorillas come high."

The greatest surprise and delight of all awaited the arrival of Bob and Jack at

Calcutta, for who should they find there but Dick Brownell and Mr. Godkin, just completing their arrangements for exporting the prizes they had secured in the East Indian jungles to America by way of England.

You can imagine how glad the friends were to meet each other again, and to find themselves all unharmed, with the most interesting of stories to exchange. The chimpanzee and gorilla were shipped with them, the four hunters taking passage on the same vessel, in order to be near their prizes and to give them their attention.

I wish I could conclude my account with a continuous record of success and gratification on the part of my employes, who had done so exceedingly well in their search for wild beasts, birds and reptiles in Asia and Africa, but, I am sorry to say, I cannot.

Toward the latter part of the voyage "Bob," the gorilla, showed signs of illness. He received every possible care, but he grew worse, and just as the shores of Old England rose to sight over the blue ocean he breathed his last.

The effort to bring a live gorilla to America had once more failed, and, as I write these closing lines, I have to repeat that success in that respect remains yet to be attained. Of course it will come sooner or later, as will many other achievements that are now deemed among the impossibilities.

With the trifling exceptions named, the rest of the valuable cargo reached this country in safety and joined my show. Among all the strange wild animals, the liveliest and brightest was "Dick," the chimpanzee. I have another, but if I happen to be present when I see you at my exhibition, I shall be pleased to point out "Dick" to you, believing you will be interested in him after learning the particulars of his capture.

He is as full of mischief and tricks as an egg is of meat. He is fond of taking a peep at himself in a mirror with which his quarters are furnished. He is frightfully homely, and I don't wonder that several times he has felt so discouraged over his unprepossessing appearance that he has smashed the little looking-glass which persisted in reflecting his lineaments so truthfully.

He is also very fond of pets, and between him and the tame rabbit, which has been placed in his quarters, a strong friendship has been formed.

As I intimated, Bob Marshall and Dick Brownell immediately entered college on their return to this country, and they are now pursuing their studies with the same vigor and persistency they showed in pursuing the wild birds, beasts and reptiles of Africa and India. They feel that they have had enough of wild life, and I am quite sure that you and I would feel the same after passing through an experience as varied and stirring as theirs has been.

Jack Harvey and Carl Godkin are among my most trusted employes, and you will admit that I am warranted in believing that nothing ever can arise to disturb the pleasant relations which have existed between us from the first.

I feel it a pleasure to acknowledge in this place my indebtedness to my friend Edward S. Ellis, A.M., for his help in the preparation of these pages. His store of

DICK AND HIS PET 487

information concerning wild animals, their haunts and habits, and his long experience as a successful writer for the young have enabled him to give me many
valuable suggestions as to arrangement, style and method of treatment.   This
acknowledgment is, therefore, due him, and is made without suggestion or wish on
his part.

CHAPTER LXXXIV.

JUST as I am about to lay down my pen, a letter comes from my esteemed publishers, in which they are kind enough to say that they believe a useful and entertaining addition to this volume will be a brief summary of the leading incidents of my life, and an expression of my views on the best means of accumulating wealth and attaining old age — two consummations which I am sure you all fervently desire, and in the achievement of which I may be able to lend you help. I sincerely hope that such may be the result of what I now submit to you.

First, respecting myself, you will allow me to quote from the remarks of President Capen, of Tufts College, Medford, Mass., in referring to my founding of the museum of natural history connected with that institution, at a cost of $55,000:

"Mr. Barnum began life in poverty, but by an energy and a spirit of enterprise almost unparalleled, even in this country, and in the face of difficulties that would have appalled most men, he conquered poverty and secured for himself a place among men of princely fortune. Through all his life he has been a man of unbounded public spirit. In the city of his adoption, he is, by unanimous consent, the foremost citizen, pouring out his money like water for every species of public improvement. In his business he has sought to combine popular amusement with popular education. He is a man of pure life, who has taught temperance by precept and example to young and old. He is a man of positive religious convictions and deep religious life."

I was born in Bethel, Ct., July 5, 1810. My father, Philo Barnum, was a tailor, a farmer, a country merchant, and sometimes a tavern-keeper, and was the son of Ephraim Barnum, who was a captain in the Revolutionary War.

I used to save my pennies when a child, until at the age of six I was the proud possessor of a silver dollar. On holidays and "training days" I peddled cakes, candies, etc., and, instead of spending money, earned it. By the time I was 12 years old, beside other property, I was the owner of a sheep and a calf, and should soon, no doubt, have become a small Crœsus, had not my father kindly permitted me to purchase my own clothing, which somewhat reduced my little store.

My father died when I was 15 years old, and left his family in very poor circumstances. I was obliged to get trusted for the pair of shoes I wore to my father's funeral. I literally began the world with nothing, and was barefooted at that.

I developed a distaste for manual labor, and was employed as clerk in a country store. I also clerked in Brooklyn, and opened a porter-house there on my own account, which I sold out not long afterward at a profit. In 1828 I returned to Bethel and opened a fruit and confectionery store, and an agency to sell lottery tickets added to my income. My interest in the lottery business, which was then legalized and regarded as respectable, was afterward greatly increased, and I estab-lished a number of agencies.

In November, 1829, I was married to Miss Charity Hallett, of Bethel, who had been until then a tailoress. I next tried my hand as an auctioneer in the book trade, traveling about the country, but was not very successful. Then my uncle, Alanson Taylor, and myself established in Bethel a country store, of which I later secured the whole control.

In a period of political excitement I wrote a number of communications to a Danbury paper, which were refused publication, and I established a paper of my own, the *Herald of Freedom*, the first number of which appeared October 19, 1831. Lacking that experience which induces caution, and without dread of consequences, I frequently laid myself open to the charge of libel, and three times in three years I was prosecuted. The last was a criminal prosecution, brought against me for stating in my paper that a man in Bethel, prominent in church, had been guilty of taking usury of an orphan boy. The truth of my statement was proved, but I was convicted and sentenced to a fine of one hundred dollars and imprisonment in the common jail for sixty days. My room in jail, however, was papered and carpeted, and I lived well. I was overwhelmed with visits of my friends. I edited my paper as usual, and received large accessions to my subscription list; and at the end of my sixty days' term the event was celebrated by a large concourse of people from the surrounding country. The court room in which I was convicted was the scene of the celebration. An ode, written for the occasion, was sung; an eloquent oration on the freedom of the press was delivered, and several hundred gentlemen afterward partook of a sumptuous dinner, followed by appropriate toasts and speeches. Then came the triumphant part of the exercises, which was reported in my paper of December 12, 1832, as follows:

"P. T. Barnum and the band of music took their seats in a coach drawn by six horses, which was preceded by forty horsemen and a marshal bearing the national standard. Immediately in the rear of the coach was the carriage of the orator and the president of the day, followed by the committee of arrangements and sixty car-riages of citizens, which joined in escorting the editor home. When the procession commenced its march amid the roar of cannon, three cheers were given by several hundred citizens who did not join the procession. The band of music continued to play a variety of national airs until their arrival in Bethel, a distance of three miles, when they struck up the beautiful and appropriate tune of 'Home, Sweet Home.' After giving three hearty cheers, the procession returned to Danbury."

I sold out my paper after an editorial career of three years, and, disposing of my interest in Bethel, moved to New York to seek my fortune. For a time I kept a small private boarding-house, and in 1835, over fifty years ago, began my long and successful career as a showman by the exhibition of a remarkable negro woman said to be 160 years old, and to have been the nurse of General Washington. For the next half dozen years I traveled with various circus and amusement combina-tions, making considerable money at times, but sinking it in unfortunate ventures.

In 1841 I determined to concentrate my energies on laying up something for the future. Scudder's American Museum in New York was for sale, and, although I had no money, I succeeded in purchasing it for $12,000, to be paid in seven annual installments. The collection was a valuable one, but had not been properly handled. I was determined on success, and, by good management, paid for the whole concern in one year from the profits of the business. I continually improved the museum, and it was the ladder by which I rose to fortune.

I thoroughly understood the value and the art of advertising, and have used printers' ink to immense advantage throughout my business life. In 1842 I introduced to the public Charles S. Stratton, the dwarf known all the world over as "General Tom Thumb," with whom I traveled extensively in this country and abroad, and made a mint of money. I selected Bridgeport, Ct., as a place for a home out of the metropolis, and had built there a magnificent residence after the general plan of the pavilion erected by George IV., and named it " Iranistan," signifying " Eastern country place."

In 1849 came the Jenny Lind tour, in which I achieved one of the greatest successes in managerial work known in the history of amusement undertakings. The Swedish nightingale gave ninety-five concerts under my control, the total receipts of which were $712,161.34, or an average of $7,496.43 per night. The next year I started a traveling museum and menagerie.

From the time of taking up my residence in Bridgeport to the present, I have done everything possible to advance the interests of that place, and in so doing have spent many thousands of dollars. In 1851 I purchased a tract of land on the east side of the river and started the city of East Bridgeport, which then became my pet scheme. In order to help build up the place by inducing a large manufacturing concern to locate there I became connected with the Jerome Clock Company and agreed to indorse its notes to the amount of $110,000, but was deceived and swindled, and became involved to the extent of over $500,000, causing my financial ruin.

After having passed the meridian of life, I found myself at the foot of the ladder again, and largely in debt at that. Offers of assistance came from far and near, but I would not accept them, and began the fight for fortune once more. I took "Tom Thumb" and went abroad, where I renewed my former successes. In 1857 my beautiful home, " Iranistan," was burned. The next year I made another foreign tour with "Tom Thumb," and then, taking the lecture platform, delivered an address on the art of money-getting to packed houses hundreds of times. I am an advocate of temperance, and have lectured many times on this subject, always free or for charitable purposes. In 1860, when all the clock indebtedness was settled, I again secured control of the American Museum, which I had lost in my financial downfall, and the press announced " Barnum on his feet again." I established agents everywhere, and searched the world for attractions for the museum, gave stage performances, and made it a wonderfully popular resort for entertainment and instruction. In 1865 the museum was destroyed by fire, but in less than four months I opened a new one.

I was elected four times to the Legislature and once to the mayoralty of Bridgeport, my support not being confined at all to party lines. In my improvements at Bridgeport I opened Sea Side Park, and when I was able built another beautiful residence by its border, naming it "Waldemere" (from three German words meaning woods by the sea), and also three cottages for my daughters, called "Petrel's Nest," "Beachcroft," and "Wavewood." One bitterly cold morning early in 1868, as I sat by my fireside looking at the morning paper, I read, "Barnum's museum totally destroyed by fire." By the burning of "Iranistan" and two museums I had lost $1,000,000. I now sold out my traveling menagerie and retired from business. But after so active a life, I was not content long to remain idle, and in 1870-71 organized a great show enterprise, combining a museum, menagerie, caravan, hippodrome and circus, which was exhibited with much profit, though at a great expense. I also purchased the building and lease on Fourteenth street, New York, known as the Hippotheatron, and established a show for the employment of two hundred of my people, who would otherwise have been idle in winter. Four weeks after its inauguration I was in New Orleans, and while reading an account of the flooding of my show grounds in that city, a telegram reached me announcing the burning of the New York establishment, by which I lost nearly $300,000. I returned to New York, and was on the road again the next spring with "Barnum's Traveling World's Fair," whose expenses were $5,000 a day, and my name has ever since been connected with the greatest show enterprises the country has seen, one marked feature of which was the transportation to America from England of the famous elephant Jumbo.

In 1873, while I was in Europe, I received intelligence of the death of my wife. In 1874 I was given a public dinner by the citizens of Bridgeport, as a recognition of my services to the city. The same year I married an English lady, the daughter of Mr. John Fish, a cotton manufacturer of Manchester. I lectured under the auspices of the Redpath Lyceum Bureau, of Boston, in 1875, on "The World and How to Live in It." Beside giving thousands of dollars' worth of land to Bridgeport for park purposes, I gave $50,000 worth of land for a cemetery, and in my native town of Bethel erected a fountain at a cost of $20,000. In my efforts to build up East Bridgeport I erected many houses and disposed of them to workingmen at cost, allowing them to pay by installments, and thus eventually own homesteads. To my large circle of friends and invited guests, the latch-string always hangs out at my residence.

I have catered to the innocent amusement of millions of people, and to my eyes the handsomest picture in all the world is an array of young and smiling faces, such as I have seen day after day, and night after night, beneath the shelter of my tents. To my ears the sweetest music is the clear, ringing laughter of the children as they give vent to their joy in my show.

While complying with the request of my publishers, I shall intrude upon their kindness, by asking space to express my views on the relations that should exist between the Church and the form of entertainment with which my life has been identified.

Years ago no two institutions were more actively antagonistic than the Church and circus. The former waged fierce and uncompromising war against the latter, the Methodist Church going so far as to make it a part of its discipline that attendance at a circus entailed forfeiture of membership. That the Church should ever tolerate, patronize or even recognize as an educator the circus was a possibility that probably entered into the dreams of no man but myself, and perhaps no man but myself believed it possible to organize a circus which should respect the Church and all pertaining to it.

In those days the circus was very justly the object of the Church's animadversions. Its spectacular attractions consisted principally of six to ten entree horses, with riders; two fairly good equestrians, whose standing feats on horseback were made on a broad pad saddle; half a dozen apprentice boys, who rode more or less (and rather less than more) and joined in flip-flaps, hand-springs, and in the afterpiece, "Billy Button, The Tailor," or "Pete Jenkins," in which drunken characters were represented and broad jokes, suited to the groundlings, were given. Its fun consisted of the clown's vulgar jests, emphasized with still more vulgar and suggestive gestures, lest providentially the point might be lost. Educational features the circus of that day had none. Its employes were mostly of the rowdy element, and it had a following of card-sharpers, pick-pockets and swindlers generally, who were countenanced by some of the circus proprietors, with whom they shared their ill-gotten gains. Its advent was dreaded by all law-abiding people, who knew that with it would inevitably come disorder, drunkenness and riot. It will scarcely be believed that it was the custom of most of such circuses to engage in advance the firemen of the town they proposed to visit to help to protect the circus company against possible attacks of the rabble, who were apt to be belligerently indignant when too outrageously victimized. Some circus proprietors paid no salary to their ticket-sellers, but let them cheat it out of their customers by giving them short change in the rush and excitement which usually prevailed around the ticket-wagon.

Every one in these enlightened days concedes that human nature imperatively demands amusement and recreation. The childish mind, to which all the world is yet fresh and interesting, and the jaded brain of the adult call with equal insistence for "something new and strange." Granted the necessity of amusements and the desirability of their being morally clean and healthful and instructive, the provider of such entertainments is a public benefactor, and may reasonably ask for his wares the countenance of the Church.

The so-called circus of to-day, with, I regret to say, some exceptions, is a widely different affair from that of the past. When under proper management it is decorous and orderly in operation and composed of features which appeal to all ages, classes and conditions. While modestly submitting to bear the generic title of circus, a genuine tent exhibition under that name must comprise a menagerie and museum, the accumulating of which necessitates a diligent searching of the whole earth at an incredible pecuniary outlay. In the proper circus of to-day the athlete demonstrates the perfection of training of which the human body is capable. His feats of strength and graceful agility please the understanding as well as the eye, and if the average small boy does stand on his head and practice turning "hand-springs" and "flip-flaps" with exasperating persistence for three weeks running after going to the circus his physique will be all the better for it. The juggler shows the marvelous precision and nicety of touch which can be acquired by patient practice. In the real circus of to-day the intelligent lover of horse-flesh will find the finest specimens of the equine race trained to do almost anything but talk. There the scientific mind is attracted by such strange examples of mechanism as the talking machine, an ingenious duplicate of the structure of the human throat, giving forth, under manipulation, a very human, if not very sweet, voice. The ethnologist finds gathered together for his leisurely inspection representatives of notable and peculiar tribes, civilized and savage, from far distant lands — types which otherwise he would never see, as they can only be sought in their native countries at the risk of life, and at an expenditure of time and money possible to very few. The menagerie of wild beasts, birds and reptiles — comprising every curious specimen of animal life from the denizens of the torrid African jungle to those of the Polar regions — form a study that will impart more valuable information in two hours than can be obtained from reading books on zoology in a year.

The morality of a genuine circus troupe compares favorably with that of any equal number of any other profession or trade. Many of them are educated and intelligent; most are loyal to strong family affections and to such domesticity as is attainable while traveling. For the rest, they are obliged to behave well. The circus proprietor has a more complete jurisdiction over his employes than any pastor over his congregation. Would any clergyman dare to punish profanity by fine, drunkenness by expulsion? which is exactly what the best type of circus proprietor can do and does. He has the whip hand, and retains during the season a proportion of the employe's salary, which is paid at the end of the season if the record is good, not otherwise. Business interests compel strict discipline, and who shall say that the employe who is compelled to behave well is not, at the end of the season, somewhat the better for eight months of compulsory sobriety, civility and orderly living?

The best circus of to-day is not a fair mark for the Church's hostility, and while the circus has advanced in merit, the Church has no less grown in tolerance. In my capacity of circus proprietor I have been the recipient of many flattering and amusing amenities on the part of the Church. As, for instance, when on Sunday evening, May 21, 1882, I entered the Church of the Messiah, New York City, Rev. Robert Collyer pastor, and quietly took a back seat only to find the keen, clear eyes of the preacher fixed upon me, and to hear his resonant voice announce, " I see P. T. Barnum in a back pew of this church, and I invite him to come forward and take a seat in my family pew. Mr. Barnum always gives me a good seat in his circus, and I want to give him as good in my church." I thought the reverend gentleman had the courage of his convictions to a most unusual degree, and I was grateful to his congregation for the gravity with which they listened to this very remarkable "pulpit notice" and made way for me as, with some embarrassment, I took the prominent seat so peremptorily indicated.

Again, a few days before my great show was to visit St. Albans, Vt., I received a letter signed by the clergy of that town reminding me that my organization was to arrive among them on Sunday morning early, and asking that I would give orders that none of the paraphernalia, wagons, etc., should be in transit between the railroad depot and the show grounds during the hours of divine service. I was punctilious in seeing that their very reasonable request was respected. Being in St. Albans myself that Sunday, I received, with my company, printed invitations to attend a prominent church. I, at least, went, and heard a very good sermon, and the preacher did not take the occasion to decry the calling I represented, as happened to Miss Emma Abbott, recently.

I will not say whether I think it was well or ill-advised of her to rise in meeting and combat the ungenerous strictures of the preacher, but I did the same thing myself (after the benediction was pronounced), under the same provocation, in Lenox, Mass., fifty-one years ago, and had a most attentive and sympathetic audience, as I doubt not Miss Abbott had.

Many prominent clergymen have written me the most cordial expressions of their approbation of my circus and of their personal pleasure in attending it.

This is what Henry Ward Beecher said:

"I should like, if I had time, to visit your gigantic combination once a week during the whole season, for there is so much to see that no one could do the matter justice in less time."

The Rev. E. H. Chapin was equally unprejudiced, for he wrote:

"My Dear Barnum: It gives me great pleasure to express my *sincere* opinion, that in the entertainments which you have furnished for the public, your patrons have always received a full and profitable money's-worth, and that they are fitted not only to amuse, but to *instruct*, and are certainly free from anything that can be in the least objectionable to any refined or religious person."

I will append only one more of the many kind notes from eminent clergymen which I have received. This is from the Rev. Theo. L. Cuyler:

"My Dear Old Friend: 'The King never dies.' This old maxim of royalty seems to apply to you as the King of Exhibitors and Caterers, not merely to the public amusement, but to popular instruction.

"Millions of 'little folks' may consider you their benefactor in affording them innocent gratification. I have several times taken my children to your museums, menageries and exhibitions, and have not observed there anything profane or impure. I especially thank you for your allegiance (both in your practice and in your business) to the principle of *total abstinence from all intoxicants*.

"With a thousand good wishes, and with kindest regards to your family, I remain,
"Yours   sincerely,   THEO. L. CUYLER."

The religious press has been no less complimentary. Perhaps my experience
has been exceptionally fortunate, but I am convinced that the Church and my circus, at least, are to-day on very good terms.

A secular recognition of my Great Show as an educator — a recognition of which
I am very proud — is contained in the following letter:

"UNITED STATES NATIONAL MUSEUM,
UNDER THE DIRECTION OF
THE SMITHSONIAN INSTITUTE,
WASHINGTON, May 1, 1882.

"DEAR MR. BARNUM: Will you do us the favor to allow Mr. Clark Mills to
make a face-mask of your countenance from which to prepare a bust for the National Museum, to be placed in our series of representations of men who have distinguished themselves for what they have done as promoters of the natural sciences.
"Very truly yours,   SPENCER BAIRD.
"P. T. BARNUM, ESQ."

And my generous foe, the late Mr. Henry Bergh, the well-known and respected
President of "The Society for the Prevention of Cruelty to Animals," with whom I
have had several tilts, said in a letter to a New York paper in the summer of 1885:
"I regard Mr. Barnum as one of the most humane and kind-hearted men living. *
* * He manages an exhibition which, in view of its vast magnitude and amazing
excellence of details, has no equal in the world."

CHAPTER LXXXV.

HOW TO GET RICH, AND HOW TO LIVE LONG AND HAPPY.

OW, as to the means of becoming rich: Those who really desire to attain an independence have only to set their minds upon it, and adopt the proper means, as they do in regard to any other object which they wish to accomplish, and the thing is easily done. But, however easy it may be found to make money, I have no doubt most people will agree it is the most difficult thing in the world to keep it.

The road to wealth is, as Dr. Franklin truly says, "as plain as the road to mill." It consists simply in expending less than we earn. Many may say, "We understand this; this is economy, and we know economy is wealth; we know we can't eat our cake and keep it also." Yet, perhaps, more failures arise from mistakes on this point than almost any other.

True economy is misapprehended, and people go through life without properly comprehending what that principle is. There are many who think that economy consists in saving cheese parings and candle ends, in cutting off twopence from the laundress' bill, and doing all sorts of little mean things. Economy is not meanness. This false economy may frequently be seen in men of business, and in those instances it often runs to writing paper. You find good business men who save all the old envelopes and scraps, and would not tear a new sheet of paper, if they could avoid it, for the world. That is all very well; they may in this way save five or ten dollars a year, but being so economical (only in note-paper) they think they can afford to waste time, to have expensive parties, and to drive their carriages. True economy consists in always making the income exceed the outgo.

The real comforts of life cost but a small portion of what most of us can earn. It is the fear of what Mrs. Grundy may say that keeps the noses of many worthy families to the grindstone. You cannot accumulate a fortune by taking the road that leads to poverty. It needs no prophet to tell us those who live fully up to their means, without any thought of a reverse in this life, can never attain a pecuniary independence.

The foundation of success in life is good health; that is the substratum of fortune. Then, how important it is to study the laws of health, which is but another name for the laws of nature. The closer we keep to the laws of nature the nearer we are to good health. Tobacco and rum should be shunned. To make money requires a clear brain. No matter how bountifully a man may be blessed with intelligence, if the brain is muddled and his judgment warped by intoxicating drinks, it is impossible for him to carry on business successfully.

The safest plan, and the one most sure of success for the young man starting in life, is to select the vocation which is most congenial to his tastes. There is as much diversity in our brains as in our countenances. Some men are born mechanics, while some have a great aversion to machinery. Unless a man enters upon a vocation intended for him by nature, and best suited to his peculiar genius, he cannot succeed. After securing the right vocation, you must be careful to select the proper location, and not begin business where there are already enough to meet all demands in the same occupation.

Young men starting in life should avoid running into debt. There is scarcely anything that drags a person down like debt. Debt robs a man of his self-respect, and makes him almost despise himself. Money is a terrible master, but a very excellent servant. It is no "eye servant." There is nothing that will work so faithfully as money when placed at interest, well secured. It works day and night, and in wet or dry weather.

When a man is in the right path he must persevere; and perseverance is sometimes but another word for self-reliance. Until you can get so you can rely upon yourself, you need not expect to succeed. What ever you do, do it with all your might. Many a man acquires a fortune by doing his business thoroughly, while his neighbor remains poor for life because he only half does it. Ambition, energy, industry and perseverance are indispensable requisites for success in business.

No man has a right to expect to succeed in life unless he understands his business, and nobody can understand his business thoroughly unless he learns it by personal application and experience. You must exercise caution in laying your plans, but be bold in carrying them out. A man who is all caution will never dare to take hold and be successful, and a man who is all boldness is merely reckless, and must eventually fall.

There is no such thing in the world as luck. If a man adopts proper methods to be successful, luck will not prevent him. If he does not succeed, there are reasons for it, although, perhaps, he may not be able to see them.

Money is good for nothing unless you know the value of it by experience. Give a boy $20,000 and put him in business, and the chances are that he will lose every dollar of it before he is a year older. Nine out of ten of the rich men of our country to-day started out in life as poor boys, with determined wills, industry, perseverance, economy and good habits.

The great ambition should be to excel all others engaged in the same occupation. Whenever you find the best doctor, best clergyman, best shoemaker, or anything else, that man is most sought for, and always has enough to do.

Every boy should learn some trade or profession. Engage in one kind of business only, and stick to it faithfully until you succeed, or until your experience shows that you should abandon it. A constant hammering on one nail will generally drive it home at last, so that it can be clinched. There is good sense in the old caution about having too many irons in the fire at once. Beware of "outside operations."

Read the newspapers, and keep thoroughly posted in regard to the transactions of the world. He who doesn't consult the newspapers will soon find himself and his business left out in the cold.

Be careful to advertise in some shape or other, because it is evident that if a man has ever so good an article for sale, and nobody knows it, it will bring him no return. The whole philosophy of life is, first sow, then reap. This principle applies to all kinds of business, and to nothing more eminently than to advertising. If a man has a really good article, there is no way in which he can reap more advantageously than by "sowing" to the public in this way. If a man has goods for sale, and he doesn't advertise them, the chances are that some day the sheriff will do it for him.

Politeness and civility are the best capital ever invested in business. Large stores, gilt signs, flaming advertisements will all prove unavailing if you or your employes treat your patrons abruptly. The more kind and liberal a man is, the more generous will be the patronage bestowed upon him.

Preserve your integrity; it is more precious than diamonds or rubies. The most difficult thing in life is to make money dishonestly. Our prisons are full of men who have attempted to follow this course. No man can be dishonest without soon being found out, and when his lack of principle is discovered, nearly every avenue to success is closed against him forever. Strict honesty not only lies at the foundation of all success in life financially, but in every other respect.

As to the means of preserving life to a green old age, I think the rules are so simple that I can add nothing that is new. You need not be told that the use of tobacco in any form, and, worse than all, the vile habit of cigarette smoking, is extremely hurtful. Alcohol is the greatest curse of the age, and there are few of my readers who have not seen examples of the moral, mental and physical ruin it has wrought.

You should be regular in your habits, moderate in eating and drinking, take abundant exercise, and above all cultivate an unvarying belief in the great truth that your life, as well as the world itself, is governed by One infinitely wiser than the wisest of us, and who "doeth all things well."

Longevity often depends more on the mind than on the food we eat. Care kills a cat. Fear, unpleasant forebodings, apprehensions, fretfulness, anger, envy, malice, and undue selfishness affect the brain, react on the stomach, produce disease, cause a morbid state of mind, constant unhappiness, and premature death. If one does right his mind should never be disturbed by anything which he cannot prevent. He should be thoroughly convinced that if he does his duty Providence will take care of the rest. and never send accident, poverty, disease, or any other apparent evil except for an ultimate good purpose. I never have a spirit of envy or malice and regard cheerfulness as wise and conducive to health and happiness. I own a small dollar book which I would not sell for a thousand dollars if I could not replace it. It is an admirable selection of fine thoughts, finely expressed by ancient and modern writers. It teaches in a marked degree the whole philosophy of living happily and living long. Its title is "Daily Strength for Daily Needs."

It is better when it can be avoided to do no mental labor in the latter part of the day, but to spend the evening in reading or recreation with pleasant companions. I am convinced that man or beast can do more labor in six consecutive days than in seven, and therefore that one day in seven should be devoted to rest of body and mind.

CHAPTER LXXXVI.

THE REASON WHY IN NATURAL HISTORY.

THE wonderful provision of nature in the adaptation of *means* to *end*, is nowhere more strikingly illustrated than in the peculiarities of structure which mark the different members of the animal kingdom, adapting each to its environment, providing the means of defense and sustenance; and in that instinctive knowledge of the hidden forces of nature which enables them to perceive the approach of storms, changes of temperature, etc., and seek means of safety. Nothing can be more interesting and instructive than to trace the *reason* of these peculiarities in animal and insect life, and thus in the book of nature read the wisdom of the Creator.

The form of question and answer has here been adopted for the reason that the facts can thus be presented in the least possible space, and in the manner best adapted to the understanding of the young.

ANIMALS.

1. *Why are there so many bodily forms in the animal creation?*

Because the various creatures which God has created have different modes of life, and the forms of their bodies will be found to present a perfect adaptation to the lives allotted to them.

Because, also, the beauty of creation depends upon the variety of objects of which it consists. And the greatness of the Creator's power is shown by the diversity of ends accomplished by different means.

2. *Why do the furs of animals become thicker in the winter than in the summer?*

Because the Creator has thus provided for the preservation of the warmth of the animals during the cold months of winter.

3. *Why have dogs and other carnivorous animals long pointed teeth projecting above the rest?*

Because as they have not hands to seize and control their food, the projecting teeth enable them to snap and hold the objects which they pursue for food.

4. *Why is the under-jaw of the hog shorter and smaller than the upper one?*

Because the animal pierces the ground with its long snout, and then the small under-jaw works freely in the furrow that has been opened in quest of food.

5. *Why have animals with long necks large throats?*

Animals that graze, or feed from the ground, generally have a more powerful muscular formation of the throat than those which feed in other positions, because a greater effort is required to force the food upward, than would be needed to convey it down.

6. *Why have otters, seals, etc., web-feet?*

Because, while the feet enable them to walk upon the land, they are equally effective in their action upon the water, and hence they are adapted to the amphibious nature of the animals to which they belong.

7. *Why do the external ears of animals of prey, such as cats, tigers, foxes, wolves, hyenas, etc., bend forward?*

Because they collect the sounds that occur in the direction of the pursuit, and enable the animal to track its prey with greater certainty.

8. *Why do the ears of animals of flight, such as hares, rabbits, deer, etc., turn backward?*

Because they thereby catch the sounds that give them warning of the approach of danger.

9. *Why has the stomach of the camel a number of distinct bags, like so many separate stomachs?*

Because water is stored up in the separate chambers of the stomach, apart from the solid aliment, so that the animal can feed, without consuming all its drink. It is thereby able to retain water to satisfy its thirst while traveling across hot deserts, where no water could be obtained.

10. *Why have the Indian hogs large horns growing from their nostrils and turning back towards their eyes?*

Because the horns serve as a defense to the eyes while the animal forces its way through the thick underwood in which it lives.

11. *Why have calves and lambs, and the young of horned cattle generally, no horns while they are young?*

Because the presence of horns would interfere with the suckling of the young animal. When, however, it is able to feed itself by browsing, then the horns begin to grow.

12. *Why cannot flesh-eating animals live upon vegetables?*

Because the gastric juice of a flesh-eating animal, being adapted to the duty which it has to perform, will not dissolve vegetable matter.

13. *Why has the mole hard and flat feet, armed with sharp nails?*

Because the animal is thereby enabled to burrow in the earth, in search for worms. Its feet are so many shovels.

14. *Why is the mole's fur exceedingly glossy and smooth?*

Because its smoothness enables it to work under ground without the soil sticking to its coat, by which its progress would be impeded. From soils of all kinds, the little worker emerges shining and clean.

15. *Why has the elephant a short, unbending neck?*

Because the elephant's head is so heavy, that it could not have been supported at the end of a long neck (or lever), without a provision of immense muscular power.

16. *Why has the elephant a trunk?*

The trunk of an elephant serves as a substitute for a neck, enabling the animal to crop the branches of trees, or to raise water from the stream.

According to Cuvier, the number of muscles in an elephant's trunk amounts to *forty thousand*, all of which are under the will, and it is to these that the proboscis of this animal owes its flexibility It can be protruded or contracted at pleasure, raised up or turned to either side, coiled round on itself or twined around any object With this instrument the elephant collects the herbage on which he feeds and puts it into his mouth, with this he strips the trees of their branches, or grasps his enemy and dashes him to the ground. But this admirable organ is not only adapted for seizing or holding substances of magnitude; it is also capable of plucking a single leaf, or of picking up a straw from the floor. The orifices of the canals of the extremity are encircled by a projecting margin, produced anteriorly into a finger-like process endowed with a high degree of sensibility and exceedingly flexible. It is at once a finger for grasping and a feeler; the division between the two nasal orifices or their elevated sides serves as a point against which to press, and thus it can pick up or hold a small coin, a bit of biscuit, or any trifling thing with the greatest ease

17. *Why do the hind-legs of elephants bend forward?*

Because the weight of the animal is so great, that when it lay down it would rise with great difficulty, if its legs bent outward, as do the legs of other animals. Being bent under the body, they have a greater power of pushing directly upward, when the powerful muscles of the thighs straighten them.

18. *Why have bats hooked claws in their wings?*

Because bats are almost destitute of legs and feet; at least those organs are included in their wings. If they alight upon the ground, they have great difficulty in again taking to the wing, as they cannot run or spring to bring their wings in action upon the air. At the angle of each wing there is placed, therefore, a bony hook, by which the bat attaches itself to the sides of rocks, caves, and buildings, laying hold of crevices, joinings, chinks, etc.; and when it takes its flight, it unhooks itself, and its wings are at once free to strike the air.

19. *Why does the bat fly by night?*

Because it lives chiefly upon moths, which are night-flying insects.

20. *Why does the bat sleep during the winter?*

Because, as the winter approaches, the moths and flying insects upon which it feeds, disappear. If, therefore, it did not sleep through the winter, it must have starved.

21. *Why do oxen, sheep, deer, etc., ruminate?*

Because they have no front teeth in the upper jaw, the place of which is occupied by a hardened gum. The first process, therefore, consists simply of cropping their food, which is passed into the paunch, to be brought up again and ground by the back teeth when the cropping process is over.

Because, in a wild state, they are constantly exposed to the attacks of carnivorous beasts, and as the mastication of the large amount of vegetable food required for their sustenance would take a considerable time, they are provided with stomachs, by which they are enabled to fill their paunches quickly, and then, retiring to a place of safety, they bring their food up again, and chew it at leisure.

22. *Why can ruminating animals recover the food from their paunches?*

Because they have a voluntary power over the muscles of the throat, by which they can bring up the food at will.

23. *Why can they keep the unchewed food in the paunch, from the "cud" they have chewed for nourishment?*

Because their stomachs are divided into three chambers: 1, the paunch, where the unchewed food is stored; 2, the reticulum, where portions of the food are received from the paunch, and moistened and rolled into a "cud," to be sent up and chewed; and 3, the psalterium, which receives the masticated food, and continues the process of digestion.

In quadrupeds the deficiency of teeth is usually *compensated* by the faculty of rumination. The sheep, deer and ox tribe are without fore-teeth in the upper jaw. These ruminate. The horse and ass are furnished with teeth in the upper jaw, and do not ruminate. In the former class the grass and hay descend into the stomachs nearly in the state in which they are cropped from the pasture, or gathered from the bundle. In the stomach, they are softened by the gastric juice, which in these animals is unusually copious. Thus softened and rendered tender, they are returned a second time to the action of the mouth, where the grinding teeth complete at their leisure the trituration which is necessary, but which was before left imperfect. I say, the trituration which is necessary, for it appears from experiments that the gastric fluid of sheep, for example, has no effect in digesting plants, unless they have been previously masticated; that it only produces a slight maceration, nearly as common water would do in a like degree of heat, but that when once vegetables are reduced to pieces by mastication, the fluid then exerts upon them its specific operation. Its first effect is to soften them, and to destroy their natural consistency, it then

goes on to dissolve them, not sparing even the toughest parts, such as the nerves of the leaves. It is very probable, that the gratification also of the animal is renewed and prolonged by this faculty. Sheep, deer and oxen appear to be in a state of enjoyment whilst they are chewing the cud. It is then, perhaps, that they best relish their food.

24. *Why do quadrupeds that are vegetable eaters feed so continually?*

Because their food contains but a small proportion of nutrition, so that it is necessary to digest a large quantity to obtain sufficient nourishment.

25. *Why do flesh-eating animals satisfy themselves with a rapid meal?*

Because the food which they eat is rich in nutritious matter, and more readily digestible than vegetable food; it does not, therefore, require the same amount of grinding with the teeth.

26. *Why do the smaller animals breed more abundantly than the larger ones?*

Because the smaller ones are designed to be the food of the larger ones, and are therefore created in numbers adapted to that end. An elephant produces but one calf; the whale but one young one; a butterfly lays six hundred eggs; silk worms lay from 1,000 to 2,000 eggs; the wasp, 5,000; the ant, 4,000 to 5,000; the queen bee, 5,000 to 6,000, or 40,000 to 50,000 in a season; and a species of white ant (*termes fatalis*) produces 86,400 eggs in a day. Birds of prey seldom produce more than two eggs; the sparrow and duck tribe frequently sit upon a dozen; in rivers there prevail a thousand minnows for one pike; and in the sea, a million of herrings for a single shark; while of the animalcules upon which the whale subsists, there must exist hundreds of millions for one whale.

27. *Why have cats, and various other animals, whiskers?*

The whiskers of cats, and of the cat tribe, are exceedingly sensitive, enabling them, when seizing their prey in the dark, to feel its position most acutely. These hairs are supplied, through their roots, with branches of the same nerves that give sensibility to the lips, and that in insects supply their "feelers."

28. *Why has the horse a smaller stomach proportionately than other animals?*

Because the horse was created for speed. Had he the ruminating stomach of the ox, he would be quite unfitted for the labor which he now so admirably performs.

29. *Why has the horse no gall-bladder?*

Because the rapid digestion of the horse, by which its fitness for speed is greatly increased, does not require the storing up of the bile as in other animals in which the digestive process is a slower operation.

30. *Why have oxen and other quadrupeds a tough ligament called the "pax-wax," running from their backs to their heads?*

Because their heads are of considerable weight; and having frequent occasion to lift them, they are provided with an elastic ligament, which is fastened at the middle of their backs, while its other extremity is attached to the head. This enables them to raise their heads easily; otherwise the effort to do so would be a work of great labor. To the horse, the pax-wax acts as a natural bearing-rein, assisting it to hold its head in that position which adds to the grace and beauty of the animal.

31. *Why have the females of the kangaroo and opossum tribes pouches, or pockets, formed in the skin of their breasts for the reception of their young?*

Because their young ones are remarkably small and helpless; in fact, more so than those of any other animal of equal proportions. Besides which, the full-grown animals have very long hind-legs, and they progress by a series of extraordinary leaps. It would consequently be impossible for their helpless young ones to follow them. God has therefore given to female kangaroos and opossums curious pockets, formed out of their own skin, in which they place their little young ones, and bear them through their surprising leaps with the greatest ease and safety.

32. *Why do animals that graze, crop the tender blades of grass, but avoid the tall stems?*

Because they are tempted by the greater sweetness and tenderness of the young blades; and in this temptation a very important end is served; for, by avoiding the stems that have grown up, the animals spare the matured plant by which seeds are borne, and by which the supply of food is to be continued.

33. *Why has the giraffe a small head?*

Because, being set upon the end of a very long neck, the animal would be unable to raise it if it were heavy.

34. *Why has the giraffe a long neck?*

Because it feeds upon the branches of tall trees.

35. *Why has the giraffe a long and flexible tongue?*

Because it is thereby enabled to lay hold of the tender twigs and branches, and draw them into its mouth, avoiding the coarser parts of the branches.

36. *Why are the nostrils of the giraffe small and narrow, and studded with hairs?*

Because the hairs and the peculiar shape of the nasal passages are designed as a protection against the insects which inhabit the boughs of the trees upon which the giraffe feeds; and also against the sands of the desert, which storms raise into almost suffocating clouds.

BIRDS.

37. *Why are birds covered with feathers?*

Because they require a high degree of warmth, on account of the activity of their muscles; but in providing that warmth it was necessary that their coats should be of the lightest material, so as not to impair their powers of flight; and feathers combine the highest warming power, with the least amount of weight.

38. *Why have ostriches small wings?*

Because, having long legs, they do not require their wings for flight; they are merely used to steady their bodies while running.

39. *Why are ostrich feathers soft and downy?*

Because, as the feathers are not employed for flight, the strength of the feathers as constructed for flying is unnecessary, and the feathers therefore consist chiefly of a soft down.

40. *Why have water-birds feathers of a close and smooth texture?*

Because such feathers keep the body of the bird warm and dry, by repelling the water from their surface. A bird could scarcely move through the water with the downy feathers of the ostrich, because of the amount of water the down would absorb.

41. *Why does a black down grow under the feathers of birds as winter approaches ?*

Because the down is a non-conductor of heat, and black the warmest color. It is therefore best adapted to keep in their bodily warmth during the cold of winter.

42. *Why have birds hard beaks ?*

Because, having no teeth, the beak enables them to seize, hold, and divide their food.

43. *Why are the beaks of birds generally long and sharp ?*

Because the greater number of birds live by picking up small objects, such as worms, insects, seeds, etc. The sharp beak, therefore, serves as a fine pincers, enabling them to take hold of their food conveniently.

44. *Why have snipes and woodcocks long tapering bills ?*

Because they live upon worms which they find in the soft mud of streams and marshy places ; their long bills, therefore, enable them to dig down into the mud after their prey.

45. *Why have woodcocks, snipes, etc., nerves running down to the extremities of their bills ?*

Because, as they dig for their prey in the soft sand and mud, they cannot see the worms upon which they live. Nerves are therefore distributed to the very point of their bills (where, in other birds, nerves are entirely absent) to enable them to prehend their food.

46. *Why have ducks and geese square-pointed bills ?*

Because they not only feed by dabbling in soft and muddy soil, but they consume a considerable quantity of green food, and their square bills enable them to crop off the blades of grass.

47. *Why has the spoon-bill a long expanded bill lined internally with sharp muscular points ?*

Because the bird lives by suction, dipping its broad bill in search of aquatic worms, mollusks, insects and the roots of weeds. The bill forms a natural spoon. and the muscular points enable the bird to filter the mud, and to retain the nourishment which it finds.

48. *Why has the spoon-bill long legs ?*

Because it wades in marshy places to find its food. Its legs are therefore long, for the purpose of keeping its body out of the water, and above the smaller aquatic plants, while it searches for its prey.

49. *Why have the parrots, etc., crooked and hard bills ?*

Because they live upon nuts, the stones of fruit, and hard seeds. The shape of the bill, therefore, enables them to hold the nut or seed firmly, and the sharp point enables them to split or remove the husks.

50. *Why can a parrot move its upper as well as its lower bill ?*

Because by that means it is enabled to bring the nut or seed nearer the fulcrum, or joint of the jaw. It therefore acquires greater power, just as with a pair of nut-crackers we obtain increased power by setting the nut near to the joint.

51. *Why are the bones of birds hollow ?*

Because they are thereby rendered lighter, and do not interfere with the flight of the bird as they would do if they were solid. Greater strength is also obtained by the cylindrical form of the bone, and a larger surface afforded for the attachment of powerful muscles.

52. *Why do all birds lay eggs ?*

Because, to bear their young in any other manner, would encumber the body, and materially interfere with their powers of flight.

As soon as an egg becomes large and heavy enough to be cumbersome to the bird, it is removed from the body. A shell, impervious to air, protects the germ of life within, until from two to twenty eggs have accumulated, and then, although laid at different intervals, their incubation commences together, and the young birds are hatched at the same time

53. *Why have birds with long legs short tails ?*

Because the tails of birds are used to guide them through the air, by a kind of steerage. When birds with long legs take to flight, they throw their legs behind, and they then serve the same purpose as a tail.

54. *Why have birds that swim upon water web-feet ?*

Because the spreading out of the toes of the bird brings the membrane between the toes into the form of a fin, or water-wing, by striking which against the water the bird propels itself along.

55. *Why have birds that swim and dive short legs ?*

Because long legs would greatly impede their motions in the water, by becoming repeatedly entangled in the weeds, and by striking against the bottom. Waders, however, require long legs because they have to move about through the tall vegetation of marshy borders.

56. Why have the feet of the heron, cormorant, etc., deep rough notches upon their under surface?

Because, as those birds live by catching fish, they are enabled by the notches in their feet, to hold the slippery creatures upon which they feed.

57. Why do woodpeckers "tap" at old trees?

Because by boring through the decayed wood, with the sharp and hard bills with which they are provided, they get at the haunts of the insects upon which they feed.

58. Why are woodpeckers' tongues about three times longer than their bills?

Because, if their bills were long, they would not bore the trees so efficiently; and when the trees are bored, and the insects alarmed, they endeavor to retreat into the hollows of the wood; but the long thin tongue of the woodpecker fixes them on its sharp horny point, and draws them into the mouth of the bird.

59. Why have birds gizzards?

Because, having no teeth, the tough and fibrous gizzards are employed to grind the food preparatory to digestion.

60. Why are small particles of sand, stone, etc., found in the gizzards of birds?

Because, by the presence of those rough particles, which become embedded in the substance of the gizzard, the food of the bird is more effectively ground.

When our fowls are abundantly supplied with meat, they soon fill their craw, but it does not immediately pass thence into the gizzard, it always enters in small quantities, in proportion to the progress of trituration; in like manner, as in a mill, a receiver is fixed above the two large stones which serve for grinding the corn, which receiver, although the corn be put into it by bushels, allows the grain to dribble only in small quantities into the central hole in the upper mill-stone

61. Why have birds of prey no gizzards?

Because their food does not require to be ground prior to digestion, as does the food of grain-eating birds.

62. Why has the pelican a large pouch under its bill?

Because it subsists upon fish, generally of the smaller kind, and uses its pouch as a net for catching them; the pouch also serves as a paunch, in which the fish are stored, until the bird ceases from the exertion of fishing, and takes its meal at leisure.

In their wild state they hover and wheel over the surface of the water watching the shoals of fish beneath, and suddenly sweeping down, bury themselves in the foaming waves, rising immediately from the water by their own buoyancy, up they soar, the pouch laden with the fish scooped up during their momentary submersion. The number of fish the pouch of this species will contain may be easily imagined when we state that it is so dilatable as to be capable of containing two gallons of water, yet the bird has the power of contracting this membraneous expansion, by wrinkling it up under the lower mandible, until it is scarcely to be seen In shallow inlets, which the pelicans often frequent, it nets its prey with great adroitness The pelican chooses remote and solitary islands, isolated rocks in the sea, the borders of lakes and rivers, as its breeding-place The nest, placed on the ground, is made of coarse grasses, and the eggs, which are white, are two or three in number While the female is incubating, the male brings fish to her in his pouch, and the young, when hatched, are assiduously attended by the parents, who feed them by pressing the pouch against the breast, so as to transfer the fish from the former into the throats of the young The action has doubtless given origin to the old fable of the pelican feeding its young with blood drawn from its own breast.

63. Why does the lower bill of the sea-crow project beyond the upper one?

Because the bird obtains his food by skimming along the water into which he dips his bill, and lifts his food out.

64. Why do the mandibles of the cross-bill overlap each other?

Because the bird requires a peculiar bill, to enable it to split seeds into halves, and to tear the open cones of the fir-tree.

INSECTS.

65. Why has the spider the power of spinning a web?

Because, as it lives upon flies, but is deficient of the power of flying in pursuit of them, it has been endowed with an instinct to spread a snare to entrap them, and with the most wonderful machinery to give that instinct effect.

There are few things better suited to remove the disgust into which young people are betrayed on the view of some natural objects, than this of the spider. They will find that the most despised creature may become a subject of admiration, and be selected by the naturalist to exhibit the marvellous works of the creation The terms given to these insects lead us to expect interesting particulars concerning them, since they have been divided into vagrants, hunters, swimmers, and water spiders, sedentary, and mason-spiders, thus evincing a variety in their condition, activity, and mode of life; and we cannot be surprised to find them varying in the performance of their vital functions (as, for example, in their mode of breathing), as well as in their extremities and instruments Of these instruments the most striking is the apparatus for spinning and weaving, by which they not only fabricate webs to entangle their prey, but form cells for their residence and concealment, sometimes living in the ground, sometimes under water, yet breathing the atmosphere Corresponding with their very singular organization are their instincts We are familiar with the watchfulness and voracity of some spiders, when their prey is indicated by the vibration of the cords of their net-work. Others have the eye and disposition of the lynx or tiger, and after crouching in concealment, leap upon their victims. Some conceal themselves under a silken hood or tube, six eyes only projecting Some bore a hole in the earth, and line it as finely as if it were done with the trowel and mortar, and then hang it with delicate curtains A very extraordinary degree of contrivance is exhibited in the trap-door spider. This door, from which it derives its name, has a frame and hinge on the mouth of the cell, and is so provided that the claw of the spider can lay hold of it, and whether she enters or goes out, the door shuts of itself But the water-spider has a domicile more curious still, it is under water, with an opening at the lower part for her exit and entrance, and although this cell be under water, it contains air like a diving-bell, so that the spider breathes the atmosphere The air is renewed in the cell in a manner not easily explained The spider comes to the surface, a bubble of air is attracted to its body, with this air she descends, and gets under her cell, when the air is disengaged and rises into the cell, and thus, though under water, she lives in the air There must be some peculiar property of the surface of this creature by which she can move in the water surrounded with an atmosphere, and live under the water breathing the air

The chief instrument by which the spider performs these wonders is the spinning apparatus The matter from which the threads are spun is the liquid contained in cells; the ducts from these cells open upon little projecting teats, and the atmosphere has so immediate an effect upon this liquid, that upon exposure to it the secretion becomes a tough and strong thread Twenty-four of these fine strands form together a thread of the thickness of that of the silk-worm We are assured that there are three different sorts of material thus produced, which are indeed required for the various purposes to which they are applied — as, for example, to mix up with the earth to form the cells, to line these cells as with fine cotton, to make light and floating threads by which they may be conveyed through the air, as well as those meshes which are so geometrically and correctly formed to entrap their prey

66. *Why have many insects a great number of eyes ?*

Because the orb of the eye is fixed ; there is therefore placed over the eye a multiple-lense, which conducts light to the eye from every direction ; so that the insect can see with a fixed eye as readily as it could have done with a moveable one. As many as fourteen hundred eyes, or inlets of light, have been counted in the head of a drone-bee. The spider has eight eyes, mounted upon different parts of the head : two in front, two in the top of the head, and two on each side.

67. *Why do certain butterflies lay their eggs upon cabbage leaves ?*

Because the cabbage leaves are the food of the young caterpillars ; and although the butterfly does not subsist herself upon the leaf, she knows by instinct that the leaf will afford food to her future young ; she therefore lays her eggs where her young ones will find food.

This explanation applies to many insects that lay their eggs upon other plants

68. *Why have insects long projections from their heads, like horns or feathers ?*

Because those organs (the antennæ), are those through which some insects hear and others feel ; and the projecting of these antennæ from their bodies probably enables them to hear or feel more acutely while their wings are in motion, without the interference of the vibrations of their wings.

69. *Why can gossamer spiders float through the air ?*

Because, having no wings, and being deficient in the active muscular powers of other spiders, they have been endowed with the power of spinning a web which is so light that it floats in the air, and bears the body of the gossamer spider from place to place. Each web acts as a balloon, and the spider attached thereto is a little aeronaut.

70. *Why do crickets make a peculiar chirping sound ?*

Because they have hard wing cases, by the friction of the edges of which they cause their peculiar noise, to make known to each other where they are, in the dark crevices in which they hide.

71. *Why has the glow-worm a brush attached to its tail ?*

Because it is necessary to keep its back very clean, that the light which its body emits may not be dimmed.

72. *Why does the glow-worm emit a light ?*

Because the female glow-worm is without wings, but the male is a winged insect. The female, therefore, is endowed with the power of displaying a phosphorescent light. The light is only visible by night, but it is, nevertheless, beautifully adapted for the purpose stated, because the male is a night-flying insect, and never ventures abroad by day.

There exists some difference of opinion between naturalists upon the uses of the light of a glow-worm, there are some who doubt that it is exhibited to attract the flying insect The objectors, however, offer no explanation of the luminous properties of the worm. Sir Charles Bell says the preponderance of the argument is decidedly in favor of the explanation we have given.

73. *Why have bees stings ?*

Because they gather and store up honey which would constantly attract other insects, and the bees would be robbed of their food but for the sting, which is given to them for protection.

74. *Why have flies fine hairs growing at the extremities of their legs ?*

Because they require to cleanse their bodies and wings and to free them from particles of dust. As they cannot turn their heads for this purpose, they have hairy feet which serve as brushes and by which any part of their bodies can be reached and cleaned.

75. *Why do the eggs of butterflies lie dormant during the winter ?*

Because the coldness of the winter would be fatal to the life of the young insects ; and the absence of vegetation would leave the caterpillars to perish of starvation, if they were developed during the winter months.

76. *Why do caterpillars appear in the spring ?*

Because the increasing warmth of the sun develops the living embryo, at the same time that it develops the vegetable germ. The warmth, therefore, that calls the caterpillar from its embryo sleep, also kindles the germinating power of the vegetable upon which it is destined to feed. The worm awakes and finds the bountiful table of nature spread for it.

77. *Why does the caterpillar eat voraciously ?*

Because it grows rapidly, and a large amount of vegetable matter is necessary to supply the rapid growth of its animal substance. Caterpil-lars in the course of a month devour 60,000 times their own weight of aliment.

78. *Why do caterpillars pass into the state of the chrysalis ?*

Because they are thereby prepared for the new existence which they are about to enjoy ; new organs must be perfected in them to adapt them to the altered conditions of their lives.

Because, also, in the transformation of their bodies, differing materially from the laws of existence that pertain to other creatures, the Creator affords another illustration of his Omnipotence.

Because, also, during the stage that the insect sleeps in the chrysalis, the flowers and their sweet juices, upon which the fly is to feed, are being prepared for it, just as, when it was sleeping in the egg, the green food was being prepared for the caterpillar. When, therefore, the beautiful fly spreads its silken wings, it finds a second time that, while it has slept, its meal has been prepared, and it now flies away joyously to feed upon the milk and honey of beautiful flowers which, at the time it passed into the chrysalis, had not yet unfolded their petals.

Paley observes, that "the metamorphosis of insects from grubs into moths and flies is an astonishing process A hairy caterpillar is transformed into a butterfly Observe the change. We have four beautiful wings where there were none before; a tubular proboscis, in the place of a mouth with jaws and teeth, six long legs, instead of fourteen feet. In another case, we see a white, smooth, soft worm, turned into a black, hard, crustaceous beetle, with gauze wings. These, as I said, are astonishing processes, and must require, as it should seem, a proportionably artificial apparatus. The hypothesis which appears to me most probable is, that in the grub there exists at the same time three animals, one within another, all nourished by the same digestion, and by a communicating circulation, but in different stages of maturity. The latest discoveries made by naturalists seem to favor this supposition The insect, already equipped with wings, is descried under the membranes both of the worm and nymph In some species, the proboscis, the antennæ, the limbs and wings of the fly, have been observed to be folded up within the body of the caterpillar; and with such nicety as to occupy a small space only under the two first wings This being so, the outermost animal, which, besides its own proper character, serves as an integument to the other two, being the farthest advanced, dies, as we suppose, and drops off first The second, the pupa or chrysalis, then offers itself to observaton This also, in its turn, dies, its dead and brittle husk falls to pieces, and makes way for the appearance of the fly or moth Now, if this be the case, or indeed whatever explication be adopted, we have a prospective contrivance of the most curious kind, we have organizations three deep; yet a vascular system, which supplies nutrition, growth, and life, to all of them together."

79. *Why does the caterpillar become torpid when passing into the state of the chrysalis ?*

Because in all probability, where the difference between the first and the ultimate form is considerable, the organs of the insect having to undergo great changes, it would suffer considerable pain. Torpor comes upon the insect, it is thrown into a state similar to that of a person who has inhaled chloroform; and after what has, in all probability, proved a pleasant dream, the insect awakes to find itself changed and beautified.

80. *Why are the pupæ of grasshoppers and other insects, when about to undergo transformation, still active and sensitive?*

Because, as there is but a slight difference between the form which they have in the pupa state, and that which they ultimately assume, they do not require the state of torpidity to save them from pain, nor to arrest their movements while their organs are being changed. With them the outer skin is thrown off, and they are then perfect insects.

81. *Why do caterpillars, when about to pass through the chrysalis state, attach themselves to the leaves of plants, etc.?*

Because they know instinctively that for a time they will be unable to control their own movements, and to avoid danger. They therefore choose secure and dry places, underneath leaves, or in the crevices of old and dry walls, and there they firmly attach themselves, to await the time of their liberation.

82. *Why do insects attach their eggs to leaves, etc.?*

Because, as the eggs have to be preserved during the winter, the insect attaches them to some surface which will be a protection to them. Generally speaking, the eggs are attached to the permanent stems of plants, and not to those leafy portions which are liable to fall and decay. The spider weaves a silken bag in which it deposits its eggs, and then it hangs the bag in a sheltered situation. Nature keeps her butterflies, moths and caterpillars locked up during the winter, in their egg-state; and we have to admire the various devices to which, if we may so speak, the same nature has resorted for the security of the egg. Many insects enclose their eggs in a silken web; others cover them with a coat of hair, torn from their own bodies; some glue them together; and others, like the moth of the silkworm, glue them to the leaves upon which they are deposited, that they may not be shaken off by the wind, or washed away by rain; some again make incisions into leaves, and hide an egg in each incision; whilst some envelope their eggs with a soft substance, which forms the first aliment of the young animal; and some again make a hole in the earth, and having stored it with a quantity of proper food, deposit their eggs in it.

83. *Why do butterflies fly by day?*

Because they are organized to enjoy light and warmth, and they live upon the sweets of flowers which by day are most accessible.

84. *Why do moths fly by night?*

Because they are organized to enjoy subdued light and cool air; and as they take very little food during the short life they have in the winged state, they find sufficient by night. Some of the moths, like that of the silk-worm, take no food from the time they escape from the chrysalis until they die.

Because, also, they form the food of bats, owls, and other of the night-flying tribes.

85. *Why are the bodies of moths generally covered with a very thick down?*

Because, as they fly by night, they are liable to the effects of cold and damp. The moths, therefore, are nearly all of them covered with a very thick down, quite distinguishable from the lighter down of butterflies.

86. *Why do moths fly against the candle flame?*

Because their eyes are organized to bear only a small amount of light. When, therefore, they come within the light of a candle, their sight is overpowered and their vision confused; and as they cannot distinguish objects, they pursue the light itself, and fly against the flame.

87. *Why do insects multiply so numerously?*

Because they form the food of larger animals, and especially of birds. A single pair of sparrows and a nest of young ones have been estimated to consume upwards of three thousand insects in a week.

88. *Why does the " death-watch " make a ticking noise?*

Because the insect is one of the beetle tribe, having a horny case upon its head, with which it taps upon any hard substance. The ticking is the call of the insect to its species, just as the noise made by the cricket is a note of communication with other crickets.

There is a superstition connected with the death-watch, which, like most superstitions, is based upon the theory of probabilities The death-watch is usually heard in the spring of the year, and a superstition runs to the effect that some one in the house will die before the year has ended. Persons who are superstitious are never very strict in the interpretation of their predictions , and therefore, whether a person dies in the house or out of it, in the same room where the death-watch was heard, or across the wide Atlantic, so that there be some kind of relationship, or even acquaintance, between the person who hears the omen, and the person dying, the event is sure to be connected with the prophetic sounds of the death-watch Little weens the small timber-boring beetle, when he is tapping gently to call his mate, and perhaps peeping into every corner and crevice to find her, that he is sending dismay into the heart of some superstitious listener, who, in ignorance of a simple fact, overwhelms herself with an imaginary grief

89. Why are insects in the first stage, after leaving the egg, said to be in the " larva " state?

Because that name is founded upon the Latin word *larva*, meaning masked, clothed as with a mask ; the term is meant to express that the future insect is diguised in its first form.

90. Why are insects in the second state said to be in the " pupa " state?

Because the term is derived from the Latin *pupa*, from a slight resemblance in the manner in which the insects are enclosed, to that in which it was the fashion of the ancients to bandage their infants.

91. Why are insects in the " pupa " stage also called " chrysalides"?

Because, as the Latin term implies, it is adorned with gems. Many chrysalides are studded with golden and pearl-like spots.

92. Why are the perfect insects said to be in the " nymph " state?

Because their joyful existence, and their beautiful forms, give them a fancied resemblance to the nymphs of the heathen mythology. The nymphs were supposed goddesses of the mountains, forests, meadows, and waters.

This term has generally, but very improperly, been also applied to the pupa state, so that pupa, chrysalis, and nymph have all been employed to represent one state. This is obviously an error, as there is nothing in the condition of the pupa or chrysalis that can at all accord with the mythological idea of a nymph, and which, in reference to the beautiful and joyous fly, finds a much truer application.

93. Whence does the snail obtain its shell?

Young snails come from the egg with a shell upon their backs.

94. How does the shell grow with the increase of size of the animal ?

The soft slime which is yielded by the body of the animal hardens upon the orifice of the shell, and thus increases its size.

95. Why is the shell spiral ?

Partly because of its original formation ; but also because, as the shell grows, the opening is elongated, and thrown up, causing the spiral body of the shell to turn, and so to wind its growth around the center.

96. Why has the snail four tentacula attached to its head ?

Because the insect, having no other limbs, is provided with those projecting members, the lower two serving as feelers and the upper two also as feelers and eyes. These, projecting in the front of the animal, impart to it a consciousness of surrounding objects, and especially of those which lie in its path.

97. Why is the snail able to move without feet ?

Because it has attached to its body a fringe of muscular skin, which is capable of considerable contraction and expansion, and by alternately stretching and shortening this, the snail is able to draw himself along.

98. Why do we see no snails in winter time ?

Because they bury themselves in the ground, or in holes, where they remain in a torpid state for several months. Before they enter into the torpid state, they form with their slimy secretion, and with some earthy matters which they collect, a strong cement with which they seal up the opening to their shells.

99. Why can snails live in shells thus sealed ?

Because they leave, in the thin wall by which they close themselves in, a small hole, too small to admit water, but large enough to let in sufficient air to carry on their feeble respiration during their winter sleep.

100. Why do insects abound in putrid waters, and in decaying substances ?

Because they have been endowed with appetites and with constitutions that enable them to live upon and to enjoy corrupt matter. In this point of view the maggots of flies are exceedingly useful ; a dead carcass is speedily threaded by them in every direction ; thus that corrupt matter which, in a large mass, would poison the air, is taken up in small portions by millions of living bodies, and by them dispersed, and becomes innoxious.

101. *Why do we see, in tanks of rain water, insects rising to the surface?*

Because numerous insects pass through their first stages of existence in water, and among them the common gnat. The gnats of the previous season having deposited their eggs on the sides of the water-butt, the warm water develops them, and the larvæ of the gnats appear.

102. *Why do they continually rise to the surface of the water ?*

Because they require to breathe air, and therefore they come up to the surface, where elevating the tube above the surface of the water, they are enabled to breathe.

103. *Why do some appear to have larger heads than others ?*

Those that have apparently larger heads, and that breathe through tubes attached to their heads, are in the pupa, or second stage of development, and underneath the large shield by which their heads are marked, their wings, feet, etc., are being formed.

104. *Why, when the water is disturbed, do the larvæ descend more rapidly than the pupæ ?*

Because the pupæ are in a torpid condition, awaiting the formation of their perfect organs.

105. *Why are the flies able to escape from the water ?*

Because, as their formation becomes perfected, and the fluids of the body of the pupa become absorbed in the production of the light texture of the wings, etc., the body and its case become lighter than the water, and rise and float upon the surface. The pupa case then forms a natural boat, from which the fly emerges ; and, spreading its wings, enters upon the final state of its existence.

This interesting metamorphosis may be seen going on in the summer time, in every pond, brook, and reservoir. A fine sunny morning calls up millions of these little boats from beneath the surface, and the diver within that wonderful little bell breaks its sealed doors, and flies away to enjoy the bright sunshine.

106. *Why are beetles denominated " coleoptera"?*

Because they have wings protected by horny sheaths ; the term coleoptera signifies wings in a sheath.

107. *Why have beetles hard, horny wing cases ?*

Because they live underground, or in holes excavated in wood, etc. If, therefore, their wings were not protected by a hard and firm covering, they would be constantly liable to destruction from the movement of the insect within hard and rough bodies.

The elytra, or scaly wings of the genus of scarabæus, or beetle, furnish an example of this kind. The true wing of the animal is a light, transparent membrane, finer than the finest gauze, and not unlike it. It is also, when expanded, in proportion to the size of the animal, very large. In order to protect this delicate structure, and, perhaps, also to preserve it in a due state of suppleness and humidity, a strong, hard case is given to it, in the shape of the horny wing which we call the elytron. When the animal is at rest, the gauze wings lie folded up under this impenetrable shield When the beetle prepares for flying, he raises the integument, and spreads out his thin membrane to the air. And it cannot be observed without admiration, what a tissue of cordage, *i e.* of muscular tendons, must run in various and complicated, but determinate directions, along this fine surface, in order to enable the animal either to gather it up into a certain precise form, whenever it desires to place its wings under the shelter which nature has given to them, or to expand again their folds when wanted for action.

In some insects, the elytra cover the whole body ; in others half ; in others only a small part of it ; but in all they completely hide and cover the true wings.

Many, or most of the beetle species lodge in holes in the earth, environed by hard, rough substances, and have frequently to squeeze their way through narrow passages, in which situation, wings so tender, and so large, could scarcely have escaped injury, without both a firm covering to defend them, and the capacity of folding themselves up under its protection.

108. *Why have many of the beetle tribe large, strong horns ?*

Because as they live in holes in the earth, or in excavations in wood, they use their horns to dig out their places of retreat.

FISHES.

109. *Why have fishes fins ?*

The fins of fishes are to them what wings and tails are to birds, enabling them to rise in the fluid in which they live by the reaction of the motions of the fins upon its substance.

110. *Why are the fins of fishes proportionately so much smaller than the wings of birds ?*

Because there is less difference between the specific gravity of the body of a fish, and the water in which it moves, than between the body of a bird, and the air on which it flies. The fish, therefore, does not require such an expanded surface to elevate it or guide it.

111. *Why have fishes scales ?*

Because scales, while they afford protection to the bodies of fish, are conveniently adapted to their motions ; and as the scales present no surface to obstruct their passage through the water, as hair or feathers would do, they evidently form the best covering for the aquatic animal.

112. *Why do fishes float in streams (when they are not swimming) with their heads toward the stream ?*

Because they breathe by the transmission of water over the surface of their gills, the water entering at the mouth, and passing over the gills behind. When, therefore, they lie motionless with their heads to the stream, they are in that position which naturally assists their breathing process.

113. *Why have fishes air-bladders ?*

Because, as the density of water varies greatly at different depths, the enlargement or contraction of the bladder regulates the relation of the specific gravity of the body of the fish to that of the water in which it moves.

114. *Why have whales a very large development of oily matter about their heads ?*

Because their heads are thereby rendered the lighter part of their bodies, and a very slight exertion on the part of the animal will bring its head to the surface to breathe air, which it constantly requires.

115. *Why have mussels strong, tendinous threads proceeding from their shells ?*

Because as they live in places that are beaten by the surf of the sea, they moor their shells by those threads to rocks and timbers.

116. *Why have cockles stiff, muscular tongues ?*

Because, having no threads to moor themselves, as the mussels have, they dig out with their tongues a shelter for themselves in the sand.

117. *Why has the whale feathery-like laminæ of whale-bone extending from its jaws ?*

Because these feathery bones, lying side by side, form a sieve, or strainer, for the large volumes of water which the whale receives into its mouth, drawing off therefrom millions of small animals, which form a jelly-like mass upon which the whale feeds. A whale has been known to weigh as much as 249 tons, and its blubber yielded 4,000 gallons of oil. How many millions of living creatures must have gone to make up that enormous mass of animal matter !

118. *Why does not the iris of the fish's eye contract ?*

Because the diminished light in water is never too strong for the retina.

119. *Why is the eye of the eel covered with a transparent horny covering ?*

Because as the eel lives in holes, and pushes its head into mud, and under stones, etc., it needed such a covering to defend the eye.

120. *Why is the whale provided with an eye having remarkably thick and strong coats ?*

Because, when he is attacked by the sword-fish and the shark, he is almost helpless against its enemies, as they fix themselves upon his huge carcass. He therefore dives with them down to a depth where the pressure of the water is so great that they cannot bear it. The eye of The whale is expressly organized to bear the immense pressure of extreme ocean depths, without impairing the sight.

121. *Why have fishes no eyelids ?*

Because the water in which they swim keeps their eyes moist. Eyelids would therefore be useless to them.

122. *Why have fishes the power of giving their eye-balls very sudden motion ?*

Because, having no eyelids (such organs being unnecessary to keep their eyes moist), they still need the power of freeing their eyes from the contact of foreign matters ; and this is secured to them by the power they have of giving the eye-ball a very rapid motion, which causes reaction in the fluid surrounding it, and sweeps the surface.

This motion may frequently be seen in the eyes of fishes, in glass globes.

123. *Why are the tails of fishes so much larger than their fins ?*

Because their tails are their chief instruments of motion, while their fins are employed simply to direct their progress, and steady their movements.

WEATHER CHANGES
AS INDICATED BY ANIMALS.

The observation of the changing phenomena which attend the various states of the weather is a very interesting study, though no general rules can be laid down that can be relied upon, because there are modifying circumstances which influence the weather in various localities and climates. To observe weather indications accurately, no phenomenon should be taken alone, but several should be regarded together. The character and the duration of the weather of the preceding days, the direction of the wind, the forms of the clouds, the indications of the barometer, the rise or fall of the thermometer, and the instinctive forewarnings of birds, beasts, insects and flowers, should all be taken into account. Although no direct material advantages attend such a study, it induces a habit of observation, and develops the inductive faculty of the mind, which, when applied to more significant things, may trace important effects to their greater causes.

124. *Why when swallows fly low may wet weather be expected ?*

Because the insects which the swallows pursue their flight are flying low, to escape the coldness of the upper regions of the atmosphere.

125. *Why do ducks and geese go to the water, and dash it over their backs, on the approach of rain ?*

Because by wetting the outer coat of their feathers before the rain falls, by sudden dashes of water over the surface, they prevent the drops of rain from penetrating to their bodies through the open and dry feathers.

126. *Why do horses and cattle stretch out their necks and snuff the air on the approach of rain ?*

Because they smell the fragrant perfume which is diffused in the air by its increasing moistness.

127. *Why may change of weather be anticipated when domestic animals are restless ?*

Because their skins are exceedingly sensitive to atmospheric influences, and they are oppressed and irritated by the changing condition of the atmosphere.

128. *Why may fine weather be expected when piders are seen busily constructing their webs ?*

Because those insects are highly sensitive to the state of the atmosphere, and when it is setting fine they build their webs, because they know instinctively that flies will be abroad.

129. *Why is wet weather to be expected when spiders hide ?*

Because it shows that they are aware that the state of the atmosphere does not favor the flight of insects.

130. *Why if gnats fly in large numbers may fine weather be expected ?*

Because it shows that they feel the state of the atmosphere to be favorable, which induces them all to leave their places of shelter.

131. *Why if owls scream during foul weather, will it change to fine ?*

Because the birds are pleasurably excited by a favorable change in the atmosphere.

132. *Why is it said that the moping of the owl foretells death ?*

Because owls scream when the weather is on the change ; and when a patient is lingering on a death-bed, the alteration in the state of the atmosphere frequently induces death, because the faint and expiring flame of life has not strength enough to adapt itself to the change.

133. *Why may wet weather be expected when spiders break off their webs, and remove them ?*

Because the insects, anticipating the approach of rain, remove their webs for preservation.

134. *Why may we expect a continuance of fine weather when bees wander far from their hives ?*

Because the bees feel instinctively that from the state of the atmosphere they may wander far in search of honey, without the danger of being overtaken by rain.

135. *Why if people feel their corns ache, and their bones rheumatic, may rain be expected ?*

Because the dampness of the atmosphere affects its pressure upon the body and causes a temporary disturbance of the system. All general disturbances of the body manifest themselves in those parts which are in a morbid state —as in a corn, a rheumatic bone, or a decayed tooth.

136. *Why if various flowers close may rain be expected ?*

Because plants are highly sensitive to atmospheric changes, and close their petals to protect their stamens.

137. *Why when moles throw up their hills may rain be expected ?*

Because the moles know instinctively that on the approach of wet, worms move in the ground ; the moles therefore become active, and form their hills.

138. *Why is a magpie, when seen alone, said to foretell bad weather ?*

Because magpies generally fly in company ; but on the approach of wet or cold, one remains in the nest to take care of the young, while the other one wanders alone in search of food.

139. *Why do sea-gulls appear numerous in fine weather ?*

Because the fishes swim near to the surface of the sea, and the birds assemble over the sea to catch the fish, instead of sitting on rocks, or wading on the shore.

140. *Why do sea-gulls fly over the land on the approach of stormy weather ?*

Because in stormy weather they cannot catch fish ; and the earth-worms come up on the land when the rain falls.

141. *Why if birds cease to sing, may wet, and probably thunder, be expected ?*

Because birds are depressed by an unfavorable change in the atmosphere, and lose those joyful spirits which give rise to their songs.

142. *Why if cattle run around in meadows, may thunder be expected ?*

Because the electrical state of the atmosphere has the effect of making them feel uneasy and irritable, and they chase each other about to get rid of the irritability.

143. *Why if birds of passage arrive early, may severe weather be expected ?*

Because it shows that the indications of unfavorable weather have set in, in the latitudes from which the birds come, and that they have taken an early flight to escape it.

144. *Why if the webs of the gossamer spider fly about in the autumn, may west winds be anticipated ?*

Because a west wind is a dry and dense wind, and suitable to the flight of the gossamer spider ; the spider feeling instinctively the dryness of the air, throws out its web, and finds it more than usually buoyant upon the dense air.

www.ingramcontent.com/pod-product-compliance
Lightning Source LLC
Chambersburg PA
CBHW082349270326
41935CB00013B/1561